# That Gentle Strength

*Historical Perspectives on Women in Christianity*

To Elizabeth
with love from John

# THAT GENTLE STRENGTH

## Historical Perspectives on Women in Christianity

*Edited with an Introduction by*
Lynda L. Coon,
Katherine J. Haldane,
and
Elisabeth W. Sommer

University Press of Virginia

CHARLOTTESVILLE AND LONDON

THE UNIVERSITY PRESS OF VIRGINIA
Copyright © 1990 by the Rector and Visitors
of the University of Virginia

*First published 1990*

Library of Congress Cataloging-in-Publication Data
That gentle strength : historical perspectives on women in
  Christianity / edited with an introduction by Lynda L. Coon,
  Katherine J. Haldane, and Elisabeth W. Sommer.
    p.  cm.
  ISBN 0-8139-1286-5
    1. Women in Christianity—History—Congresses.   I. Coon, Lynda L.
  II. Haldane, Katherine J.   III. Sommer, Elisabeth W.
  BV639.W7T42   1990
  270'.082—dc20                                        90-36977
                                                          CIP

Printed in the United States of America

# Contents

# Acknowledgments

The editors wish to express their thanks to the many people who gave us their help and support in the preparation of this volume. Susan Harvey, Duane Osheim, Alexander Sedgwick, and Erik Midelfort read drafts of the introduction and made valuable suggestions. Tom Noble also contributed to the early stages of this project. Joseph Miller and Robert Cross helped with the difficult process of selecting essays. Elizabeth Stovall and Kathleen Miller, the secretaries of the Corcoran Department of History at the University of Virginia, were exceedingly patient and helpful beyond the call of duty. Kimberly Reiter not only provided the title of the book, but she and Jena Gaines were a much needed source of friendship and support. They and Mary Walker were also instrumental in the early work from which this volume developed.

The book would be much less polished without the indispensable editorial work and thought-provoking comments of Ellen Litwicki and Beth Plummer. Marilyn Appleby graciously provided the print from which the jacket design was made, and her help is greatly appreciated. We especially want to thank John McGuigan of the University Press of Virginia for his willingness to bring this book to press.

# That Gentle Strength

*Historical Perspectives on Women in Christianity*

I

*Lynda L. Coon, Katherine J. Haldane,*
*and Elisabeth W. Sommer*

# Introduction

CHRISTIANITY HAS PROVIDED A PLACE for woman for which she is fitted, and in which she shines; but take her out of that place, and her lustre pales and sheds a feeble and sickly ray. Or, to change the metaphor, woman is a plant, which in its own greenhouse seclusion will put forth all its brilliant colors and all its sweet perfume; but remove it from the protection of its own floral home into the common garden and open field, where hardier flowers will grow and thrive, its beauty fades and its odor is diminished. Neither reason nor Christianity invites woman to the professor's chair, nor conducts her to the bar, nor makes her welcome to the pulpit, nor admits her to the place of ordinary magistracy.[1]

John Angell James (1785–1859), an English Victorian minister, thus identified the essential paradox of women's position within Christianity. Although women were perceived as upholding and exemplifying the virtues of the church, they were excluded from active participation in institutional power. James simply expressed the dominant perception that women's relation to Christianity was essentially passive. Recently, however, this characterization of female religiosity has been challenged by the recognition that, although their role has been obscured by both a lack of sources and institutional biases, women have been at the forefront of Christian leadership. The title of this volume, *That Gentle Strength*, juxtaposes the traditional concept of women as "soft" and "yielding" with a suggestion of their "power" and "authority." This collection of essays explores the historic roles of women in the Christian church and examines how their spirituality both reflected and shaped not only the female experience but the universal Christian experience. The focus of this study is Western Christianity, from the early Christians to the late Victorians.[2] The essays in this collection are designed not to provide a comprehensive examination of women in Christianity but simply to explore a sample of the "varieties of religious experience" of Christian women and to establish a history of their continuing conflicts, struggles, and achievements.

The relationship of women and Christianity can be approached both from within the confines of religious orders and from lay piety. Women have exerted a special influence on Christian life and have been profoundly affected by spirituality, but the exact nature of this relationship has yet to be fully understood. Holy women throughout history have struggled over the nature of women's calling within the church. Christianity has been both a liberating force for women and the cause of their oppression. Jesus envisioned a community of equals, with no distinction as to gender, status, or race. Elisabeth Schüssler Fiorenza has shown that early Christians attempted to live in this type of alternative community where women held powerful leadership positions.[3] Second- and third-century theologians reformulated the first-century position of Christian women in response to outside criticisms of the public role of women and to the patriarchal environment of Greco-Roman society. Eventually this patriarchal system, reflected in Aristotle's definition of marriage as "the union of natural ruler and subject," was incorporated into Christian theology.

A conflict therefore arose over the emancipating nature of Christ's call to all people as equals, which the restrictions placed on women's activity within the church seemed to deny. This tension increased with the rise of the cult of Mary, with its emphasis on the superior purity of virginal women.[4] The great mystic Teresa of Avila (1515–82) agonized over this precise tension in *The Way of Perfection*:

When You were in the world, Lord, You did not despise women, but did always help them and show them great compassion. You did find more faith and no less love in them than in men, and one of them was Your most sacred Mother, from whose merits we derive merit, and whose habit we wear, though our sins make us unworthy to do so. We can do nothing in public that is of any use to You, nor dare we speak of some of the truths over which we weep in secret, lest You should not hear this our just petition. Yet, Lord, I cannot believe this of Your goodness and righteousness, for You are a righteous Judge, not like judges in the world, who, being after all, men and sons of Adam, refuse to consider any woman's virtue as above suspicion. Yes, my King, but the day will come when all will be known. I am not speaking on my own account, for the whole world is already aware of my wickedness, and I am glad that it should become known; but, when I see what the times are like, I feel it is not right to repel spirits which are virtuous and brave, even though they be the spirits of women.[5]

Only in rare instances can we find a clear example of a woman, such as Teresa of Avila, expressing a real problem facing holy women. One of their most intense conflicts was the struggle between what women believed to be their orthodox role and the conviction that in fact, through Christ, God maintained a close relationship with women. Both Christ and Paul included women in their ministry.[6] The existence of this conflict should give us reason to pause from imposing the modern obsession with authority and power on earlier holy women. Some of these women did obtain spiritual authority (and at times temporal as well), for example Catherine of Siena and Angélique Arnauld, but this did not necessarily result from a desire for power. Susan Harvey and Rosemary Keller in their essays both discuss the importance of a spiritual calling in determining women's sphere of activity. Women's relationship to Christ was often the center of their thought.

Early studies of women attempted to discover the *vox feminae*, the voice of women. Much of the past feminist scholarship on women and religion has been polemical, perhaps necessarily so. Its purpose was to raise the consciousness of scholars of religion as to the involvement and impact women have had and continue to have on the theological, the spiritual, and the institutional aspects of church life. By identifying a long-standing active role for women in Christianity, much of this literature strove to establish a precedent for the contemporary leadership and participation of women in Christianity.[7] Rosemary Ruether has proposed a rereading of Christian texts with a recognition of male bias. Rather than rejecting Christianity, Ruether has drawn out of the texts "things they never said before." On the other hand, radical feminists, such as Mary Daly, have rejected the message of Christianity because of its inherent androcentric-patriarchial bias. The revolutionary work of Elisabeth Schüssler Fiorenza has reconstructed the *memoria passionis* (memory of suffering) of Christian women. Fiorenza has maintained the necessity of revitalizing the role of women in the early church. The accomplishments of these authors have been extremely important to the feminist movement and have reworked Christian scholarship.

Recent scholarship has explored women and Christianity within the historical context. In the process scholars have illuminated a more active role for women and have identified a unique female spirituality. Rudolph M. Bell proposed in *Holy Anorexia* that in the late Middle Ages, holy women practiced rigorous asceticism in an attempt to obliterate "femaleness."[8] Through self-starvation and mutilation, the late medieval female saint reinforced the negative image of the female body. Bell believes that this particular form of piety grew out of a popular concept of woman as Eve. On the more positive side, women used their asceticism and "holy" modes of behavior to gain an autonomous role outside of the traditional family. More recently, Caroline Bynum in *Holy Feast and Holy Fast* looked at the same problem, concentrating more particularly on the image of eating.[9] Bynum argues that the female perception of holiness differed in part because of the unique female experience. Whereas men gave up wealth, which was their source of power, in order to pursue the *vita apostolica*,[10] women gave up food, over which they had control.

The question of female uniqueness in some ways is the crux of the current research. The fact that research indicates that female piety possesses an autonomous form, enables (and encourages) scholarly exploration of this subject to bridge both time and place. The issue of "masculine" and "feminine" spiritual and societal roles forms a dominant theme throughout this collection. The essays indicate that the question of the proper relation of the sexes to each other and to God shaped attitudes toward female piety in a number of ways. Primary among them was the desire for a separate sphere where women's particular gifts could flourish, and where women and men would be protected from each other. Although this resulted in the cloistering of women, it is clear that the religious life often provided an alternative to the domestic world. Yet because of limits placed on female authority outside of the convent (largely as a result of the perception of women as weak and in need of guidance), women such as Teresa of Avila often found it difficult to pursue their spiritual calling. How the essays in this collection address these interrelated problems is the burden of the remainder of this introduction.

DEFINING THE FEMININE

Late antiquity was a crucial period in the development of Christian perceptions of masculine and feminine. Elizabeth Clark once noted that women were both God's "good gift to men—and the curse of the world."[11] Eve lost paradise. The Virgin could regain paradise. The early church fathers defined spheres of activity for holy men and women that were distinct, in theory, yet not always so in reality. Influential ascetics such as Jerome wrote both in condemnation and admiration of the feminine and of specific aristocratic women. Clearly, Christian intellectuals were ambiguous about the role of women in the church.

Regulation and rebellion form the central issues in Elizabeth Clark's essay on early Christian women. Clark discusses the ways in which women were viewed as rebels and as heroines. Christianity redefined the late antique community. Yet at the same time Christianity retained aspects of traditional Greco-Roman social and political institutions as well as their cultural conventions concerning the masculine and feminine. Women typically were praised by the church fathers when they exercised fidelity within marriage and submitted to their husbands' will. Submission, compunction, nurturing, obedience, humility, and purity were generally characterized as positive feminine characteristics.[12] The lurking presence of Eve, however, contributed to other less positive female traits such as weak flesh, moral depravity, quarrelsomeness, and ostentation. Masculine qualities, in contrast to the feminine, included intellectual talent, strength in action, and the ability to exercise public power. Yet in late antiquity masculine and feminine were not synonymous with male and female since female martyrs, penitents, pilgrims, and ascetics were often venerated for their manly strength.[13] Thus, through the patristic definition of masculine and feminine, late antiquity set the stage for future differentiation of gender roles.

Susan Harvey offers an innovative approach to the interpretation of symbolic texts. Harvey discusses the ways in which the image of women in early Byzantine hagiography differs from women's actual experience. Interestingly, even those Byzantine hagiographers most determined to exclude women from their worthy and pious subject matter were unable to dismiss females from their texts. Hagiography became the genre that revealed the heroic spirituality of extraordinary women and the actions of ordinary women. Understanding gender in Byzantine hagiography is a complex subject. As Susan Harvey notes, women were sanctified "within a masculine framework." In other words, women who were able to transcend female weakness and achieve true piety were no longer truly feminine. Byzantine topoi portray the most dramatic hagiographical reversals: saintly harlots and transvestites as well as violated virgins. Susan Harvey makes several important points about the tension that existed between the hagiographer and the women who filled his accounts of saintly men and women. In theory, women were the evil temptation, yet many times the relationships between men and women in Byzantine hagiography were sympathetically drawn. The real women encountered by male hagiographers molded their total image of women, which was neither dismally negative nor idealistically positive. A careful and creative reading of these symbolic texts reveals visions of women that contradict the image the hagiographers wished to portray. This incongruity is both the crux of hagiographical texts as well as a source of their amazing characterizations of women, heroic as well as ordinary.

The issue of the feminine and the masculine is also central to Diane Mockridge's essay. The role of gender and its influence on the writing of saints' lives has until very recently been ignored by historians. Mockridge provides a way to look at gender and image. Although Clark and Harvey show that late antique hagiographers were not reluctant to describe women in masculine terms, the opposite was true of the late Middle Ages, according to Mockridge. Rather than depicting heroic female ascetics as manly, late medieval hagiographers chose to describe both male and female saints as brides or friends of Christ. Even with this feminization of language in saints' vitae, however, male hagiographers were hesitant to depict male saints as submissive, a feminine characteristic.[14] Mockridge speculates that the shift in hagiographic imagery resulted from the twelfth-century emphasis on a more intimate relationship with Christ, best expressed in sexual or affectionate terms.[15]

Thus far the essays discussed deal mainly with women outside of the family: virgins and widows. When the Protestant Reformation rejected the cloister, it gave marriage and family new prominence in theological debate.[16] Keith Moxey's work supplies a basis for understanding the secular setting in which women sought to exercise a spiritual role during this period. Moxey looks at Reformation broadsheets dealing with marriage and concludes that in the context of the Protestant family, women were to be tamed. From his observations, it appears that while Protestants legitimized sexuality and the family, they continued to feel threatened by female power (and especially female sexuality) and took steps to insure that women would remain within the home, which was to be their special sphere.

Thomas Head reinforces this interpretation of the effect of the Protestant elevation of marriage on the position of women. The Reformation initially loosened traditional social and gender boundaries. Just as in the period of the early church, married women assumed a more public role in religion. They began to participate in the theological debates over questions raised by Luther and others. Head looks at the response of both female Catholics and Protestants to the Reformation. The Catholic definition of the Virgin as the female ideal allowed women to exercise some measure of spiritual authority within the convent. On the other hand, marriage was viewed as, at best, a necessary evil. The nuns studied by Alexander Sedgwick, for example, equated marriage with death. Agnes Arnauld, a nun at Port-Royal, hastily wrote to her nephew, Antoine Le Maistre, when she learned of his upcoming marriage: "Thus have I spoken to you about marriage, which is not contemptible in itself, but in comparison to the ecclesiastical order, which is an association of the living whereas the other [marriage] constitutes the company of the dead." [17]

Head demonstrates that although Protestantism gave women positive secular roles (as wives and mothers), its rejection of monastic piety made holding any unique spiritual office problematic. There was no specific institutional place wherein women could profess spirituality. The Protestant response to the initial breakdown of traditional social roles was to de-emphasize the public role of women. The reformers believed that the ideal place for woman was at her husband's side, managing the home and raising the children. This definition of the proper feminine sphere left precious little room for an autonomous position within the church, nor did Protestant theologians seek to identify a specifically feminine piety. This did not hold true for the women themselves, however. Head shows that in the debates between Catholic and Protestant women in the early years of the Reformation, both sides sought in different ways to maintain a peculiar spiritual role for women.

Even though Catholicism allowed women a greater spiritual role, they still faced limitations dictated by assumptions about the feminine character and the proper role for the female. Rudolph Bell in his essay points out the difficulties faced by the truly pious woman who attempted to conduct her married life according to the strict dictates of the marriage manuals that were widely available for the first time in the sixteenth century. She could not have escaped the litany of the dangers of lust and her own responsibility for maintaining sexual purity within the connubial bedchamber. At the same time, she was depicted as the weaker vessel, whose very physical presence was a potential danger to her own and her husband's salvation.

The problems did not end within the safety of the convent. Alexander Sedgwick concentrates on a group of nuns who sought reform within the confines of orthodox Catholicism. While some religious and secular leaders supported the nuns in their reform movement, those who opposed them were particularly angry because of the determined resistance they encountered from mere women. Therefore, they made it clear to the sisters that it was not the place of females to meddle in theology.

Just as the Reformation redefined the relationship of women and Christianity, so too did the dramatic events of the American Revolution and the onset of industrialization. Rosemary Keller sees a rethinking of women's roles in the era of the American Revolution. Although women were still consigned to the home, domesticity was becoming a profession equal to the public careers pursued by men. Women like Abigail Adams persevered on the domestic front, training the children and freeing their husbands from the responsibilities of the household so that men could fully concentrate on the war effort. For Abigail Adams the American

Revolution was a "holy war"; her faith in the revolution was an out-growth of her faith in God. Her commitment to the Revolution and to religion led her to conceive of women's career as providing the moral basis of a secular nation. Women's position was understood, not as in-ferior but as equal. Its focus was domestic, but its spirit was political, as evidenced by the life of Abigail Adams. Keller describes one woman's response to the situation created by the Revolution, and her own answer to the question of gender roles in the Christian life. Abigail Adams was perhaps not a typical eighteenth-century woman, nor were her beliefs necessarily held by others of her sex. Yet her conviction that women were called to provide the spiritual backbone of the nation placed their religious role into a larger, national picture.

Abigail Adams's thought grew out of her experience in the American Revolution. She recognized that the formation of a new nation required a spiritual guidance that women could provide in the home. Similarly, the nineteenth century saw the rise of a new industrial society that also needed women's spiritual direction. Thus, religion in the Victorian period continued to be regarded as women's sphere, usually within the confines of the home.[18]

Industrialization gave new prominence to the middle-class home by separating economic and domestic life. Women were moral and spiri-tual guardians of the middle-class family in the face of a changing world that was perceived as being tainted by avarice and worldly concerns. Although Adams's conception of domesticity answered a specific need in revolutionary America, the "cult of domesticity" came into its own in the nineteenth century in both America and Britain, as a response to industrialization. The Victorians institutionalized Adams's thought, with the result that the household career of women became a positive role for many. Elizabeth Fox-Genovese shows how antebellum slave-holding women saw their religious life as an outgrowth of their societal and familial roles. To be a good Christian meant to fulfill the specific positions God ordained for them as wives, mothers, and mistresses.

Yet because of a fear of the results of women's departure from the home, which could mean the removal of the spiritual protector, Vic-torian society barred women from most alternative careers. Stepping outside the haven of the home could corrupt women's "pure" nature and thus undermine the moral foundation of Victorian culture. More than in any other period, Victorian women and men agreed that women were the more spiritual sex. But because their spiritual role was based in the home, they could not exercise public authority.

Many Victorians were seeking spiritual options to orthodox Christianity, however. The nineteenth century saw an intense crisis of faith, which was in fact a step toward the twentieth-century secularization of society. The new, primarily German, Higher Criticism of the Bible, combined with fresh scientific discoveries, called into question long-accepted beliefs about God and his relationship with the world. Consequently, many Victorians found themselves unable to believe in the traditional Christian faith. Some attempted to find alternatives; rationalism, positivism, and spiritualism were among the choices. Spiritualism was an attempt to find a scientific confirmation of the existence of the hereafter, in a world that seemed increasingly mechanistic and removed from any sort of spiritual forces.

Mary Walker points out that within the spiritualist movement, the association of women with the supernatural was viewed both positively and negatively. Because of the perception of females as prone to visions and hysteria, the predominance of women in the spiritualist movement seemed to invalidate any claim it might hold to scientific truth. Paradoxically, this caused many within the movement to deny that supernatural manifestations were any more prevalent among women than men, which in effect denied the existence of any unique feminine spirituality.

## A SEPARATE SPHERE

Theological and metaphysical conceptions of masculine and feminine character distinctions frequently led to differentiation of the roles proper to men and to women. This had a concrete effect on ecclesiastical institutions and on the daily life of the laity. Physical separation was the most extreme manifestation of perceived gender differences.

The perception of the feminine fostered a physical institution that was designed to keep the sexes separated. The church fathers who upheld virginity as the greatest Christian virtue, such as Chrysostom and Jerome, constantly fretted about the role of women in religion. Women also hesitated to fulfill God's work. Catherine of Siena once lamented: "My very sex, as I need not tell you, puts many obstacles in the way. The world has no use for women in work such as that, and propriety forbids a woman to mix so freely in the company of men." [19] Women were prominent in the early church, yet their very presence was scandalous. In the church hierarchy, women held an ambiguous and ill-defined place. Late antique holy men were not only to avoid conversing with women, they were not even to cast an eye upon them. One desert hermit achieved fame by periodically inhabiting 106 towns without having any "traffic" with a woman. [20] The male ascetics who controlled the church hierarchy feared female sexuality. Separation of the sexes remained the ideal, but in reality women worked with men. Thus the separation was only theoretical.[21]

The essays by Graciela Daichman and Duane Osheim examine popular attitudes toward the cloister and the administrative reality behind the containment of nuns and pious laywomen. Professor Daichman investigates the reported scandalous behavior in English convents in the late Middle Ages. Alongside women who desired to express their spirituality within the confines of the convent lived the excess daughters of noble families, unmarriageable daughters, and women who had been involved in illicit love affairs or rebellious political activity. Scandals arose, at least in part, because even those who lacked a vocation could not abandon the convent without being labeled apostate. Osheim and Daichman both note in their essays that convents were often seen as an institutionalization of women's stereotypical bad characteristics: quarrelsomeness, sensuality, ostentation. Still, the cloister remained the symbolic focus of late medieval female spirituality.

Osheim notes that in late medieval Italy it was Bernadino da Siena's *madonna clausura* ("lady cloister") that formed the ideal of female spirituality. The *madonna clausura* herself was to avoid the presence of all except the angels. The ideal lay female religious lived as a recluse in her own household, exercising the virtues of fasting and ascetic rigor and avoiding luxury. According to Osheim, the reason behind the enthusiasm for domestic spirituality in Italy was not a lack of space in its numerous convents or a domination of those convents by the wealthy. Rather, many Italian women desired to free themselves from the confines of cloister and from clerical manipulation. Ideally, women, because of their inherent weakness and their suspect sexuality, were to remain separate from men, especially ordained men. The visitation records cited by Daichman and the variety of synodal statutes, parish records, sermons, and confessors' manuals used by Osheim show this hierarchical emphasis on separation. Walls, gates, locks, and guards were indispensable aspects of female spirituality, as Daichman makes clear. Women were not to wander.

Both essays, however, attest to the ineffectiveness of these efforts to control the behavior of female religious. Nuns and tertiaries shared conviviality with both women and men, much to the scandal of contemporary society. Daichman gives examples of nuns engaging in drinking and eating with noble guests as well as dancing, singing, and luting with friars. Fear of conviviality led to an obsession with strict separation. The topoi and exaggerations of female decadence found by Professor Daichman in the episcopal records reiterate this fear.

Rudolph Bell's research likewise reveals a continued distrust of female sexuality and a preference for the state of chastity. In a sense, women were to be cloistered even within marriage. Priests who heard confession from women remained on vigilant guard against their own flesh when confronted with the temptation of proximity. Thus the barrier between holy men and women was still very much in place in the sixteenth century, at least among Catholics.

## WOMEN AND AUTHORITY

The Byzantine theologian Chrysostom's assessment of the proper role for women expresses how perceptions of the female character resulted in their exclusion from public ecclesiastical authority: "Indeed, this is a work of God's love and wisdom that he who is skilled at the greater things is downright inept and useless in the performance of the less important ones, so that the woman's service is necessary. For if the man were adapted to undertake both sorts of activities, the female sex could easily be despised. Conversely, if the more important, most beneficial concerns were turned over to the woman, she would go quite mad." [22]

Women were condemned if they sought an active role in hierarchical leadership. Elizabeth Clark notes that late antique heresies often offered women leadership roles, a fact that intensified orthodox polemics against heretical groups. The "madness" of heretical groups who allowed women to exercise power was apparent to Chrysostom. Rebellion and usurpation of male authority by women was indeed a dangerous thing. Hagiographers continually associated unsuitable female behavior with heresy. Susan Harvey describes several fascinating instances where women usurped male roles and suffered for their presumption. Byzantine hagiography, as Harvey reminds us, served a didactic purpose, including reinforcing an awareness of "woman's place." This fact was especially apparent when the women in hagiographic texts appeared to ignore their proper roles in favor of manly action. Women who achieved a measure of authority were "textually" corrected and reminded of their weak flesh. Women who were too actively involved in financially supporting saintly men scandalized contemporary society. As Professor Osheim shows, the conviviality between men and women sometimes demolished the fine line between female spirituality and heresy, or even witchcraft. [23] Women's attempts to exercise independent judgment could also demolish this line. The nuns of Port-Royal faced harsh persecution and even accusations of witchcraft when they resisted ecclesiastical authority.

Male suspicion of female authority often made it difficult for women to identify the role God designated for them within Christianity. Chrysostom in the fourth century rationalized women's ministry with Paul by maintaining that their presence was only due to the angelic nature of the church. Chrysostom's discomfort with contemporary women's activity is not unique to late antiquity. In the Reformation, as Thomas Head shows, the only way M. Dentière could attempt to justify her public teaching was to claim the inspiration of the Holy Spirit, as did her Catholic and Anabaptist counterparts. Even then, Calvin succeeded in silencing her. The Protestant reformers attacked Marie Dentière through her husband by claiming that she was a bad influence on him. Eventually they accused him of writing one of her treatises defending women's right to speak out on issues of faith, despite her protests that she alone was responsible.

The nuns studied by Professor Sedgwick found themselves forced to defy the male members of their family and the ecclesiastical hierarchy in order to carry out the reforms to which they saw themselves led by divine inspiration. The focus then became whether to obey God or man. As Sedgwick indicates, however, the issue was a complicated one, because the nuns were told that their defiance of accepted authority was in fact unchristian. This caused conflict among them. Some argued in favor of submitting on the grounds that public defiance was indicative of the sin of pride. Others, however, held that to submit would be to betray their holy calling to reform. Sedgwick's portrayal of the split among the nuns provides an excellent example of the dilemma faced by holy women in their desire to serve Christ to the fullest.

Yet the perception of a distinct female piety could also provide a life outside of traditional domesticity. This gave women a sense of their unique worth. Christianity in late antiquity redefined and legitimized the status of the widow and the unmarried virgin, as Elizabeth Clark discovers. Christianity also gave women visibility, granted widows sustenance, provided an alternative to remarriage, and offered young women an escape from restrictive domestic roles. Celibate women lived a life that was symbolically opposed to childbearing and domesticity. Through asceticism women could "storm the gates of heaven" and avoid a more traditional lifestyle. Byzantine hagiography, as Susan Harvey demonstrates, gives us positive images of women as well as examples of women who possessed extraordinary miraculous and ascetic powers. These saintly women became models of behavior for all Christian women. Early medieval abbesses exercised authority through the administration of vast agrarian estates and often served as patrons and educators of local communities. Osheim proposes, though, that in the late Middle Ages it was the strictness of the cloister and not the desire for power via ordination

that drove many Italian women to the semireligious groups that were
extremely popular at that time.

Abigail Adams clearly was not seeking power for women, and she
obviously upheld traditional domesticity, though with a new emphasis.
Adams saw her identity as inseparable from that of her husband. At
the same time, however, Adams realized that fulfilling woman's special
responsibilities could bring a certain amount of independence and autonomy. She passionately believed that women's execution of their tasks
entitled them to fuller political rights, a belief not shared by her husband
and his colleagues.

As Professor Fox-Genovese found, most southern slaveholding women
also valued traditional domesticity, believing that the male-dominated
society was part of a biblically ordained patriarchy which also legitima-
tized slavery. The loss of the Civil War and the subsequent destruction of
the slave society forced many women to reevaluate the received tradition
concerning God's earthly hierarchy.

Southern women were part of an extremely conservative environment
and were heavily socialized in a white man's culture. Women from urban,
industrial backgrounds also questioned their traditional societal roles.
Most Victorians believed woman's special moral and spiritual nature
made her confinement to the home a societal necessity. Yet many found
this concept too narrow and turned to the women's rights movement,
which gained momentum throughout the second half of the nineteenth
century. This movement did not provide the only alternative. In theory
women were restricted to the home, yet in both Britain and America,
the very exercise of their special mission as spiritual and moral leaders
led many to a more visible and active role in society, without any necessary reliance on the women's movement. This slowly helped to transform
contemporary attitudes about their sex.[24] Hannah More and Catherine
Booth are but two examples. Vanessa Dickerson shows that spiritualism
could serve as a means of escape from the confines of the "angel in the
house" ideal. Attempts of mediums and believers in the supernatural to
reach and be reached by the otherworld led directly to a more public life
in this world.

## CONCLUSION

Clearly the separation of the masculine from the feminine played the
predominant part in the development of religious roles for men and
women. From late antiquity to Victorian Britain, recognizable patterns
emerge. Definitions of the feminine arose from the fact that women were

daughters of both Eve and Mary. Eve's nature represented lust and moral
weakness, but Eve's earthiness was redeemed by the purity of Mary.[25]
Both the lust and the purity of women led to the separation of the sexes,
exclusion of women from public authority, and the virtual cloistering of
married women within the household. Yet at the same time the gospel
provided the basis for female claims to a special relationship with God,
as Teresa of Avila proclaimed.[26] And as Susan Harvey has demonstrated,
woman and woman's body could symbolize the evil and purity inherent
in humanity, thus "woman" could symbolize "humanity."[27] These essays
demonstrate the tenacity of certain societal and theological concepts.

Individual research on women's Christianity tends to be fragmented;
one scholar looks at antiquity, another examines the Victorians. Yet
Christianity's influence has covered a vast period of time. Christianity
was a living, powerful force in late antiquity, in the Middle Ages, and in
the industrialized nineteenth century. The editors of this volume seek to
place these individual studies within a wider focus: to examine how relationships between men and women in the church have developed over
the long history of the church, how one age has influenced the next, and
how the situation of our own time is a product of earlier developments.
Today's perceptions of gender derive from the past Christian mentality
toward the relationship of the sexes. Furthermore, Elaine Pagels has
proposed that Western government has been shaped by Augustine's interpretation of the archetypal relationship between man and woman, the
Fall.[28] Finally, the study of women in the church is the history of an out-
group. As such, this *memoria passionis* of women also has relevance for
minorities.

The study of Christian women is a delicate one. The ambivalence of
the church fathers and of society toward women, the "good gift" and
"great evil," makes any scholarly investigation of holy women difficult.
Because of the ambiguity of contemporary society the critical issue arises
of how to extract the female voice from sources written by men and
dominated by societal notions of the masculine and the feminine. The
essays in this collection and current scholarship present a methodology
by which we may partially recover the *vox feminae*. In regard to the
hagiographical texts, current research has shown that it is possible to
distinguish between the hagiographer's image and the saint herself. Because the authors of saints' lives focus on the ideal woman, the method
used in hagiographical studies can be applied to the study of other types
of sources in other periods. The problem of the idealized woman is universal, as is evident in the opinion of the Victorian minister John Angell
James. Therefore the need to distinguish between the ideal and reality

is also universal. These essays offer methodologies for making such a distinction.

However, other historiographical problems exist. Neither James's view of the male-dominated hierarchy, nor the feminist polemic, nor the current separation of two spiritualities, male and female, accurately portrays the historic reality. In theory, men and women have been institutionally separate from one another. Yet as the essays demonstrate, this separation seldom was a reality. Since female spirituality was never isolated from male spirituality it is most fruitful to study the one in the context of the other. In addition, such an approach is the only way to determine the extent to which feminine spirituality was uniquely female. It is important to recognize the unique contribution of women to Christian development, but it is equally important to understand the context within which this contribution was enacted. Elisabeth Schüssler Fiorenza has best defined the goal of current scholarship: "To reconstruct early Christian history as women's history in order not only to restore women's stories to early Christian history but also to reclaim this history as the history of women and men."[29]

## NOTES

1 / John Angell James (1785–1859), *Female Piety; or The Young Woman's Friend and Guide Through Life to Immortality* (New York, 1854), 90.

2 / The Victorian spiritualists may not appear at first to be part of this group. The spiritualists are an example of the modern movement away from Christianity. Yet Christian thought shaped Victorian mentality toward gender, even for those who did not consider themselves Christians. Victorian women faced the same dilemmas as early Christian women because societal perceptions of gender affect basic social relationships.

3 / Elisabeth Schüssler Fiorenza, *In Memory of Her: A Feminist Theological Reconstruction of Christian Origins* (New York: Crossroad, 1983).

4 / Yet it has been noted by feminist scholars that the cult of the Virgin also had a negative impact on female spirituality. See Julia Kristeva, "Stabat Mater," in *The Kristeva Reader*, ed. Toril Moi, trans. Leon S. Roudiez (Oxford: Basil Blackwell, 1986), 160–86.

5 / E. Allison Peers, trans. *The Complete Works of Saint Teresa of Jesus*, vol. 2. *The Way of Perfection* (London: Sheed and Ward, 1946), 13.

6 / For an excellent discussion of the role of women in the Gospels and in the Epistles, see Judith L. Kovacs, "Women in the New Testament," in *What the Bible Really Says*, ed. Morton Smith (New York: Harper and Row, 1989).

7 / For Fiorenza's work, see n. 3 above. Mary Daly has proclaimed that "the entire conceptual systems of theology and ethics, developed under the conditions of patriarchy, have been the products of males and tend to serve the interests of sexist society." Further, Daly emphasized that "there exists a world wide phenomenon of sexual cast" (*Beyond God the Father: Toward a Philosophy of Women's Liberation* [Boston: Beacon

Press, 1973], 4). Also by Mary Daly, *The Church and the Second Sex of Radical Feminism* (New York: Harper and Row, 1968) and *Gynecology, the Metaethics of Radical Feminism* (Boston: Beacon Press, 1978). Rosemary Ruether has also written a great deal on women and religion. See *Mary, the Feminine Face of the Church* (Philadelphia: Westminister Press, 1977); *New Woman, New Earth: Sexist Ideologies and Human Liberation* (New York: Seabury Press, 1975); *Religion and Sexism: Images of Women in the Jewish and Christian Traditions* (New York: Simon and Schuster, 1974); *Sexism and God-Talk: Toward a Feminist Theology* (Boston: Beacon Press, 1983); Ruether, ed., *Woman-Church: Theology and Practice of Feminist Liturgical Communities* (New York: Harper and Row, 1985); Ruether, ed., with Eleanor McLaughlin, *Women of Spirit: Female Leadership in the Jewish and Christian Traditions* (New York: Simon and Schuster, 1979); and Ruether, ed. and comp., *Womanguides: Readings toward a Feminist Theology* (Boston: Beacon Press, 1985).

8 / Rudolph Bell, *Holy Anorexia* (Chicago: Univ. of Chicago Press, 1985).

9 / Caroline Bynum, *Holy Feast and Holy Fast: The Religious Significance of Food to Medieval Women* (Berkeley and Los Angeles: Univ. of California Press, 1987).

10 / See Lester K. Little, *Religious Poverty and the Profit Economy in Medieval Europe* (Ithaca: Cornell Univ. Press, 1978).

11 / Elizabeth Clark, *Women in the Early Church*, Message of the Fathers of the Church Series, vol. 13 (Wilmington, Del.: Michael Glazier, 1983), 15.

12 / Catherine of Siena once described humility as "the foster mother and nurse of charity, and with the same milk she feeds the virtue of obedience" (*The Dialoge of Saint Catherine of Siena*, trans. Algar Thorold [Rockford, Ill.: Tan Books and Publishers, 1974], 284).

13 / Caroline Bynum defines "masculine and feminine" as the asymmetrical juxtapositioning of "intellect/body, active/passive, rational/irrational, reason/emotion, self-control/lust, judgment/mercy, and order/disorder" (*Gender and Religion: On the Complexity of Symbols*, ed. Bynum, Steven Harrell, and Paula Richman [Boston: Beacon Press, 1986], 257). A perfect example of manly strength can be found in the desert corpus. A female hermit, Sarah, was confronted one day by two famous male ascetics who had decided to humiliate her: "So they said to her, 'Be careful not to become conceited thinking to yourself: Look how the anchorites are coming to see me, a mere woman.' But amma Sarah said to them 'According to nature I am a woman, but not according to my thoughts.'" She also said to the brothers, "It is I who am a man, you who are women" (*Apophthegmata Paturm* [text Migne, *Patrologia Graeca* 65.419–20], Sarah 4:9, trans. Benedicta Ward, in *The Desert Christian: Sayings of the Desert Fathers* [New York: Macmillan, 1975], p. 230). Because of the humble status of women in late antiquity their humility became the perfect device to criticize prideful male ascetics.

14 / See Caroline Bynum, *Jesus as Mother: Studies in the Spirituality of the High Middle Ages* (Berkeley and Los Angeles: Univ. of California Press, 1982) and Bynum, Harrell, and Richman, eds., *Gender and Religion*, as well as Eleanor McLaughlin, "Women, Power and the Pursuit of Holiness," in Ruether and McLaughlin, eds., *Women of Spirit*, 100–130.

15 / For a discussion of the sexual language used by late medieval female mystics, see Luce Irigaray, "La Mysterique," in *Speculum of the Other*

*Women*, trans. Gillian C. Gill (Ithaca: Cornell Univ. Press, 1985), 191–202.

16 / For the new prominence of the family in Italian secular life see David Herlihy, *The Family in Renaissance Italy* (Arlington Heights, Ill.: Forum Press, 1974) and Herlihy and Christiane Klapisch-Zuber, *Tuscans and their Families: A Study of the Florentine Catasto of 1427* (New Haven: Yale Univ. Press, 1985). For the Reformation family, see Steven E. Ozment, *When Fathers Ruled: Family Life in Reformation Europe* (Cambridge: Harvard Univ. Press, 1983).

17 / See Alexander Sedgwick's essay "The Nuns of Port-Royal: A Study of Female Spirituality in Seventeenth-Century France," this volume.

18 / This is not to say that women had no public religious role. Many, such as the Methodist women preachers of late eighteenth-century Britain, played a significant part in the evangelical movement. Others were active in religiously flavored associations including the temperance and anti-slavery societies. See Mary P. Ryan, *Cradle of the Middle Class: The Family in Oneida County, New York, 1790–1865* (New York: Cambridge Univ. Press, 1981).

19 / Raymond of Capua, "The Life of Catherine of Siena," in *The Life of Catherine of Siena*, trans. Conleth Kearns (Wilmington, Del.: Michael Glazier, 1980), 116–17.

20 / Palladius, *Lausiac History*, 71:2. Text in Migne, *Patrologia Graeca*, 34.1256, trans. Robert T. Meyer, Ancient Christian Writers Series, no. 34 (New York: Newman Press, 1964), 153.

21 / Much of late antique and medieval hagiographical literature can be viewed as an extension of the *vita Christi*. Christ numbered women among his disciples. Paul included women among his missionaries. Thus it is not surprising that holy men and women maintained intimate relationships despite a theoretical separation and the raised eyebrows of society. The early church fathers, while often the greatest proponents of *virginitas*, nevertheless surrounded themselves with women (e.g., Jerome, Paula, and Eustochium; Chrysostom and Olympias; Melania and Rufinus). This created a tense situation because proximity invited temptation. The tension in turn led the church fathers often to be overtly hostile to women and to emphasize to them the role of Eve in the Fall. This attitude continued to plague holy women throughout the period covered in this volume. For early holy women, see Rosemary Ruether, "Mothers of the Church: Ascetic Women in the Late Patristic Age," in *Women of Spirit*, 72–98. For a discussion of hagiography as "the literary arsenal for the authors of saints' lives," see Jean LeClercq, "L'écriture sainte dans l'hagiographie monastique du Haut Moyen Âge," in *La Bibbia nell'alto medioevo*, Settimane di Studio del Centro Italiano di Studi sull'Alto Medioevo (Spoleto: Presso la Sede del Centro, 1963), 103–28.

22 / Text from Migne, *Patrologia Graeca*, 51.230, trans. Elizabeth Clark, "The Kind of Women Who Ought to Be Taken as Wives," in *Women in the Early Church*, 37. Monasticism did offer women a leadership role in the office of abbess. Yet late antique and early medieval convents were under strict supervision of male superiors and confessors. This supervision was intensified by Boniface's *periculoso et detestabili* cited by both Osheim and Daichman. However, in the early Middle Ages, abbesses could exercise private power through control of agrarian estates and patronage of local communities. See Jo Ann McNamara and Suzanne

Wemple, "The Power of Women through the Family in Medieval Europe: 500–1100," *Feminist Studies* 1 (1972): 126–41, and Janemarie Luecke, "The Unique Experience of Anglo-Saxon Nuns," in *Peaceweavers*, Cistercian Studies Series, no. 72 (Kalamazoo, Mich.: Cistercian Publications, 1987), 55–65.

23 / Catherine of Siena also was investigated for witchcraft.

24 / See F. K. Prochaska, *Women and Philanthropy in Nineteenth-Century England* (Oxford: Clarendon Press, 1980); Gail Malmgreen, ed., *Religion in the Lives of English Women, 1760–1930* (London: Croom Helm, 1986); and Martha Vicinus, *Independent Women: Work and Community for Single Women, 1850–1920* (London: Virago Press, 1985).

25 / For the classic study of the inability of women to escape the paradoxical "feminine" ideal of mother and asexual being, see Julia Kristeva, "Stabat Mater," 160–86.

26 / Christianity developed both in response to heresy and to outside criticism. The early prominence and visibility of women in the Christian community led to hostile attacks by pagan critics. Paul's radical statement, "In Christ there is neither male nor female" (Galatians 3:28) was altered to fit societal concepts of the masculine and the feminine. This fact is evident in the missionary activity of Paul, who on the one hand included women in his early community and later restricted their behavior. See Constance F. Parvey, "The Theology and Leadership of Women in the New Testament," in *Religion and Sexism*, ed. Rosemary Ruether, 117–49. See also Robert L. Wilken, *The Christians as the Romans Saw Them* (New Haven: Yale Univ. Press, 1984). Wilken studies the way in which Christianity evolved in response to criticism. Pagans, such as Celsus, were suspicious of Christianity's inclusion of "credulous" women.

27 / See Benedicta Ward, *Harlots of the Desert: A Study of Repentance in Early Monastic Sources* (Oxford: Mowbray, 1987) and Marina Warner, *All Alone of Her Sex: The Myth and Cult of the Virgin Mary* (New York: Vintage, 1983).

28 / Elaine Pagels, *Adam, Eve, and the Serpent* (New York: Random House, 1988).

29 / Fiorenza, *In Memory of Her*, xiv.

## 2

*Elizabeth A. Clark*

# Early Christian Women: Sources and Interpretation

TO RECONSTRUCT THE HISTORY OF WOMEN in a distant era for which the sources are few, the gaps enormous, and the rhetoric tendentious is a daunting project for even the most intrepid scholar. To be sure, there remains from the early Christian era a scant—very scant—handful of texts composed by women. Little extant patristic literature concerns real women, however, and the few we can unearth are almost invariably elites. The great mass of unexceptional women remains unknown and probably unknowable, barring the discovery of new sources.

Despite this bleak assessment of our materials, we should make creative use of what we have. We can, for example, locate certain types of early Christian literature that are richer in information about women. These usually are the "lower" genres: letters, homilies, pilgrimage accounts, martyrologies, hagiography, and the apocryphal acts. Moreover, official sources, such as church histories, the canons of church councils, and church orders often provide both narrations about and prescriptions regarding women, the latter of which, through an imaginative reading, hint at women's actual activities. The "higher" genres of early Christian literature, such as theological treatises, however, tend not to supply useful information for our purpose, although they sometimes reveal the church fathers' normative views on women in general, particularly through their exegesis of key biblical verses.

Material pertaining to women also tends to cluster around certain issues: the constitution of appropriate roles for women within the household and the church, heresy, martyrdom, pilgrimage, asceticism, and the deeds of imperial women. The last constitutes a species of political writing from a Christian slant: women who assisted the orthodox church, such as Constantine's mother Helena, are heralded, whereas empresses who favored alleged heretics (such as the Arian-supporter Justina), or brought ill-fate on notable churchmen (such as Eudoxia, who prompted the ouster of John Chrysostom from the bishopric of Constantinople), are excoriated by the early church historians.[1]

Most striking, the other issues mentioned—especially roles, heresy, martyrdom, and asceticism—pivot on the interrelated themes of regulation and rebellion. Whether or not women were easily regulatable, and that against which they rebelled, were the two decisive questions that govern the reactions to women of the male writers who provide the overwhelming bulk of our literary evidence. Regulation is especially demanded in two areas: within the family and within the leadership of the church. Here, the traditional hierarchical structures of Greco-Roman society prevailed, and Christianity made few early inroads into the existing order. But for heresy, martyrdom, and asceticism, rebellion was the issue. Here, women were judged by what they rebelled *against:* if it was the mainline orthodox church (so seen in retrospect, of course), they were condemned. If, however, they rebelled against social and political structures deemed by churchmen to be tainted or even outrightly evil, they were rather exalted as true heroines of the faith.

To put it differently: in areas in which Christianity retained structures like those of the dominant social order (namely, in marriage and institutional leadership), few if any new avenues were opened to Christian women. But in those areas in which Christianity most dramatically took a stand against the norms and mores of ancient society, women appear in the front ranks and are resoundingly praised for a resistance that, if conducted against the structures of marriage or church leadership, would have been just as resoundingly deplored. Patronage, a highly traditional institution of ancient society, furnishes a major exception to the scheme I propose, for it provided leverage for some elite Christian women to break through the older structures: a fascinating case of how, ironically, tradition can be manipulated to counter tradition.

Let us begin with marriage, an area that early Christian male writers, like their pagan counterparts, thought demanded careful regulation. Whatever the antifamilial slant of Jesus' teachings as attested in the Gospels, marriage as an institution showed little sign of vanishing, given the nonappearance of the expected eschaton. Two innovations—the only significant ones—in early Christian marital ethics were the single standard of sexual morality and, more gradually, the condemnation of divorce and remarriage.[2] Although Roman philosophers also counseled the sexual chastity of the husband as well as of the wife, their admonitions appear not to have made much impact upon practice.[3] From the earliest Christian writings onward, however, a unanimous voice calls for absolute marital fidelity from both partners. Thus Paul does not hesitate to startle his Corinthian audience by applying Jesus' words on marriage, themselves borrowed from Genesis ("the two shall become one"), to describe the union of a man with a *prostitute*—the point being that sexual union with *any* woman makes a man "one flesh" with her.[4] For Paul, that God has "bought" Christians and made their bodies temples of the Holy Spirit means that no Christian male may frequent prostitutes.[5] Marriage ordains that the wife "rules over" the husband's body to the same extent that he does hers.[6] In the late fourth century, John Chrysostom reminds his audience that this demand for sexual fidelity is the *only* point at which there is equality between husband and wife.[7] Even if the law of the Roman state punishes only a wife's adultery, the law of God is different: it decrees punishment for the husband's adultery as well, Chrysostom intones.[8] Similarly, he argues, young men as well as young women should remain virginal until marriage.[9]

A second point at which Christian teaching on marriage came to challenge traditional views was the stronger prohibitions on divorce and remarriage. Jesus' alleged teaching on divorce—that only on grounds of a wife's unchastity could a man seek divorce—ran up against Roman law and custom on two counts: the narrowness of the grounds and the sex of the agent.[10] Paul, addressing a wider Greco-Roman audience, assumes that divorce can be sought on other grounds and that women may initiate the action, although he prefers that married couples stay together.[11] How much the Christian moralists' condemnation of divorce and remarriage was strengthened in the next few centuries is well illustrated by the example of Jerome's eulogy on Fabiola, an aristocrat of the gens Fabia: to Jerome's acute embarrassment, she had divorced her first, loutish husband and remarried soon thereafter. Jerome's best exoneration of his friend and patron is to claim that she did not know that "the laws of Christ are different from the laws of Caesar," and that since she was sexually restless, she might have "played the courtesan" if she had not remarried. The "stain of her defilement," Jerome hastens to add, was removed by her public penance in the Lateran basilica, by a later life of pious deeds, and by the mercy of the Good Shepherd, Christ.[12]

Despite these Christian innovations in marital ethics, the ordering of the household deemed normal by late ancient pagan society tended to prevail in Christianity as well. Even by the turn of the second century, Christian writers had renounced Paul's preference for virginity to counsel instead wifely submission. Women were meekly to obey their husbands so that "the word of God may not be discredited," so that the women would "give the enemy no occasion to revile us"—hints that good domestic order was seen as necessary for Christianity's successful mission to the outside world.[13] Likewise, Christian wives were enjoined to be submissive to their husbands so that by their "reverent and chaste behavior" the nonbelieving husband might be won for the Christian cause.[14] Discreet and modest wives thus stand as exemplary apologists for the new faith. Such attitudes also seem to undergird the counsels to women in Clement of Alexandria's treatise *The Instructor*, in which "Christian behavior" appears to be largely identifiable with "good manners."[15]

But such an apologetic rationale was not the only one put forward by churchmen for submissive female behavior—indeed, it would no longer be appropriate once Christianity became the favored religion of the Roman Empire in the fourth century. Stronger justifications were needed for traditional matronly subordination. One such justification was constructed within the pages of the New Testament itself and was repeated endlessly in the centuries to follow: because woman was created after man and for him, and because she had led him into the first sin in Eden, she was to accept the rule of her husband as a chastening penalty.[16] This interpretation of Genesis 2 and 3—which rather overlooks the simultaneous creation of the sexes in Genesis 1—provided the theological rationale for later patristic writers' stress on male domination in marriage.[17] To be sure, they pressed this theme as part of their propaganda to encourage women's adoption of the ascetic life—the life that would free them from submission to husbands.[18] Yet the propaganda had a real-life correlate. Augustine, for example, held up the example of his own mother to his readers, a wife who bore her husband's hot temper and infidelities with nary a murmur against him.[19] Likewise, he was quick to reproach contemporary women who attempted to shake off a husband's authority for the sake of espousing asceticism: married women are in subjection to their husbands, he asserts, and must remain that way.[20] Thus the patristic evidence suggests that traditional Greco-Roman marriage ideals received minimal revision by early Christian writers.

The same holds true for the notion that leadership was to be retained almost exclusively in the hands of males. The New Testament evidence on women's leadership in the early Christian movement is disappointingly vague. Romans 16, with its list of women and men who worked, along with Paul, in the early Christian communities is evidence that they were involved in some activities—but which ones? Most tantalizing in the list is Phoebe, a *diakonos* from the church of Cenchreae—but what was a *diakonos* in the earliest decades of the Christian movement?[21] Similarly, it is not clear whether the women mentioned in the midst of a somewhat later New Testament discussion about requirements for deacons refers to *female* deacons, or merely to wives of male deacons.[22] The evidence can be read in more than one way.

Whatever the situation of women as leaders in the first-century church (and strong arguments for their leadership have been advanced by scholars such as Elisabeth Schüssler Fiorenza), women's admission to the priesthood was roundly condemned by male churchmen from the late second century onward.[23] In part, this exclusion appears to have been motivated by a desire to distinguish mainstream Catholic Christianity from various schismatic and heretical sects, some of which apparently allowed women prophetic and priestly functions. The Montanists, for example, exalted two women leaders as prophetes; and Marcosians, Marcionites, and Carpocratians are among the sects which the church fathers fault for allowing women to serve in priestly and other leadership positions.[24] Catholic Christianity, by contrast, allowed women to join such groups as the widows, or later, the deaconesses.[25] The rationale for having deaconesses, however—as given by male writers—emphasizes that the office was only a concession dictated by circumstances: male priests could not appropriately visit women alone, or touch parts of women's bodies during their anointing at baptism.[26] Thus even the office of deaconess was seen by some male authors as a stopgap measure, dictated only by propriety. Whether the deaconesses themselves viewed the matter in the same way seems unlikely.

By the later fourth century, women found new roles as monastic leaders—again, a role that a man could not appropriately assume, for too close contact with even ascetic women was thought to endanger his purity.[27] Several such women are known to us from the fourth to the early sixth centuries: Mary, the sister of Pachomius; Melania the Elder; Paula; Macrina, sister of Gregory of Nyssa and Basil of Caesarea; Olympias of Constantinople; Caesaria, sister of Caesarius of Arles.[28]

What is notable about several instances of Christian women's leadership, however, is the way in which their leadership and their patronage are intertwined. Thus, turning back to the pages of the New Testament, many (but not all) of the women noted as workers in the early Christian communities were also those who owned houses in which the Christian group in their area met. Attestation of this phenomenon exists for Aphia in Colossae, Prisca / Priscilla (along with husband Aquila) in Ephesus, Nympha in Laodicea, and Lydia in Philippi.[29] Later, women who became heads of convents often were the donors who paid for the construction of the monastery; in some cases, they are said to have left endowments for the operation of the monasteries after their deaths.[30] Thus the role of patron blends with that of institutional leader. Indeed, it would be a challenging project to compile the list of women known from early Christian annals who were recognized as Christian leaders *apart* from any known patronage function: I suspect that it might be rather short. Insofar as patronage was one of the few ways in antiquity for women to assume a public role, Christian women of means simply employed the existing social structures to advance the church's cause—and probably their own personal causes as well.[31]

If on the issues of marriage and church leadership patristic Christianity remained resolutely traditional, on other fronts there were ways for Christian women to make their mark: through support of alleged heretics, through martyrdom, and through asceticism. Of course, when such making a mark was in support of heresy, the woman's rebellion against the orthodox church was roundly condemned—but when that same resistance was directed to the service of ideals approved by male church leaders, it was applauded as the fruit of a "manly" spirit.

From the New Testament times onward, male Christian writers fretted about the supposed tendency of women to lapse into heterodox views. Already by the turn to the second century, the author of 1 Timothy complained that widows had "strayed after Satan," and that "weak women," "who will listen to anybody and can never arrive at a knowledge of the truth," were being led theologically astray by sham teachers who invaded their households.[32] In a brilliant article, Jouette Bassler has advanced the theory that these Christian women may indeed have been attracted to the so-called heretical movements (some of which appear to have been an early form of Gnosticism) by the larger roles available to them there.[33] When the churchmen of 1 Timothy attempted to impose stricter "eligibility" requirements on these widows, thus cutting down on the number of women who could be granted a special role within the "mainstream" church, they only exacerbated the situation they wished to correct: widows pushed out of roles within the developing Catholic church might well look for a warmer reception elsewhere.

From the second century on, we hear a litany of complaints from the church fathers against women's predilection to side with schismatics and heretics. That women assumed roles of leadership in the Montanist sect shocked early Christian writers.[34] Male gnostic leaders likewise were faulted for the prominence of females both within their ranks and within their myths.[35] Women of the imperial family in the fourth century, sometimes to the dismay of Catholic writers, sided with the Arians—for example, the empresses Eusebia and Justina. Priscillian, a Spanish heretic whose theology echoed themes reminiscent of Gnosticism, also

had notable women followers, one of whom, Euchrotia, had the ill fortune to be executed along with him in A.D. 385.[36] Slightly later, the
proponents of Origen's theology were labeled heretics—but that did not
dispel the support of the feisty and wealthy Melania the Elder.[37] And even
women who deemed themselves the pinnacles of Christian orthodoxy
were counted among the supporters of Pelagius' theology.[38] The fact that
many of these women commanded considerable financial resources made
their support of heretics all the more galling to mainstream churchmen,
who doubtless would have preferred that patronage be put solely at the
disposal of Catholic orthodoxy.

Martyrdom and asceticism, however, two other avenues of rebellion
open to early Christian women, were lauded by Christian authors. Both
martyrdom and asceticism represented strong attacks upon the prevailing sociopolitical structures of late pagan society. Although *we* may well
wonder how being martyred could be seen as a positive career path, so to
speak, Christians of the second through the early fourth centuries so saw
it. Not only did later Christians exalt these martyrs; the women and men
themselves are always represented in the martyr acts as joyfully giving
themselves to the Roman (or other) persecutors, remaining steadfast in
the Christian cause.

Among the more interesting features of the martyr accounts are that
not just women, but women of all social classes, are represented in
them. Thus the letter detailing the persecution of Christians in Lyons
and Vienne in A.D. 177 counts among the martyrs there both a slave girl,
Blandina, and her mistress.[39] The first martyrs of North Africa of whom
we know, the martyrs of Scillium put to death in A.D. 180, counted five
women among the twelve martyrs named, although we do not know their
social class.[40] Notable among third-century North African martyrs were
Perpetua and Felicitas: the former, from a good family, while the latter
was a slave.[41] We do not know the exact social status of the Thessaloni-
kan martyrs Agape, Irene, and Chione, put to death in A.D. 304, but in
their martyr account they are said to have abandoned "their family, property, and possessions" for the love of God.[42] The Persian and Arabian
female Christian martyrs and ascetics whose accounts Susan Ashbrook
Harvey and Sebastian Brock have recently translated also seem to come
from diverse social backgrounds. Some of the women are put to death
along with their servants; the martyr Anahid is the daughter of a Zoroas-
trian priest; and Ruhm, eventually martyred after refusing the proposal
of a king, is said to have been "of high standing," a standing attested to
by the notice that she had never shown her face outside the house.[43]

Although women martyrs are represented at their trials as calmly refusing to deny their Christian commitment, their steadfastness itself was seen as an act of defiance. Sometimes the defiance was directed against family members as well as against the interrogating officials: so we see in the case of Perpetua, who enraged her pagan father by claiming that she could no more cease to be a Christian than a waterpot could abandon its nature.[44] Some of the women politely aver that while they honor Caesar as Caesar, they cannot give him their highest allegiance, for this belongs to God.[45] Others defy their torturers with mockery: so the Persian martyr Anahid, who offers her severed breasts to her torturer with the words "Seeing that you very much wanted them, O Magian, here they are, do with them whatever takes your fancy. If I have any other limbs that you would like, give the order and I will cut them off and put them in front of you. I will not hold back anything I have from your banquet."[46] Bodies could be flayed and tossed by wild animals, limbs amputated—but the spirits of these women could not be broken. Such women proved invincible to the highest powers of state.

If martyrdom provided one framework within which Christian women's rejection of the political order could be manifested as fully and gloriously as men's, asceticism provided another. Indeed, male writers from the fourth century onward make explicit that asceticism provided a new arena for Christian combat once martyrdom was no longer an option.[47] In the earlier martyr accounts themselves, asceticism and martyrdom are closely aligned: sexual coercion or sentence to prostitution is often the threatened fate of a woman who refused to renounce her Christianity. Such themes appear in the martyrdoms of Potamiaena and of Irene; in the acts of the Persian and Arabian martyrs, forced marriage is seen as the equivalent of sexual coercion.[48] And in the Apocryphal Acts, with their fictional heroines, a woman can be made subject to persecution when she refuses marriage or marital relations.[49]

In the ascetic literature of the fourth and fifth centuries, we find the theme of women's defiance similarly construed. Here, the women who are cast as the most ardent revolutionaries are from the elite class, no doubt because they have the most to revolt *against* in the institution of marriage. For women from the lower social classes, renunciation may in practice have required less since there was less to renounce.[50] Indeed, for some of them, monasticism might represent an improvement of their social and material circumstances—a point about which Augustine worried.[51]

For aristocratic women, however, ascetic renunciation was both a significant religious choice and an act of rebellion against the social order.

Often represented as coming from small families, with only one or no siblings, these women's bodies were needed by their parents to consolidate power, property, wealth. Their refusal to cooperate with their parents' marital designs for them was a rebellion against both family and state. Since their defiance was manifested in ways that materially benefited the church and religious institutions, however, their pious biographers exalt their behavior—seen by the larger society as aberrant—as the height of pious sanctity.

Even though the conditions of marriage had been modified by later antiquity to favor the female more fully than earlier, aristocratic girls were still pawns in parental schemes to ensure suitable transmission of property within the senatorial class.[52] Church writers such as John Chrysostom provide evidence that upper-class girls may have had little say in the marriages arranged for them by their parents—and this despite the fact that by later antiquity, "consent" was supposed to be an important factor in Roman marriage law.[53] In his treatise *On Virginity* (written to lure girls away from marriage and toward the ascetic life) Chrysostom depicts the young girl trembling in anxiety at the choice of spouse her parents may make on her behalf. He imagines her asking, "What husband will [I] get? Will he not be low-born, dishonorable, arrogant, deceitful, boastful, rash, jealous, penurious, stupid, wicked, hard-hearted, effeminate?" Chrysostom compares her state of soul to that of a slave ignorant of who his future master will be. The suitors present their cases, the family accepts and rejects proposals. Since the girl is shut indoors, she has no way to ascertain the habits and appearance of the suitors her parents entertain.[54] Such is Chrysostom's rendition of the fate of aristocratic maidens.

That husbands of aristocratic girls were apt to be considerably older than they—despite the general tendency for the ages of spouses to be more approximate than in earlier time—is suggested by a variety of patristic evidence, both didactic and biographical.[55] On the didactic side, for example, Chrysostom counsels the husband to "regulate and direct" his bride since she is "wanting in wisdom." He is to teach her "as if he had an image given into his hands to mold." The husband is enjoined to make speeches to the young and tender maiden that will befit one whose temper is like a child's. Chrysostom provides a sample speech for the groom that begins, "I have taken thee, my child, to be partner of my life."[56]

On the biographical side, we can note that the vitae of women such as Olympias of Constantinople and Melania the Elder suggest that they were married as teenagers to men considerably older: we infer this from the important imperial and civic posts the husbands held, and from the fact that they died within a few years of the marriages.[57]

The feistiness of some of these aristocratic women as Christian ascetics is notable. Take the case of Olympias, deaconess of Constantinople and best friend of John Chrysostom in the last years of the fourth and the opening years of the fifth centuries. Orphaned at an early age, Olympias stemmed from a family which exhibited the extremely rapid upward mobility open to Christians in Constantine's Eastern capital. Her maternal grandfather Ablabius had not been from aristocratic stock, but was elevated to the senatorial aristocracy by Constantine in that emperor's bid to form a new, Christian senate for his recently founded capital city, where Ablabius served as praetorian prefect and as consul.[58] Both of Ablabius' daughters married well, and their families must have further enhanced the property and wealth that Ablabius had accrued.[59] When Olympias' parents died, the prefect of Constantinople himself served as her guardian.[60] She was raised so as to make her a desirable mate for a leading senator—and indeed her husband of very brief duration, Nebridius, was such: he was appointed prefect of Constantinople in 386, a year after their marriage.[61] When he died shortly thereafter, Olympias was the sole heir of a vast fortune.[62] She opted for Christian asceticism, and here her troubles began.

The Emperor Theodosius I himself tried to force her into a marriage with one of his own relatives, which he doubtless (and correctly) understood would be financially advantageous for his family. When Olympias refused, she was punished by having her property put under guardianship so that she could not give it all to the church.[63] (When I speak of her property, I mean something beyond what most of us today would think imaginable: one recent reckoning of her donations to the church in present-day American dollars estimates the amount at 900 million dollars, not counting the extensive real estate she also gave.)[64] Eventually Theodosius relented, and Olympias was allowed to be ordained as a deaconess, although she was underage for such a position.[65] We are told that she "maintained" Nectarius, then the bishop of Constantinople, as well as the operations of the Constantinople church during the time Chrysostom reigned.[66] She then had built, and assumed the headship of, a monastery for women in Constantinople that housed 250 women.[67]

Other accounts of ascetic women in this era also sound the note of resistance. Sometimes the defiance was more explicitly of family than was the case with the orphaned Olympias. Jerome's friend in Rome, Marcella, turned down a proposal from an elderly and wealthy ex-consul. When asked the reason by her mother, who apparently favored the union, Marcella reportedly replied, "If I wanted to marry rather than dedicate myself to perpetual chastity, I'd look for a husband, not for an inheritance."[68]

Another example is provided by Melania the Younger, only daughter of an aristocratic family that wished to consolidate its already vast resources by marrying her to her cousin.[69] Although forced into the marriage (according to her biographer), she defied her parents' command to bathe at the public baths, and on more than one occasion, attempted to flee her marriage.[70] Her struggle to retain her property so that she might use it for Christian causes engaged her in a battle against her husband's brother which took the intervention of the imperial court to settle.[71] Her vita further reports that the city prefect of Rome at the time of Alaric's initial onslaughts on the city attempted to confiscate her property, probably—so we infer from other sources—to dispel the Gothic threat with a bribe.[72] (She was saved from the latter confiscation by the murder of the prefect during a bread riot, an episode smugly reported by her biographer.)[73] Toward the end of her life, she trekked from Jerusalem to Constantinople to wrest a deathbed confession of Christianity from her still pagan uncle, who was in Constantinople on a high-level diplomatic mission.[74] The money she had been able to rescue from the hands of relatives and city prefects—and what income from property was left after the Gothic sack of Rome—she used for building monasteries in North Africa and Jerusalem, as well as for other Christian causes.[75] Money that would, in earlier generations, have enriched one's descendants, supported civic institutions, and refurbished public buildings has here been withdrawn from public circulation—the financial parallel to the withdrawal of the female body from the breeding of future aristocrats.[76]

That such a withholding of the female body from social use has radical feminist implications has been well noted by Gayle Rubin in her now-classic essay "The Traffic in Women: Notes on the 'Political Economy' of Sex."[77] Providing (among other points) a feminist interpretation of Claude Levi-Strauss's *Elementary Forms of Kinship* and of Marcel Mauss's *The Gift: Forms and Functions of Exchange in Archaic Societies*, Rubin writes:

> If it is women who are being transacted, then it is the men who give and take them who are linked, the women being a conduit of a relationship rather than a partner to it. The exchange of women does not necessarily imply that women are objectified, in the modern sense, since objects in the primitive world are imbued with highly personal qualities. But it does imply a distinction between gift and giver. If women are the gifts, then it is men who are the exchange partners. And it is the partners, not the

presents, upon whom reciprocal exchange confers its quasi-mystical power of social linkage. The relations of such a system are such that women are in no position to realize the benefits of their own circulation. As long as the relations specify that men exchange women, it is men who are the beneficiaries of the product of such exchanges—social organization.[78]

At the conclusion of her provocative essay, Rubin provides an agenda for future research. Her list of topics to be explored includes the following:

> Traditional concerns of anthropology and social science—such as the evolution of social stratification and the origin of the state—must be reworked to include the implications of matrilateral cross-cousin marriage, surplus extracted in the form of daughters, the conversion of female labor into male wealth, the conversion of female lives into marriage alliances, the contribution of marriage to political power, and the transformations which all of these varied aspects of society have undergone in the course of time.[79]

That part of Rubin's agenda might find rich sources in the ascetic literature of late antiquity, I hope I have made evident. The success of early Christian women in working against the social and political order of their day thus appears more notable than their accommodation, whether forced or voluntary, to the traditional structures of marriage and to their exclusion from the main seats of power within the church.

## NOTES

1 / For Helena, see Eusebius, *Vita Constantini* 3, 41–46, text in J. P. Migne, ed., *Patrologia Graeca* (Paris, 1857–66) 20, cols. 1101–5 (hereafter cited as *PG*). See also Socrates, *Historia ecclesiastica* 1, 17 (*PG* 67, cols. 117–21) and Sozomen, *Historia ecclesiastica* 2, 1–2 (*PG* 67, cols. 929–36). For Justina, see Socrates, *Historia ecclesiastica* 5, 11 (*PG* 67, col. 596), Sozomen, *Historia ecclesiastica* 7, 13 (*PG* 67, cols. 1447–49), and Ambrose, *Epistula* 20 (= 76), 18, text in *Corpus Scriptorum Ecclesisticorum Latinorum* (Vienna, 1866–) 82[3], 118 (hereafter *CSEL*). For Eudoxia's role in the expulsion of Chrysostom from Constantinople, see Socrates, *Historia ecclesiastica* 6, 15; 18 (*PG* 67, cols. 708–12), Sozomen, *Historia ecclesiastica* 8, 16; 20 (*PG* 67, col. 1557), and Palladius, *Dialogus de vita S. Joannis Chrysostomi* 30, ed. P. R. Coleman-Norton (Cambridge: Cambridge Univ. Press, 1928), 51.

2 / Many verses can be adduced that illustrate views ascribed to Jesus on divorce, and on marital and sexual morality: Matt. 10:34–39 ‖ Luke 14:26–27; Mark 3:31–35 ‖ Matt. 12:46–50 ‖ Luke 8:19–21; Mark 13:12–13 ‖ Matt. 24:21 ‖ Luke 21:16; Luke 11:27; Luke 23:28–29; Mark 12:25 ‖ Matt. 22:30 ‖ Luke 20:34–36; Matt. 19:10–12; cf. Mark 3:19b–

21. See Derrick Sherwin Bailey, *Sexual Relation in Christian Thought* (New York: Harper and Row, 1959), 11; Jean Gaudemet, "Droit romain et principes canoniques en matière de mariage au Bas-Empire," in his *Sociétés et mariage*, Recherches institutionnelles 4 (Strasbourg: Cerdic-Publications, 1980), 122.

3 / Musonius Rufus, 12. Text in Cora Lutz, *Musonius Rufus, "The Roman Socrates"* (New Haven: Yale Univ. Press, 1947), 84–87.

4 / Gen. 2:24, cited in Matt. 19:5 ∥ Mark 10:8; cf. its later use in Eph. 5:31, also to apply to marriage.

5 / 1 Cor. 6:15–20.

6 / 1 Cor. 7:4.

7 / John Chrysostom, *Propter fornicationes uxorem* 4 (*PG* 51, col. 214); *Homilia 19 I Cor.* 1 (*PG* 61, col. 152).

8 / John Chrysostom, *Homilia 5 I Thess.*, 2 (*PG* 62, col. 425); *Propter fornicationes uxorem* 2 (*PG* 51, col. 214).

9 / John Chrysostom, *De Anna* 1, 6 (*PG* 54, cols. 642–43); *Homilia 59 Matt.* 7 (*PG* 58, cols. 582–83); *Homilia 5 I Thess.* 3 (*PG* 62, col. 426); *De inani gloria* 53; 81; 82, text in *Sources Chrétiennes* (Paris: Editions du Cerf, 1943–) 188, 152, 186–90 (hereafter *SC*); cf. Jean Dumortier, "Le Mariage dans les milieux chrétiennes d'Antioche et de Byzance d'après Saint Jean Chrysostome," *Lettres d'Humanité* 6 (1947): 111.

10 / On Roman marriage law, see Riccardo Orestona, *La struttura giuridica del matrimonio romano dal diritto classico al diritto giustinianeo* 1 (Milano: Antonio Giuffrè, 1951); idem, "Alcune considerazioni sui rapporti fra matrimonio cristiano e matrimonio romano nell' età postclassica," in *Scritti di diritto romano in honore di Contardo Ferrini*, ed. Gian Gualberto Archi, (Milano: Ulrico Hoepli, 1946), 345–82; Emilio Albertario, *Studi di diritto romano* 1 (Milano: Antonio Giuffrè, 1933), esp. chaps. 10–12; Percy Ellwood Corbett, *The Roman Law of Marriage* (Oxford: Clarendon Press, 1930); Jean Gaudemet, *Sociétés et Mariage*; Kunkel's article "Matrimonium," in A. Pauly and G. Wissowa, *Realencyclopädie der classischen Altertumswissenschaft* 14, 2 (Stuttgart, 1893–), 2259–86; Albertio's article "Matrimonio," in *Enciclopedia Italiana* 22 (1934), 580–81; Hans Julius Wolff, "Doctrinal Trends in Postclassical Roman Marriage Law," *Zeitschrift der Savigny-Stiftung für Rechtsgeschichte*, Romanistiche Abteilung 67 (1950), 261–391; Alan Watson, *The Law of Persons in the Later Roman Republic* (Oxford: Clarendon Press, 1967), esp. chaps. 1–7; A. Esmein, *Le Mariage en droit canonique*, 2d ed. (Paris: Librairie du Recueil Sirey, 1928), and Jane E. Gardner, *Women in Roman Law and Society* (Bloomington and Indianapolis: Indiana Univ. Press, 1986), esp. chaps. 3–5. For Christian modifications see Henri Crouzel, *Mariage et divorce, célibat et caractère sacerdotaux dans l'église ancienne* Etudes d'histoire du culte et des institutions chrétiennes 2 (Torino: Bottega d'Erasmo, 1982), pt. 1.

11 / 1 Cor. 7:12–16, 27.

12 / Jerome, *Epistle* 77, 1; 2; 12 (*CSEL* 55, 37–38, 48–49).

13 / Titus 2:5; 1 Tim. 5:14b. See Elisabeth Schüssler Fiorenza, *In Memory of Her: A Feminist Theological Reconstruction of Christian Origins* (New York: Crossroad, 1983), esp. chap. 7; David L. Balch, *"Let Wives Be Submissive . . .": The Domestic Code in I Peter.* Society of Biblical Literature Monograph Series 26 (Chico, Calif.: Scholars Press, 1981), esp. chap. 8.

14 / 1 Pet. 3:1–2; cf. Balch, *"Let Wives be Submissive,"* chap. 8.

15 / Clement of Alexandria, *Paedagogus* II, 2, 33; 7, 54; 10, 109–10, 114; 13, 122–28; III, 2, 5–9. Text in *Die Griechische Christliche Schriftsteller der ersten drei Jahrhunderte* (Leipzig: J. C. Hinrich, 1913) 12, 176, 190, 222–23, 225, 230–33, 238–41 (hereafter *GCS*).

16 / 1 Tim. 2:11–14; cf. Gen. 2–3.

17 / For example, John Chrysostom, *Homilia 9 I Tim.* 1 (*PG* 62, col. 544); *Homilia 14 Gen.* 4 (*PG* 53, col. 115); *Homilia 26 I Cor.* 2 (*PG* 61, col. 215); Ambrose, *De paradiso* 14, 72 (*CSEL* 32, 329).

18 / For example, John Chrysostom, *De non iterando coniugio* 5 (*SC* 138, 1881); Jerome, *Adversus Helvidium* 20–21, text in J. P. Migne, ed., *Patrologia Latina* (Paris, 1844–66) 23, 213–16 (hereafter *PL*).

19 / Augustine, *Confessions* IX, 9, 19, text in *Corpus Scriptorum Christianorum, Series Latina* (Turnholt: Typograph Brepolis editores Pontificii, 1953–) 27, 145 (hereafter *CCL*).

20 / Augustine, *Epistle* 262 (*CSEL* 57, 621–31).

21 / Rom. 15:3, 6, 12 and 16:1–2.

22 / 1 Tim. 3:11. Given the views of the author of 1 Timothy, probably the latter.

23 / Elisabeth Schüssler Fiorenza, "Women in the Pre-Pauline and Pauline Churches," *Union Seminary Quarterly Review* 33 (1978): 153–66; idem, *In Memory of Her*, esp. chap. 5.

24 / Hippolytus, *Refutatio* 8, 19 (*GCS* 26, 238); Eusebius, *Historia ecclesiastica* 5, 16 (*PG* 20, cols. 469–72); Epiphanius, *Panarion* 49, 1–2 (*PG* 41, cols. 880–81); Hippolytus, *Refutatio* 6, 40 (*GCS* 26, 171–72); Irenaeus, *Adversus haereses* I, 13, 1–2 (*PG* 7, cols. 577–81); Epiphanius, *Panarion* 42, 4 (*PG* 41, col. 700); Irenaeus, *Adversus haereses* I, 25, 6 (*PG* 7, col. 685); Tertullian, *De praescriptione haereticorum* 41 (*PL* 2, cols. 68–69).

25 / For a convenient collection of the patristic references, see Roger Gryson, *The Ministry of Women in the Early Church*, trans. J. Laporte and M. L. Hall (Collegeville, Minn.: Liturgical Press, 1980).

26 / *Constitutiones apostolorum* 3, 16, text in F. X. Funk, ed., *Didascalia et Constitutiones apostolorum* (Paderborn: Ferdinand Schoeningh, 1905) I, 209, 211.

27 / *Vitae patrum* V, 4, 61 (*PL* 73, col. 872); *Vita Pachomii* 27 (Bohairic), text in *Corpus Scriptorum Christianorum Orientalium, Scriptores Coptici* (Louvain: E. Peeters, 1906–) 7, 26–28 (hereafter *CSCO*).

28 / *Vita Pachomii* 27 (Bohairic) (*CSCO*, 7, 26–27); Palladius, *Historia Lausiaca* 46, text ed. Cuthbert Butler, *Historia Lausiaca: The Lausiac History of Palladius* (Cambridge: Cambridge Univ. Press, 1898–1904), 135–36; Jerome, *Epistle* 108, 20 (*CSEL* 55, 334–36); Gregory of Nyssa, *Vita Macrinae* (*PG* 46, 969 ff.); *Vita Olympiadis* 6–7 (*SC* 13 bis, 418–20); see Caesarius of Arles, *Regula sanctarum virginum*, in G. Morin ed., *Sancti Caesarii Episcopi Arlatensis Opera* (Martioli, 1942), 129–44, letters to his sister, Caesaria.

29 / Phile. 2; 1 Cor. 16:19; Rom. 16:5; Col. 4:15; Acts 16:14.

30 / On Paula, Jerome, *Epistle* 108, 14; 20 (*CSEL* 55, 325, 334–36); on Melania the Elder, Palladius, *Historia Lausiaca* 46; 54 (Butler 135–36, 148).

31 / See Elizabeth A. Clark, "Patrons, Not Priests: Gender and Power in Late Ancient Christianity," *Gender & History* 2 (1990).

32 / 1 Tim. 5:15, 3:6–7.

33 / Jouette M. Bassler, "The Widows' Tale: A Fresh Look at I Tim. 5:3–16," *Journal of Biblical Literature* 103 (1984): 23–41.

34 / Hippolytus, *Refutatio* 8, 19 (*GCS* 26, 238).

35 / For example, Irenaeus, *Adversus haereses* 1, 1–8 (Valentinians); 13 (Marcosians); 23 (Simonians); 30 (Sethians) (*PG* 7, cols. 445–537, 577–92, 669–73, 694–704).

36 / On women's involvement with heresy, see Sozomen, *Historia ecclesiastica* 3, 1 (*PG* 67, col. 1033); Ambrose, *Epistle* 20 ‖ 76, 18 (*CSEL* 823, 118); Sozomen, *Historia ecclesiastica* 7, 13 (*PG* 67, cols. 1447–49). For the fullest treatment of Priscillianism, see Henry Chadwick, *Priscillian of Avila: The Occult and the Charismatic in the Early Church* (Oxford: Clarendon Press, 1976). Also see Jerome, *Epistle* 133, 4 (*CSEL* 56, 245).

37 / For a summary of the evidence, see Elizabeth A. Clark, *The Life of Melania the Younger: Introduction, Translation, and Commentary* (New York and Toronto: Edwin Mellen Press, 1984), 141–43.

38 / Pelagius, *Epistula ad Demetriadem* (*PL* 30, cols. 16–46). For Augustine's fears regarding the Anician women, also see Peter Brown, "The Patrons of Pelagius: The Roman Aristocracy between East and West," *Journal of Theological Studies*, n.s. 21 (1970): 56–72 (reprinted in *Religion and Society in the Age of Saint Augustine* [New York: Harper and Row, 1972], 208–26), and Augustine, *De bono viduitatis* 17, 21 (*CSEL* 41, 329), and *Epistle* 188 (*CSEL* 57, 119–30).

39 / The account of the martyrs of Lyons is preserved in Eusebius, *Historia ecclesiastica* V, 1, 3–2, 8, text in Herbert Musurillo, trans., *The Acts of the Christian Martyrs* (Oxford: Clarendon Press, 1972), 66–67.

40 / *Passio Sanctorum Scillitanorum* 1, 16 (Musurillo 86–89).

41 / *Passio Sanctarum Perpetuae et Felicitatis* 2 (Musurillo 108–9).

42 / *Martyrion tōn Hagiōn Agapēs, Eirēnēs, kai Chionēs* 1 (Musurillo 280–81).

43 / "The Martyrdom of Tarbo, her Sister, and her Servant," translation in Sebastian P. Brock and Susan Ashbrook Harvey, *Holy Women of the Syrian Orient*, Transformations of the Classical Heritage 13 (Berkeley: Univ. of California Press, 1987), 73–76; "Anahid" (Brock and Harvey 82–99); and "Women Martyrs of Najran" (Brock and Harvey 108, 111–15).

44 / *Passio Sanctarum Perpetuae et Felicitatis* 3 (Musurillo 108–9).

45 / For example, Donata in *Passio Sanctorum Scillitanorum* 9 (Musurillo 88–89).

46 / "Persian Martyrs" (Brock and Harvey 95).

47 / For the classic argument, see Edward E. Malone, *The Monk and the Martyr: The Monk as the Successor of the Martyr*, The Catholic University of America Studies in Christian Antiquity 12 (Washington, D.C.: Catholic Univ. of America Press, 1950).

48 / *Martyrion tōn Hagiōn Potamainēs kai Basileidou* 2 (Musurillo 132–33); *Martyrion tōn Hagiōn Agapēs, Eirēnēs, kai Chiones* 5, 8 (Musurillo 290–91); and, for example, the martyrdoms of Martha, Tarbo, Thekla, and Anahid, "Persian Martyrs" (Brock and Harvey, 67–73, 73–76, 78–81, 82–99).

49 / Especially Thecla in *Acta Pauli* 20–22, 27–38, in R. Lipsius and M. Bonnet, *Acta Apostolorum apocrypha* (rpt. Hildesheim: George Olms, 1959) I, 248–51, 254–64.

50 / Nicely illustrated by the rejoinder of the aristocrat-turned-ascetic to the simple Egyptian monk in *Vitae patrum* V, 10, 76 (*PL* 73, cols. 925–27).

51 / Augustine, *De opere monachorum* 22 (25) (*PL* 40, col. 568); *Epistle* 211, 6 (*CSEL* 57, 360–61).

52 / David Herlihy, *Medieval Households* (Cambridge: Harvard Univ. Press, 1985), 14–16.
53 / See esp. Josef Huber, *Der Ehekonsens in Römichen Recht, Studien zu seinem Begriffsgehalt im der Klassik und zur Frage seines Wandels in der Nachklassik*, Analecta Gregoriana 204 (Roma: Università Gregoriana Editrice, 1977); Giuseppe d'Ercole, "Il consenso degli sposi e la perpetuità del matrimonio nel diritto romano e nei Padri della Chiesa," *Studia et documenta historiae et iuris* 5 (1939): 18–75; Susan Treggiari, "Consent to Roman Marriage: Some Aspects of Law and Reality," *Echos du Monde Classique / Classical Views* 26 (1982): 34–44. For a summary of opinions, see Elizabeth A. Clark, "'Adam's Only Companion': Augustine and the Early Christian Debate on Marriage," *Recherches Augustiniennes* 21 (1986): 158–61.
54 / John Chrysostom, *De virginitate* 57 (SC 125, 308).
55 / Herlihy, *Medieval Households*, 19, and M. K. Hopkins, "The Age of Roman Girls at Marriage," *Population Studies* 18 (1965): 321.
56 / John Chrysostom, *Homilia* 20, *Eph.* 8–9 (PG 62, cols. 146–48).
57 / *Vita Olympiadis* 2 (SC 13 bis, 410); Palladius, *Historia Lausiaca* 46; 56 (Butler 134, 149–50).
58 / See A. H. M. Jones, J. R. Martindale, and J. Morris, *The Prosopography of the Later Roman Empire*, vol. 1: *A.D. 260–395* (Cambridge: Cambridge Univ. Press, 1971), 3–4; *Vita Olympiadis* 2 (SC 13 bis, 408–10).
59 / Ammianus Marcellinus XX, 11, 3.
60 / *Vita Olympiadis* 2 (SC 13 [2d ed.], 410); Gregory of Nazianzen, *Epistle* 193 (PG 37, cols. 315–17) (the inference is that Procopius was Olympias's guardian).
61 / *Vita Olympiadis* 2 (SC 13 [2d ed.], 410); Palladius, *Dialogus* 56 (Coleman-Norton 98).
62 / *Historia Lausiaca* 56, 1 (Butler 150); *Vita Olympiadis* 2 (SC 13 [2d ed.], 410).
63' / *Vita Olympiadis* 3–4 (SC 13 [2d ed.], 410–14).
64 / *Vita Olympiadis* 5 (SC 13 [2d ed.], 416): 10,000 pounds of gold, 20,000 of silver, plus real estate in Thrace, Galatia, Cappadocia Prima, Bithynia, and Constantinople.
65 / *Vita Olympiadis* 5–6 (SC 13 [2d ed.], 414, 418). For sixty as the age of ordination of deaconesses, see Basil, *Epistle* 199, 24 (PG 32, col. 723); *Codex Theodosianus* XVI, 2, 27. The Council of Chalcedon in 451 proclaimed 40 to be a suitable age (canon 15).
66 / Palladius, *Dialogus* 61 (Coleman-Norton 110); *Vita Olympiadis* 14 (SC 13 [2d ed.], 436).
67 / *Vita Olympiadis* 6 (SC 13 [2d ed.], 418–20).
68 / Jerome, *Epistle* 127, 2 (CSEL 56, 146).
69 / *Vita Melaniae Junioris* 1 (SC 90, 130); for the family tree, see stemmata 20 and 30 in *Prosopography* I, 1142, 1147.
70 / *Vita Melaniae Junioris* 2 (SC 90, 132) and 4 (SC 90, 132).
71 / *Vita Melaniae Junioris* 10–12 (SC 90, 144–52).
72 / For a discussion of some of the recent hypotheses and an analysis of the evidence, see Clark, *The Life of Melania the Younger*, 101–9.
73 / *Vita Melaniae Junioris* 19 (SC 90, 166).
74 / *Vita Melaniae Junioris* 50; 54–55 (SC 90, 224, 234–38).
75 / *Vita Melaniae Junioris* 10–14; 22; 41; 49 (SC 90, 144–56, 172, 204–6, 220–22).

76 / Melania's vita states that she was forced by her husband to bear two children to inherit their property before he would consider a vow of chastity. She bore the two children, both of whom died. So anxious was her husband for her mental and physical health that he, too, pledged himself to chastity (*Vita Melaniae Junioris* 1; 3; 5; 6 [SC 90, 132, 134–38]).

77 / Gayle Rubin, "The Traffic in Women: Notes on the 'Political Economy' of Sex," in Rayna R. Reiter, ed., *Toward an Anthropology of Women* (New York: Monthly Review Press, 1975), 157–210.

78 / Ibid., 174.

79 / Ibid., 210.

## 3

*Susan Ashbrook Harvey*

## Women in Early
## Byzantine Hagiography:
## Reversing the Story

MUCH HAS BEEN WRITTEN ABOUT WOMEN in Byzantine history.[1] In recent years, the use of hagiography as a source for this study has become popular, both for what it tells us about women saints and for its incidental depictions of women's lives.[2] The dangers of historical method are here well known: first, that hagiography is a symbolic form of literary discourse for which the question of historicity matters only in relation to the story's meaning; and second, that hagiography even when written about women is most often written by men. During the early Byzantine period in particular, hagiography is almost exclusively the product of male writers. For that period we have little if any writing by women to compare with what hagiography says about them, and the editorial presence of male authors is invariably and overtly felt. In the case of historical women, one can find severe tension between the attitude of the writer and the career he is describing. In the case of legendary women, one often confronts a model consciously molded to conform to certain social expectations.

I would like to examine what early Byzantine hagiography between the fourth and seventh centuries tells us about women, on its own terms. Rather than seeking historical data, I am interested in hagiography's depiction of women according to its own purpose as symbolic literature. From this view, the interplay between historical and legendary material, between event and image, becomes highly fluid; they are often interchangeable. Because hagiography is a didactic literature, what it describes is never sufficient to account for its message. It teaches a theological moral to every story it tells, and it is that moral which this paper seeks to understand.

I turn first to a brief review of the hagiographer's purpose and method, with the specific tradition of early Byzantine hagiography in mind.

The primary concern of hagiography is the encounter of the human and the holy.[3] The saint embodies divine presence in the world and enacts divine agency. In its turn, hagiography tells the story of the saint as a means for revealing God's truth and purpose. Closely tied in function, saint and story contain in each occurrence Christianity's own story.

Thus the saint is understood to be the true disciple of Christ. The Gospels had defined discipleship as the imitation of Christ—doing what he had done—and by that imitation gaining the power to accomplish those same actions by which he himself had made known God's redeeming grace: feeding the hungry, healing the sick, exorcizing demons, teaching, guiding, and exercising authority over a world in which people themselves had little control. In both the natural and human realms, the saint could restore a fallen existence: rain could be brought in times of drought, taxes remitted in times of hardship. The saint was known by actions, understood in the most tangibly concrete sense: the saint's activity made the saint's identity.

In turn, it was the hagiographer's task to make that activity known for what it really was: God's presence and work in the midst of human life. Just as the saint imitated Christ in action, the hagiographer imitated Christ's story in the telling. The gospel model is always the form that dictates the hagiographer's text. This works at various levels. In legend, hagiography is often a variation on the gospel story itself. In its biographical form, hagiography will tell the saint's story using the gospel as a lens through which to understand the career of the subject. In this way, the hagiographer can in effect "construct" the saint, fitting the story into a prescribed form. While the results tell us the theological meaning of the saint's career, we may lose sight of what actually took place.

But hagiography performed a function. It identified where and how the divine was at work, and it did so by telling the story of the holy one, imitating the activity of the gospel text. Its purpose was that of the Gospels: not simply to reveal the work of salvation that had taken place, but further, to show how that work could be done—to inspire imitation on the part of those who heard the story. Just as the story imitated the Gospel, just as the saint imitated Christ, the believer could imitate the saint's story—the saint's activity—and so bring anew the playing out of the salvation drama. In the person of the saint, as in the person of Christ, story and action become inseparable. The function of hagiography is to make this identification happen.

It is here that we see how the line between legend and history becomes irrelevant. Far more important is the way in which person and story, saint and hagiography, perform the same task. Thus, for example, Theodoret of Cyrrhus tells us in his *Historia Religiosa* that he writes hagiography about both men and women so that people will have both male and female models to imitate.[4] He describes the imitation of actual encounters: the holy woman Domnina imitated the way of life pursued by the hermit Maron and therein gained her own sanctity.[5] Having imitated a holy man, she became a model also for women who came to her. Theodoret's desire is that his audience will imitate the stories he tells just as if they had actually met his subjects.[6] Responding to such a desire, St. Melania the Younger was an avid reader of saints' lives throughout her career, and self-consciously sought to imitate what she read.[7]

Did she read about real or legendary women? The question is meaningless. In the vita of the legendary St. Eugenia, the saint was converted to Christianity by reading the story of the legendary St. Thecla.[8] But in the *Life of St. Macrina* by her brother Gregory of Nyssa, we are told how important the model of Thecla was for the life of this real woman, and how Macrina herself, imitating her model, became the model for others.[9] So, too, is Thecla important as a model in the epic romance about St. Febronia,[10] and for the hagiographer of Olympias, friend and sustainer of John Chrysostom.[11] Hagiography, whether telling the stories of real or legendary women, gave women a model to imitate in their own lives that included them as women in the work that God intended and performed. This alone granted hagiography a position of serious efficacy as a social force; the extent to which it could be successful may be sensed, for example, in the article by Elizabeth Clark in this collection.[12]

Early Byzantine hagiography about historical women was, above all, a literature of paradox. Against all odds, we are told, women were worth writing about. The fact was that a model for holy women existed, in story and in reality. In legend, St. Thecla beat up men who attacked her and slew wild animals with a single glance;[13] St. Mary of Egypt levitated and walked on water.[14] In reality, holy women founded and ran monasteries for both women and men;[15] established and conducted social service networks for whole cities;[16] ran underground railways for religious refugees;[17] fought the Roman Senate[18] or the emperor himself;[19] were notable scholars[20] and teachers;[21] wore iron chains so heavy that men could barely lift them,[22] and followed such severe ascetic regimes that men were jealous.[23]

Sometimes the considerable impact of these women stemmed from high social status: the impressive accomplishments of aristocratic holy women have been well treated by recent scholars.[24] Sometimes women earned their positions of authority and influence by the impact of their actions. Matrona's many friends in high places—including two empresses—seem to have been gained by the simple force of her teaching and works.[25] The holy woman Susan ran away from her noble family as a child, changed her name, and entered a convent in Palestine as a person with no identity or history. Years later, under extreme conditions of religious persecution, Susan was recruited (much against her will) to direct a monastic community of women and men in Egypt—both the monks and nuns wanted her not because of who she was but because of what she had achieved.[26] More pointedly, the holy woman Euphemia and her daughter Maria worked for their living in the city of Amida. Maria spun yarn which Euphemia sold to feed the hungry and tend the sick.[27] Some of the citizens complained, among other reasons, because Euphemia left her daughter alone all day to spin while she herself went out to work.[28]

In other words, holy women did what holy men did; and it is clear from their vitae (as well as other documents) that in so doing they were often a source of distress to the men in authority over them, and to the men who wrote about them. That is, it is clear that holy women often did what they wanted to do, on their own terms. Here the issue of imitation, or models, cannot be overestimated.

Still, the real holy women we hear about do not seem to have thought about breaking out of social or cultural oppression, as we might think of such activity. It was not a sense of self or self-worth that led them outside their normal boundaries—quite the opposite. It was the sense that God had called them to do particular work; therefore, they must do it. This was a bypassing of the self, or rendering the self irrelevant. Thus Susan, the unwilling monastic leader of men and women, hid her face completely from men throughout her career, fearing both that she might cause harm to a man and might suffer it herself; yet one day she explained to a discouraged monk how she found the strength to battle demons. "I am aware that the strength of the Lord surrounds my weakness like a wall of bronze, and there is no other power that can rise against it."[29] So, too, did Euphemia explain why she and her daughter would not accept help with their work, or an easier occupation (perhaps even a more acceptable one): "God gives me strength, and that poor girl who is with me, so that we may work for our own needs and minister to our brothers according to our strength."[30] What mattered was not who one was, a woman, but the vocation to which one was called.

The apparent paradox of women's behavior was mirrored in its literary expression: paradox characterized early Byzantine hagiographical language about women. Here, in the language of the hagiography itself, we confront the heavy-handed presence of male writers at every level. We see it first at the basic level of literary formulas. The topoi used to distinguish hagiography about women from that about men are variations on a simple theme: although inferior to men as a lot, women can sometimes achieve lives worth imitating—worth telling—and this alone is cause for wonder.

Thus hagiographers felt compelled to justify telling a woman's story, despite the apostolic injunction that in Christ there is neither male nor female (Gal. 3:28) which was often cited for support.[31] Theodoret of Cyrrhus commented in his *Historia Religiosa* that holy women are worthy of greater praise than men, because they have had to overcome a weaker nature.[32] John of Ephesus insisted that he had not lowered the standards of his hagiographical collection, the *Lives of the Eastern Saints*, when he chose to include stories of women.[33] Palladius claimed that he included women in his *Lausiac History* "so that no one could plead as an excuse that women are too weak to practice virtue successfully."[34] Indeed, the fact that women might be successful could itself be a lesson. The east Syrian writer Martyrius (Sahdona) prefaced his portrait of the holy woman Shirin with these words: "But why should I talk just about men? Let us examine the weak nature of the frail female sex to see whether the beauty of the virtuous life is not also revealed to us in the godlike women who trampled on sin and Satan. I myself am ashamed to gaze on their valiant deeds when I consider the laxity of us men; but it is right that this beauty should be made public—to our greater confusion, and to the glory of those women."[35]

It was a short step from this topos to the next: women who achieved sanctity had surpassed their sex, reversing the pattern of their gender. How else to account for the remarkable deeds of "weak, feeble, frail women"?[36] Gregory of Nyssa hesitated to call his sister Macrina a woman, not knowing "if it is right to use that natural designation for one who went beyond the nature of a woman."[37] Palladius called Melania the Elder "that female man of God."[38] Melania the Younger was received by the monks of Cellia "as if she were a man. In truth, she had been detached from the female nature and had acquired a masculine disposition, or rather, a heavenly one."[39] John of Ephesus described Mary the Anchorite as "a woman who by nature only carried the form of females, but who also carried in herself the way of life and soul and will not only of ordinary men, but of strong and valiant men."[40]

Each holy woman is presented as the exception to her kind, so much so, that she ceases to be of her own kind, becoming instead an honorary

male. No matter how many virtuous women were found—Theodoret, for example, mentions convents with "hundreds" of exemplary women;[41] Palladius claimed that Ancyra alone had "thousands" of excellent virgins, "remarkable women indeed"[42]—each one was an exception. To view holy women in this way curtailed their impact on societal attitudes. The image of women as a whole remained unredeemed.

Hagiographies about men present the same problematic, and paradoxical, view. The notion that women by nature continue the work of Eve is ubiquitous. Exhorting that even the sight of a woman represents destruction for men is a constant topos in these texts. John Moschus told the story of Abba Thomas, whose antipathy to women was such that when he was buried the earth around his body spat out any women buried nearby.[43] Of course, this topos was more than a literary commonplace. Cyril of Scythopolis in his *Lives* of Saints Euthymius and Sabas reported that women were not the only people denied access to their monasteries: beardless men—eunuchs and young boys—merely because they resembled women were also a source of grave concern, and were sometimes banned.[44]

But the hagiographers betray themselves. Cyril of Scythopolis included no women subjects in his *Lives of Palestinian Saints* (despite the many famous convents of the Judean desert).[45] Yet he reports that two of his subjects, Theodosius and Theognius, were led to their holy careers by female spiritual mentors, whose names he nonetheless does not consider worth reporting.46 In his *Life of John the Hesychast*, another young man is brought to the religious life by a pious nun, Basilina, to whom John would not deign to grant an audience.[47] Cyril himself was brought to his ecclesiastical vocation by the piety of both his parents.[48] So, too, did Theodoret of Cyrrhus meet several of his subjects because of his mother's concern for her own and her son's spiritual guidance.[49]

More pointed is this paradox as it appears in hagiographic stereotype. John Moschus, for one, presents women in a singularly monotonous view: in his *Pratum Spirituale*, women are almost invariably presented as the source of sexual temptation for men—and this they are frequently.[50] However, John himself undermines the force of this view. The prostitutes he writes about have often turned to that profession because of simple hunger, or destitution.[51] Repeatedly, the women who represent temptation for the monks are themselves virtuous, and are not the source of the temptation, which is rather the devil himself. Instead, they talk the passion-crazed monks out of their attempted rapes, exhorting them on the meaning of their vocational vows and what the loss of their religious careers would mean for the future of their souls.[52] These women save men from themselves. Moschus may present women as the ever-threatening downfall of holy men, but he also tells us women are not in fact the problem. They may even be the solution. In terms of lust, they come off as far more virtuous than the holy men who are his subjects. Palladius, in two similar stories, had stated that even where holy women led impeccably exemplary lives, their beauty led men to suspect the worst.[53]

The motif of the virtuous woman saving the lustful man could, however, take a more ominous tone. The holy woman Alexandra lived immured in a tomb for some years. Asked by Melania the Elder why she had chosen this course, she replied, "A man was distracted in mind because of me, and rather than scandalize a soul made in the image of God, I betook myself alive to a tomb, lest I seem to cause him suffering or reject him."[54] In a similar story, John Moschus wrote of a woman recluse relentlessly pursued by an infatuated ("possessed") young man. When she asked what had caused his passion, he replied that it was her eyes; at once she took up her spindle and blinded herself. Immediately struck with compunction, the man left for Scete and went on to become an exemplary monk.[55]

Initially these two stories are striking for the self-sacrifice of these women, who save the souls of men when they themselves are innocent of any wrongdoing. But while this too represents the *imitatio Christi,* Moschus' story with its more lurid turn to self-mutilation also points to a higher moral. Clearly the real purpose of this story lies in its final sentence: this man was converted to the desert life (a happy ending). Yet his conversion was at the hands of a woman who, although in every respect a virtuous religious, had nearly caused his downfall through no fault of her own. Here, perhaps, we face the true image of women as helpless: only able to save men by their own destruction.

But as we have seen, early Byzantine hagiography rarely represents women as helpless. For example, we are sometimes given the picture that convents of nuns are disastrous places because, as groups of women, they epitomize all the sins of the weaker gender—thus requiring the intervention of wise male guidance.[56] Far more often, the convent is portrayed as a place where women can find a rich and meaningful life of friendships, education, and freedom from men, whether fathers, husbands, brothers, or sons.[57] Indeed, hagiography of real men and women no less than its counterpart in legend portrays the holy person as humanity was created to be: an image of God fallen and now restored.

Our hagiographies of women show us women who command significant roles in their communities, both religious and secular, and who exercise a great variety of talents and strengths. They break down the social norms without appearing to do so because of the way in which their behavior is presented and perceived: stemming from a divine calling rather than their own initiatives, and above all exceptional to their own nature.

In the background scenery of these hagiographies and those about holy men, we are shown the women, both lay and religious, who made up the surrounding Christian communities. They are pious. They take their children and their husbands, as well as themselves, to visit their local holy men and women. They take them for cures when they are sick, and for teaching when they are well. They themselves come especially often to be healed of sterility or to be exorcized of demons. They influence their families and peers to lead more virtuous lives; they lead them into holy vocations. They are often of great significance in the religious lives of others, and our hagiographers may even stress this. Yet they are rarely named, and their own stories are rarely told. We have far fewer hagiographies about women than we do about men. But above all, women are not shown to be of a different ilk from their sisters who achieve the status of sanctity and merit being called saints. That is, women shown in their ordinary lives, whether as religious or as lay women, are not shown to be what the stereotypical image of women claims. They are not shown to be weak, feeble, or frail, endlessly lustful or eternally endangering the souls of men. Here again we confront the problem of paradox. Even hagiography as it is written by men does not succeed in portraying women in accord with its own claims.

It is this paradox of image and experience, of language and action, that can perhaps explain an otherwise curious account in John of Ephesus' *Lives of the Eastern Saints*. In this story, Satan works to defeat holy men through the image of the Blessed Virgin Mary.[58] Two monks in north Mesopotamia were especially known for their work as exorcists. One night Satan took a young Greek girl, herself possessed, who had come to the monks for healing. "Clothing her in awe-striking forms of phantasmal rays," the demons led her to the chapel to sit on the bishop's throne, and then filled the room with fantastic light and images "as if they were angels." Other demons went to wake the two unwitting monks, telling them the Virgin Mary had appeared in the chapel with a heavenly host, and had been sent especially to them. Rushing to the chapel, overcome by a vision of fantastic light and radiance flashing from and around the girl, they prostrated themselves at her feet. She announced her identity as Mary and claimed to have been sent by Christ to ordain them presbyters. This she did, the two monks kneeling before her in obeisance. At once the vision faded, and the horrified men found themselves at the feet of a simple Greek girl. Fleeing in anguish, they made confession, served three years penance, and spent the rest of their lives seeking to atone for their sacrilege.

It is a curious story, both for its telling and for its message. The girl herself is the exact picture of most women who pass through hagiographical stories: she is nameless, possessed by demons, seeking a cure from holy men. She has no story, just as she has no name. John specifically tells us that she was "unaware even herself" of what was happening, and that "the demon spoke through her." Through no will of her own, no knowledge of her own, and no fault of her own, she was the downfall of two earnest monks. With no apparent alternative, she was quite simply "the devil's gateway."[59] But what was the sin, and how was it performed? Strikingly, we are given no hint of sexual wrongdoing or temptation. On the contrary, the monks had thought themselves in the presence of the Virgin and approached her with appropriate humility and reverence. These monks sinned theologically: a woman ordained them. This was indeed the work of the devil.

What can we make of this story? John of Ephesus is one of our most "reliable" hagiographers. A historian of note in his own right, he was also primarily concerned with holding together the beleagured and persecuted Monophysite community of his day.[60] His hagiographical collection was intended to praise those men and women whose hard work at the grass-roots level kept the movement alive; some of our finest and most insightful portraits of sixth-century holy women come from his pen.[61] Indeed, John's holy women are nothing if not competent, talented, smart, and effective.

This may well be the point. John tells us, for example, that the holy women Euphemia and her daughter Maria were arrested during the Monophysite persecutions, because of their work with religious refugees and the leadership they practiced among the Monophysite faithful in the city of Amida. The informers had told the Chalcedonian officials, "These women are upsetting this city—why, the citizens revere and honor them more than the bishops!"[62] The riots following their arrest forced the authorities to exile the women rather than imprison them. The work of real women did beg the question: their own lives belied the social and ecclesiastical curtailment of their place. Hence hagiography becomes a place where people were reminded of what women's roles ought to be, even when their activity might seem to point to other conclusions. Writing in a situation of crisis, John of Ephesus knew that the work of women was crucial for the survival of the Monophysites, as it had been for the early church in its centuries of martyrdom and persecution. The story of our two hapless monks is a story about the insidious dangers of women's competency, at a time when their talents were sorely needed and witnessed.

But the question lingered even where such urgency was not present. In the legendary *Life of Mary of Egypt*, the priest Zosimos confronts in Mary, a former harlot, a sanctity he has never found elsewhere. In fitting recognition of that sanctity, he, a priest, asks her blessing, "Since grace is not recognized by rank but by the way of the Spirit, bless me, yourself, for God's sake; and grant a prayer for the one who seeks your succour." [63]

Early Byzantine hagiography presents a picture of paradox about women, whether writing about women saints or ordinary women, women as they are actually encountered or commonly stereotyped. In this, it opens to us a cultural conflict we know all too well. But hagiography is more than a social document about its culture. It is a form of theology, and it presents a theology of activity. Further, it is entirely self-conscious as a literary form. The very paradox that characterizes women's portrayal in these texts is in fact the whole point, of the texts and of their message.

We have already mentioned that each saint and each saint's story replays the salvation drama. What is that drama? For the Byzantine church it is at heart a drama of reversal—reversing our state of sin to one of salvation: returning to the paradise we lost, recovering the image of God in which we were made. Biblical images for such an understanding abound—the lion becomes the lamb, water becomes wine, death becomes life. By its sin humanity had overturned the created order; by the salvation of Christ, all was returned to its true nature, including humanity. In the saints, hagiography tells us, we see that promise fulfilled.

In its love for typological symmetry, the early Byzantine world looked continually for images of reversal by which to ponder the meaning of the salvation event. Women represented just this reversal. As women had been the source of sin through Eve, they could also be the source of salvation through Mary, the Second Eve.[64] In hagiography, women become the weak made strong, the unworthy made worthy, the foolish made wise, the sensual made spiritual. They are the type of humanity redeemed because they are so often the symbol of humanity lost. The paradox of language and content we have considered thus far expresses exactly this theological understanding. But we may see it best when we look at those hagiographical motifs that present the harshest stereotypes of women.[65]

The theme of the reformed harlot was a favorite one in Byzantine saints' lives; as such, it was based both on stereotype and on genuine experience. The whore who renounced her ways and undertook severe, mortifying penance was invariably cited as an edifying example for other Christians, a frequent motif in homily as well as hagiography.[66] But the harlot in the extremity of her chastisement bore the full weight of the abhorrence of sexuality that the church focused on women.[67] The legend of the prostitute Thaïs is a typical example.[68] When she had confessed her sins, the abbott had Thaïs sealed in a windowless cell, saying that its filth would be a match for her own. Forbidden even to lift her hands to God or take his name upon her lips, she was allowed only to face the east and pray for mercy. After three years she was taken from her cell, herself unwilling, and readmitted to the communion of the church. Shortly thereafter she died.

The legend of Thaïs represented the most brutal aspect of this motif. No doubt its most influential form was the story of Mary of Egypt, a prostitute from Alexandria who worked her passage to Jerusalem for fun, and was there converted at the doors of the cathedral.[69] Repenting of her former life, Mary set off across the Jordan and lived in the desert, a hermit unknown and unseen by any other creature, human or animal. After some years the priest Zosimos was wandering in the desert and found her; he extracted her story with difficulty, receiving it with wonder. In return, Mary asked that he bring her the sacraments. After taking communion at his hands, she died. Although popular in the West as well, Mary became the great symbol of repentance for the Orthodox church, which annually celebrates her story twice: not only on her feast day (April 1) but also as part of the Lenten cycle, as the prelude to Holy Week.[70]

As Sister Benedicta Ward has shown,[71] the image of the reformed harlot stood for the fundamental state of humankind and its call to repentance, following traditional biblical imagery that used the metaphor of harlotry to describe faithlessness toward God on the part of Israel or the church.[72] But it was also an image that spoke to the church's deep-seated disdain (and distrust) of women's sexuality. This image combined with the imagery and language of gender reversal that was used to praise holy women and produced the hagiographic motif of the transvestite saint, a theme that became a common one in Byzantine legends of holy women,

*Sexuality, rather than femininity!*

*being a snake?*

flourishing in particular between the fifth and ninth centuries.[73] Its real starting point in popular literature was the story of Pelagia, renowned courtesan of Antioch.[74] Converted suddenly and in spectacular manner by the bishop Nonnus, Pelagia received baptism, freed her slaves, gave away her wealth, and secretly departed. She lived out her career in the guise of a eunuch recluse named Pelagius on the Mount of Olives, especially venerated for his holy way of life. At her death, her true identity was discovered amidst mingled cries of horror and astonishment. "Praise to You, Lord," the bishops marveled, weeping, "how many hidden saints you have on the earth—and not just men, but women as well!"[75]

Pelagia's story was captivating, and become one of the most popular in the Christian Middle Ages; and it inspired many variations in many other languages.[76] These saints were women who chose to pursue their religious vocation disguised as monks and whose sanctity derived from living, literally, as men; the masquerade seems never to have happened in reverse. The ruse was inevitably discovered when the ascetic died, if not before, and invariably received with an exclamation such as that made over the body of Pelagia: here, truly, were women who had risen to glory! The stories are often blatantly allegorical: these women chose to disguise themselves as men, to "become" men, because they could not serve God adequately as women. In the words of St. Eugenia, "For by nature I am a woman. And I was not able to fulfill the desire of my soul regarding the fear of God, unless I changed myself into this chaste and honorable and excellent guise."[77] Men were worthier than women, monks were holier than nuns. Nor was this theme found only in legend; real women followed Pelagia's choice.[78]

In the legends and stories that developed around the transvestite motif, the emphasis most often lay on the saint's life in disguise, and her most wondrous deeds derived from that pretense. But in the case of St. Pelagia, in many ways the starting point of it all, little is said of her adopted life—only that she became holy, served the faithful accordingly, and died undiscovered then to be revealed. The story's accent and detail come in its first part, concerning her life as a prostitute and the spectacle of her conversion. Pelagia's reform and subsequent transformation express a meaning similar to that of the stories of Thaïs or Mary of Egypt. In repenting of her sins as harlot, Pelagia took upon herself what the church often saw as the sin of womankind: sexuality polluted. And so pure was Pelagia's conversion, so perfect her dedication to God, that not only was her former life abandoned, and not only her former self, but even more, her former sex. Her transformation was complete and of singular significance by virtue solely of her previous life. Indeed, Pelagia's repentance attained such a level that only a man could have achieved it—or so the story's sense.

The image of the transvestite saint, then, allowed the Byzantine church the appearance of praising women in dramatic terms. But the terms were the institution's own, and served its interests. A choice of language such as Palladius' for Melania the Elder—"that female man of God"—in fact diminished the saint's actual accomplishments by devaluing her essential humanity. The church was thus able to curtail for women the enormous power and authority accessible to ascetics in the early Byzantine world. For its part, the lay populace felt no shame in honoring those whose service was effective in its midst, whether holy women or holy men. It was precisely at this point that the counteraction of the church institution functioned to curb women's impact, by sanctifying women within a masculine framework. Still, these stories express, even more poignantly, the ambiguity inherent in their own existence; for the fact remains that they were written to glorify women. Indeed, the dilemma of women and sanctity for the early Byzantine church may be summed up in the image of the transvestite saint: despite real and literary attempts to the contrary, in the end it was her true identity as a woman which was, by necessity, duly and appropriately honored. These women were canonized as women.[79]

But women in their identification with sexuality were not condemned categorically, despite the frequency with which one hears the familiar discussion. The Byzantine East presented a more positive picture (or at least more positively ambiguous) than the Latin West, with regard to the nature of human sexuality and its place in the created order.[80] If the transvestite motif gave graphic articulation to the view of women's nature and its means of redemption, the theme of sexual violence against women did so with more surprising results. The story of St. Febronia is an example.

Febronia was said to have been martyred by Roman officials around the year 300, though her vita dates from the late sixth or early seventh century.[81] The story tells of a woman raised from birth in a convent near Nisibis, especially renowned for her ascetic discipline and her capacity to teach. But the mark of her sanctity was the fact that Febronia had never seen a man, nor been seen by one. The arrival of Roman soldiers, however, led to her imprisonment and death by slow torture, much of it sexual, as a warning to other Christians in the area.

A major theme of Febronia's vita lies in the tension between Christian purity (symbolized by her physical and social virginity), and pagan corruption (in the form of the Romans' alternative offer, that she could live if she would marry one of their officials). The sexual torture in the story describes this symbolism sharply. Febronia's purity is such that the use of her body as a sexual object does not convey sin, as women's sexuality is wont to do. Rather, in this martyrdom it was specifically her body in its sexual identification that brought salvation.

Thus in this text, we have a rarely heard sentiment in early Christian writings, when Febronia declares that she is not ashamed of her naked body.[82] Stripped and humiliated by the soldiers in the public stadium as a prelude to torture, Febronia called to the judge Selenus, "Even if you should have me stripped completely naked, I would not think anything of this nakedness, for there is but one Creator of males and of females."[83] The following interchange ensues: "'You impudent woman,' exclaimed Selenus, 'you deserve every kind of disgrace. I know very well that you are proud of your shapely features, and that is why you do not think it a shame or disgrace to stand there with your body naked; you even imagine it adds to your splendor.' Febronia replied, 'Listen, judge, my Lord God knows that I have never seen a man's face up to this very moment, and just because I have fallen into your hands I am called a shameless and impudent woman! You stupid and imperceptive man!'"[84]

In fitting homage, this text claims to have been written by a woman—an event remarkable in itself in antiquity—Thomaïs, a nun of Febronia's convent who later became the abbess. Literarily, the female authorship underscores the story's central theme of purity and defilement, but it also results in an impressive characterization of women. The vita places great emphasis on women's friendships with each other. Moreover, the women in the story are seen to be well educated, intellectually sophisticated, and courageous in the largest sense. The standard hagiographical practice of presenting women saints as individuals who are exceptions to the rule of their kind is missing here. Febronia is presented as a special woman among many fine women.[85]

Febronia's is not a singular case, though it is a profound one; nor is this notion of women's sexuality as a God-given source of pride merely a literary concession to theology. When the reports of the sixth-century Najran martyrs reached Byzantium, they contained powerful accounts of the Christian women involved.[86] But the words of the troublesome serving woman Mahya stand out. Stripped naked in the public square by her torturers, Mahya had called to the king, "It is to your shame . . . that you have done this; I am not ashamed myself . . . for I am a woman—such as was created by God."[87]

The motif of sexual torture occurs in varying degrees of extremity in a number of female martyrs' passions, crossing a spectrum from humilia-

*Sexual torture, rape, torture motha hon awarted both m.F. Christians* ✓

tion to rape to sexual mutilation by the severing of the woman's breasts (as in Febronia's vita).[88] While we have historical evidence that both women and men were subjected to sexual torture during the early Christian experience of martyrdom,[89] the motif occurs almost exclusively in texts about women and is developed as a specific literary mechanism only in those texts.[90] The important issue here is the use of the image literarily—in these texts it has a function as an image rather than as an act. From this view, a text such as Febronia's vita contains a stunning reworking of Christianity's traditional image of women's bodies. The female body, normally the source of sin (Eve), here becomes the source of salvation (Mary). Since in martyrdom it is the actual suffering death of the martyr that effects the salvific force of the act, in these martyr texts it is the woman's body as a sexual body that achieves salvation— and the martyr's death bears upon the salvation of all.

The motif of the reformed harlot and its extension into that of the transvestite saint offer us the traditionally degrading stereotypes of women familiar in early Christian society. But they also offer us the theological resolution of those views, by completing the stories in each instance with the full redemption of the saint as a human being and specifically as a woman. In the instance of Febronia and other related texts that use the literary motif of sexual torture, we are reminded that *by nature* women too were created in the image of God; and when human nature is as it should be that nature is good, as it was created.

In martyrdom by sexual torture, sexuality becomes not the source of sin but of salvation. With the reformed harlot, true repentance redeems the furthest degree of degradation. In the transvestite saint, repentance renders one unrecognizable to one's former life; but the redemption that follows reveals one's true and natural self. In each instance, the hagiographical motif that first served to separate women from humanity (men), ultimately serves to reconcile them.

Early Byzantine hagiography displays full awareness of its inherent self-contradictions on the subject of women. It tells us that women are unworthy by nature, become worthy by what they do, and nonetheless remain unworthy because of who they are. It tells us women can do and be the very things it tells us they are incapable of doing and being; and it declares this irresolvable conundrum the basic fact of women's lives.

Further, this literature presents women symbolically with motifs that restrict their identities as persons to their particular identity as sexual persons. More than popular stories in their own right, the imagery of

the virgin in her purity or violation, the reformed harlot, and the transvestite saint pervade hagiographical language about women even where
the stories are not about these themes. For the early Byzantine church,
women's bodies symbolized with acute clarity the conditions of purity
and perdition, to such an extent that they represent that condition for
the whole of humankind. Thus, women's stories of salvation—hagiography—could (and did) convey the truth of humanity's salvation with
particular force. Our hagiographers liked to claim that women could display this grace more than men because they deserved it less. The paradox
of these texts is their message: women's stories are in fact humanity's
own story.

Two final images from early Byzantine hagiography serve to measure
the enormity of this theological understanding. The first concerns a real
woman. When Melania the Younger died, she was buried in the clothes
of other saints, both male and female. Her hagiographer tells us, "It was
fitting that she be buried in the garments of those whose virtues she had
acquired while she was living."[91] Scholars have sometimes questioned
whether hagiography tells more than one story, or describes more than
one saint.[92] Since the Christian is called to imitate one model alone, the
answer of course is no. In the act of her burial as recorded in her vita,
Melania thus achieved the reality of sanctity: the reception or absorp-
tion (but not the annihilation) of her particular identity, as a woman,
as an individual, into the corporate identity of humanity redeemed, the
company of saints.

The second image is from the legend of Mary of Egypt. When the priest
Zosimos asked to hear her story, Mary began to tell it and then balked,
overcome with fear and shame. But Zosimos, "watering the ground with
tears, said to her, 'For God's sake, speak, Mother; go on and do not
break the thread of your life-giving narrative.'"[93] Zosimos knew that
Mary's story held life, for him and for all; and he went forth to pro-
claim her "life-giving narrative" to the world. This was the method and
message of Byzantine hagiography: the saint was the story embodied—
humanity redeemed—and the story was the Word.

### NOTES

1 / See, e.g., Catia Galatariotou, "Byzantine Women's Monastic Commu-
nities: The Evidence of the Typika," *Jahrbuch der Österreichischen
Byzantinistik* 38 (1988): 263–90; idem, "Holy Women and Witches:
Aspects of Byzantine Conceptions of Gender," *Byzantine and Modern
Greek Studies* 9 (1984–85): 55–94; Dorothy deF. Abrahamse, "Women's
Monasticism in the Middle Byzantine Period: Problems and Prospects,"

*Byzantinische Forschungen* 9 (1985): 35–58; Angeliki E. Laiou, "Observations on the Life and Ideology of Byzantine Women," *Byzantinische Forschungen* 9 (1985): 59–102; idem, "The Role of Women in Byzantine Society," XVI Internationaler Byzantinistenkongress, Akten I/1, *Jahrbuch der Österreichischen Byzantinistik* 31, no. 1 (1981): 233–60 and "Addendum to the Report on the Role of Women in Byzantine Society," XVI Int. Byz. Akten II/1, *Jahrbuch der Österreichischen Byzantinistik* 32, no. 1 (1982): 198–204; Alice-Mary Talbot, "Late Byzantine Nuns: By Choice or Necessity?" *Byzantinische Forschungen* 9 (1985): 103–17; Judith Herrin, "In Search of Byzantine Women: Three Avenues of Approach," in *Images of Women in Antiquity*, ed. Averil Cameron and Amelie Kuhrt (London: Croom Helm, 1983), 167–89; idem, "Women and the Faith in Icons in Early Christianity," in *Culture, Ideology, and Politics*, ed. Raphael Samuel and Gareth Stedman Jones (London and Boston: Routledge and Kegan Paul, 1983), 56–83; Joëlle Beauchamp, "La situation juridique de la femme à Byzance," *Cahiers de civilisation médiévale Xe–XIIe siècles* 20 (1977): 145–76; J. Grosdidier de Matons, "La femme dans l'empire byzantine," in *Histoire mondiale de la femme*, ed. Pierre Grimal (Paris: Nouvelle librairie de France, 1967), 3: 11–43; and Georgina Buckler, "Women in Byzantine Law about 1100 A.D.," *Byzantion* 11 (1936): 391–416. Part 1 of *Byzantinische Forschungen* 9 (1985) is devoted to women and monasticism in the Byzantine Empire; of the six papers contained therein, I have noted here only those that most pertain to issues raised here.

2 /  Especially important is the work of Evelyne Patlagean, *Structure sociale, famille, chrétienté à Byzance: IVe–XIe siècle* (London: Variorum Reprints, 1981); idem, *Pauvreté économique et pauvreté sociale à Byzance IVe–VIIe siècle*, Civilisations et Société 48 (Paris and LaHaye: Mouton, 1977), esp. 113–55. See also *From Pagan Rome to Byzantium*, ed. Paul Veyne, tr. Arthur Goldhammer, vol. 1 of *A History of Private Life*, ed. Philippe Ariès and Georges Duby (Cambridge and London: Harvard Univ. Press, Belknap Press, 1987); Talbot, "Late Byzantine Nuns"; Abrahamse, "Women's Monasticism in the Middle Byzantine Period"; Herrin, "In Search of Byzantine Women" and "Women and the Faith in Icons." For the bridge period of late antiquity and early Byzantium, Elizabeth A. Clark, *Ascetic Piety and Women's Faith: Essays on Late Ancient Christianity* (Lewiston and Queenston: Edwin Mellen, 1986); and idem, *Jerome, Chrysostom, and Friends: Essays and Translations* (New York and Toronto: Edwin Mellen, 1979) are particularly helpful.

3 /  The bibliography on hagiography is enormous. Classic introductions are in Hippolyte Delehaye, *The Legends of the Saints*, trans. Donald Attwater (New York: Fordham Univ. Press, 1962) and René Aigrain, *L'Hagiographie: ses sources, ses méthodes, son histoire* (Paris: Bloud et Gay, 1953). For Byzantine hagiography, the most important works are the seminal article by Evelyne Patlagean, "A Byzance: ancienne hagiographie et histoire sociale," *Annales: e.s.c.* 23 (1968): 106–26, English tr. "Ancient Byzantine Hagiography and Social History," in *Saints and Their Cults: Studies in Religious Sociology, Folklore and History*, ed. Stephen Wilson (Cambridge: Cambridge Univ. Press, 1983), 101–21; and François Halkin, "L'hagiographie byzantine au service de l'histoire," in *Thirteenth International Congress of Byzantine Studies, Oxford 1966, Main Papers XI*, ed. Joan M. Hussey, Dmitri Obolensky, and Steven

Runciman (London and New York: Oxford Univ. Press, 1966), 1–10. Wilson, *Saints and Their Cults*, contains extensive and useful bibliographies, as does Alison Goddard Elliott, *Roads to Paradise: Reading the Lives of the Early Saints* (Hanover and London: Univ. Press of New England, 1987). Elliott's book, however, is mainly concerned with later Latin hagiography and its impact on medieval Western literature.

4 / Theodoret of Cyrrus, *Historia Religiosa*, Prologue, and chapters 29.7, 30.7. The text is in *Théodoret de Cyr, Histoire des moines de Syrie*, ed. and trans. Pierre Canivet and Alice Leroy-Molinghen, Sources Chrétiennes 234 and 257 (Paris: Les Editions du Cerf, 1977–79); English trans. by R. M. Price, *Theodoret of Cyrrhus, A History of the Monks of Syria*, Cistercian Studies 88 (Kalamazoo: Cistercian Publications, 1985). Theodoret wrote the *Historia Religiosa* in the 440s; for the date, see the indispensable commentary by Pierre Canivet, *Le monachisme syrien selon Théodoret de Cyr*, Théologie Historique 42 (Paris: Editions Beauchesne, 1977), 27–35.

5 / Theodoret, *Historia Religiosa*, ch. 30.

6 / Ibid., ch. 30.7.

7 / *Vita S. Melaniae*. For the text see Denys Gorce, *Vie de Sainte Mélanie*, Sources Chrétiennes 90 (Paris: Les Editions du Cerf, 1962); English trans. in Elizabeth A. Clark, *The Life of Melania the Younger: Introduction, Translation, and Commentary* (New York and Toronto: Edwin Mellen, 1984). Melania lived c. 385–439; her vita, by her longtime friend the priest Gerontius, was composed around the year 452. See the extensive commentary in Clark, *Melania the Younger*. Melania was also deeply influenced by her grandmother and namesake Melania the Elder, who died in 410.

8 / Eugenia: François Halkin, *Bibliotheca Hagiographica Graeca*, 3d ed., Subsidia Hagiographica 8a (Bruxelles: Société des Bollandistes, 1957) and idem, *Novum Auctarium Bibliothecae Hagiographicae Graecae*, Sub. Hag. 65 (Bruxelles: Société des Bollandistes, 1984) (citation numbers correspond in both collections), 607–8; Paul Peeters, *Bibliotheca Hagiographica Orientalis*, Sub. Hag. 10 (Bruxelles: Société des Bollandistes, 1910; rpt. 1954), 281–84; *Bibliotheca Hagiographica Latina Antiquae et Mediae Aetatis*, Sub. Hag. 6 (Bruxelles: Société des Bollandistes, 1898–99; rpt. 1949), and *Bibliotheca Hagiographica Latina Supplementi*, Sub. Hag. 12 (Bruxelles: Société des Bollandistes, 1911), 2666–70. She was said to have been martyred under Diocletian (284–305). Thecla: *Bibliotheca Hagiographica Graeca*, 1710–22; *Bibliotheca Hagiographica Orientalis*, 1152–56; *Bibliotheca Hagiographica Latina*, 8020–25. Thecla was the companion of the Apostle Paul, and her story dates back to the second century *Acts of Paul*, for which see *New Testament Apocrypha*, ed. Edgar Hennecke and Wilhelm Schneemelcher, trans. R. McL. Wilson (Philadelphia: Westminster, 1963), 2: 322–90, especially 330–33 and 353–64. Saint Thecla exerted prodigious influence in the Christian East through both her story (especially important in its fifth-century form) and cult; Gilbert Dagron, *Vie et miracles de sainte Thècle: Texte grec, traduction, et commentaire*, Sub. Hag. 62 (Bruxelles: Société des Bollandistes, 1978).

9 / Gregory of Nyssa, *Vita S. Macrinae*, ed. Virginia W. Callahan, in *Gregorii Nysseni Opera*, ed. Werner Jaeger, vol. 8, pt. 1, *Opera Ascetica* (Leiden: E. J. Brill, 1952), 347–414; English trans. in Virginia W. Calla-

han, *Saint Gregory of Nyssa: Ascetical Works*, Fathers of the Church 58 (Washington: Catholic Univ. Press, 1967), 161–91. Macrina lived c. 327–80; her brother composed her vita not long after she died.

10  /  Febronia: *Bibliotheca Hagiographica Graeca*, 659; *Bibliotheca Hagiographica Orientalis*, 302–3; *Bibliotheca Hagiographica Latina*, 2843–44. Although she was said to have been martyred c. 300, her vita probably dates from the late sixth or early seventh centuries. I follow the Syriac text (whence the legend moved westward), here citing Thecla's model for Febronia at sec. 19. The text is edited in Paul Bedjan, *Acta Martyrum et Sanctorum*, vol. 5 (Paris and Leipzig: O. Harrassowitz, 1895; rpt. Hildersheim: Georg Olms, 1968), 573–615; English trans. in Sebastian P. Brock and Susan Ashbrook Harvey, *Holy Women of the Syrian Orient* (Berkeley and Los Angeles: Univ. of California Press, 1987), 150–76.

11  /  *Vita S. Olympiadis*, 1. For the text see Anne-Marie Malingrey, *Jean Chrysostome: Lettres à Olympias*, 2d ed., Sources Chrétiennes 13 bis (Paris: Les Editions du Cerf, 1968), 393–449; English trans. in Clark, *Jerome, Chrysostom, and Friends*, 127–44. Olympias lived c. 366–408; her vita was composed by an anonymous author probably in the fifth century.

12  /  On the concept of imitation in this regard, see above all Peter Brown, "The Saint as Exemplar in Late Antiquity," *Representations* 1, no. 2 (1983): 1–25. More generally on the place of the holy man or woman as it was established for the Byzantine world, see idem, *Society and the Holy in Late Antiquity* (Berkeley and Los Angeles: Univ. of California Press, 1982).

13  /  *Vita S. Theclae.*

14  /  Mary of Egypt: *Bibliotheca Hagiographica Graeca*, 1041–44; *Bibliotheca Hagiographica Orientalis*, 683–87; *Bibliotheca Hagiographica Latina*, 5415–21. I follow the Greek text edited in J. P. Migne, *Patrologiae cursus completus . . . Series Graeca* (hereafter *Patrologia Graeca*), vol. 87, pt. 3 (Paris, 1865), cols. 3697–3726. There is an English translation of the Latin version, with an excellent introduction, in Benedicta Ward, *Harlots of the Desert: A Study of Repentance in Early Christian Monastic Sources*, Cistercian Studies 106 (Kalamazoo: Cistercian Publications, 1987), 26–56. Mary's story seems to date from the sixth century.

15  /  Examples are legion: for example, Melania the Elder and Melania the Younger, their contemporary Paula, Macrina, Olympias, Matrona, Caesaria.

16  /  An especially vivid example is that of the sixth-century holy woman Euphemia in the city of Amida; her life is told in *John of Ephesus, Lives of the Eastern Saints*, ed. and trans. E. W. Brooks, in *Patrologia Orientalis*, ed. R. Graffin and F. Nau, vols. 17–19 (Paris: Firmin-Didot, 1923–25), ch. 12, at *Patrologia Orientalis* 17, pp. 166–86. An English translation of her life is also available in Brock and Harvey, *Holy Women*, 124–33. John of Ephesus wrote his *Lives* in the late 560s. But consider also the "social work" described in the *Life of Olympias*, or, e.g., Palladius, *Lausiac History*, sec. 67. For the text of Palladius, see Cuthbert Butler, *The Lausiac History of Palladius*, 2 vols. (Cambridge, 1898–1904), trans. and annot. Robert T. Meyer, *Palladius: The Lausiac History*, Ancient Christian Writers 34 (New York: Newman Press, 1964). Palladius wrote the *Lausiac History* probably in the 420s; its influence

on monastic hagiography was almost as extensive as that of the *Life of Antony of Egypt*.

17 / John of Ephesus, *Lives*, 12; Palladius, *Lausiac History*, secs. 63 and 64.

18 / Palladius, *Lausiac History*, secs. 46, 54 (Melania the Elder).

19 / *Life of Olympias*; Anastasia, a sixth-century patrician: *Bibliotheca Hagiographica Graeca*, 79–80; *Bibliotheca Hagiographica Orientalis*, 242. There is an English translation of the Syriac version of Anastasia's story in Brock and Harvey, *Holy Women*, 142–49.

20 / Both Melania the Elder (Palladius, *Lausiac History*, sec. 55) and Melania the Younger (*Life of Melania the Younger*); Caesaria, another sixth-century patrician (John of Ephesus, *Lives*, 54, *Patrologia Orientalis* 19, 185–91).

21 / Macrina (*Life of Macrina*); Matrona: *Bibliotheca Hagiographica Graeca*, 1221–23. Matrona lived c. 425–524; the vita prima may date from the mid-sixth century. Her extraordinary vita and its later versions are discussed in Eva C. Topping, "St. Matrona and Her Friends: Sisterhood in Byzantium," in *Kathegetria: Essays Presented to Joan Hussey on her Eightieth Birthday*, ed. J. Chrysostomides (London: Porphyrogenitos Press, 1989), 211–24. Febronia is portrayed as a great teacher of both religious and lay women (*Life of Febronia*).

22 / Marana and Cyra, in Theodoret, *Historia Religiosa*, 29.

23 / Palladius, *Lausiac History*, 20; Theodoret, *Historia Religiosa*, 29, 30; John of Ephesus, *Lives*, 12, 27, 54.

24 / E.g., Clark, *Ascetic Piety and Women's Faith*; Kenneth G. Holum, *Theodosian Empresses: Women and Imperial Dominion in Late Antiquity* (Berkeley and Los Angeles: Univ. of California Press, 1982).

25 / See the discussion in Topping, "St. Matrona and Her Friends."

26 / John of Ephesus, *Lives*, 27, *Patrologia Orientalis* 18, 541–58. This *Life* is also translated in Brock and Harvey, *Holy Women*, 133–41.

27 / John of Ephesus, *Lives*, 12.

28 / Ibid., *Patrologia Orientalis* 17, 174–75 (Brock and Harvey, *Holy Women*, 128).

29 / John of Ephesus, *Lives*, 27, *Patrologia Orientalis* 18, 557 (Brock and Harvey, *Holy Women*, 140).

30 / John of Ephesus, *Lives*, 12, *Patrologia Orientalis* 17, 176 (Brock and Harvey, *Holy Women*, 128).

31 / Theodoret, *Historia Religiosa*, 30.5; John of Ephesus, *Lives*, 12, *Patrologia Orientalis* 17, 166.

32 / Theodoret, *Historia Religiosa*, 29.1.

33 / John of Ephesus, *Lives*, 12, *Patrologia Orientalis* 17, 166–67.

34 / Palladius, *Lausiac History*, 41.1 (Meyer, *Palladius*, 117).

35 / Brock and Harvey, *Holy Women*, 178. Martyrius wrote during the seventh century.

36 / John of Ephesus, *Lives*, 27, *Patrologia Orientalis* 18, 541.

37 / *Life of Macrina*, in Callahan, *Saint Gregory of Nyssa*, 163.

38 / Palladius, *Lausiac History*, 9; Meyer, *Palladius*, 43.

39 / *Life of Melania the Younger*, sec. 39; Clark, *Melania the Younger*, 53–54.

40 / John of Ephesus, *Lives*, 28, *Patrologia Orientalis* 17, 559.

41 / Theodoret, *Historia Religiosa*, 30.4–5.

42 / Palladius, *Lausiac History*, 67.

43 / John Moschus, *Pratum Spirituale*, 88, text in *Patrologia Graeca* 87, pt. 3, cols. 2851–3112, trans. M.-J. Rouët de Journel, *Jean Moschus, Le Pré*

*Spirituel*, Sources Chrétiennes (Paris: Les Editions du Cerf, 1946). John wrote in the early seventh century. See Henry Chadwick, "John Moschus and his Friend Sophronius the Sophist," *Journal of Theological Studies* 25 (1974): 41–74.

44 / Cyril of Scythopolis, *Vita S. Euthymii*, 16, 31; *Vita S. Sabae*, 7, 69. The texts are in Eduard Schwartz, *Kyrillos von Skythopolis*, Texte und Untersuchungen zur Geschichte der altchristlichen Literatur 49, pt. 2 (Leipzig: J. C. Hinrichs, 1939); trans. in André-Jean Festugière, *Les Moines de Palestine*, vol. 3, parts 1–3 of idem, *Les Moines d'Orient* (Paris: Les Editions du Cerf, 1962–63). Cyril wrote in the latter sixth century. See the introductions in Schwartz, *Kyrillos von Skythopolis*, and Festugière, *Les Moines de Palestine*; and above all, Bernard Flusin, *Miracle et Histoire dans l'oeuvre de Cyrille de Scythopolis* (Paris: Etudes Augustiniennes, 1983). Banning women from monasteries and saints' enclosures was common practice at this time.

45 / Cyril does record a version of the story of Mary of Egypt about an anonymous woman hermit, setting it in the Judaean wilderness: *Vita S. Kyriaki*, 18–19. There may not have been convents in the specific geographical area Cyril writes about outside Jerusalem, but the convents in and around the Holy City and elsewhere in Palestine were well known.

46 / *Vita S. Theodosii*, 1, *Vita S. Theognii*.

47 / *Vita S. Johannis Hesychasti*, 23–24.

48 / As he himself describes: e.g., *Vita S. Sabae*, 75, *Vita S. Johannis Hesychasti*, 30.

49 / Theodoret, *Historia Religiosa*, 9, 13. Every hagiography used in this study describes instances of women—mothers, sisters, or religious—providing spiritual direction for men.

50 / John Moschus, *Pratum*, 3, 14, 19, 31, 39, 45, 60, 75, 76, 78, 88, 135, 136, 152, 179, 188, 189, 204, 205, 206, 207, 217.

51 / Ibid., 136, 186, 207; cf. the ready conversion of the prostitutes in 31 and 32.

52 / Ibid., 39, 60, 75, 78, 179, 204, 205.

53 / Palladius, *Lausiac History*, 59.2, 63.

54 / Palladius, *Lausiac History*, 5.2; Meyer, *Palladius*, 36–37.

55 / *Pratum*, 60; cf. 179.

56 / Palladius, *Lausiac History*, 29, 30, 33, 34; John Moschus, *Pratum*, 128, 135.

57 / E.g., in the vitae of Macrina, Melania the Younger, Olympias, Matrona; Palladius, *Lausiac History*, 59.1, 67; Theodoret, *Historia Religiosa*, 30.4; John of Ephesus, *Lives*, 27 and 54.

58 / John of Ephesus, *Lives*, 15, *Patrologia Orientalis* 17, 220–28.

59 / Tertullian, *De cultu feminarum*, 1.1.

60 / On John of Ephesus' career as monk, writer, bishop, and spokesman for the Monophysites, see Ernst Honigmann, *Evêques et évêchés Monophysites d'Asie antérieure au VIe siècle*, Corpus Scriptorum Christianorum Orientalium vol. 127, Subsidia 2 (Louvain: Imprimerie Orientaliste, 1951), 207–15.

61 / See Susan Ashbrook Harvey, *Asceticism and Society in Crisis: John of Ephesus and the "Lives of the Eastern Saints"* (Berkeley and Los Angeles: Univ. of California Press, 1990).

62 / John of Ephesus, *Lives*, 12, *Patrologia Orientalis* 17, 182 (Brock and Harvey, *Holy Women*, 131).

63 / *Vita*, para. 13, col. 3708B. Cf. Palladius, *Lausiac History*, 34, where Abba Piteroum begs the blessing of the nun who was a holy fool.

64 / See John Meyendorff, *Byzantine Theology: Historical Trends and Doctrinal Themes*, 2d rev. ed. (New York: Fordham Univ. Press, 1983), 146–49; Hilda Graef, "The Theme of the Second Eve in Some Byzantine Sermons on the Assumption," *Studia Patristica* 9, ed. F. L. Cross, Texte und Untersuchungen zur Geschichte der altchristlichen Literatur 94 (Berlin: Akademie-Verlag, 1966), 224–30; and for examples that set the early Byzantine pattern on this theme, Robert Murray, "Mary, the Second Eve in the Early Syriac Fathers," *Eastern Churches Review* 3 (1971): 372–84.

65 / Probably the two most common images of women saints in early Byzantine literature, as for the early church, are those of Bride of Christ and Soldier. These images are ubiquitous for both women and men, and indeed are largely interchangeable. The images I am singling out for treatment in this study are those specifically used for women, which thus serve to differentiate them from men in the context of sanctity. The images of Bride and Soldier are discussed in a different context by Diane Mockridge elsewhere in this collection.

66 / See especially Benedicta Ward, *Harlots of the Desert*, for a superb analysis of this motif and its varied meanings.

67 / Rosemary Radford Ruether, "Misogynism and Virginal Feminism in the Fathers of the Church," in *Religion and Sexism: Images of Women in the Jewish and Christian Traditions*, ed. Ruether (New York: Simon and Schuster, 1974), 150–83, outlines the main patristic material that lay behind this view.

68 / Thaïs: *Bibliotheca Hagiographica Graeca*, 1695–97; *Bibliotheca Hagiographica Orientalis*, 1137; *Bibliotheca Hagiographica Latina*, 8012–19. An English translation of the Latin is in Ward, *Harlots*, 76–84. The story is set in the fourth century, and began to circulate not long thereafter.

69 / See above, n. 14.

70 / See the discussion in Ward, *Harlots*, 26–34. An English version of the Orthodox services for the Sunday of Mary of Egypt (the fifth Sunday in Lent) may be found in *The Lenten Triodion*, trans. Mother Mary and Archimandrite Kallistos Ware (London and Boston: Faber and Faber, 1984), 447–63.

71 / Ward, *Harlots*. Some related material is covered in idem, "Apophthegmata Matrum," *Studia Patristica* 16, pt. 2, ed. E. A. Livingstone, Texte und Untersuchungen zur Geschichte der altchristlichen Literatur 129 (Berlin: Akademie-Verlag, 1985), 63–66.

72 / Especially the prophets, as, e.g., Hosea and Ezekiel.

73 / By far the best treatment is that of Evelyne Patlagean, "L'histoire de la femme déguisée en moine et l'évolution de la sainteté féminine à Byzance," *Studi Medievali* 17 (1976): 597–623. Also helpful are Khalifa A. Bennasser, *Gender and Sanctity in Early Byzantine Monasticism: A Study in the Phenomenon of Female Ascetics in Male Monastic Habit* (Ann Arbor: University Microfilms, 1984); and Marie Delcourt, "Female Saints in Masculine Clothing," in idem, *Hermaphrodite: Myths and Rituals of the Bisexual Figure in Classical Antiquity*, trans. Jennifer Nicholson (London: Studio Books, 1961), 84–102. The roots of the motif date back to the *Acts of Paul*, where Thecla dressed in men's clothing to travel as a missionary.

74 / Pelagia: *Bibliotheca Hagiographica Graeca*, 1478–79; *Bibliotheca Hagiographica Orientalis*, 919; *Bibliotheca Hagiographica Latina*, 6605–11. See above all Pierre Petitmengin, ed., *Pélagie la Pénitente: métamorphoses d'une legende*, 2 vols. (Paris: Etudes Augustiniennes, 1981–84), which includes editions of the Greek, Latin, Syriac, Arabic, Armenian, Georgian, and Slavonic texts. English translations are available of the Syriac in Brock and Harvey, *Holy Women*, 40–62; and of the Latin in Ward, *Harlots*, 57–65 and in Helen Waddell, *The Desert Fathers* (London: Constable, 1936), 267–81. The story dates from the early fifth century.

75 / So the Syriac; Brock and Harvey, *Holy Women*, 61.

76 / Discussed in detail in Patlagean, "La femme déguisée" and Bennasser, *Gender and Sanctity*.

77 / So the Syriac version, ed. and trans. in Agnes Smith Lewis, *Select Narrations of Holy Women by John the Stylite of Beth-Mar-Quanun*, Studia Sinaitica 9–10 (London, 1900); text in 9, pp. 1–48, trans. in 10, pp. 1–35. Here quoted from Studia Sinaitica 10, p. 20. This is probably an older version than the Greek Metaphrastic text in *Patrologia Graeca*, vol. 116 (Paris, 1891), cols. 609–52.

78 / E.g., Anastasia and Matrona; for their texts, see above, notes 19 and 21.

79 / Of course, at this point no legal process for "canonization" existed; I use the term to refer to the church's glorification and commemoration of those it considered saints. Patlagean, "La femme déguiseé," sees the ultimate resolution of the transvestite motif in the symbol of androgyny, particularly as carried in the Gnostic tradition that opposites must be reconciled for salvation to happen. The full complexity of this Gnostic material is only now being assessed; see esp. Jorunn Jacobsen Buckley, *Female Fault and Fulfilment in Gnosticism* (Chapel Hill: Univ. of North Carolina Press, 1986). Patlagean's argument is compelling, but I do not agree that the transvestite image is an androgynous one. Ancient writers knew the difference. These saints are not described with androgynous language; nor is the language of Gal. 3:28 used. In the stories, they are women who become men, literally as well as figuratively; and are then known in their true identity as women.

80 / For the patristic roots of this difference, see Ruether, "Misogynism and Virginal Feminism." The Orthodox church never accepted the Augustinian notion of Original Sin, and that accounts for a lot. See Meyendorff, *Byzantine Theology*, 143–46. Consider, e.g., that the Orthodox also accept married clergy.

81 / For the texts see n. 10. Febronia's cult is still an important one for Christian women in the Middle East; see Elijba Gülcan, "The Renewal of Monastic Life for Women in a Monastery in Tur Abdin," *Sobornost* 7, no. 4 (1977): 288–98.

82 / Cf. the shame of her nakedness expressed by Mary of Egypt when Zosimos found her (*Vita S. Mariae Aegyptae*, para. 12, *Patrologia Graeca* 87, pt. 3, col. 3705 C–D).

83 / *Vita S. Febroniae*, sec. 23; Brock and Harvey, *Holy Women*, 165.

84 / *Vita S. Febroniae*, sec. 24; Brock and Harvey, *Holy Women*, 166.

85 / Cf. the consideration of female authorship for the *Life of Matrona* in Topping, "St. Matrona and Her Friends."

86 / The original texts are Syriac; these are edited and translated with full discussions in Irfan Shahid, *The Martyrs of Najran*, Sub. Hag. 49 (Bruxelles: Société des Bollandistes, 1971), and Axel Moberg, *The Book of*

*the Himyarites: Fragments of a Hitherto Unknown Syriac Work* (Lund: C. W. K. Gleerup, 1924). Greek and Latin versions are usually found listed under St. Arethas and his Companions: *Bibliotheca Hagiographica Graeca*, 166–67; *Bibliotheca Hagiographica Latina*, 671. Some of the Syriac texts about these women martyrs are translated in Brock and Harvey, *Holy Women*, 100–121.

87 / Simeon of Beth Arsham, sec. xx; Brock and Harvey, *Holy Women*, 110.

88 / E.g., the cases of Febronia, Mahya, and Anahid are translated in Brock and Harvey, *Holy Women*; Palladius, *Lausiac History*, 3 (Potamiaena) and 65 (unnamed virgin); Barbara, in John the Stylite, *Select Narrations*, Studia Sinaitica 10, 77–84; Theodosia, in Eusebius of Caesarea, *Martyrs of Palestine*, 7.2, trans. in H. J. Lawlor and J. E. L. Oulton, *Eusebius of Caesarea, the Ecclesiastical History and the Martyrs of Palestine* (London: SPCK, 1954).

89 / Eusebius, *Ecclesiastical History*, 8.12.7 and *Martyrs of Palestine*, 7.4.

90 / The torture of women by sexual mutilation becomes a part of the Western iconographic tradition of women martyrs, perhaps best known in the depictions of St. Agatha.

91 / *Vita S. Melaniae*, sec. 69; Clark, *Melania the Younger*, 81–82. The English translation implies that the clothes were from both women and men, but this is explicit in the Greek; see the text in Gorce, *Vie de Sainte Mélanie*, 268–70.

92 / E.g., Flusin, *Miracle et Histoire*, 87–137; Benedicta Ward, *Miracles and the Medieval Mind: Theories, Record and Event 1000–1215*, rev. ed. (Philadelphia: Univ. of Pennsylvania Press, 1987), 166–71.

93 / So the Latin as translated by Ward, *Harlots*, 45; it is virtually identical to the Greek, at para. 20, *Patrologia Graeca* 87, pt. 3, col. 3712B.

## 4

*Diane L. Mockridge*

## Marital Imagery in Six
## Late Twelfth- and Early
## Thirteenth-Century Vitae
## of Female Saints

EVERY CULTURE PRODUCES ITS OWN unique stories. Studying how people tell their tales—the language they use and the symbolism they employ—reveals much about how they perceive and make sense of their world. When studying medieval religious culture, saints' lives (vitae), the stories of holy women and men, are invaluable in ascertaining medieval models of female and male sanctity, perceptions of God, and attitudes about the proper relationship the believer should have with God. As these perceptions changed over the course of the Middle Ages, so did the stories of the saints. Twice-told tales of saints' lives, then, can be used as barometers of religious attitudes because these retold hagiographies reflect mimetically the current perceptions of the time.

I shall focus on the small changes introduced by six twelfth- and thirteenth-century vernacular hagiographers as they retold three Latin vitae of female saints.[1] Compared here are the tenth- and eleventh-century Latin vitae, upon which the vernacular renditions were most probably based, of Saints Juliana of Nicomedia, Margaret of Antioch, and Katherine of Alexandria with the earliest versions that appeared between circa 1150 and 1225 in both Old French and Middle English.[2] The three Latin vitae chosen were mature versions of the legends, rather than the original brief notices that appeared in either Greek or Latin within a century or two after the deaths of these virgin martyrs in the fourth century.[3] Upon superficial examination, these mature Latin vitae seem identical to their later vernacular redactions, so much so that many scholars have called these vernacular versions mere translations of the Latin.[4] But if one does a close textual analysis of these works, subtle changes in words and phrases *do* appear between the Latin and vernacular versions of the lives of Juliana, Margaret, and Katherine.

The most important changes made by the late twelfth- and early thirteenth-century vernacular hagiographers in rewriting the tenth- and eleventh-century Latin vitae involve changes in the portrayal of the saint. The six vernacular hagiographers examined are more apt to portray the female saints as brides of Christ than are the three Latin biographers. Marital imagery abounds in the six works, both in places where in the Latin none existed before and in places where previously there had been martial imagery. The nuptial imagery in the vernacular texts is further enhanced by the characterization of the women as lovers or friends of Christ.[5]

In all six vernacular texts, the saints are said to be brides of Christ, either through an explicit statement to that effect or by characterizing Christ as their husband. This is true, for example, in the vernacular versions of the legend of St. Juliana of Nicomedia where marital imagery is used to depict Juliana as Christ's bride. In the Latin version of the legend, the story centers around Eleusius' (a pagan senator of Nicomedia) desire to wed the virgin Juliana and her refusal due to her Christian beliefs. The Latin vita depicts Juliana as steadfast in her beliefs and courageous in her ability to withstand torture and martyrdom. She describes herself as Christ's champion when she says to Eleusius, "In the Name of my Lord Jesus Christ, I shall overcome your savage spirit and make your father, Satan, redden with shame. I will find courage in the sight of my Lord Jesus Christ."[6] However, the Latin version does not soften the portrayal of Juliana the soldier of Christ. Despite the repeated discussion of the issue of marriage in the Latin version, the anonymous author of that work never applied marital imagery to Juliana nor did the author use it to characterize the relationship thought to be appropriate between Juliana and Christ.

In contrast, the vernacular hagiographers of the legend take full advantage of the marriage debate that occurs in the story and use it to depict Juliana as Christ's bride. In both the Old French and the Middle English versions Juliana declares that she "seeks no other spouse" (Old French) and that she is already "espoused to one . . . who is unlike him [Eleusius] and all worldly men" (Middle English).[7] After such declarations, both versions underscore the nuptial imagery being applied to Juliana and Christ by having Juliana's father demand to know where her "secret spouse" (Old French) is and who her husband is "to which she is wedded" (Middle English).[8] We elsewhere find both the Old French and Middle English hagiographers directly stating that Juliana is "God's spouse" (Old French) and his "bride" (Middle English).[9] The effect of the addition of marital imagery and the deletion of such ideas as being Christ's champion as well as the use of words which imply a romantic involvement between Juliana and Christ—the Middle English addition that Juliana was "Jesus Christ's lover" and the Old French addition that Juliana was "Jesus Christ's friend"—results in new versions of the legend which retain the basic story and characterization of Juliana and point at the same time to a new model of female sanctity.[10]

The vernacular redactions of the legend of St. Margaret also show a new interest in depicting a holy woman as a bride of Christ. Where the tenth-century Latin version by Theotimus begins by describing Margaret as a fighter ("I wrote down all that the blessed Margaret suffered, how she fought the devil, defeated him and was crowned"), the twelfth-century Old French version by Wace begins by describing Margaret as a spouse ("I will tell you the life of a virgin, of a most holy maiden, who had her love turned toward God the highest. . . . She was God's hand-maiden and spouse, willingly and well she guarded her chastity for him and devoted herself to him").[11]

In addition to the substitutions of one image for another that occur when the vernacular redactors "translate" the Latin into their native tongues, we also have cases where the vernacular hagiographers add new material to a scene. For example, toward the end of the Latin version of the legend of St. Margaret, Christ says to Margaret, "Come quickly to the place prepared for you. For I am with you and I will open for you the door of the kingdom of heaven."[12] The Middle English hagiographer turns this speech into a moving epithalamium which has language reminiscent of that in the Song of Songs: "Come now, bride, to your bridegroom. Come, love, to your life, for I expect your coming: brightest bedroom abides you. Love, come quickly to me. Come now to my kingdom. Leave the common people so low, you shall wield with me all that I own, brightest of brides."[13] As with the vernacular legends of St. Juliana, the Old French and Middle English versions of St. Margaret also repeatedly refer to Margaret's love of Christ, and call her his "friend."[14]

The vernacular treatments of the St. Katherine legend also show the inclusion of marital imagery, some replacing what had previously been martial imagery. For example, where Katherine in the Latin base text says, "My God cannot abandon his soldiers amidst hunger and tribulation," in the Old French twelfth-century version she says, "My spouse, my good friend, fed me very well."[15] As in the vernacular legends of Juliana and Margaret, numerous references in the Old French and Middle English versions of the Katherine legend make it clear that Katherine is Christ's spouse.[16] While there are a few instances of the use of bridal imagery in the base Latin text, the more frequent use of bridal images in the Old French and Middle English versions suggests that this model of female sanctity was becoming more popular.[17]

Nearly as important as the changes made by the vernacular hagiographers in their portrayal of the female saints are the changes they made in their portrayal of God the Father and God the Son. The Middle English and Old French hagiographers emphasize the humanity in God and Christ. Where the Latin versions portray God as an all-powerful king, the vernacular versions depict him instead as a merciful and loving father. The awe-inspiring deity of the earlier Latin accounts gives way in the vernacular versions to the approachable God who is a healer and a comforter. For example, in the Latin version of the life of St. Juliana, Juliana asks God to help her and reveal who the demon is who is tormenting her in prison: "O Lord, God of heaven and earth, do not desert me or let your handmaiden perish. Strengthen my heart in your might and show me, as one who trusts in your Name, who it is that speaks such things and urges me to worship idols."[18] Juliana, perceiving her God as a god of strength, asks to be *strengthened* by his *might*. This perception of God undergoes a transformation in the early thirteenth-century Old French version. There she says, "Lord, the savior of orphans, you who are their true father, merciful to the sinners, and good medicine to the suffering, and just to all the poor and good protector of all the serfs, Beautiful Lord God! Judge me according to how I place my faith in you. Now judge me as you can and as you know and as you wish. Of this mockery you have guided me well, so that I am not sullied by anything. Now allow me Lord this gift by your most holy name: This one [the demon] cannot part from me, nor go outside the prison until I know well who gave him this message."[19] This god is not a god of strength but a lord of mercy, a father who loves his children, and who empathizes with the poor and weak.

This humanization of God is also apparent in the Margaret legend. In the tenth-century Latin version by Theotimus, Margaret defends her belief in God by saying to the emperor Olybrius, "I worship and call upon him, at whom the earth trembles, of whom the sea is afraid, whom the winds and every creature fear, whose kingdom endures forever."[20] The Middle English twelfth-century version changes this to "Him alone I love and believe in, who has power over and directs through his will the winds and weathers, and all that is set upon with sea and with sun, both above and beneath, all bow to him and bend. To add to this he is so mighty and so powerful, the loveliest to look upon and sweetest to smell; nor can his sweet savour, nor his almighty might, nor his spotless lovely body ever more lessen or perish, for he never perishes, but lives always in honor, and all who live in him last ever more."[21] The Latin version portrays God in terms of the response he evokes. God is all-powerful because everything is afraid of him and thus in a subordinate position to him. The Middle English account, however, embellishes the Latin description of God to the extent that a different picture emerges. In the first part of this description God controls but does not threaten his creation. But the vernacular hagiographer goes further and consciously adds new qualities that tone down the image of the all-powerful God. God is now, in addition to mighty, the loveliest to look at and the sweetest to smell. These qualities are repeated a second time at the end of the passage. The effect of these additions is to change the fear-inspiring God of Theotimus' day into a God who, while still powerful, is now approachable and has human qualities. These two new qualities, moreover, are noteworthy in that these are characteristics one would use to describe an object of love. The most direct change the Middle English hagiographer made in this passage was to have Margaret say she "loved" God rather than she "worshipped" him, revealing a new intimate relationship envisaged between the believer and God.

But before examining the new dynamic between the believer and God, which is the third significant change the vernacular hagiographers introduce into their versions of the legends, it is necessary to look at the new perceptions of God the Son. As with the perceptions of God the Father, Christ's portrayal changes also; the triumphant Christ who conquers death by living eternally is replaced by the suffering Christ who humbled himself out of love for humanity. For example, where Juliana in the Latin version describes Jesus as a god who "lives forever and reigns in heaven," in the corresponding Old French and Middle English sections, respectively, she describes him as the savior who "created me and you out of nothing, and on the cross redeemed us" and the Son of God who "to redeem mankind, which must otherwise have been lost, gave up his life on the cross."[22] Unlike the Latin version in which Christ was portrayed as the eternal king, the vernacular versions portray him as a suffering man.

The shift of emphasis apparent in these hagiographies corresponds to the larger change that occurred between the early and high Middle Ages regarding the atonement theory. According to the classic theory of atonement prevalent in the early Middle Ages, a cosmic battle took place between God and Satan over the human soul.[23] God the all-powerful and wise sent his only son to defeat Satan because humans were unable to effect their own salvation. By making his son human, God tricked Satan into believing that Jesus was under his power, and thus committing the crime of executing him. But this act was one of treason as Christ had never submitted himself to the devil. Thus by killing Christ, Satan had committed the ultimate crime and God could rightfully punish and defeat him forever. By this scenario God had successfully outwitted Satan.[24] As historian Richard Southern says of this theory, "That God should become Man was a great mystery, a majestic, awe-inspiring act."[25]

This early-medieval perception of Christ gave way in the late eleventh and early twelfth centuries to a new view of the deity that stressed his humanity. Scholars have credited St. Anselm (1033–1109) with this movement's start. In *Cur Deus Homo* (1098) Anselm presents a new theory of atonement, known both as the satisfaction theory and the juridical theory. He does not discuss the role of Satan, as the classic theory did; instead he discusses the event in terms of Original Sin. Anselm concluded that because a human, Adam, committed the Original Sin, the "debt" incurred by this deed had to be paid in order for humankind to be saved. Since a man committed the sin, another *man* would have to make satisfactory reparation for it. But since humans were tainted and incapable of attaining their own salvation, there was only one man who could help them—a man who was also a God. So God became human in order to save humankind.[26]

The essence of Anselm's theory is thus at odds with the earlier classic theory of atonement. Where the classic theory stresses Christ's heroism in battle, his supernatural abilities, and his triumphant nature, the juridical theory stresses his humanness, his suffering, and his love for humanity. The twelfth-century rejection of the classic theory in favor of the juridical theory is encapsulated in a digression in Clemence's Old French version of the Katherine legend, which has no equivalent passage in the Latin. In discussing why God became human, Clemence asserts that "God could well by his strength or by his will alone cure the world of the Enemy, but by greater justice made it so that a man avenged man; what man forfeited, man made reparations for."[27]

The changes that occurred in both the portrayal of the female saints as well as God affected the portrayal of the resultant *relationship* between the saint and God. In examining this third significant change which the vernacular hagiographers introduced into their texts, we need to keep in mind the widespread use of nuptial imagery in these texts. For in expressing the new relationship between the believer and Christ envisaged by the vernacular hagiographers, the marriage metaphor occupies a central place. With the change from martial imagery to marital, the vernacular hagiographers make possible a new dynamic of divine and human interaction. Where once there was a relationship of subordination, there is now one of mutuality. Passive worship of a distant Godhead is replaced by active love of an accessible being. An intellectual comprehension of religious truths is replaced by the need for an emotional experience of oneness with God.

All of these changes can be seen when comparing the Latin texts with their vernacular redactions. For example, evidence of the new mutuality of the relationship can be seen when one compares the Latin line in the legend of St. Margaret, "She was filled with the Holy Spirit," with Wace's Old French rendition of this which starts with "She was filled with the Holy Spirit, she was the handmaiden and lover of God," and ends with a statement not seen in the Latin: "She loved God and God loved her, she gave him all her heart; she adored God and she held God dear, he returned to her a very good reward."[28] The shift from passive belief in God to active love of him is seen when comparing the speech Juliana makes in Latin which rejects the pagan Eleusius' marriage offer because it required her to give up her Christian beliefs with its Old French and Middle English counterparts. Where the Latin has Juliana say, "I speak the truth and do not lie when I say I will suffer every trial and judgment joyfully. I will not abandon the teaching of my Lord Jesus Christ," the Old French version has her say, "I adore him and so believe in him and give my trust to him in everything. I don't fear you or any other."[29] In Latin, Juliana asserts that she will not abandon Christ's *teachings*—a statement which is both negatively expressed and impersonal—while in Old French she positively proclaims her *love* of *him*. The nature of Juliana's faith has changed, as seen here in the shift from the Latin Juliana who responds to Christ with her mind to the Old French Juliana who worships from her heart.

The Middle English version of this sentence also shows the same shift. In this version Juliana says, "I wish for him to know this . . . that I am espoused to one, whom I will truly without falsehood love, who is unlike him and all worldly men, nor will I ever more deny nor desert him for wealth or for joy, for woe nor for misery that you may do me."[30] Passive acceptance of Christ's *dictates* are here replaced by a heartfelt binding commitment to Christ *himself,* her husband.

Even the nature of worship, which reveals aspects of the relationship thought to be appropriate between a believer and God, has changed between the Latin texts and their vernacular redactions. A demon in the Latin version of the Juliana legend describes the act of worship as follows: "[One] begins to pray, to listen to the Holy Scriptures and to receive the Divine Mystery."[31] The Old French version changes the act substantially: "[One should] conduct oneself very simply, and sigh very tenderly, and look at the crucifix upon which we killed Jesus, and cry and lament over one's sins."[32] Where the Latin shows a passive believer who listens to and receives divine illumination, the vernacular shows a new tendency toward active participation in worship. The ideal Christian, as portrayed here, is one who *longs* for Christ. It is no longer enough to simply *receive* the divine mystery, one must attain a heightened emotional state in order to join with Christ in a mystical union. Worship itself has become an act of love.

These, then, are the three major changes the six vernacular hagiographers make while reworking their Latin base texts. It seems that the vernacular hagiographers changed the received material as they did because they wished, perhaps unconsciously, to portray their own new perceptions of God and sanctity. In common with other contemporary portrayals of believers, saints, and God, the portrayals discussed here are more in tune with the type of spirituality current in the high Middle Ages than they are with earlier medieval spirituality. High medieval spirituality is centered on a recognition of God's humanity, a belief in the possibility of a mystical union, and a desire for an emotional and personal form of worship.

In order to understand the significance of these new religious attitudes prevalent in the high Middle Ages, we must look briefly at the basic characteristics of early medieval spirituality. The classic theory of atonement as well as artistic depictions of the crucifixion in the early Middle Ages sees Christ as a deity who is all-powerful. Christ was victorious in the great cosmic battle against Satan, and was triumphant over death on the cross. In artistic depictions of what is known as the "Triumphant Christ," Christ's body is erect on the cross, his head is held up straight, his eyes are open, and he shows no sign of pain. He is fully clothed in the garb of a king, including a real gold crown upon his head. The reaction that this type of representation evokes is one of awe, mimetically reflecting the attitudes of many believers toward God at this time. Just as the act of incarnation was a deed for humans to admire, so too was Christ's triumph over death. As historian Richard Southern says, "Until [the late eleventh century], the most powerful representation of the crucifixion in Western Europe had expressed the sense of that remote and majestic act of Divine power."[33]

Given this early medieval perception of God, it makes sense that many believers in the early Middle Ages would perceive themselves as soldiers in God's army. Carolyn Bynum, in her study of the use of feminine images in twelfth-century spiritual writings, says that "images of warfare

—which were to medieval people clearly male images—were dominant in the monastic spirituality of the tenth and eleventh centuries."[34] John Bugge, in his study of the medieval ideal of virginity, discusses at length the notion of being a *miles Christi* (a soldier of Christ), a role particularly attractive to monks in the early Middle Ages. He says at that time it was "the belief in more than just a figurative or symbolic way [that] the man who chooses the life of a monk has enlisted for battle as a *miles Christi*."[35]

As previously mentioned, this early medieval perception of God gave way in the late eleventh and early twelfth centuries to a new view of the deity that stressed his humanity. Both St. Anselm's juridical theory of atonement and high medieval artistic depictions of the crucifixion show this new interest in Christ's humanness and his suffering. As Bugge says of Anselm's theory, "The effect of the juridical view of atonement was to throw the weight of emphasis upon Christ's humanity, somewhat at the expense of his divinity. . . . The juridical theory also allowed for an entirely new category of speculation over the meaning of the redemption: The severity of Christ's passion and death seemed the proof of a corresponding intensity in his love for the human race. The suffering Jesus became the centerpiece of medieval piety; the theme was based on the belief that he had undergone the torments of the passion for the purpose of winning man's love."[36] These ideas are given concrete form in art in the new representation of Christ on the cross, known as the "Suffering Christ." Christ is seen literally hanging on the cross, his body emaciated, his arms sagging, his wounds bleeding, his head drooping, his eyes closed, with a look of intense anguish on his face. Gone is the garb of the king as in the earlier depictions of the triumphant Christ; in its place is a loin cloth, and on his head is a crown of thorns.[37] Christ's humanness is emphasized in this depiction, not his otherworldiness as in the earlier representation. But most importantly, the reaction elicited by this type of portrayal is at odds with that of the earlier depiction. The suffering Christ evokes pity, not awe, from its viewers. Seeing concretely that Christ suffered out of love for humanity, the viewer cannot help but respond emotionally in return. The observer literally participates in Christ's passion instead of feeling removed from it as in earlier representations.

The humanization of Christ resulted in a changed perception not only of Christ's basic attributes but also of believers' views of themselves in relation to God. As mentioned, many Christians in the early Middle Ages viewed God as a king and a victorious commander, and subsequently saw themselves as soldiers of God enlisted to carry on the cosmic battle against evil. But, as Bugge says, "with the growth in popularity of the juridical atonement, the idea that salvation history was to be conceived of as a kind of *agon,* together with the notion that the monk was the soldier of Christ, receded as inevitably as did the concept of *Christus Victor* [the victorious Christ]." [38] In place of these ideas, new ones arose in the twelfth century based on the notion of Christ's humanity: "This 'humanization' of Christ allowed for one other extremely important attribution; it permitted the believer to focus on what the unerring fixation upon his divinity had all but obscured, the fact of Christ's human sexuality. . . . By the twelfth century . . . the Anselmian view of the atonement had removed the obstacle, as it were, to seeing Christ as a man, both human and male. The importance of this sequence of events is that it opened the way to speaking of Christ in the metaphorical terms of human sexual love." [39] We find with increasing frequency in the high Middle Ages that believers will envision their relationship to Christ as analogous to a human marriage. The believer, male or female, is the bride and Christ is the bridegroom. The metaphor comes, of course, from the Song of Songs. The notion becomes more popular in the twelfth century when both the Song of Songs and St. Bernard of Clairvaux's commentaries on them were widely read, and even available in the vernacular. [40] Although the analogy was sometimes employed in religious writing before the twelfth century, "in the early Middle Ages it was more often the concept of the soldier, not that of the bride, to which male monasticism turned for the more authentic expression of its traditional world view." [41]

What was it about the image of the bride which made it so attractive that even some males could identify themselves with it? At the heart of the metaphor was the notion that just as the bride and bridegroom in the Song of Songs were united in a loving bond, so too would the believer and Christ be conjoined. The high medieval emphasis on Christ's humanity had made the deity much more accessible than in the previous era. The emphasis on his humanity combined with the heart-rending portrayals of him in art resulted in the desire on the part of many believers to have a personal encounter with the deity. That desire for mystical union was expressed in analogies drawn from human experience, the most profound of which was love.

The changes just delineated between early and high medieval spirituality indicate that there is a clear correspondence between the current perceptions of God and sanctity with the current portrayals in medieval hagiography of saints, God, and their resultant relationships. In the Latin vitae of the tenth and eleventh centuries, the portrayals of the saints, the view of God, and the notion of the proper relationship between a believer and God all reflect the early medieval perception of God as a powerful commander, of believers as soldiers of God, and of proper worship as awe and distant admiration of the Godhead. Likewise, the portrayals in the vernacular hagiographies reflect the high medieval perception of God as a loving comforter, of believers as brides of Christ, and of proper worship as love and intimacy with Christ.[42]

We have just seen the general correspondence between these six portrayals and various aspects of high medieval spirituality. But to focus a bit more closely on the vernacular hagiographers' use of bridal imagery and its subsequent effect on the portrayal of these saints, we need to see whether the issue of gender made a difference or not. That is, did the gender of the saints affect their portrayal? Did the gender of the hagiographer? To answer the first question, comparisons will be made between these reworked vitae of women and fifteen reworked Old French vitae of men composed in the twelfth century.[43] The second question can be addressed briefly.

Unfortunately, there is not enough evidence to see whether the gender of the author is a factor in the changing portrayal of the saints in these texts. Of the six vernacular hagiographers examined, only two are known by name: Clemence of Barking and Wace. While these are obviously not a significant sample, when one compares their reworkings of a Latin text, few differences occur. Both Clemence and Wace pare down the use of military images found in the Latin exemplar. And both add nuptial imagery where none had existed before. Both stick very closely to the original story, grafting on new imagery and ideas while retaining the narrative structure of the Latin work. The changes they introduce reflect the new attitudes toward God and sanctity just delineated. The only substantial difference between their recastings of the legends is that Clemence's work is longer and more digressive, but this clearly has little to do with the gender of the author.

Finding little difference between the types of changes Clemence and Wace introduce into their texts fits the overall pattern Bynum discovered concerning the "feminization of language" in the high Middle Ages. Many scholars have noted an increase in the use of female imagery in texts starting in the twelfth century. While Bynum says that bridal imagery, which she sees as an example of the feminization of language, is more common in thirteenth- and fourteenth-century texts by female authors (she does not mention the twelfth century), she makes it clear overall that "such language [feminine language] is in *no* way the special preserve of female writers."[44] Nor did women find such language particularly compelling—in fact it seems "they were less attracted [to it] than men."[45]

We may now return to the first question: Did the gender of the saints have an effect on their portrayal? As with the reworked vitae of the female saints, the reworked vitae of the male saints reveal perceptions of God and sanctity that seem consistent with high medieval affective spirituality. All but one of the works (which was less than 500 lines) speak of the saints' love of God or vice versa. Most of them use the phrase "for the love of God" so frequently that it becomes a cliché. Seven of the Old French male lives mention that the saint was God's friend or that God was the saint's friend. To give just a few examples: the anonymous author of what is known as the first Old French version of the St. Alexis legend declares that "he [Alexis] loves God more than all his family."[46] The line has no equivalent in the Latin base text. In that work the author also uses the expression "for the love of God" a few times, a phrase that also has no Latin equivalent.[47] In Benedeit's Anglo-Norman *Voyage of St. Brendan* Jesus is described as a "tender and ready friend," while the Latin source makes no mention of this.[48] As with the reworked vitae of the female saints, those of the male saints reveal their hagiographers' desire to portray the relationship between their subject and God as a close one involving loving bonds.

What is interesting about these fifteen Old French vitae is that despite their repeated use of the phrase "for the love of God," the repeated mention of the mutuality of the love between the saint and God, and the repeated declaration of the friendship between the saint and God, not one of them employs marital imagery in discussing these bonds. Compared to the widespread use of nuptial imagery which occurred in the six vernacular vitae of the women, it appears that the lack of that imagery in the vitae of the men is due to the gender of the saint being portrayed.

Perhaps the best piece of evidence on this point involves two compositions by Wace, his *Vie de Sainte Marguerite* and his *Vie de St. Nicolas*. Wace uses the tenth-century Latin vita of Margaret by Theotimus, and the ninth-century Latin vita of Nicholas by John the Deacon as his exemplars. When portraying a female saint, Wace uses the word *spouse* three times, and the word *friend* twice—and none of those words appeared in the Latin original.[49] When portraying a male saint, however, Wace never uses the word *spouse,* or even *friend*. Despite the fact that his *Life of Nicholas* is twice as long as his *Life of Margaret*, Wace has only six references concerning the mutuality of God and Nicholas's love, compared to nine references concerning God and Margaret.[50] Examining how one author portrays both a male and female saint seems to show, then, that gender is a factor at work in determining the type of imagery employed in the portrayal of the saint.

It is unclear why some twelfth-century vernacular hagiographers readily portrayed their female subjects as brides of Christ but were unable to use the same imagery to portray their male subjects. Medieval men were known, on occasion, to have described themselves as brides. As Bynum says, "We have many examples of monks describing themselves or their souls as brides of Christ—that is, as female."[51] In her critique of Victor Turner's theory of liminality, Bynum shows that male lives, as lived and told, between the twelfth and fifteenth centuries, often involve sex-role reversals. She cites, for example, Bonaventure's life of St. Francis, where during Francis's central crises he is depicted as nude, weak, and female.[52] She explains this phenomenon here and in her article on female imagery in late medieval writing when she says, "The male writer who saw his soul as a bride of God or his religious role as womanly submission and humility was conscious of using an image of reversal. He sought reversal because reversal and renunciation were at the heart of a religion whose dominant symbol is the cross—life achieved through death."[53]

But it is one thing when a medieval man or his biographer deliberately uses images of reversal to show renunciation of the world and submission to God, and quite another when a hagiographer uses symbolism to show a relationship of mutuality or union with God.[54] As Bynum mentions, twelfth-century religious writers frequently used physical metaphors drawn from human relationships to make the close bond between the believer and God concrete.[55] Rather than changing their own gender, male Cistercian writers were known to describe God as female—as a mother—to show the intimate union they envisaged between themselves and God.[56] As the rewritten vitae of the men we examined were concerned with showing the saints' love of God and vice versa, they were more interested in metaphors that stressed union and not ones that stressed, for their male subjects, reversal or subordination. As a result, the most frequently used metaphor for both the male saint and Christ in these texts was simply "friend."[57]

Another factor that might be at work here is the rising influence of canon law about marriage. During the twelfth century, Gratian asserted that a marriage was not valid until it had been consummated (although others argued that the mutual promise to be married constituted a marriage).[58] If our hagiographers concurred with Gratian, then only women would be capable of completing a true marriage to the male Christ.

Again, given the popularity of symbolism drawn from human relationships and, as we have seen, the hagiographers' use of passionate sexual
language when discussing that relationship in marital terms, perhaps
the hagiographers felt that bridal metaphors were inapplicable to men.[59]
Whatever their reasons, at least in the case of twice-told tales, it seems
that hagiographers of the late twelfth and early thirteenth centuries were
more apt to show women, and not men, as brides of Christ.

## NOTES

I would like to thank Lynda L. Coon, Kathy Haldane, Elisabeth Sommer, and
the graduate students in the Corcoran Department of History, University of Virginia, for inviting me to give this paper. Thanks also go to Susan Harvey and Tom
Head for their suggestions for revisions. I am indebted to Val Krueger for typing
(and retyping) this paper. Special thanks go to my husband, Mark Lindquist, for
his editorial assistance. Any remaining errors are, obviously, my own.

1  /  This paper is a very brief summary of my dissertation, "From Christ's
Soldier to His Bride: Changes in the Portrayal of Women Saints in Medieval Hagiography," Ph.D. diss., Duke Univ., 1984.

2  /  The following texts were used: for the vitae of St. Juliana of Nicomedia,
the Latin text, "Acta Auctore Anonymo," in *Acta Sanctorum . . . ,* ed.
Joannes Bollandus (Paris, 1863–1940), 875–78; the Old French text, "Vie
de Sainte Juliane," in *Li ver del juise,* ed. Hugo von Feilitzen (Upsala,
1883), 3–24; the Middle English text, *Pe Liflade of St. Juliana from
Two Old English Manuscripts of 1230 A.D. with Renderings into Modern English by the Rev. O. Cockayne and Edmund Brock,* ed. Oswald
Cockayne (London, 1872). For the vitae of St. Margaret of Antioch, the
Latin text, "Passio Sanctae Margarite Virginis que passa est in Anti-
ochia civitate sub Olibrio Prefecto XIII kalendas Augusti," in Wace, *La
Vie de Sainte Marguerite,* ed. Elizabeth A. Francis (Paris: Champion,
1932), 2–56; the Old French text, Wace, *La Vie de Sainte Marguerite,*
ed. Elizabeth A. Francis (Paris: Champion, 1932); the Middle English
text, *Seinte Marherete: The Meiden and Martyr,* ed. Frances M. Mack
(London: Oxford Univ. Press, 1934). For the vitae of St. Katherine of
Alexandria, the Latin text, "Passio Sanctae Katerine Virginis," in *Dvĕ
verse starofrancouzské Legendy o sv. Kateřině Alexandrinské,* ed. J. U.
Jarnik (Prague, 1894), 1–80; the Old French text, Clemence of Barking,
*The Life of St. Catherine,* ed. William MacBain (Oxford: Published for
the Anglo-Norman Text Society by Basil Blackwell, 1964); the Middle
English texts, *The Life of St. Katherine from the Royal MS 17 A xxvii,
&c., with its Latin Original from the Cotton MS Caligula A. viii, &c.,*
ed. Eugen Einenkel (London, 1884) and *Seinte Katerine,* ed. Eric J. Dob-
son and Simonne R. Th. O. d'Ardenne (Oxford: Oxford Univ. Press,
1981).

3  /  The rationale behind this selection process was the fear of comparing,
as it were, apples and oranges if the earliest brief notices were compared
with the high medieval legends. A saint's life does change substantially
over the course of its evolution. However, if one restricts oneself to
changes made after the legend has reached maturity—after the incorpo-

ration of the significant events and associations made with that particular saint—the results are changes in degree rather than in kind.

4 / This makes sense, because the vernacular hagiographers themselves claim that they are faithfully translating the Latin into their native tongue. For example, Clemence of Barking says, "I want to translate the life from Latin to bring it into romance so that it (will) be more pleasing to those hearing it" (*Life of St. Catherine*, 2: "voil translater la vie, / De latin respundre en rumanz / Pur ço que plus plaise as oianz"). The translations of this Old French text are by Paul Shullenberger.

5 / As will be seen through various textual examples, the six vernacular hagiographers examined here characterize marriages between the saints and Christ as involving loving bonds. While this portrayal of love in marriage may reflect the six authors' views concerning *spiritual* marriages, one should *not* conclude that this portrayal also reflects their attitudes toward either ideal or real marriages in the high Middle Ages. This paper does not intend to draw conclusions about the reality of European marriages in the twelfth and thirteenth centuries.

6 / This translation of the Latin legend is called "The Acts of Saint Juliana," in *Sources and Analogues of Old English Poetry: The Major Latin Texts in Translation*, trans. Michael J. B. Allen and Daniel G. Calder (Totowa, N.J.: Rowman and Littlefield, 1976), 122–32. This particular passage is on page 124. In Latin, this is from "Acta Auctore Anonymo," 875: "Sed ego in nomine Domini mei Jesu Christi vincam mentem tuam inhumanam, et faciam erubescere patrem tuum satanam, et inveniam fiduciam in conspectu Domini mei Jesu Christi."

7 / "Vie de Sainte Juliana," 8: "ne quier avoir altre espose." The translations of this Old French text are my own. *Liflade of St. Juliana*, 15: "ich am tu an iweddet . . . þat is unlich him 7 alle worltliche men." The translations of this Middle English text are my own.

8 / "Vie de Sainte Juliana," 9: "espous celeement." *Liflade of St. Juliana*, 15: "Ant hwet is he þes were þat tu art to iweddet."

9 / "Vie de Sainte Juliane," 9: "la deu espose." *Liflade of St. Juliana*, 31: "brud."

10 / *Liflade of St. Juliana*, 9: "ihesu cristes leofmon." "Vie de Sainte Juliane," 8: "deu amie." "Amie" is a significant word in all three of the Old French texts examined here. Frederic Godefroy, in his *Dictionnaire de l'ancienne langue française*, 10 vols. (Paris, 1881–1902) translates it as both "friend" and "lover".

11 / "Passio Sanctae Margarite," 4: "Scripsi omnia quibus passa est beatissima Margarita, quomodo pugnavit contra demonem et vicit eum et coronata est." The translations of this Latin text are my own. Wace, *Vie de Marguerite*, 3: "Dirai d'un virge la vie, / D'une damoisele saintime / Qui s'amor ot vers Deu hautisme. . . . / Ancele Deu fu et espouse / Volentiers et bien li garda / Sa castée, se li voua." The translations of this Old French text are my own.

12 / "Passio Sanctae Margarite," 52: "Veni celerius in locum tibi preparatum. Ego enim tecum sum, et aperiam tibi ianuam regni celorum."

13 / *Seinte Marherete*, 48: "Cum nu . . . brud, to þi brudgume. Cum leof, to þi lif, for ich copni þi cume: brihtest bur abitd te. Leof, hihe þe to me. Cum nu to mi kinedom. Leaf þet leode se lah, 7 tu schalt wealde wið me al þet ich i wald ah, alre burde brihtest." The translations of this Middle English text are my own.

14 / See for example, Wace, *Vie de Marguerite*, 5, 15, 27, 29; *Seinte Marherete*, 8, 12, 36.

15 / "Passio Sanctae Katerine Virginis," 58: "(Deus meus) suos milites in fame et tribulatione deserere nescit." The translations of this Latin text are my own. Clemence of Barking, *Life of Catherine*, 61: "mun espus, mun bon ami / Tres bien me put."

16 / See for example, Clemence of Barking, *Life of Catherine*, 5–6, 19, 43–44, 52, 83; *Life of St. Katherine*, 71–72.

17 / See "Passio Sanctae Katerine Virginis," 13, 41–42.

18 / "Acts of St. Juliana," 126; "Acta Auctore Anonymo," 876: "Domine Deus coeli et terrae, ne deseras me, neque permittas perire ancillam tuam: sed confirma cor meum in virtute tua: et confidenti in nomine tuo significa mihi quis est iste, qui mihi talia loquitur, et persuadet idola adorare."

19 / "Vie de Sainte Juliane," 12–13: "Sire, vrais salvere / as orfenins ki es vrais pere / merciables as pecheors, / et bons mies as doleros, / et justeciers de toz parvers, / et bons garanz a toz tes sers, / beaz sires deus! ajue moi, / enssi cum je moi fie en toi; / or m'ajue si cum tu pues, / et cum tu seis et cum tu vus; / de truske ci m'as bien conduite, / si ke de rien ne sui sorduite, / or m'otroie sire! cest don / par lo taen saintisme non, / ke cist ne puist de moi partir, / ne de la chartre fors issir, / tant cum je bien conoisse et sache, / ki li charjat icest message."

20 / "Passio Sanctae Margarite," 12: "ego illum (adoro ac invoco) quem terra contremiscit, mare formidat, quem timent venti et omnis creatura, cuius regnum permanet in secula seculorum."

21 / *Seinte Marherete*, 11: "Him ane ich luuie ant habbe to bileaue, þe welt 7 wisseð þurh his wit windes 7 te weteres, 7 al þat biset is mit see ant mit sunne. Buuem ba ant bineoðen, al buheð him 7 beieð. Teken þis, þat he is so mihti ant so meinful, he is leoflukest lif for to lokin uppon 7 swotest to smeallen: ne his swote sauur, ne his almihti mihte, ne his makelese lufsumlec ne mei neauer lutlin ne aliggen; for he ne alið neauer, ah liueð aa in are, 7 al þat in him lið, leasteð aa mare."

22 / "Acts of Saint Juliana," 123; "Acta Auctore Anonymo," 875: "Qui vivit semper et regnat in coelis." "Vie de Sainte Juliane," 9: "Ki moi et toi de nient format, / et en la croiz nos rachata." *Liflade of St. Juliana*, 15–17: "þat forte alesen moncun þat schulde beon forloren al; lette lif o rode."

23 / Gustaf Aulén, *Christus Victor: An Historical Study of the Three Main Types of the Idea of Atonement* (New York: Macmillan, 1951), 36–41.

24 / This summary is taken from Aulén, *Christus Victor*, 16–80, and from Richard W. Southern, *The Making of the Middle Ages* (New Haven: Yale Univ. Press, 1953), 234–36.

25 / Southern, *Making of the Middle Ages*, 235.

26 / Aulén, *Christus Victor*, 81–92.

27 / Clemence of Barking, *Life of Catherine*, 32: "Bien poust Deus par poesté / U par sule sa volenté / Guarir le mund de l'Enimi, / Mais par greinur dreit le fist si, / Que un hume l'ume venjast; / Ço que hume forfist, hume amendast."

28 / "Passio Sanctae Margarite," 4: "Illa de Spiritu sancto erat repleta." Wace, *Vie de Marguerite*, 5, 7: "Del Saint Espir fu replenie, / Ancele Deu fu et amie. . . . / Ele ama Deu et Deu l'ama, / Trestot son cuer li adona; / Deu aora et Deu ot chier, / Il l'en rendi mult bon loier."

29 / "Acts of St. Juliana," 123; "Acta Auctore Anonymo," 875: "Verum dico

et non mentior, quia omnem quaestionem et omnia judicia gratanter sustineo, nec recedam a Domini mei Jesu Christi praecepto." "Vie de Sainte Juliane," 9: "Je l'ador et si lo croi / e lui m'afi de tot en tot, / ne toi, ne altre ne redot."

30 / *Liflade of St. Juliana*, 15: "Ich chulle þat he wite hit ful wel, ich am tu an iweddet þat ich chulle treowliche wiðute leas luuien. þat is unlich him 7 alle worltliche men. ne nulle ich neauer mare him lihen ne leauen. for weole ne for wunne. for wa ne for wontreaðe þat ȝe me mahen wurchen."

31 / "Acts of St. Juliana," 127; "Acta Auctore Anonymo," 876–77: "ierit orare, et sanctas Scripturas audire, et communicare divinum mysterium, ab illo praecipites effugamur."

32 / "Vie de Sainte Juliane," 18: "contenir mut simplement / et sospireir mut tenrement / et regardeir lo crucefis, / cum Jhesus fut par lui ocis, / et les pechiez ploreir et plaindre."

33 / Here again I am summarizing Southern's overall argument. This quotation is from page 237. See also Colin Morris, *The Discovery of the Individual, 1050–1200* (New York: Harper and Row, 1972), 23. There are, of course, as Southern himself acknowledges, examples of the "Triumphant Christ" which were produced later than the last part of the eleventh century. There are also examples of the "Suffering Christ," discussed later in this paper, which were produced earlier than the twelfth century. As with some of the other points I am making, I am here arguing a matter of degrees, not of absolutes.

34 / Caroline Walker Bynum, *Jesus as Mother: Studies in the Spirituality of the High Middle Ages* (Berkeley and Los Angeles: Univ. of California Press, 1982), 139. See also her citation of Barbara Rosenwein and Lester Little, "Social Meanings in the Monastic and Mendicant Spiritualities," *Past and Present* 63 (May 1974): 20–32.

35 / John Bugge, *Virginitas: An Essay in the History of a Medieval Ideal* (The Hague: Martinud Nijhoff, 1975), 47.

36 / Ibid., 82.

37 / Southern, *Making of the Middle Ages*, 237; Morris, *Discovery of the Individual*, 140.

38 / Bugge, *Virginitas*, 82.

39 / Ibid., 83.

40 / Ibid., 90, and Jean Leclercq, *The Love of Learning and the Desire for God: A Study of Monastic Culture* (New York: Fordham Univ. Press, 1960), 106.

41 / Bugge, *Virginitas*, 79.

42 / Again, these observations are not meant as absolute strictures. There is not just one perception of God current at any given time period. But it is possible to make general statements about the pattern historians have seen in the extant religious writings of the time and thus I am in agreement with Southern, Bynum, etc., who have discussed the characteristics of this religiosity of the high Middle Ages and have labeled it a time of "affective spirituality."

43 / The fifteen Old French saints' lives I examined are of: Alexis I, in *The Life of St. Alexius in the Old French Version of the Hildesheim Manuscript*, ed. Carl L. Odenkirchen (Brookline, Mass.: Classical Folia Editions, 1978), 92–140; Alexis II, in *La Vie de Saint Alexis*, ed. G. Paris and L. Pannier (Paris, 1872), 222–60; Bon, in *Adgar's Marienlegenden*, ed. Carl Neuhaus (Heilbronn, 1886), 115–21; Brendan, in *The Anglo-Norman Voyage of St. Brendan by Benedeit*, ed. E. G. R. Waters

(Oxford: Clarendon Press, 1928), 3–94; Edmund I, in *La Passiun de Seint Edmund*, ed. Judith Grant (London: Anglo-Norman Text Society, 1978), 65–122; Edmund II, in *La Vie Seint Edmund le Rei, poème anglo-normand du XIIème siècle par Denis Piramus*, ed. Hilding Kjellman (Göteburg: Wettergren and Kerbor, 1935), 3–155; George I, in *Les Oeuvres de Simund de Freine*, ed. John Matzke (Paris: Société des Anciens Textes Français, 1909), 61–117; George II, in *La Vie de la Vierge Marie, par Wace, suivie de la Vie de Saint Georges*, ed. V. Luzarche (Tours, 1858) [Luzarche incorrectly attributed this version to Wace]; Giles, in *La Vie de saint Gilles par Guillaume de Berneville, poème du XIIème siècle publié d'après le manuscrit unique de Florence*, ed. Gaston Paris and Alphonse Bos (Paris, 1881), 1–115; Gregory, in *La Vie du Pape Saint Gregoire Huit Versions françaises médiévales de la légende du bon pécheur*, ed. Hendrik Bastiaan Sol (Amsterdam: Rodopi, 1977), 2–362; Laurence, in *La Vie de Saint Laurent: An Anglo-Norman Poem of the Twelfth Century*, ed. D. W. Russell (London: Anglo-Norman Text Society, 1976), 33–58; Nicholas, in *La Vie de Saint Nicolas par Wace*, ed. E. Ronsjö, Etudes romanes de Lund, no. 5 (Lund: Gleerup and Munksgaard, 1942), 113–74; Theophile, in *Adgar's Marienlegenden*, ed. Carl Neuhaus (Heilbronn, 1886), 79–115; Becket I, in *La Vie de Saint Thomas le martyr par Guernes de Pont-Sainte-Maxence*, ed. E. Walberg (Paris: Champion, 1922), 3–209; and Becket II, in *La Vie de Thomas Becket par Beneit*, ed. Borje Schlyter, Etudes romanes de Lund, no. 4 (Lund: Gleerup and Munksgaard, 1941), 77–161. See also Phyllis Johnson and Brigitte Cazelles, *Le Vain Siècle Guerpir: A Literary Approach to Sainthood through Old French Hagiography of the Twelfth Century* (Chapel Hill: North Carolina Studies in Romance Languages and Literatures, 1979) for more information about these vitae and their editions.

44 / Bynum, *Jesus as Mother*, 140.

45 / Ibid., 141; Bynum, " '. . . And Woman His Humanity': Female Imagery in the Religious Writing of the Later Middle Ages," in Bynum, Stevan Harrell, and Paula Richman, eds., *Gender and Religion: On the Complexity of Symbols* (Boston: Beacon Press, 1986), 258–59.

46 / *The Life of St. Alexius*, 111. See page 110 for the Old French line: "Plus aimet Deu que tut sun linage."

47 / Ibid., 109, 129.

48 / Benedeit, *Voyage of St. Brendan*, 23: "douz e prest amis." The translation of this Old French text is my own.

49 / Wace, *Vie de Marguerite*, 3, 29, 51, 5, 17.

50 / Ibid., 3, 7, 15, 21–23, 27, 49–51, 56; Wace, *Vie de Saint Nicolas*, 116, 118, 141, 158, 166, 173.

51 / Bynum, *Jesus as Mother*, 161.

52 / Caroline Walker Bynum, "Women's Stories, Women's Symbols: A Critique of Victor Turner's Theory of Liminality," in Robert Moore and Frank Reynolds, eds., *Anthropology and the Study of Religion* (Chicago: Center for the Scientific Study of Religion, 1984), 109.

53 / Bynum, "Female Imagery in Religious Writing," 273.

54 / Bynum discusses how male authors used "femaleness" as the ultimate metaphor for worldly renunciation and submission to God. In doing so, they claimed a "superior lowliness" to real women: "When male writers took femaleness as an image to describe their renunciation of the world, they sometimes said explicitly that women were too weak to be women" (Bynum, "Female Imagery in Religious Writing," 269).

55 / Bynum, *Jesus as Mother*, 161.
56 / Ibid., 110–69.
57 / See Benedeit, *Voyage of St. Brendan*, 33; *Passiun de Seint Edmund*, 117; Piramus, *Vie de Seint Edmund le Rei*, 92, 98–99, 106, 116; Guillaume de Berneville, *Vie de saint Gilles*, 15; *Vie de Théophile*, 86, 92, 109, 110; Guernes de Pont-Sainte-Maxence, *Vie de Saint Thomas le martyr*, 77, 80, 171; Beneit, *Vie de Thomas Becket*, 125, 154.
58 / Thomas Head, "Marriage to Christ as Legal Contract in the *Vita* of Christina of Markyate" (Paper delivered at the American Catholic Historical Association, April 1987), 11.
59 / I am grateful to both Everett Crosby and Tom Head for this suggestion. For a variety of reasons, including England's unique reception of St. Bernard's commentaries on the Song of Songs, John Bugge thinks that the bridal metaphor was gender-specific by the late twelfth century in England: "It became unthinkable to speak of the monk as the 'bride of Christ'" (Bugge, *Virginitas*, 96; see also 109, 135, 137).

5

*Duane J. Osheim*

## The Place of Women
## in the Late Medieval
## Italian Church

THERE ARE A VARIETY OF WAYS to think about the place of women in the
late medieval church. Yet in one way or another most eventually return
to what German historians since the nineteenth century have called the
"women's question." When *die Frauenfrage* was first raised, the issue was
to explain the numbers and varieties of religious institutions for women
in the late Middle Ages—and particularly the Beguinages, associations
for women who lived and worked together in communities following
a semimonastic form of life. Beguines followed no set rule and could
leave the community and even marry. Scholars initially concluded that
since Beguinages, unlike convents, were not the exclusive preserves of
the aristocracy, they offered well-to-do urban fathers a safe haven for
daughters they were unwilling or unable to dower and marry off. By
the 1930s, however, the question had been reformulated to examine the
role of women in the spiritual flowering of the twelfth and thirteenth
centuries. As marginal individuals par excellence, females were seen as
essential actors in the creation of vernacular spiritual literature and in
the formation of a number of religious movements—both heretical and
orthodox. And in a recent variant, female participation in the heretical movements, especially the Albigensians of southern France and the
Waldensians of northern Italy, was explained by the heretics' willingness
to make no distinction between male and female, thus allowing women
to assume positions of importance within the movement. And a leit motif
is the issue of how the female experience of religious life differed from
that of males; that is, to what extent were women merely objects in a
system of behavior defined and manipulated by males?[1]

These variants of the "female question," all underline the social, cultural, and religious significance of women's role in late medieval society. Yet institutions and phenomena through which historians can approach these questions differ in various parts of Europe. England, for

example, seems to have had an unusually large number of anchoresses in the thirteenth and fourteenth centuries.[2] In the Low Countries and the Rhineland, on the other hand, one finds many more beguinages than elsewhere.[3] In much of the south of France, of course, Cathars predominated to the point that until the mid-thirteenth century they were the ones who founded and supervised convents.[4] And finally in Italy, where convents were numerous, socially homogeneous, and small, a majority of women may have chosen the semireligious status of penitents and *conversae* attached to hospitals, monasteries, and even to convents themselves.[5] None of these forms of life, of course, were entirely absent from any part of Europe. The specific roles women adopted, however, depended largely on what was possible in a particular context. For that reason it will be worthwhile to look at one region of Europe, Italy, asking what was the place religiously concerned women claimed for themselves in the society of the late Middle Ages?

A first issue that must be addressed is women's place as defined by church leaders. Administrators were very active in late medieval Italy. Regulating and defining were the order of the day. As in the rest of Europe, the Italian church of the thirteenth and fourteenth centuries experienced a massive attempt to restructure and define organization and behavior at the parish level. It is probably not accidental that substantial documentation about the organization and functioning of parishes first survives from the thirteenth century and after.[6] And, of course, after the Fourth Lateran Council, bishops and parish priests were made ever more aware of their responsibilities to lead and discipline their flocks—most notably through the imposition of required annual confession and communion.[7]

In the flurry of reforming and organizing, Italian bishops largely followed the lead established by the papacy. According to Edith Pasztor's recent study, thirteenth-century popes treated religious women as a juridical and not a spiritual problem.[8] Because of the fragility of their sex, women could not preach and had to be protected and isolated. Pasztor concludes that late medieval popes increasingly viewed female religious with a fear and suspicion that built to Boniface VIII's bull *Periculoso et detestabili*. Women were to be kept isolated and under control. It is ironic that in an age reaching from St. Clare to St. Catherine, the papacy, like the mendicant orders, concluded that women were on the whole an unnecessary temptation to religious males and outside of the mainstream of ecclesiastical life.

Women seem equally marginal to the administrators of local churches, at least as their concerns are mirrored in surviving episcopal parchments and curial records. Bishops and their vicars expended a great deal of energy in two areas. The first was the organization and administration of the episcopal patrimony, a combination of lands, rents, feudal and spiritual dues, and jurisdictions. Bishops felt themselves challenged and harassed and sometimes even under siege by increasingly self-conscious and powerful communal governments which viewed political, economic, and religious life as part of their responsibility. Bishops also worked energetically to hold together and revitalize the network of local churches spread throughout their dioceses. Parishioners, on the one hand, claimed the right to name parish priests, to supervise the patrimony, and to organize local feasts. And, on the other, monasteries and eventually mendicants claimed the rights to preach, to hear confessions, and to bury the dead.[9] Episcopal administrators apparently had little time or energy left for women. The nature of episcopal concerns is clear in the bishop's books of Città di Castello. Officials oversaw traditional convents, lay sisters, and especially the unusually large numbers of recluses in and around the city. In most cases administrators said they were acting in response to reports of scandalous behavior. The amount of episcopal supervision in Città di Castello, however, was probably not typical. In most dioceses one finds occasional references to male guardians and confessors for convents; curial officers sometimes acted to force disaffected nuns to return to their convents. In most surviving episcopal acts, women, and especially religious women, rarely appear.[10]

It may be naive to look for a coherent view of diocesan values in administrative records which, for the most part, react to juridical and bureaucratic challenges. Yet the image of women as marginal to ecclesiastical life is little changed by an inspection of surviving synodal statutes and episcopal visitations. Synodal laws that did deal with issues like usury, gambling, sorcery, and clerical behavior had little to say specifically about women. Except in cases where men and women were treated together (as in the regulation of lay brothers and lay sisters), women are rarely mentioned. The Lucchese synod of 1308 brought up nuns almost as an afterthought and only to specify that neither lay men nor women were to visit convents without an episcopal license.[11] Fourteenth-century synodalia from Florence and Fiesole treat women in the same context, defining more and more specifically when and where confessors could enter the convent, the size and location of grates through which women could communicate with the outside world, and under what conditions nuns could leave the convent (only if accompanied and if they returned the same day).[12] The only other references are to what are called "suspect lay sisters." These are not women who fraudulently claimed religious status to escape taxes (which is what the phrase *conversus suspectus* would mean in a male context), but sexually suspect women, like whores and concubines of parish priests, who were the cause of scandal within the parish community. Women who offered the occasion for scandal and sin were clearly on the mind of Archbishop Andrea Della Torre of Genoa, who repeatedly ordered that healthy women not be allowed to confess at home or in other "occult" places.[13] Most extant visitations say comparatively little about lay or religious women. During the thirteenth and fourteenth centuries, the emphasis was on parish priests and their behavior. Women were easily missed. Only in Città di Castello was there a special visitor to inspect the numerous recluses. Bishops and their administrators, it seems, followed the papal lead and viewed religious women as the wise virgins of Matthew 25 who awaited the bridegroom with both lamp and oil. Yet in a telling reinterpretation, popes and bishops added that because of the fragility of their sex, religious women could only be wise virgins if isolated and protected by an ecclesiastical hierarchy.[14] *Joining of forces . . .*

Spiritual leaders agreed with administrators that there should be a separate and cloistered female spirituality, but they had little to say publicly about what that spirituality should be. Like all other Christians, nuns were required to confess regularly. Exempt convents, of the Cistercians for example, had confessors named by the male abbots to whom these nuns were subject. And the bishop appointed confessors for convents under his supervision.[15] Yet from handbooks of instruction for confessors, it seems clear that cloistered nuns were not expected to have to deal with the same sorts of complex moral issues which burdened the laity. In addition to issues of birth control and infanticide, female behavior became problematical when a wife failed to convince her husband to change his ways. For as Thomas of Cobham observed, "No priest can soften the heart of a man as effectively as his wife can." This was, he added, a woman's spiritual duty.[16] To be sure, exceptional women like St. Catherine of Siena received advice and council from confessors, yet Thomas of Cobham's handbook probably accurately reflects the advice most women received.

In many respects, preachers treated women the same way. Of sermons preached to Beguines in late thirteenth-century Paris, Nicole Bériou observed that whether widow or virgin, the safest path for a woman was cloistering and obedience to a superior.[17] There is no study similar to Bériou's for Italy. Popular preachers there tended to concentrate on local political issues, public morality, and domestic problems.[18] There is

little information about what sorts of sermons were directed at cloistered nuns. Archbishop Federigo Visconti of Pisa did preach before nuns
during a tour of the churches of his diocese.[19] Live correctly, he urged
them, avoid luxury in the convent. But most of the archbishop's time
and attention was devoted to political problems in Pisa, male ecclesiastical institutions, and to the laity. It was his hope and expectation that
he could bring about a renewal in his diocese. In his sermons and his
synods he emphasized renewed discipline in local churches and a clergy
who could lead the laity by example.

The archbishop's sentiments were not unlike those of his fellow
townsmen Giordano da Rivalta, a Dominican whose cycles of sermons
preached in early fourteenth-century Florence have survived. Speaking
throughout the city, Giordano concentrated on the threat of heresy, the
instability of local politics, and the questionable ethics of merchants. Several of his sermons are recorded as having been delivered at convents.
It seems, however, they were mostly delivered in the piazzas beside the
convents. The preacher's muffled words, if heard at all, only reached the
nuns from across the high convent walls. When Giordano did address
his words to women, it was to underline the common themes of wealth,
ostentation, and superstition. They come to sermons only to show off
their beauty and their wealth. Too many women, he concluded, drive
their husbands into usurious practices in order to satisfy female vanity.
Giordano's folk commonplace, of course, formed the basis for Machia-
velli's comic masterpiece *Belfagor*.[20]

Early in the fifteenth century San Bernardino of Siena echoed the same
sentiments.[21] He chided women for coming forward in expensive clothes
and wigs. But he did include in his cycle of sermons a long discussion
on marriage and female piety. Like many other of the mendicants he had
a basically positive view of marriage. He urged widows who felt emotionally compelled to remarry to do so and to ignore wicked tongues.[22]
But he did advise those who could live chastely, to maintain themselves
in what he called "true widowhood." Having lost their husbands they
should devote themselves completely to God. Bernardino advised them
to shun public appearances, even public sermons in church. They should
be cloistered, but in their own homes. Beautiful and young though they
might be, they should tame their flesh. Fasting, discipline, and avoiding the luxury of featherbeds were the first steps. Those who can read,
should read the canonical hours; others should simply recite Paternos-
ters and Ave Marias at the appropriate times. Those who do so, he says,
will be semireligious. This sort of life is, in fact, what Bernardino recommended to all women. In a sermon on the meaning of the virgins of

Psalm 45 who accompany the prince's bride, he explained that the first is *"madonna clausura"*—who will keep all but the angels from the presence of the Blessed Virgin. Bernardino urged that women accept the same sort of protection, avoiding those who would enter their houses as well as people they would meet on the streets. This done, Bernardino, like many other mendicants of the late Middle Ages, would consider these women to be following a religious vocation.[23]

There is a narrowness of vision among the moralists which reminds one of the administrators. While most moralists and preachers distinguished clearly among nobles, merchants, and peasants, they usually ignored social differences in the cases of women and simply discussed virgins, married women, and widows.[24] When moralists did consider what would be most beneficial to women who wish to be spiritual, they returned again and again to separation and closure. Penitential discipline, prayer, and keeping the canonical hours were important, but, as San Bernardino said, first comes *"madonna clausura."*

This emphasis on separation did take root in the female population of Italy, but not always to the extent or in the way that preachers had hoped. Women tended to mark their separation symbolically, by the adoption of a distinctive habit even as they continued to move about much more than churchmen wished. It has been suggested, in fact, that the more strictly administrators tried to enforce separation and cloister, the more likely women were to join semilay penitential groups or become recluses in private houses.[25] The famous like St. Catherine or the Blessed Angela of Foligno and the less famous traveled on pilgrimage and visited church dignitaries, going to Assisi, to Rome, even to the isolated shrine of St. Michael in the mountains of southern Italy. They moved spiritually as well. Many, like Angela of Foligno, had been married and raised families.[26] Concerned women often began as pilgrims, sometimes becoming recluses, then penitents, and perhaps finally entering houses as professed nuns.[27] And they moved about as they and their friends met in churches, hospitals, convents, and even private homes to discuss moral and spiritual problems.

Clearly the actions of administrators and the thoughts of the moralists tell us little of the places women made for themselves. As a first step to understanding the place of women, we can create a sort of spatial continuum that extends out from the convent to private homes and at each station along the way we will find women who in one sense or another considered themselves to be separated from the secular world and following a religious life.

The convent is, of course, the most obvious place for religious women.

Late medieval Italian convents, it seems, were likely to have had between ten and twenty professed nuns.[28] These would be cared for by four or five servants, usually hired on contract. While the number and the strength of female religious houses in northern Europe seem to have declined in the late Middle Ages, women's houses in Italy may have continued to grow. In Florence, at least, the number of convents grew modestly in the fourteenth and fifteenth centuries. Just over one percent of the female population of Florence in the 1330s were professed nuns, and that number probably had doubled by the early fifteenth century.[29] It is never easy to know who entered convents, but since a nun was expected to bring a dowry sufficient to support her, urban and rural elites probably supplied the majority of the nuns. By the fifteenth century it was commonplace (if naive) to consider convents to be safe places for the well-to-do to leave unmarried daughters—a function convents continued to fulfill more and more explicitly in the sixteenth and seventeenth centuries.

The isolation of the convent was often broken by nonprofessed lay sisters (called *conversae, oblatae* or *devotae*).[30] These were not simply lower-class servants. Like the lay brothers and sisters attached to monasteries, hospitals, and even parish churches, they were a heterogeneous group that included some who considered work with their own hands to be a religious vocation; there were others who had given properties to the convent and who wished to live in a semireligious retirement in the cloister or perhaps in a house beside the convent. These semireligious followed a very simple rule, perhaps coming once daily to the church or perhaps only reciting a Paternoster. An important identifying mark was their habit, usually a variant of the clothing mandated for the fully professed members of the institution to which they were attached. By the oath they took, these women promised stability of place and obedience to the abbess. In practice they tended to have the run of the district.[31] Some who called themselves lay sisters even continued to live at home with husband and family, maintaining possession of property and even practicing a trade.

Lay sisters in Italy do not at all fit the traditional monastic definition of lay brothers and sisters as merely semireligious servants. They are much closer in status and behavior to members of what eventually became the Order of Penitents, associations of pious men and women found especially in the Romagna, Lombardy, and the Veneto. These men and women took the status of voluntary penitents, which required one to make a public confession of sin and adopt a religious habit. Penitents lived at home but renounced commercial activities, public office, and the right to bear arms. Married penitents also gave up the right of remarriage and promised continence during parts of the year. Penitents described themselves with a dizzying number of names; they wore a wide variety of costumes; and they manifested their piety in many different ways. The one common element was that by costume and by custom they could be seen to be different from the population at large. By the beginning of the fourteenth century, most of these penitents had been amalgamated and organized into the semireligious Third Orders of the Franciscans and Dominicans.[32]

And at the final point along our continuum we find informal recluses. These women, many of whom would eventually become penitents, join a Third Order, or even become professed nuns, began their spiritual journeys simply by closing themselves off in their own homes. The most dramatic may well be the Blessed Umiliana dei Cerchi, a well-to-do Florentine matron who on the death of her husband turned her back on her children and retreated to a life of penance isolated even from members of her own family.[33] From lay sisters to recluses, Italian women seemed to prefer a style of spiritual life that included distinctive clothing and a variety of penitential acts ranging from pilgrimage to fasting. It was these activities and not cloistering that separated them from other members of the laity.

In one sense Italian women seemed to be responding vigorously to the mendicant call to a life lived in a sort of imitation of Christ. Yet they continued to engender suspicion in diocesan authorities and especially in the Inquisition. The reason was that in their unregulated conviviality and their concern to discuss moral and ethical issues they were easily confused with the heretical groups that flourished in the thirteenth and fourteenth centuries.[34] It is, in fact, their relationship to heretical groups that allows us to know something about those mute women whose lives were never the subject of hagiographers.

Inquisitors needed to know who belonged to suspect groups, what they believed, and how they acted on those beliefs. Victims of the Inquisition offer a convincing portrait of the places in which religious women could be found in Italian society. The Guglielmites of Milan are an ideal subject. They were quite similar to the spiritual families which often surrounded Italian holy women.[35] They were pious women and men who formed themselves around a woman they knew as Guglielma la Boema. That is, Wilma the Bohemian, so called because she was said to have been the daughter of the king of Bohemia.[36] Soon after her arrival in Milan (probably in the 1260s) she associated herself with the wealthy Cistercian monastery of Santa Maria Chiaravalle, possibly as a lay sister. At the time of her death she was living in one of the monastery's houses in the Milanese suburb of San Pietro al Orto. Because of her reputation for sanctity, she was soon surrounded by a group of pious clergy, laymen, and especially women. Her inner circle of followers probably contained about 40 people while 120 or more participated in solemn festivals in her memory. It is no longer possible to know exactly what she said or did. It was probably that combination of example, moral exhortation, and even wonder-working that thirteenth-century Italians expected of saints. One of her followers reported that she had warned him of the dangers of usury; another that he was never so sad or depressed that he did not feel better after a visit with her.[37] After her death in about 1281 the monks of Chiaravalle promoted her cult and seemed well on the way to having her beatified.

Their attempts to promote her cult failed; in fact, as a result of an investigation of her followers in 1300 she was declared a heretic and her bones were disinterred and burned. The reason for the abrupt change in Guglielma's fortunes was that inquisitors discovered that beginning about five years before her death and continuing for the next twenty-six years a few of her followers began to claim that Guglielma was the Holy Spirit incarnate![38] There has been a long debate on the sources and the extent of the Guglielmite heresy. But from the actions of the inquisitor, it seems fair to say that most of her circle remained fascinated but unconvinced by the extreme claims. The heterodox Guglielmites believed that she had instituted a new age of the Holy Spirit complete with a female pope, cardinals, and priests. After her death she would soon return again and convert the Saracens and the Jews. Guglielma's followers seem to have derived and amplified their beliefs from a combination of Joachimite prophecy and ideas current among heretics of the Free Spirit, Waldensians, and Cathars. While some of her followers were clearly heretical, Guglielma and a majority of her followers may well have been completely orthodox. A monk of Chiaravalle reported that once in exasperation she said "that she was of flesh and bone, and that she brought a son with her to Milan; and that she was not what they thought she was. And unless they did penance for what they said [*de illis verbis*] about her, they would go to Hell."[39] And on her deathbed she complained to those of her followers who thought she had received the stigmata, "You are incredulous. You do not see what you think you see."[40]

In the process of investigating Guglielma and her followers, however, inquisitors created a precious description of one circle of pious women and men which included Cistercians, Third Order Dominicans, parish priests, and Humiliati as well as laywomen and men. Because the Guglielmites included orthodox as well as heretics, and because they were supported by the Cistercians (and possibly even the Franciscans), they can give us an idea of the sort of spiritual place women made for themselves in late medieval Italy. Many aspects of the life followed by the Guglielmites were typical of groups surrounding many Italian *beati*.

The Guglielmites, like many similar groups, often gathered for meals and discussion. Manfreda, a member of the Humiliati and the woman who was to be the popess in the new age to come, admitted that she often met with men and women of the sect at her convent and elsewhere. Perhaps recalling the rules of cloister, she claimed she only shared meals with women, never with the men. But in fact, eating together was one of the important things the group did. In acts prefiguring the modern American church potluck supper, members often brought bread, wine, and other foods for meals to be taken in a variety of localities. It was after such a meal, probably eaten in the garden beside the house of a believer, that Manfreda made her strongest claims about Guglielma and the things to come. And on the anniversary of Guglielma's death, when the inner circle went to the monastery of Chiaravalle where their saint was buried, the abbot himself provided an elaborate meal. Feasting was to create more than just good cheer. It affirmed concord and family feeling. At a time when the group was sharply riven by Manfreda's claims, she chided them: "You eat from one loaf and you drink the same wine, but you are not of one heart or of one will."[41] To share bread and wine, it should be noted, is a common Italian definition of a family. And family was how the Guglielmites would, on occasion, describe themselves.

Gatherings of Guglielma's family often centered on what should be called *paraliturgical* functions.[42] The term is meant to include a number of activities which are not central to the Christian cult, but which add to it and provide a means of participation to those who are not in priestly orders. Guglielmites painted banners with their saint's image and provided altar paraments for several of the churches in which they were accustomed to meet; they placed a fresco of St. Catherine of Alexandria at Gugliema's tomb. When Guglielma's body was moved from a temporary burial in the Milanese suburbs to Chiaravalle, members of the group moved the body into the chapel of the lay brothers at Chiaravalle, washed her body with wine and water, and dressed her in a habit of silk before her final burial. Several members admitted having certain books about Guglielma; Manfreda herself composed a liturgy for the saint; and one priest acknowledged that several songs sung about Guglielma's deity were composed by him.[43]

A few of the activities were clearly magical. For example, some involved the water and wine with which the saint had been washed or hosts that had been consecrated over Guglielma's tomb.[44] Most, however, were of a type encouraged by churchmen. It was when the leaders of the heretical wing of the Guglielmites moved beyond the paraliturgical that they were in trouble. Manfreda and her male associate Andrea Saramita were the two who claimed that Guglielma had appeared to them after her death. Manfreda proclaimed herself the new popess.[45] As popess and first priest of the new age, Manfreda covertly said mass and distributed the host in several Milanese churches, including a chapel at Chiaravalle.[46]

Manfreda's declaration of the new age and new order caused dissension in the group, but even those who doubted her claim were unable to challenge her directly.[47] The reason that this was so lies at the heart of the issue of authority within orthodox and heterodox groups like the Guglielmites. It is by now a commonplace that those who cannot participate in the priestly hierarchy depend for religious authority on charisma. The initial interest in Guglielma seems to have been based in part on the wonders she worked. Later, when Andrea and Manfreda tried to convince the others of the new age to come, their authority was based on visions. Andrea explained that Guglielma appeared to him while he was at prayer before her tomb. She ordered him to carry the message back to her followers. Manfreda made a similar claim; according to a witness she made the following statement after a dinner meeting, "Our Lady [Guglielma] said to me that I must say these words to you . . . that she is the Holy Spirit." There was consternation and disbelief in the group until, as one witness reported, they received a sign: "Lady Carabella was using her cloak as a cushion; and when she arose she found that the clasp and draw-strings [*fibialia sive corda*] of the cloak had been tied into three knots, in a way which they had not been previously. . . . And many of those gathered there, including this witness, believed that this was a great miracle." [48]

We might find it rather less than a *magnum miraculum*, yet it does underline the source of authority or the manner in which authority could be verified. And we should add that these sorts of visions and miracles were not uncommon among female religious leaders. The Blessed Cristina of Santa Croce Valldarno reported to the elders of her village that she had a vision of the exact house which they would purchase and endow as a convent for her and her followers. The elders hastened to comply.[49]

The Guglielmites were not as fortunate as the Blessed Cristina and her circle. Authorities had monitored the Guglielmites for over twenty-six years. Andrea Saramita and Manfreda had been forced to abjure once in the 1290s. When, after the turn of the century, the extent of their continued beliefs in a new age became known, they and several of their followers were relaxed to the secular arm and Guglielma's body was exhumed and burned. This effectively removed the leaders and destroyed the shrine around which the sect had flourished.

It might be worthwhile now to consider briefly what a survey of the place of women in the Italian church adds to various discussions of the "women's problem." It has been generally accepted for some time that one cannot argue that Beguines or any of the other semireligious movements for females can be explained simply because of the exclusiveness of convents. In the Italian context, we probably can go even further. There does not seem to have been any shortage of places in convents. It seems rather that many women preferred to take a semireligious vow and join a Third Order or a penitential group that did not require tight cloistering and control.[50] To be a lay sister, a penitent, or member of a Third Order implied a particular conception of the nature of an evangelical or Christlike life. And the primary difference between the church's vision of a religious life for women and the place these women created for themselves was cloistering. It should be remembered that St. Clare would have preferred to lead an evangelical life like that of Francis. It was only in deference to the saint that she agreed to the strict cloistering that became the hallmark of the Poor Clares of St. Damian. Numerous married couples who became lay brothers and sisters wanted their daughters to have the option to become either nuns or lay sisters, whichever they preferred. Convents, hospitals, even monasteries were surrounded by large numbers of men and women from all classes who were living a religious life as they chose to define it. Italian convents as the only option for the daughters of the urban and rural elites are probably more typical of the fifteenth and succeeding centuries than of the late Middle Ages.[51]

The Guglielmites also give us faint echoes of the roles the semireligious movements and the women in them may have played in late medieval Italian culture. Guglielma's cult, for example, did spawn a number of books, probably of legends, in addition to the liturgy and the songs. Inquisition records unfortunately tell us nothing of the quality or nature of these documents. But it seems likely that they imitated what they knew of ecclesiastical writings just as they created paraments, banners, and frescoes of the type typically found in churches. The experience of the Guglielmites is similar to what is known of other heretical groups and about the books laymen generally would have known.[52] Just as in later periods, it seems likely that the sorts of literature that appealed immediately to the laity were devotional in nature. To the extent female religious popularized certain types of devotions, they probably did contribute to popular literary culture.[53]

The Italian experience casts doubt on the extent to which women yearned for full ecclesiastical status. As I mentioned earlier, one line of research has suggested that women were drawn to heretical movements because they were not dominated by a male priesthood. Manfreda, the popess, clearly did wish to be a priest. Yet within the Guglielmites as a whole, and within other early fourteenth-century heretical groups, a desire for ordination is not particularly evident.[54] And the tendency of the penitents and the lay brothers and sisters to avoid full ecclesiastical profession suggests that many may have defined full ecclesiastical status in terms of penitential practices. We may also wish to question just what was unique about the female position in the medieval church. While certain practices, such as fasting, may have held more appeal for women than for men, the role of recluse, penitent, lay sister or brother, or professed religious was open to both sexes. Lay sisters and brothers, penitents, professed monks and friars, and concerned members of the laity all can be found in Guglielma's group. Similar individuals lived in and around convents, monasteries, and hospitals. Lists of oblates and penitents as well as Inquisition records show that there were large numbers of women involved, but they were at best a slight numerical majority.[55]

The question we have posed concerning the place of women is, of course, an administrator's question and I have given the response of an institutional historian. Women do not, in this sense at least, represent a fourth estate separated by sex from those who pray, fight, or work.[56] Bishops were most interested in maintaining the distinctions between lay and cleric, and inquisitors the uniqueness of the sacrament of ordination. This last may be what was distinctive about women. Their spiritual options were truncated. Lacking ordination, which in any case may have appealed only to a minority of spiritually concerned women, the best women could hope for was participation in semireligious groups with paraliturgical functions. This they shared with laymen. Both were outside the formal structures; both emphasized informal bonds of charity and association; and both adapted many ecclesiastical forms to their own uses. Yet there were still differences between men and women. Depositions by Florentine Cathars underline again and again difference between the male and the female roles. Women could be perfects. They did move from house to house within their shadowy community. But, it seems, the missionaries everyone wanted to meet were men. Orthodox confraternities which included women as well as men still restricted the activities in which women were allowed to participate. And in Venice public processions by the scuole were limited to men. Thus, even as laymen and women worked out a satisfactory religious life outside of strict clerical control, differences of gender persisted.[57]

NOTES

1 / Ernest W. McDonnell, *The Beguines and Beghards in Medieval Culture* (1954; rpt. New York: Octagon Books, 1969), esp. 81–100; Grado Giovanni Merlo, *Eretici ed inquisitori nella società piemontese del Trecento* (Turin: Claudiana, 1977); Gottfried Koch, "La donna nel Catarismo e nel Valdismo medievali," in *Medioevo ereticale*, ed. Ovidio Capitani (Bologna: Il Mulino, 1977), 245–75; Shulamith Shahar, *The Fourth Estate: A History of Women in the Middle Ages* (London and New York: Methuen, 1983); Genevieve Hasenohr, "La vie quotidienne de la femme vue par l'église: L'enseignement des 'Journées Chrétiennes' de la fin du moyen-âge," in *Frau und spätmittelalterlicher Alltag*, Internationaler Kongress Krems an der Donau 2. bis 5. Oktober 1984 (Vienna: Verlag der Östreichischen Akademie der Wissenschaften, 1986), 19–101; Gabriella Severino Polica, "Cultura ecclesiastica e culture subalterne: rileggendo alcuni saggi di H. Grundmann," *Studi Storici* 23 (1982): 137–66.

2 / Ann K. Warren, *Anchorites and Their Patrons in Medieval England* (Berkeley and Los Angeles: Univ. of California Press, 1985), 19–22.

3 / McDonnell, *Beguines and Beghards*, 4–7; Robert E. Lerner, "Beguines and Beghards," in *Dictionary of the Middle Ages* (New York: Charles Scribner's Sons, 1983).

4 / Koch, "La donna nel Catarismo," 252–58.

5 / See the essays collected in *Il movimento religioso femminile in Umbria nei secoli XIII–XIV*, Atti del Convegno internazionale di studio nell'ambito delle celebrazioni per l'VIII centenario della nascita di S. Franciso d'Assisi, Città di Castello, 27–28–29 ottobre, 1982, ed. Roberto Rusconi (Perugia: Regione dell'Umbria and Florence: La Nuova Italia, 1984) and esp. Giovanna Casagrande "Forme di vita religiosa femminile nell' area di Città di Castello nel sec. XIII," 150–52.

6 / On parish structure see Mauro Ronzani, "Aspetti e problemi delle pievi e delle parrocchie cittadine nell'Italia centro-settentrionale," in *Pievi e parrocchie in Italia nel basso medioevo (sec. XIII–XV)*, Atti del VI Convegno di storia della Chiesa in Italia (Firenze, 21–25 sett. 1981), 2 vols., Italia Sacra, vols. 35–36 (Rome: Herder, 1984), 1:307–49; and Dietrich Kurze, *Pfarrerwahlen im Mittelalter*, Forschungen zur kirchlichen Rechtsgeschichte und zum Kirchenrecht, vol. 6 (Cologne and Graz: Böhlau, 1966), 96–140 on late medieval Italy.

7 / On the politics of spiritual and administrative reform see Helene Tillmann, *Pope Innocent III* (Amsterdam and New York: North Holland Publishing Co., 1980), 189–227.

8 / Edith Pasztor, "I papi del duecento e trecento di fronte alla vita religiosa femminile," in *Il movimento religioso femminile*, 29–65 and esp. 33–42.

9 / Duane J. Osheim, *An Italian Lordship: The Bishopric of Lucca in the Late Middle Ages*, Publications of the Center for Medieval and Renais-

sance Studies, UCLA, vol. 11 (Berkeley and Los Angeles: Univ. of California Press, 1977), 70–85; George W. Dameron, "Episcopal Lordship in the Diocese of Florence and the Origins of the Commune of San Casciano Val di Pesa, 1230–1247," *Journal of Medieval History* 12 (1986): 135–54; Cinzio Violante, "Pievi e parrocchie dalla fine del X all'inizio del XIII secolo," *Le istituzioni ecclesiastiche della "Societas Christiana" dei secoli XI–XII, diocesi, pievi e parrocchie*, Atti della sesta Settimana internazionale di Studio, Milano, 1–7 settembre 1974 (Milan: Vita e Pensiero, 1977), 643–799, who emphasizes the struggle against monastic claims especially during the twelfth century.

10 / Casagrande, "Forme di vita religiosa femminile," 129–30, 149–52; for an example of episcopal business see Gero Dolezalek, ed., *Das Imbreviaturbuch des Erzbischöflichen Gerichtsnotars Hubaldus aus Pisa, Mai bis August 1230*, Forschungen zur neueren Privatsrechtgeschichte, vol. 13 (Cologne: Böhlau, 1969).

11 / Raoul Manselli, "La sinodo lucchese di Enrico del Caretto," in *Miscellanea Gilles Gérard Meersseman*, 2 vols., Italia Sacra, vols. 15–16 (Padua: Antenore, 1970), 1:197–246, on convents see rubrics 71 and 73, 242–44.

12 / Richard Trexler, *Synodal Law in Florence and Fiesole, 1306–1518*, Studi e Testi, vol. 268 (Vatican City: Biblioteka Apostolica Vaticana, 1971), 92.213–17, 261–62.

13 / Ibid., 247 and 261; Domenico Cambiaso, "Sinodi genovesi antichi," *Atti della R. Deputazione di Storia Patria per la Liguria* 68 (1939): 63–65, 76–77; Enzo Virgili, "La sinodo dell'arcivescovo Federigo Visconti (1258)," *Studi storici in memoria di Natale Caturegli* (Pisa: Pacini, 1976) [also published as *Bollettino Storico Pisano* 44–45 (1975–76)] 480.

14 / Casagrande, "Forme di vita religiosa femminile," 129–30; Noemi Meoni, "Visite pastorali a Cortona nel Trecento," *Archivio Storico Italiano* 129 (1972): 200–204, 216 where convents were visited. But at Ivrea behavior of the male clergy was the issue and female convents seem to have been ignored. See Ilo Vignono ed., *Visite pastorali in diocesi di Ivrea negli anni 1329 e 1346*, Thesaurus Ecclesiarum Italiae, vol. 1, pt. 3 (Rome: Edizione di storia e letteratura, 1980), xxvii, 5, 20; Pasztor, "I papi del duecento."

15 / Duane J. Osheim, "Conversion, *Conversi*, and the Christian Life in Late Medieval Tuscany," *Speculum* 58 (1983): 368–90, esp. 373; Catherine E. Boyd, *A Cistercian Nunnery in Medieval Italy, the Story of Rifreddo in Saluzzo, 1220–1300* (Cambridge: Harvard Univ. Press, 1943), 106–8.

16 / Thomas de Chobham, *Thomae de Chobham summa confessorum*, ed. F. Broomfield (Louvain: Editions Nauwelaerts and Paris: Béatrice Nauwelaerts, 1968), 375; On Thomas and the role of women, see Sharon Farmer, "Persuasive Voices: Clerical Images of Medieval Wives," *Speculum* 61 (1986): 517–43.

17 / "La prédication au béguinage de Paris pendant l'annee liturgique 1272–1273," *Recerches augustinnienes* 13 (1978): 105–229, esp. 181–82.

18 / Carlo Delcorno, *Giordano da Pisa e l'antica predicazione volgare*, Biblioteca di Lettere italiane, vol. 40 (Florence: L. S. Olschki, 1975), 50–51; on preaching in Europe generally see Hasenohr, "La vie quotidienne de la femme," 19–101; Alberto Forni, "Kerygma e adattamento: Aspetti della predicazione cattolica nei secoli XIII e XIV," *Bullettino dell'Istituto Storico Italiano per il Medio Evo e Archivio Muratoriano* 89 (1980–81): 261–348; and D. L. d'Avray, *The Preaching of the Friars, Sermons Dif-*

*fused from Paris before 1300* (Oxford: Clarendon Press and New York: Oxford Univ. Press, 1985).

19 / On the general tenor of the archbishop's sermons, see Celestino Piana, "I sermoni di Federico Visconti, arcivescovo di Pisa," *Rivista di Storia della Chiesa in Italia* 6 (1952): 231–48.

20 / Delcorno, *Giordano da Pisa*, esp. 50–51, 67, 68–69, 70, 123.

21 / Iris Origo, *The World of San Bernardino* (New York: Harcourt, Brace and World, 1962), 43–75, on Bernardino's attitudes toward women; the sermons discussed in this paragraph are in San Bernardino da Siena, *Le prediche volgari*, ed. Pietro Bargellini (Rome and Milan: Rizzoli, 1936), 166–67, 172, 364, 462–63, 473, 477, 666, and esp. 467–70.

22 / Ibid., 166–67.

23 / Ibid., p. 463 ("ella è mezza religiosa").

24 / This is the recurring theme in Hasenohr, "La vie quotidienne de la femme"; see also Bériou, "La predication," 181, who says that distinctions by status and knowledge were always subordinated to distinctions between widows and virgins.

25 / Mario Sensi, "Incarcerate e recluse in Umbria nei secoli XIII–XIV: un brizzocaggio centro-italiano," in *Il movimento religioso femminile*, 85–121; and more generally, André Vauchez, *Les laïcs au Moyen Age, pratiques et experiences religieuses* (Paris: Cerf, 1987), 100–107, Vauchez suggests that the decline of the Domenican Third Order can be dated from the attempts of the master-general to impose clerical control.

26 / G. Petrocchi, "Angela da Foligno," *Dizionario biografico degli Italiani* (Rome: Istituto della Enciclopedia italiana, 1960).

27 / On the variety of experiences see, e.g., Robert Brentano, "Catherine of Siena and Margery Kempe, and a caterva virginum," in *Atti del Simposio internazionale Cateriniano-Bernardiniano, Siena 17–20 aprile 1980*, ed. Domenico Maffei e Paolo Nardi (Siena: Accademia senese degli Intronati, 1982), 45–55; and Arnold Esch, "Tre santi ed il loro ambiente sociale a Roma: S. Francesca Romana, S. Brigida di Svezia, e S. Caternina da Siena," ibid., 89–120; and Claudio Leonardi, "Santità femminile, santità ecclesiastica," *Il movimento religiosa femminile*, 19–26.

28 / Information is fragmentary and difficult to come by, but see, e.g., Boyd, *A Cistercian Nunnery*, 106–8; and Giovanna Casagrande and Paola Monacchia, "Il monastero di Santa Giuliana a Perugia nel secolo XIII," *Benedictina* 27 (1980): 526, 530; Francesco Coradini, "Visita pastorale del sec. XV fatta dal vescovo Accaioli (1461–73) alle chiese, cappelle, monasteri e ospedali di Arezzo," *Atti e memorie dell'Accademia petrarca di scienza, lettere ed arti* 39 (1968–69): 334–35; and Luigi Pesce, *La chiesa di Treviso nel primo quattrocento*, 3 vols., Italia sacra, vols. 37–39 (Rome: Herder, 1987), 1:591–634.

29 / Richard C. Trexler, "Le célebat à la fin du Moyen-Age: Les religieuses de Florence," *Annales, ESC* 27 (1972): 1329–50 and esp. 1330–35; Alison Luchs, *Cestello, A Cistercian Church of the Florentine Renaissance* (New York and London: Garland, 1977), 6, 8–9, 132 n. 21; and Gene Brucker, *Renaissance Florence*, 2d ed. (Berkeley: Univ. of California Press, 1983), 191–94.

30 / Duane J. Osheim, "Conversion"; Antonio Rigon, "Penitenti e laici devoti fra mondo monastico-canonicale e ordini mendicanti: qualche esempio in area veneta e mantovana," *Ricerche di storia sociale e religiosa* 17–18 (1980): 52–59.

31 / Osheim, "Conversion," 383–84; *Visite pastorali in diocesi di Ivrea,*

134; Antonio Rigon, "I penitenti di San Francesco a Padova nel XIV e XV secolo," in *Il movimento francescano della penitenza nella società medioevale*, ed. Mariano D'Alatri, Atti del Terzo Convegno di studi francescani, Padova, 25–26–27 settembre 1979 (Rome: Istituto storico dei Capuccini, 1980), 289.

32 / On the debate over the nature of the Order of Penitents and its relationship to the Franciscans, see the articles collected in *Il movimento francescano della penitenza*.

33 / Anna Benvenuti Papi, "Umiliana dei Cerchi, nascita di un culto nella Firenze del dugento," *Studi Francescani* 77 (1980): 87–117, esp. 110 ff. underscoring the desire of many women to experiment outside for formal orders and institutions.

34 / Meoni, "Visite pastorali a Cortona," 203; Grado G. Merlo, "Pluralità di esperienze penitenziali nel Piemonte del secolo XIV," in *Il movimento francescano della penitenza*, 159–71.

35 / Benvenuti Papi, "Umiliana dei Cerchi," 111–12; Brentano, "Catherine of Siena," 47; Giovanni Vitolo, "Eremitismo, Cenobitismo e religiosità laicale nel mezzogiorno medievale aproposito di alcuni recenti pubblicazioni," *Benedictina* 30 (1983): 538–39.

36 / The most recent account is Patrizia Maria Costa, *Guglielma la Boema, L'"eretica" di Chiaravalle* (Milan: NED, 1985), which includes a very complete bibliography.

37 / F. Tocco, "Il processo dei Guglielmiti," *Rendiconti della R. Accademia dei Lincei, Atti della classe di scienze morali*, 5th ser., 5 (1899): 377, 424.

38 / There has been a rather wide-ranging debate over the origins and significance of the claims made by two of her followers. On the debate see most recently Stephen Wesseley, "The Thirteenth-Century Guglielmites: Salvation through Women," in *Medieval Women*, ed. Derek Baker, Studies in Church History Subsidia, vol. 1 (Oxford: Basil Blackwell, 1978), 289–303 and Margorie Reeves, *The Influence of Prophecy in the later Middle Ages* (Oxford: Clarendon Press, 1969), 248–49. For a good narrative of the affair, Henry Charles Lea, *A History of the Inquisition of the Middle Ages*, 3 vols. (New York, 1888), 1:90–99; it should be noted, however, that Lea did not have the benefit of Tocco's edition of the trial. The most complete treatment remains Gerolamo Biscaro, "Guglielma la Boema e i Guglielmiti," *Archivio Storico Lombardo* 57 (1930): 1–67. Although I remain unconvinced by his suggestion that Guglielma was the only member of the circle smart enough to have thought up the odd mix of Joachite and Free Spirit speculations current in the group, Biscaro's is the basic position taken by Wesseley "Guglielmites." It is unlikely that any further sources will be found, and thus Guglielma and the theology of her followers will remain a subject of controversy.

39 / Tocco, "Il processo dei Guglielmiti," 461–62; Guglielma rejected these claims several times; see, e.g., 446 and most emphatically 334 "ite, non sum deus." One must admit, however, that within the context of an inquisition process witnesses may not always tell the truth.

40 / Ibid., 371.

41 / Ibid., 429. The inquisition document merely refers to Manfreda as one who officiated "just as the pope does." The term *popess,* however, catches the sense of a world turned upside down which was clearly part of the appeal of the radical Guglielmites.

42 / Robert W. Scribner, *Popular Culture and Popular Movements in Reformation Germany* (Ronceverte, W.Va.: Hambledon Press, 1987), 22. This

essay was first published as "Ritual and Popular Belief in Catholic Germany at the Time of the Reformation," *Journal of Ecclesiastical History* 35 (1984): 47–77.

43 / Tocco, "Il processo dei Guglielmiti," 317, 322, 329, 331, 333, 427.

44 / Ibid., 326, 353, 376.

45 / Ibid., 383. Manfreda di Pirovano and Andrea Saramita both admitted to having made these claims, but both said they were instructed to do so by Guglielma, who appeared to them in visions after her death. Manfreda's relationship to the Visconti family caused Matteo Visconti no small amount of trouble in the 1320s. She may have been the inspiration for the Popess in the Visconti Tarot cards; see Michael Dummett, *The Visconti-Sforza Tarot Cards* (New York: Braziller, 1986), 106.

46 / Tocco, "Il processo dei Guglielmiti," 316–17, 326, 335, 351–52.

47 / Ibid., 331, 368, and esp. 420.

48 / Ibid., 418.

49 / Chechi, Vincenzo, *Una fondatrice toscana del secolo XIII e le sue costituzioni (S. Cristina da S. Croce sull'Arno)* (Florence: Tipografia Ettore Rinaldi, 1927), 23.

50 / Brentano, "Catherine of Siena," 75–83; Vauchez, *Les Laïcs*, 102–4 is particularly convincing on this point.

51 / David Herlihy and Christianne Klapisch-Zuber, *Les Toscains et leurs Familles: Une étude du Catasto florentin de 1427* (Paris: Presses de la Fondation Nationale des sciences Politiques, 1978), 580–81.

52 / Tocco, "Il processo dei Guglielmiti," 317, 427; and Polica, "Cultura ecclesiastica," 162–65; Vauchez, *Les laïcs*, 101, on the tendency of the laity to imitate and appropriate ecclesiastical dress and behavior.

53 / Polica, "Cultura ecclesiastica," 161.

54 / Inquisitors wanted very much to know which liturgical functions Manfreda had appropriated. She was the only member of the sect, however, who seems to have done so. On the liturgical and paraliturgical practices of women, see Wesseley, "Salvation," 293, and Reeves, *Influence*, 248–49, among others.

55 / Costa, *Guglielma la boema*, 52; Merlo, *Eretici*, 49–51; see esp. the documentary appendix of Felice Tocco, *Quel che non c'è nella Divina Comedia, o Dante e l'eresia* (Bologna, 1899), 32–78.

56 / It is Shulamith Shahar's thesis that the female experience was fundamentally different from that of males, *The Fourth Estate*.

57 / For discussions of women in heretical groups, see Merlo, *Eretici*, 49–51; on women in Venetian confraternities, see Lia Sbriziolo, "Per la storia delle confraternite veneziane," *Atti dell'Istituto veneto di scienze lettere ed arti* 126 (1967–68): 405–42.

6

*Graciela S. Daichman*

## Misconduct in the Medieval Nunnery: Fact, Not Fiction

IN A LILY GARDEN THE BRIDEGROOM IS FILLED WITH DELIGHT, and finds pleasure in gathering lilies above all other flowers. It is therefore needful to enclose this garden by the defence of shrewd and sharp discipline, as the Paradise of God was enclosed by angelic care and the flaming sword, lest an entrance be opened to the serpent into the same."[1] So says Archbishop Johannis Peckam in his injunctions to Romsey Abbey after a visitation in the year 1283. By the thirteenth century the golden age of monasticism was a thing of the past. Misconduct in the nunnery, sporadic and worrisome to the church hierarchy in the early Middle Ages, had at first consisted mainly of such mildly reprehensible transgressions as lateness to chapel and incidents of quarreling among the sisters. Gradually, however, monastic misconduct took on an uglier turn with reports of incontinence and childbearing in the convent becoming increasingly frequent. It is important to remember at all times, though, that the episcopal visitation reports and their attendant injunctions as well as all other documents recording life in the nunnery dwell only on the faults of the community and not on its virtues. Because "what is virtuous and good and regular is left unrecorded, whilst what is evil and irregular and faulty is prominently brought forward, that it may be corrected," the view such documents afford is unavoidably one-sided.[2] The majority of professed women were deeply devoted and unswerving in their commitment to the religious life; yet it was the bad apples who got the attention of the church authorities. Reports of errant behavior in the nunnery date as far back as the beginning of the twelfth century although they do not become common until the beginning of the fourteenth, increasing in number and severity throughout the entire fifteenth century. Profligate nuns were not a rare phenomenon in the Middle Ages; they were, instead, a matter of intense concern to the guardians of the spiritual life. The frequency and number of reported cases of errant behavior in the nunnery makes it imperative to choose a viable mode of dealing with them for our present purposes. To make the project manageable, I have limited most of my references to misconduct in the nunneries of England with only a few examples from others elsewhere.

An early example of immorality in the convent is that of certain nuns of Amesbury, one of the oldest and most prestigious houses in England, which fell into bad times in the last quarter of the twelfth century. According to the records, the convent was dissolved in 1189 after the abbess was said to have given birth three times and a large number of the sisters were found to be leading sinful lives: "The nuns of Amesbury, some thirty in number for the turpitude of their life, the dissolution of their order, and public scandal (*infamia*) were, by the mandate of Pope Alexander, with assent of his father king Henry and by the care of Richard Archbishop of Canterbury, . . . removed from their monastery and placed in other monasteries."[3] Corruption at every level was reported in one religious house after another. The episcopal visitation reports read like catalogues of sins ranging, as mentioned above, from infractions to the lesser points of the monastic rule to blatant disregard for the most basic moral tenets of the religious life: preserving the chastity of the *sponsae Dei*.

The decline in the morals at the nunnery has to do with the circumstances under which women entered the convent. From earliest times admission had been restricted to upper-class women, basically because only the affluent could afford the "dowry" demanded by each house. Moreover, "the very uselessness of a noble lady for any occupation other than marriage and motherhood made the convent a significant outlet for the unwanted and unmarriageable daughters of upper-class families."[4] The custom in large families of sending one or more daughters to the convent was so established as to inspire a popular proverb of the time: "Aut virum aut murum oportet mulierem habere" (a woman ought to have either a husband or a wall).[5] Sometimes young girls were made to enter the religious life much before they could possibly understand the consequences of such a commitment. Thus, many an angry prelate felt compelled to fulminate against the practices, as one put it, of using the cloister as "a dumping ground for portionless children of good families," while another speaks of "daughters of noble families dumped into a convent."[6]

Although some of the young nuns adapted quite well to the life of the community—the only one they ever got to know—in others the results could be disastrous as in the case of a nun in the double monastery of Watton. Placed there at the age of four, the child grew into "a frivolous and lascivious young woman who resisted all efforts at correction and remained without inclination for monastic life or love for God."[7] Pregnant by a Gilbertine canon at the monastery, she was involved together with her lover in a gruesome episode which ended in castration for him and public dishonor for her and some of her fellow nuns.

An interesting phenomenon that brought even more young women to the convent was the custom throughout the twelfth and thirteenth centuries of many fairly well-off fathers to establish small, slightly endowed nunneries with the sole purpose of providing their surplus daughters with a place to live. From a long list of nuns from the *Records* of Romsey Abbey for the year 1333, for example, "it may be gathered that the country gentlefolk and the officials of bishops and nobles found in Romsey a home for many of their daughters."[8] At the same time, because religious communities were always in need of financial support, they welcomed other women too often just as unsuited for the religious life as the unwillingly professed child-nuns. Among these were a number of wealthy widows who, in search of a safe haven from the incessant turmoil of the medieval world, would either take the veil at a nunnery they had previously favored or set up one in their own name. Naturally, such inmates, long used to positions of authority and prestige, had considerable trouble adjusting to the life of austerity and service to God that the convent demanded and often had little interest in giving up the privileges of their rank. Sometimes the church itself contributed to the favoritism these women felt was their due. Thus,

> in 1289 the general of the Dominican Order gave to the nuns of Saint Lambert instructions on how to treat Countess Agnes of Orlamünde after her acceptance by the convent: "If she does not want to eat with the convent-community, she may enjoy the privileges of the infirmary. Her name is not to be entered on the lists for service; she is to be entitled to sleep on cushions, is not to be called up for the daily reading of the chapters and is not to be burdened with work. All this is to be granted to her and to any person of higher rank, even to all those who come to the convent from a more refined way of living, and it is not to be deemed a violation of the rules."[9]

As a result of the special treatment either received or demanded by this special breed of nuns, quarrels frequently arose between them and their abbesses, often equally high-minded and domineering, a situation that diverted considerable energy and time from conventual business and bitterly divided the community. Monastic discipline was naturally the victim in such cases, much to the dismay of the diocesan bishops without whose patient intercession the feuding could drag on for years, particularly when it was the superior herself who "sowed discord among the sisters saying, 'Thus and thus spake such an one of you.'"[10]

Among other women entering the medieval nunnery for reasons unrelated to a religious vocation were the daughters of the newly established class of nouveaux riches. Eager to imitate one more practice of the nobility, these families also sent their daughters to the convent with little regard for either calling or preference. There is no particular record of how many such young nuns conducted themselves with proper decorum once professed, but obviously, as in the case of the daughters of the upper class, only those taking the veil in response to a genuine spiritual urge could become true religious.

Probably equally unsuited for convent life were the women forced into the convent by external circumstances, social, political, or economic. Such were the relatives of vanquished leaders who would then linger there, "immured" for all time and deprived of any rights by the enemies of their lords. Sempringham, for instance, "was in high favour with the three Edwards, who sent thither wives and daughters of their chief enemies. Wencilian, daughter of Llewellyn, prince of Wales, was sent to Sempringham as a little child, after her father's death in 1283. . . . In 1322, by order of the Parliament at York, Margaret, countess of Cornwall, was sent to live at Sempringham among the nuns. In 1324, Joan, daughter of Roger Mortimer, was received at the priory. Two daughters of the elder Hugh Despenser were also sent to take the veil at Sempringham."[11] By a twist of fate, sometimes such noble inmates were joined by the illegitimate offspring of their own fathers or even of the clergy themselves, as was the case of Cardinal Wolsey's own daughter, a nun of Shaftesbury at the time of the Dissolution of the monasteries.

Withering away in the nunnery too were girls afflicted by deformities or incurable diseases which rendered them a burden to families who could not—or would not—care for them.

> *Now earth to earth in convent walls*
> *To earth in churchyard sod.*
> *I was not good enough for man,*
> *And so am given to God,*

sings a girl in an anonymous medieval song.[12] In 1441 the prioress of Ankerwyke was accused by one of the sisters before Bishop Alnwick of accepting as novices "quasi idiotas et alias inhabiles" (some that are almost witless and others that are incapable).[13]

It is obvious that it was not only the sisters who were guilty of breaking monastic law with a variety of transgressions but their superiors
too. This startling realization leads us to wonder about the moral fiber
of these women appointed to lead communities made up of such dis-
parate, troubled, often reluctant members. Medieval abbesses seem to
have been mostly aristocratic, temperamental, rather formidable women
whose conduct set the norm for the nuns in their care. An abbess was
landlord of all estates and properties of her house, and as a lady of noble
birth she "wielded notable power and influence. The apogee of authority
was reached in the tenth and eleventh centuries by the abbesses of royal
nunneries in Saxony who reigned over vast tracts of land; as barons of
the king they summoned their own armed knights to war, and they held
their own courts. The abbesses of Quedlinburg and Gandersheim struck
their own coins. Royal abbesses were even called to the Imperial Diet. . . .
Sometimes these abbesses took an active part in politics, like German
emperor Otto III's aunt, Matilda, abbess of Quedlinburg, who served
unofficially as regent."[14] Some superiors were quite autocratic and rebellious—after a 1492 visitation by Cardinal Morton, for example, the
abbess of Romsey said that "when the inquiry was finished, she would
do as she had done before."[15] Doña Sancha García, abbess of the Spanish convent of Las Huelgas from 1207 to 1230, "even went so far as to
take upon herself the same powers as an abbot—including his sacerdotal
authority—and presumed to hear confessions and bless novices."[16]

Abbesses remained in office for life or until they resigned or were removed under some extraordinary circumstance, such as embezzlement
of conventual funds or clearly immoral conduct. Although the majority
of medieval abbesses—and prioressess—were women of strong moral
principles, a number of them deviated from the right path and were
not circumspect about it. Prioress Denise Lewelyck of Markyate "was
accused of having broken her vow of chastity, to the very evil example
of her sisters," and was forced to resign after a board of inquiry found
her guilty of consorting with Richard, the steward of the priory.[17] Joan
de Barton, prioress of Moxby, resigned from her post and the records
indicate that "the reason for the resignation is apparent from a penance
enjoined upon her for having been guilty *super lapsu carnis* (of a lapse
of the flesh) with the chaplain, Laurence de Systeford."[18] A twelfth-
century German abbess was severely reprimanded by Pope Eugenius III
for turning her house into a brothel, and Bishop Henry of Liège was
accused of having lived with two or three abbesses and a nun among his
concubines.[19] Because their lodgings were separate and they could eat
and entertain there, some superiors were tempted to indulge in luxuries

that directly contradicted the monastic vow of poverty. At Eastbourne, for example, the bishop found in 1441 that "the prioress's extravagance had run the house into debt. . . . She was constantly out of the convent, feasted sumptuously wherever she went, and wore a mantle . . . [with] fur trimmings."[20] Bishop Alnwick's records indicate that in the same year, and also at Ankerwyke, "the prioress wears golden rings exceedingly costly with divers precious stones, and also girdles silvered and gilded over and silken veils . . . and has on her neck a long silken band, in English lace, which hangs down upon her breast, and theron a golden ring with one diamond."[21]

Naturally, moral turpitude was a much more serious charge against a superior than indulgence in rich clothes and finery. After a visit to the Priory of Redlingfield in Suffolk, the bishop's deputies conducted an inquiry into the conduct of the prioress, Isabel Hermyte, who confessed among other things that "she had been alone with Thomas Langelond, bailiff, in private and suspicious places, such as a small hall with windows closed, 'and sub heggerowes'; that no annual account had been rendered; that obits had been neglected; that goods had been alienated, and trees cut down and sold without knowledge or consent of the convent; and that she was not religious or honest in conversation."[22] A twelfth-century abbess of Amesbury "was accused of incontinence and her evil ways were followed by the nuns," and in 1316 Alice de Chilterne, prioress of Whitehall, "stood publicly charged with the crime of incontinence with John de Passelewe, chaplain."[23] During a 1396 visitation the bishop was informed that the prioress of Arden in Yorkshire "was defamed with a certain John Beaver, a married man, that they had slept together in a house at night, and that on one occasion they lay alone together within the priory, in the prioress's chamber."[24] At St. Ouen-de-Rouen, Odo de Cluny found that "the prioress was ill-famed with Renaud, priest of Ourcy; Perronelle de Dreux, the abbess, was much defamed, as of old, with Raoul de Maintru."[25] As late as the year 1501, on a visit to Romsey Abbey the commissary of the prior of Canterbury learnt of "a great scandal [that] had arisen concerning the Abbess and Master Bryce *super mala et suspecta conversatione*; and that lately, at the instigation of Master Bryce, the Abbess had been negligent in correcting the sisters."[26] During a 1440 episcopal visitation to Gracedieu the nuns complained that the prioress "goes out to work in autumn alone with sir Henry, he reaping the harvest and she binding the sheaves, and at evening she comes riding behind him on the same horse. She is overfriendly with him and has been since the doings aforesaid." To add insult to injury, "of her trust in her own judgement she holds the rest of her sisters in contempt."[27] Sister Juliane Wolfe indicated to Bishop Alnwick on a 1442 visitation to Catesby that the prioress was in the habit of going "by herself to the town of Catesby to the gardens with one man alone, a priest, by name William Taylour." She added, too, that "the prioress did threaten that, if the nuns disclosed aught in the visitation, they should pay for it in prison"![28]

Since the well-being of the convent was closely linked to the character and ability of its superior, not only would reprobate abbesses confer a bad name on their house (in 1440, Dame Agnes Marcham, placed in Leicester Abbey at thirteen, decided not to become a professed nun there because of what she called "the ill fame which is current thereabout concerning that place") but their improper conduct was bound to affect that of the sisters in their charge.[29] Thus, Joan Tates, a nun of Redlingfield, upon "being questioned as to incontinence, said that it was provoked by the bad example of the prioress."[30] Errant behavior, though, did not always disqualify these ladies: in 1472 Abbess Elizabeth Broke of Romsey requested from the bishop absolution from "adultery with one John Placy" and she was not only absolved but reelected![31] It may be interesting to note here that not only were certain abbesses and prioresses accused of immorality by their nuns, but some seemed to have been truly despotic, causing the sisters considerable grief, if we are to believe their complaints. While one is merely said to treat "her sisters in harsh wise," another "is so harsh and headstrong that she may in no wise be appeased" and when "enraged against any of the nuns, [she] calls them whores and pulls them by the hair, even in quire"![32]

The reported abuses in the nunnery prompted irate prelates to fulminate against them with incredible ferocity on occasion: "Convents resemble brothels rather than hallowed cloisters . . . their doors are open, even by night itself, to clergy and laity, indiscriminately, whomsoever it may please the sisters to admit"; "nowadays the cloisters of nuns have become as it were brothels of harlots"; "the nuns sometimes prostitute themselves abominably."[33]

Even though we do not need to accept as unquestionable truth the accusations and excoriations of the male members of the church whose misogynistic bias was legendary, the evidence recorded in the documents that have come down to us corroborates the charges of monastic misconduct. Moreover, although some of the erring sisters came from the smaller, less prestigious houses, others belonged to the wealthiest, most prominent English abbeys such as Shaftesbury, Godstow, and Amesbury. Therefore, although it would be unfair to level a charge of generalized immorality against any particular nunnery, some seem to have had more wayward nuns than others. At St. Aubin in 1254, for instance, "Alice of Rouen is incontinent; she has again given birth to a son," according to Archbishop Odo de Cluny. (The "again" tells its own story.) In 1269 the same archbishop's diary records: "We visited the nunnery of Bival, and found some of the nuns defamed of the vice of incontinence."[34]

At Cannington Priory a commission sent by the archbishop of Shrewsbury found that "two of the nuns, Matilda Pulham and Alice Northlode . . . were known, to the violation of their monastic vow and the shame of their sex, to keep company with . . . sundry suspected women . . . and by their sensuality brought disgrace upon their vow and a scandal on their house."[35] At Easebourne one of the nuns testified during an episcopal visitation that sister Philippa King had had relations with "a certain 'brother William Cotnall'" and that, together with sister Joan Portsmouth, a chaplain, and one of the earl of Arundel's retainers, they had left the convent after giving birth to one or more children.[36] Actually, according to the *Victoria History of the Counties of England*, "it would almost seem that this remote priory served as a kind of reformatory for young women of good family who had strayed from the path of virtue."[37] The sections on religious houses in this collection provide, in fact, some of the most vividly detailed accounts of the transgressions in a number of English nunneries as well as the circumstances under which they were committed. Notice this entry quoted in the *Victoria History* from Archbishop Thoresby's register: "On December 8, 1358," Alice de Reygate, a nun of Hampole, "with weeping countenance, had prostrated herself at his feet, confessing that she had broken the vow of her profession and been guilty of immorality with an unmarried man."[38]

At Arden Priory, Archbishop Greenfield had "dealt with the case of Joan de Punchardon, one of the nuns, who had become a mother" in 1306, while at Hampole, Isabella Folifayt had been found guilty of incest with Thomas de Raynevill in 1324.[39] Here we must note the peculiar use of the word *incest*, employed in its medieval religious sense of "intercourse between persons who were both under ecclesiastical vows and thus in the relation of spiritual father and daughter, or brother and sister."[40] Thus, "he who corrupteth a nun commiteth incest," says a fourteenth-century gloss of Gratian's *Decretum*, "for she is the bride of God, who is our Father."[41]

Documents from three German nunneries contain similar reports of gross abuses by some of the inmates. In the convent of Sonnenburg, in the Pusterthal, Bishop Nicholas Cusanus found that "the young daughters of the Tyrolese nobility led the freest and most luxurious life under cover of the veil," while in an Augustinian monastery in Friesland, priests and lay brothers were accused of "keeping nuns with them . . . with whom they slept and sometimes begat children."[42] Almost at the end of the Middle Ages, at the convent of Söflingen near Ulm, the convent's patron, Count Eberhard of Würtemberg, lamented that the nuns were leading "an unclean and ungodly life." Truly a mild indictment considering that during a 1484 visitation the bishop's commission found several pregnant nuns and also confiscated a number of love letters. In the following extract from one of them, an unidentified correspondent who signs himself A.E.L.B. writes to sister Adele Ehinger: "And, my love, . . . let me be recommended to you, as my love is yours and shall remain yours. See to it, my love, that I can talk to you tomorrow as much as my heart desires."[43]

It may at this point help us to understand better the possible reasons for such heinous breaches of the church's moral code to explore the identity of the men capable of seducing a bride of Christ. It is important to keep in mind that although some of the less worldly sisters may have fallen to the charm of a prospective suitor, most of the historical evidence available seems to indicate that this was seldom the case. Scarcely ever was a religious woman either seduced or forced to submit to the sexual advances of an opportunistic lover; the punishment imposed by the church on those found guilty of violating a nun was severe enough to discourage most would-be assailants. Such a vile crime was regarded with extreme repugnance by the state as well as the church, and under a law passed by Edward I, the ravisher had to make restitution to the convent somehow and could also be condemned to three years in prison. If the accused failed to prove his innocence before the bishop by submitting the required number of witnesses that could attest to it, he would be excommunicated if unrepentant or given a penance if remorseful. In case of the latter, the punishment could be quite harsh, as proved by this fragment from a 1286 letter from the Register of Godfrey Giffard, bishop of Worcester to his relative Sir Osbert Giffard, accused of abducting and seducing two nuns of Wylton:

> The bishop enjoined upon him that he should restore the aforesaid sisters and all goods of the monastery withdrawn and should make all the satisfaction that he possibly could to the abbess and the convent. And that on Ash Wednesday in the Church of Salisbury, the said crime being solemnly published before the clergy and people, he should humbly permit himself to be taken to the door of the church, with bare feet, in mourning raiment and uncovered head, with other penitents and should be beaten with sticks about the church on three holy days and on three Tuesdays through the market of Salisbury and so often and in like manner about the church of

Wylton and through the market there; and he should be likewise beaten about the church of Amesbury and the market there and about the church of Shaftesbury and the market there. In his clothing from henceforth there shall not appear any cloaks of lamb's wool, gilt spurs or horse trappings, or girdle of a knight, unless in the meantime he should obtain special grace of the king, but he shall journey to the Holy Land and there serve for three years.[44]

Awareness, then, of the consequences that a love affair with a nun could bring, makes us wonder once more who were these men willing to lead—or follow—a religious woman into sin. According to the documents that have come down to us, the lovers were for the most part men with easy access to the nunnery, such as Richard Gray, a lodger with his wife at St. Michael's, Stamford, who, in 1442 "begot offspring of dame Elizabeth Wylugby, nun in that place," or Geoffrey de Eston, bailiff of Bulmershire, found guilty of incest with Clarice de Speton of Arden Priory in 1311.[45] The lover could sometimes be one of the men allowed into the inner sanctum of the convent for needed repairs as was the case in Watton, where a nun became involved with a worker "and the two contrived to meet frequently out of doors until at last the nun's condition became obvious."[46] On occasion, too, a wandering minstrel's art and allure may have captivated the heart of an amorous sister. In fact, a 1440 visitation by Bishop Alnwick to St. Michael's, Stamford, reports that "one Agnes, a nun of that place, has gone away in apostasy cleaving to a harp player."[47]

The most common liaison, however, seems to have been between nuns and priests, since the vicars, chaplains, and chantry priests who moved about the convent had perfectly easy and justified access to it. Furthermore, because these men were all under the same vow of celibacy as the nuns, they knew very well how to break it, and they could practically tempt and absolve a sinner in the same breath. There is strong evidence in the historical documents and the literature of the Middle Ages that priestly corruption was rampant. The affairs between men and women of the cloth aroused the fury and condemnation of every guardian of monastic morals, among them St. Catherine of Siena, who accuses nuns of leading a wanton life, engaging in affairs with the monks assigned to the nunnery as spiritual advisors: "In miserable fashion they fulfill their lusts; and the fruits which appear are such as I know well you have seen, children to wit."[48] Sometimes the priestly lover did not belong to the nunnery but lived in a nearby village where he might be a clerk or a vicar. At the priory of Villa Arcelli in 1249, for instance, Archbishop Eude Rigaud of Rouen found, among other abuses, that "the Prior of Gisorcium is always coming to the house for Idonia. Philippa de Rouen is suspected with a priest of Suentre, of the diocese of Chartres; Marguerita, the treasuress, with Richard de Geneville, a clerk, Agnes de Fontenei, with a priest of Guerreville, diocese of Chartres. . . . Jacqueline came back pregnant from visiting a certain chaplain, who was expelled from his house on account of this. Also, Agnes de Mont Sec was suspected with the same."[49]

At Nunkeeling Priory in York, "Avice de Lelle was strictly forbidden to go outside the inner cloister of the house in any manner, or to talk to Robert de Eton, chaplain. . . . She had confessed incontinence." At Keldholme Priory, also in York, "Archbishop Melton wrote to the prioress and convent directing them to compel Mary de Holm to undergo the penance enjoined her for the vice of incontinence by her with Sir William Lyly, chaplain."[50] At Swine Priory in 1310 Archbishop Greenfield wrote a letter to Roger de Driffield, abbot of Meaux, "concerning Brother Robert de Merflet and Stepen de Ulram his fellow monks, who have been guilty of incontinence and incest with Elizabeth de Rude, nun of Swine."[51] Ironically, one of the worst offenders seems to have been John Stafford, archbishop of Canterbury, accused of "procreating a son and a daughter by a nun" when he was bishop of Bath and Wells in 1443.[52]

Evidence of this seemingly widespread abuse can only make us wonder how the church would punish such abominable conduct by its daughters. Interestingly enough, impunity seems to have been pretty much the order of the day, provided the sinner repented and returned to the fold. The unexpected leniency toward reprobate sisters in light of the severity of the punishments meted out to their lovers can probably be explained by the fact that the church, beset with incidents of monastic abuse, was coming more and more to regard scandal as worse than sin, and would attempt, whenever possible, to conceal a nun's errant behavior. The fact that episcopal visitations, practically the only means of exposing sinners to the proper authorities, took place only every few years made it fairly easy to keep rumors of illicit affairs under wraps except, of course, when a sister became pregnant as a consequence of her trespass. There are practically no official records of abortions in medieval nunneries; a deterrent, of course, may have been that "in the Middle Ages, the potions given to cause an abortion were considered a murderous act, and anyone guilty of such a crime was given capital punishment."[53] As to the fate of the chil-

dren born in the convent, the records are quite hazy, although according
to the thirteenth-century reverend Augustus Jessop, "the offspring died
immediately after."⁵⁴ Some, however, must have survived.

Even though the church, no matter how harassed, seemed to treat
profligate nuns with incredible forbearance, there was one sin it was reluctant to pardon, and this was apostasy, or abandoning the convent to
return to the world. An apostate nun broke all monastic vows. Were she
allowed to remain unpunished, her example could have been followed by
countless other sisters who may have been waging similar wars in their
own souls. In order to prevent apostates from remaining at large in the
world, the church reached out with a mighty arm and through a combination of threats and pleas generally succeeded in luring them back to
the nunnery. When all else failed, the help of the state's machinery was
enlisted to bring the sinners back. Such was the fate suffered by Mary
de Felton, of the Minoresses Without Algate; in 1385 the king "ordered
his sergeant-at-arms to arrest . . . Mary de Felton and deliver her to the
abbess for punishment."⁵⁵

Taking into account then the fact that the odds were pretty much
against her when a nun left the convent, between the years 1290 and
1360 the records for the diocese of Lincoln, for example, show a surprising number of apostates. In 1269 Prioress Agnes Bowes abandoned the
convent of St. Michael to which Wothorpe Priory was annexed later and
in 1300 Joan de Fynnemere from Sewardsley "is said to have abandoned
her habit and returned to a secular life."⁵⁶ In 1358 a nun from Goring
"apparently fled with someone who was also under a vow of celibacy, as
her sin is called 'incest'," and in 1336 and 1337 one sister left Markyate
and another one St. Leonard's.⁵⁷ At the Abbey of Delapré, "the bishop in
1300 issued a mandate to the archdeacon of Northampton to denounce
Isabel de Clouville, Maud Rychemers, and Ermentrude de Newark, professed nuns of Delapré, who had discarded the habit of religion and
notoriously lived a secular life as apostate nuns. . . . In 1311 another sister, Agnes de Landwath, was denounced for apostasy and for forsaking
the habit of religion."⁵⁸ More than a hundred years later, at Ankerwyke
Priory, Bishop Alnwick notes in 1441 that "six nuns have now left the
house in apostasy."⁵⁹ Among the recorded cases of apostasy which have
come down to us in considerable detail, one of the most complex and
colorful ones is probably that of Agnes de Flixthorpe, also known as
Agnes de Wissendum, a nun of St. Michael's, Stamford, whose tragic
story begins to unravel in 1309 when Bishop Dalderby excommunicated
her for apostasy. Brought back to the convent by the sheriff of Notting-
ham, Agnes refused to repent and by order of the bishop was then placed

in a room with her legs fettered as punishment. In 1312, after a year's confinement in a remote little Devonshire priory, Agnes broke down and declared her repentance but was still kept in solitary confinement until 1314, at which time she was considered "cured" and allowed to return to Stamford. The diagnosis, however, was premature because two years later Agnes had once again abandoned the convent leaving behind her a life she probably should never have entered.[60] Nothing more is said about the unfortunate Agnes in the records, and how she spent the rest of her life is left to the imagination.

Searching for an answer to the mounting and seemingly unsolvable question of the sins of the professed, church authorities throughout the centuries appear to have agreed that the *radix malorum* of monastic misconduct was the nuns' habit of wandering outside the cloister. "It would have been no unusual circumstance . . . to meet a sister of Canyngton or Buckland in the busy streets of Taunton or Bridgwater. . . . Actually some of the sisters . . . were accustomed to wander through the streets and lanes of Ivelcestre . . . and sometimes, which was worse, did without scruple or fear enter into the houses of secular and suspected persons, . . . to the scandal of holy religion and the manifest peril of their own souls."[61] A thirteenth-century prioress of Ramsey Abbey complains that "the nuns frequent taverns, and continually go into town without leave," and on a 1303 visit to Greenfield Priory, Bishop Dalderby heard that the prioress "had been absent from the house for two years."[62] A 1440 episcopal visitation report of Heynings Priory reveals that "the nuns have access too often to the house of the treasurer of Lincoln, abiding there sometimes for a week."[63] At Gracedieu in 1441 the prioress sometimes gave sisters "leave to visit their parents for seven or eight days," and at Markyate the prioress complained to the bishop during a 1442 visitation that "sometimes the nuns, when they visit their parents and friends, do stay with them for seven or eight days, not counting the days for their journey on the way there and back."[64] At Nuncoton Priory the prioress indicated to the bishop in 1440 that "the nuns when they visit their friends in the country do make long tarrying, even for a week, before they return to the monastery."[65]

In vain did the church try to use its power and resources to keep its daughters within the cloister. Those who had chosen a life of seclusion in the nunnery in pursuit of a true religious vocation needed no encouragement to persevere in their vow of claustration. It was the others, for whom the lure of the world never ceased, who disregarded the injunctions of the bishops and remained undaunted by the threat of punishment which could range from reprimands to "enclosure for two years within the outer gate of the Priory" in the case of the nuns of Polslo, near Exeter, as dictated by Bishop Stapeldon in January 1320.[66]

The conventual records and the bishops' visitation reports note that nuns went on visits to sick relatives, business trips, and pilgrimages; sometimes they went to weddings, christenings, and funerals, each time renewing those ties with the world that many found difficult to break. The need to secure an income for the community and to buy and provide for it was so pressing that the sisters were constantly requesting permission to leave the convent. The fear that wandering in towns or spending too much time at friends' or relatives' would lead to greater abuses elicited from the bishops countless injunctions, the tenor of which whether in English or Latin was generally the same: "It is forbidden to eat, drink or spend the night in the town of Ramsey"; "no nun is to go out except in staid company, nor is she to stay with secular folk beyond three days."[67] Or it could be, "we wish and ordain that no sister of the monastery leave the cloister without permission from the prioress."[68]

Occasionally, the bishops' worst fears were confirmed; in 1442, for example, a nun of Catesby Priory "did pass the night with the Austin friars at Northampton and did dance and play the lute with them in the same place until midnight, and on the night following she passed the night with the friars preachers at Northampton, luting, and dancing in like manner."[69] Such inexcusable behavior did have precedents, though; a century earlier Bishop Berthold of Strassbourg wrote: "We strictly forbid dancing to all ladies of any nunnery . . . and especially in public. . . . Let any superior who dances publicly henceforth . . . incur the sentence of *ipso facto* excommunication."[70]

By the end of the thirteenth century the abuses caused by the nuns' disregard for the rule of claustration seem to have reached such proportions that, despite previous papal fulminations, in 1298 Pope Boniface VIII proclaimed his famous statute on monastic enclosure based on the sixty-sixth chapter of the Benedictine Rule. The text of the bull was widely quoted throughout the next two hundred years as a deterrent to monastic wandering, especially the section beginning:

> Desiring to provide for the perilous and detestable state of certain nuns, who, having slackened the reins of decency and having shamelessly cast aside the modesty of their order and of their sex, sometimes gad about outside their monasteries in the dwellings of secular persons, and frequently admit suspected persons within the same monasteries, to the opprobrium of religion and to the scandal of very many persons; we by the present constitution, which shall be irrefragably valid, decree with healthful intent

that all and sundry nuns, present and future, to whatever order they belong and in whatever part of the world, shall henceforth remain perpetually enclosed within their monasteries.[71]

The injunction that nuns should remain within their convents, repeated through the centuries, may actually be seen as the most powerful indication of its failure. As late as 1498 the General Chapter of the Dominican Order warned that "the going abroad of nuns from their nunneries is not without grievous peril and scandal to the Order" and that "the nunneries are fallen so low—*adeo collapsas*—that they are indiscriminately open to persons of both sexes."[72]

Monastic rule specifically forbade conversation between the sisters and the stream of noble visitors descending with implacable regularity on the convent. Although the bishops spoke out with great passion against the practice, permission was seldom denied to persons of rank wishing to sojourn in the nunnery. In October 1391, for example, Queen Anne was given "indult to enter as often as she pleased with a suite of fifty honest persons of either sex any monastery of enclosed religious women and to eat and drink therein."[73] Inevitably, the visitors' presence would disrupt the often tenuous discipline of the house, bringing the nuns unbearably close to the temptations of a world many of them had been forced to leave. Furthermore, a 1442 episcopal visitation to Catesby revealed that the sisters themselves sometimes received "persons for whom they sent and with whom they [hold] parleyings and conversations," and that "secular folk often have recourse to the nuns' chambers within the cloister, and talkings and junketings take place there."[74] As was customary, some of the more affluent visitors came accompanied by a number of servants and followers. On a 1311 visitation to Romsey Abbey, Bishop Henry Wolcott complained about some who were "pregnant, incontinent and quarrelsome."[75] (Much like some of the nuns themselves?) At Nunburnholme Priory, scandal having arisen from the frequent gossiping between certain nuns and the secular persons attending some noble visitors, "the prioress and sub-prioress were ordered by the Archbishop not to allow such access to the nuns."[76]

In their never-ending effort to curb the abuses prompted by the need to entertain noble company, the bishops were constantly issuing new injunctions or refurbishing old rules that had been allowed to expire. One such was the Cistercian statute establishing that nuns were forbidden to eat with secular guests "on account of the perils which beset cloistered persons if they live among the gentiles, and lest their good manners be corrupted by evil communication." [77] Such possibility is confirmed by an injunction from Archbishop Alnwick after a 1440 visitation to Gracedieu Priory: "A Frenchwoman who dwells in the priory should be removed because of the unseemliness of her life, for she receives all alike to her embraces." [78]

As in the case of the wandering nuns, no matter how stern the warnings or how severe the punishment—"ordered (on pain of excommunication and deposition of the Abbess, Prioress, and greater officials of the Convent, if they be found disobedient or negligent in this) that secular women, married and single staying there, from the time of the receipt of these presents, shall be wholly removed from the Abbey without hope of return," according to an injunction from Bishop Henry Woodlock to Romsey Abbey in 1311—the influx of visitors to the nunnery did not seem to abate. [79] In 1411 Theobald lamented before the Council of Constance that convents were frequented "as if they were public places, even more than the theatres." [80] By 1441, however, nothing seemed to have changed and during a visitation to Godstow the abbess complained that she could not "restrain students from Oxford from having common access in her despite to the monastery and the cloister precincts." [81] The nuns' habit of welcoming visitors to the convent without regard for either rule or propriety had already prompted the French abbot Gilles li Muisis to write in his embittered prelate's attack on ecclesiastical corruption called *Lamentations* (c. 1350): "Some folk are welcomed into nunneries, and no order is kept in giving folk good cheer; they go thither gladly and often and at many times; but the young are better welcomed there than the bald-headed." [82]

The records also reveal that had it been possible to keep visitors away from the dorter and the cloisters, the nuns would have still found a way to circumvent restrictions by quietly slipping out to the guest house. Thus, during a visitation to Heynings Priory in 1440, sister Alice Leget reported that "the nuns do hold drinkings of evening in the guestchamber even after compline, especially when their friends come to visit them." [83] Faced with the nuns' resourceful resistance to their regulations against receiving visitors, the bishops apparently tried to restrict at least the length and location of the visits. Seculars were forbidden to enter the convent after sunset or curfew, while at the same time the most elaborate arrangements were made to lock and unlock the doors of the nunnery. An injunction at Romsey Abbey commanded: "The doors of the cloister (of) the dormitory shall be kept at the proper hours and closed, and especially after compline," and another called for the door near the altar of the Holy Rood called " 'the rede dore' " to be "wholly closed and locked and nailed to the wall with bolts and iron nails."[84] At Esholt and Sinningthwaite, Archbishop Lee commanded that the prioress should furnish enough locks and keys for the convent doors, so the latter could be locked every night immediately after compline; the doors were to remain locked until six o'clock in the morning in summer and seven in winter. The prioress was enjoined to retain the keys in her possession or "commit the custody of them to such a discreet and religious sister that no fault nor negligence may be imputed to the prioress."[85] At times the ordinances became so severe that the nuns must have felt like prisoners; in 1441, for example, "to prevent the Benedictine nuns (of Augsburg) from receiving friends in their convent and from going out as freely as though they had not been cloistered, the iron railings had to be replaced by walls, and then the walls had to be built higher and guarded by town soldiers."[86] In an attempt to guard the purity of the monastic vow and keep the sisters from temptation, in 1311 Bishop Henry of Winchester even went so far as to decree at Romsey Abbey that "curtains shall be removed for ever from before the beds of the nuns."[87]

Despite pressure and precautions, however, the world continued to penetrate the cloister. Determined to preserve a measure of control over the affairs at the nunnery, though, the authorities passed regulations to prevent any secret communication between nuns and seculars in secluded corners or through darkened windows. Thus, an episcopal injunction from Romsey Abbey "admonished William Scott, kinsman of Master William Brian Esthorp, that he should not have access to any nun nor hold communication with her at the kitchen window nor at any other place either in his own person or through some other person, on pain of excommunication."[88] Dean Kentwode of St. Helens enjoined the prioress and convent that "none of them speak nor commune with a secular person, nor send or receive letters, missives or gifts of any secular person."[89]

On the occasions when visitors were admitted to the nunnery, the rules established that before speaking with them, the sisters needed permission from their superior. Some injunctions, however, went unheeded, such as Archbishop Peckham's to the nuns of Romsey Abbey not "to hold converse with any man save either in their parlour or in the side of the church next to the cloister. And in order that all suspicion may henceforth be removed, we order that any nun about to speak with any man, save in the matter of confession, have with her two companions to hear her conversation, in order that they may either be edified by useful words, if these are forthcoming, or hinder evil words, lest evil communications corrupt good manners."[90] During a 1442 visitation to Markyate, the prioress complained to the bishop that "the nuns do sometimes talk with secular folk, with no other nun to hear or see what they say or do," while sister Joan Marchaunt said "the nuns hold speech with secular folk with the prioress's permission, when [none] other is in hearing, but at their wish and will." Such communications prompted the bishop to enjoin the prioress not to allow the nuns to engage in conversation with seculars when alone, "ne that ye suffre none of your sustres to receyve ne sende owte lettres, tokens ne gyftes."[91]

So incensed were some church fathers at the abuses to which the un-fettered contact with men led certain nuns that their censure at times could become vituperation: "Another cause Religious is conversation with nuns. For in the convent they have their lady-devotees—with whom they too often talk too long without witnesses, extorting rather than ob-taining leave from the superiors. There are undisciplined laughter and ogling glances exchanged; there are words of levity and vanity and car-nality, and amorous touches; there are hearts aflame with fire, and every window open to the deadly things around."[92] As usual, though, some recalcitrant sisters would find a way to satisfy their longings for the for-bidden, and messages as well as gifts were exchanged despite injunctions to the contrary. Thus, at Romsey Abbey, the vicar-general "enjoined Agnes, wife of William Coke, cook of the Monastery, that she shall not be messenger or bearer of messages or signs between any nun and any lay person on pain of excommunication" and "Elizabeth Rowthall and Agnes Skelyng, fratresses, to see the window of the kitchen closed and locked at the proper time, because the nuns have been used to hold communication with lay people at the said window."[93]

If we trust the historical evidence that has come down to us, then, there is little doubt that as we approach the end of the Middle Ages, the monastic ideal was harder and harder to attain. Intended originally as enclaves of peace and devotion during one of the most turbulent periods of mankind, the medieval convents, like the church, were torn by inner struggles reflecting the turmoil of the time. However, when we look at reports of misconduct in the nunnery, it is essential to keep in mind that they come from over three hundred years of monastic existence when "good" nuns performed their duties and remained unswervingly faith-ful to their vows. Furthermore, because the present paper for obvious reasons demanded considerable selectivity in its choice of incidents of misconduct in the convent, the image evoked throughout has been care-fully conditioned. Let not the transgressions, no matter how real, detract from the magnificence of the institution of monasticism itself, which sur-vived nuns ill-equipped for religion and dissension among them; abuse and apostasy, temptations and opprobrium, disreputable superiors and unprincipled priests. While seemingly unstoppable social, political, and economic forces were resulting in momentous changes in the world of the Middle Ages, the nunnery was equally affected by them, yet managed to remain the sole center of education for women as well as the only viable alternative for the unmarried, the widowed, and those on whom society turned its back with or without justification. Because the documents record only the actions of the wicked sisters while the truly dedicated ones lived out their lives in blissful oblivion ignored by the bishops and content with their lot, we may feel inclined to concur with the historian's remark: "Happy the nunnery that has no history."[94]

## NOTES

An earlier version of this essay appeared as chapter 1 of *Wayward Nuns in Medieval Literature* (Syracuse: Syracuse Univ. Press, 1986) and is reprinted here with the permission of Syracuse University Press.

1 / Quoted in *Records of Romsey Abbey*, ed. G. D. Liveing (Winchester: Warren and Son, 1912), 82.

2 / Ibid., 94.

3 / *Calendar of Documents Preserved in France*, ed. J. Horace Round (1899; rpt. Nendeln, Liechstenstein: Kraus Reprint, 1967), 1: 384.

4 / Angela M. Lucas, *Women in the Middle Ages* (New York: St. Martin's, 1983), 51.

5 / Jean Baptiste Thiers, *Traité de la Cloture des Religieuses* (Paris, 1681), quoted by Eileen Power, *Medieval English Nunneries* (1922; rpt. New York: Biblo and Tannen, 1964), 342 n. 3.

6 / Quoted by G. G. Coulton, *Five Centuries of Religion* (Cambridge: Cambridge Univ. Press, 1950), 2: 61, 4: 26.

7 / Giles Constable, "Aelred of Rivaulx and the Nun of Watton," in *Medieval Women*, ed. Derek Baker (1978; rpt. Oxford: Basil Blackwell, 1981), 207.

8 / *Records of Romsey Abbey*, 99.

9 / Quoted by Sibylle Harksen, *Women in the Middle Ages* (New York and London: Abner Schram, 1975), 30–31.

10 / *Records of Visitations Held by William Alnwick, Bishop of Lincoln: 1436 to 1439*, vol. 2 of *Visitations of Religious Houses in the Diocese of Lincoln*, ed. A. Hamilton Thompson, Lincoln Record Society and Canterbury and York Society (Lincoln: The Societies, 1914–29), 48.

11 / *Victoria History of the Counties of England: Lincoln* (London: Constable, 1907), 2: 184, hereafter cited as *VCH*.

12 / Quoted by Power, *Medieval English Nunneries*, 31.

13 / *Visitations of Religious Houses*, 2: 4.

14 / Frances and Joseph Gies, *Women in the Middle Ages* (New York: Crowell, 1978), 65–66.

15 / *Records of Romsey Abbey*, 220.

16 / Quoted in Sally Thompson, "The Problem of the Cistercian Nuns," in Baker, *Medieval Women*.

17  /  *VCH: Bedfordshire*, 1: 360; also in *Visitations of Religious Houses*, 1: 82–86.
18  /  *VCH: York*, 3: 240.
19  /  Coulton, *Five Centuries*, 2: 300.
20  /  Quoted by G. G. Coulton, "The Truth about Monasteries," in his *Ten Medieval Studies* (Cambridge: Cambridge Univ. Press, 1930), 92.
21  /  *Visitations of Religious Houses*, 2: 5.
22  /  *VCH: Suffolk*, 2: 84.
23  /  Lina Eckenstein, *Woman under Monasticism* (Cambridge, England, 1896), 205; *The Medieval Nunneries of the County of Somerset and Diocese of Bath and Wells*, ed. Thomas Hugo (London, 1867), 24.
24  /  *VCH: York*, 3: 114.
25  /  Quoted by Coulton, *Five Centuries*, 2: 213.
26  /  Quoted in *Records of Romsey Abbey*, 223.
27  /  *Visitations of Religious Houses*, 2: 123.
28  /  Ibid., 47.
29  /  Ibid., 217.
30  /  *VCH: Suffolk*, 2: 84.
31  /  *Records of Romsey Abbey*, 214.
32  /  *Visitations of Religious Houses*, 2: 4, 48, 47.
33  /  St. Brigitta of Sweden, *Revelations*; Jean Gerson, *Compendious Declaration of the Defects of Ecclesiastics*; Johan Nider, *Reformatione Religiosorum*, quoted in Coulton, *Five Centuries*, 2: 566, 589, 591.
34  /  Quoted ibid., 213.
35  /  *Medieval Nunneries of the County of Somerset*, 30–32.
36  /  Quoted by Henry O. Taylor, *The Medieval Mind*, 4th ed. (London: Macmillan, 1927), 2: 495–96.
37  /  *VCH: York*, 3: 85.
38  /  Ibid., 164.
39  /  Ibid., 113, 164.
40  /  Power, *Medieval English Nunneries*, 459 n. 2.
41  /  Quoted by Coulton, *Five Centuries*, 2: 154 n. 3.
42  /  E. Vansteenberghe, *Le Cardinal Nicolas de Cues* (1920), quoted in Coulton, *Five Centuries*, 4: 133, 1: 408.
43  /  Harksen, *Women in the Middle Ages*, 31.
44  /  Godfrey Giffard, archbishop of Worcester, *Register: 1268–1302*, ed. J. W. Willis Bund (Oxford: James Parker, 1902), 278–80.
45  /  *Visitations of Religious Houses*, 3: 352; *VCH: York*, 3: 113.
46  /  Eckenstein, *Woman under Monasticism*, 219.
47  /  *Visitations of Religious Houses*, 3: 348.
48  /  Santa Caterina da Siena, *Libro della Divina Dottrina*. Quoted and trans. Coulton, *Five Centuries*, 2: 547.
49  /  Eude Rigaud, Archeveque de Rouen, *Regestrum Visitationum: 1248–1269*, ed. Thomas Bonin (Rouen, 1852), 1: 43. My translation.
50  /  *VCH: York*, 2: 121, 169.
51  /  Ibid., 3: 181.
52  /  Thomas Gascoigne, *Locie Libro Veritatum*, ed. J. E. Thorold Rogers. Quoted by Power, *Medieval English Nunneries*, 447 n. 6.
53  /  Rigaud, *Regestrum*, 1: 255 n. 1.
54  /  *Visitations of the Diocese of Norwich: 1492–1532*, ed. August Jessop, Camden Society, n.s. 43 (Westminster, 1888), 109.
55  /  *VCH: London*, 1: 518.
56  /  *VCH: Northampton*, 2: 101, 126.

57 / VCH: Oxford, 2: 10 (see 13 n. 40 for religious meaning of incest); Bedford, 1: 360; Lincoln, 2: 179.
58 / VCH: Northampton, 2: 114.
59 / Visitations of Religious Houses, 2: 3.
60 / For more incidents of apostasy see diocesan episcopal registers and VCH.
61 / Medieval Nunneries of the County of Somerset, 24.
62 / Records of Romsey Abbey, 218; VCH: London, 2: 150.
63 / Visitations of Religious Houses, 2: 132.
64 / Ibid., 122, 3: 228.
65 / Ibid., 3: 250.
66 / Medieval Nunneries of the County of Somerset, 62–63.
67 / Quoted in Records of Romsey Abbey, 101, 84.
68 / William Wickwane, archbishop of York, Register: 1279–1285, Surtees Society 114 (London: The Society, 1904), 141.
69 / Visitations of Religious Houses, 2: 50.
70 / Coulton, Five Centuries, 2: 569.
71 / Simonis de Gandavo, bishop of Salisbury: Register: 1297–1315, Canterbury and York Society 40–41 (Oxford: Oxford Univ. Press, 1934), 1: 10–11. Quoted and trans. Power, Medieval English Nunneries, 344.
72 / Quoted by Coulton, Five Centuries, 2: 194.
73 / Papal Letters, vol. 4 of Calendar of Entries in the Papal Registers, ed. W. H. Bliss (London, 1893), 397.
74 / Visitations of Religious Houses, 2: 47, 46.
75 / Records of Romsey Abbey, 104.
76 / VCH: York, 3: 119.
77 / Cited by Coulton, Five Centuries, 1: 404.
78 / Visitations of Religious Houses, 2: 122.
79 / Records of Romsey Abbey, 102.
80 / Coulton, Five Centuries, 2: 587.
81 / Visitations of Religious Houses, 2: 114.
82 / Trans. Coulton, Five Centuries, 2: 557.
83 / Visitations of Religious Houses, 2: 133–34.
84 / Records of Romsey Abbey, 103, 230.
85 / Yorkshire Archaeological Journal 16, quoted by Power, Medieval English Nunneries, 402. See also Visitations of Religious Houses, 2: 116, and Records of Romsey Abbey, 103.
86 / Vansteenberghe, 118. Quoted by Coulton, Five Centuries, 4: 133.
87 / Records of Romsey Abbey, 104.
88 / Ibid., 232.
89 / Monasticon Anglicanum, ed. Sir William Dugdale (London, 1846), 4: 554.
90 / Johannis Peckham, Archiepiscopi Cantuarensis: 1279–92, Registrum Epistolarum (London, 1882), 2: 664.
91 / Visitations of Religious Houses, 3: 228, 229, 230.
92 / Alvarus Pelagius, Lib. II, art. xxiv, fol. 130, quoted in translation by Coulton, Five Centuries, 2: 546–47.
93 / Records of Romsey Abbey, 232, 231.
94 / Power, Medieval English Nunneries, 473.

## 7

*Rudolph M. Bell*

## Telling Her Sins:
## Male Confessors and
## Female Penitents in
## Catholic Reformation Italy

IN 1216 THE FOURTH LATERAN COUNCIL DECREED that all the faithful of Latin Christendom henceforth must tell their sins at least once each year. The person designated to hear this confession was the parish priest, and only with his explicit permission might the sinner confess to some other authorized cleric. This institutionalization and codification of penance gradually replaced a variety of public and private modes of expiating sin and expressing contrition. In the centuries ahead there would still be bands of penitents wearing special garb, flagellating themselves, or undertaking arduous pilgrimages, but no amount of public display could substitute for the required auricular confession and absolution by a priest. The written confession, although never again to achieve the exquisite expressive form and impact of Augustine's early exemplar, would continue as a literary motif, but it too could not displace the requirement to recount orally and in person the sins committed.[1]

Christian instruction required the penitent to go beyond a general hatred of sin and sense of remorse. Priests were guided on how to lead the penitent through a detailed, specific recollection of each occasion of sin—what prior actions had led up to it, what emotions surged while committing it, when remorse set in, whether the resolve truly was there to avoid a similar temptation in the future. The mechanical listings of sins and fixed appropriate penances found so commonly in medieval penitentials were to be avoided; instead, the priest, once he became thoroughly familiar with the explicit circumstances of the sinner, was to teach, support, punish, and implore him or her in order that the transgression not be repeated.[2]

We cannot know the percentage of parish priests who actually understood what was expected of them and who had the patience and skill to serve as effective confessors. No doubt a great many of the faithful lined up once a year, quickly mumbled a list of sins committed and how many times each, substituted a standardized act of contrition for a careful examination of conscience, were assigned a perfunctory penance, and received a formulary absolution. The widespread resort to traveling confessors may be taken as evidence of the deficiencies of the typical parish priest, although other factors clearly were involved in their popularity, most notably the power relationship and embarrassment necessarily involved when a sinner's only alternative was to reveal inner secrets to someone who was also a neighbor.[3]

As with so many other medieval church practices, by the sixteenth century auricular confession annually to the local priest had lost much of its focus, vigor, and intent. Protestants swept it away as one of many Roman doctrinal addenda having little or no biblical foundation, replacing it in some instances with forms of public interrogation, confession, humiliation, and punishment that make the Roman confessional look rather benign. Be that as it may, Reformation Catholic leaders reaffirmed the legitimacy of the Fourth Lateran Council decrees and sought to make them efficacious as well.[4]

To do so, they now had at their disposal the printing press. Elizabeth Eisenstein's formulation, widely acknowledged but less than fully applied, is especially appropriate here. The scribe culture of medieval Europe gave way to the print culture of the Reformation. On the Italian peninsula, the Roman Church used every means at its disposal to control the printed word, drawing up an index of prohibited books, prosecuting heretical or deviant authors and publishers, seizing suspect literature, and distributing extensively its own views.[5]

Books and pamphlets aimed both at parish priests and at the laity poured forth, written in the vernacular in plain words. More clearly than ever before, the shepherds and their flocks would know exactly what sin was and how to avoid its occasion. Printed hastily on inexpensive paper, without quality binding or attractive frontispiece, and written by clerics of no particular literary elegance, only a tiny fraction of this outpouring remains available to us. Even what little there is has not attracted much interest from scholars. Bibliophiles hardly can be expected to put precious resources into adding such materials to their collections; exempla in monasteries sometimes are inaccessible; students of sixteenth-century literature have seemingly richer areas of concern; and often the content of these works may offend polite sensibilities without the saving grace of being truly erotic. Whatever the reasons for past neglect of this genre, it deserves a fresh look in the light of a social historian's concern with gender images and realities.[6]

The present essay is part of a larger study of how sixteenth-century men and women understood themselves and each other as men and women. The authorities who shaped, or at least attempted to shape, prescriptive gender images were many, including physicians and quacks purveying secret medicinals; writers of farmers' almanacs, poetry, plays, and public recitations; secular marriage counselors; artists and composers; and teachers of dance and cooking to name only a few. Among these authorities, of course, were the clerics, and it is their views that concern us here.

Brother Cherubino da Siena dictated his *Rules of Married Life* in the latter half of the fifteenth century, a product of the waning years of the scribe culture, but his work was an instant success in the new print culture and underwent several editions. Although most of these disappeared over the centuries, there is no reason to doubt the litterateur Carlo Negroni's assertion that this early manual of marital advice enjoyed considerable popularity in sixteenth-century Italy. Its style is colloquial in the extreme, often using the familiar *tu* form to cajole, admonish, and threaten married men, and especially married women, to behave themselves with decency and modesty. The manual is devoted almost entirely to questions of sexual behavior, a subject also of major concern in the confessors' guides and other materials we shall consider shortly.[7]

Brother Cherubino's little book shares the Christian tradition that the object of marriage is procreation, and often his particular exhortations refer back to this tradition; more interesting is his emphasis, hardly unique but very revealing about popular images of gender, on how men and women must rise above their animal instincts and cultivate their higher intellect. To encourage the faithful toward this goal, he reasons with his male readers, whereas he exhorts and shames their wives. A husband's first duty is to instruct his wife, by reading to her this work and similar writings. Secondly, he must correct and castigate her, and lastly he must provide for her maintenance. The good wife (addressed as "tu, figliuola mia") must fear her husband and do nothing to displease him or make him jealous. Her second duty is to attend to all the housework (a clear indication here that the intended audience lacks servants and is not aristocratic or patrician); lastly, if she sees her husband slipping into some sinful activity she should "sweetly and pleasingly" try to talk him into better ways.[8]

Then, a long chapter begins by addressing both husband and wife in familiar fashion, urging them to observe three mutual obligations: cordiality, living under one roof, and fulfilling the marriage debt. Brother Cherubino moves through the first two obligations in perfunctory fashion before turning in the last two-thirds of his book to its main subject, detailed advice on proper sexual behavior. Hardly a fit topic for public discourse, it was ideally suited to the print culture. Virtually everything Cherubino has to say may be found in earlier writings. The novelty is the medium, not the message. What educated clerics always could have known, and what modern scholars have documented thoroughly, became accessible to ordinary Christian men and women.

A wife's body belongs to her husband, and his to her; thus, either may initiate, and must not be denied, a legitimate request to engage in sexual intercourse. Four rules govern whether such a request is legitimate: intention, timing, place, and mode. The intent to conceive a child of course is legitimate, but Brother Cherubino adds three additional good intentions. The marital debt is of a contractual nature and each partner is obligated to pay it, just as would be the case with any other debt. The nearest analogy would be to the right of a banker to call for immediate payment of a demand loan, one with an infinite principal. Another legitimate intention is to ward off one's own temptation to fornicate with someone else or engage in other sinful behavior. Finally, a spouse may demand sexual intercourse in order to keep her or his partner from sinful thoughts and actions. "I tell you, little daughter of mine, if you think your husband is chasing after other women . . . have sex with him; that certainly is not sinful, but highly meritorious."[9]

The second rule concerns timing. It requires married couples to abstain from sexual activity during prescribed times of the year: Sundays and other feast days of holy obligation, all of Lent and vigils of feast days, and around the time of receiving communion. Brother Cherubino tells his readers that the church fathers are not in complete agreement about the number of days of sexual abstinence appropriate when receiving communion; some say at least eight days, others less. He urges a practice of three days before and three days after communion, and then adds a special plea to husbands. "If your wife wants to receive communion three or four or ten times each year, help her along, comfort her, do this favor for the service of God. . . . Leave her alone at least three days before and three days after communion; in this way you will share in the good she is doing."[10] In addition to these fixed times of abstinence, the demand of the marital debt is not legitimate during pregnancy, after childbirth until the mother enters church for purification, while breastfeeding, while menstruating, and during the time between the arrangement of a marriage contract and its official blessing by a priest.

The rule concerning place brings Brother Cherubino not only to such obvious matters as no sexual activity in churches, open fields, and public squares, but also to prohibitions on oral and anal intercourse. Here he does not address husbands at all, and instead pleads with wives, reminding them of the scandalous behavior recounted to San Bernardino of Siena by a woman married for six years who remained a virgin because her husband used her only like a man. "And if because you do not consent to this horrible evil your husband tears you apart, cheer up and tell him you wish to become a martyr and truly to go to your eternal life. And if already you have fallen into this sin . . . go to confession, otherwise the devil will carry you off." [11]

Finally the cleric comes to the rule of modality, excusing himself for entering upon such a delicate question by invoking the precedents of such angelic virgins as Thomas Aquinas and Saint Bonaventure, and by pointing out that unless his readers know what is right and what is wrong they will not be able to make a good confession. He warns first against excessive frequency, and tells husbands that just as a bull who defeats an adversary for the right to a cow and then copulates with the animal is so weakened that he loses the next battle with the same opponent, so also does sexual intercourse drain natural male vigor. Many are the husbands who have become insane or blind as a result of too much sexual activity; ten blood-lettings drain male vitality far less than one coition. Frequent intercourse leads to an early death; better to take a hint from the continent elephant or the sterile mule. Sex empties a man of virtue and spiritual vitality, and renders his offspring weak, sickly, and shortlived. Notwithstanding this logic, Brother Cherubino refuses to give advice about how much is too much, citing but not fully approving Boezio's recommendation of once a month and San Bernardino's suggestion to sleep in separate beds, and conceding that sexual needs vary considerably from one person to another.[12]

Whereas the discussion of frequency is addressed entirely to husbands, the friar's next topic, "situation," presumes that wives control the circumstances and are in need of his advice. During sexual intercourse the woman should face the sky and her husband the earth; other positions tend to inhibit conception, and, moreover, they lead to libidinous, sinful feelings. Inverted and lateral situations may be legitimate if necessitated by a physical handicap, but what excuse can there be for standing or sitting? Similarly, the chest and belly of the husband must touch the same parts of his wife's body. "If you have fallen [into situational sin] in the past, go to confession, and in the future watch out not to do it again." [13] While engaging in intercourse, husband and wife must look at each other face to face, like friends not like enemies, beasts, or dogs. "Oh beast, aren't you ashamed of yourself? And you, ribald wife, aren't you ashamed of consenting to him?" [14] Sexual activity should not involve the eyes, the nose, the ears, the mouth, the tongue or any other part of the body meant for other purposes and in no way necessary for procreation. Yes, a wife may look at her husband's private parts if he is ill, but to do so for excitement is a sin. "Never allow yourself, you woman, to be seen in the nude by your husband." [15] Soaps and perfumes are fine for removing bad odors, but sinful if meant to arouse. Kissing is allowed, but not with the tongue, and only mouth-to-mouth. "*Oimè!* The devil knows how to do so much between husband and wife; he makes them touch and kiss not only the honest parts but the dishonest ones as well. Even just to think about it, I am overwhelmed by horror, fright and bewilderment. . . . You call this *holy matrimony*?" [16] On a calmer note, Brother Cherubino goes on to urge wives not to indulge their husbands' requests to prepare spicy foods and special drinks aimed at improving sexual performance.

The friar then returns to more familiar themes. Husbands must ejaculate only into the appropriate vessel and wives must do nothing to inhibit conception or to induce abortion. Adultery by either partner cancels the right of the guilty party to claim the marital debt but does not remove the obligation to pay upon request. Finally, sexual intercourse is prohibited among couples whose marriage is juridically invalid because of consanguinity, bigamy, murder of the partner's former spouse, or a prior vow of chastity.

The pious wife familiar with Brother Cherubino's advice, or with similar admonitions available in the expanding written media, must have approached confession with some trepidation. Anonymity was unlikely; the closed confessional box with a small sliding door between the priest and his penitent began to be used only in the late sixteenth century, and then primarily in large cities. These were ordered to be placed in a prominent, highly visible place, and their purpose may have been more to prevent abuses, or the hint of abuses, perpetrated by clerics upon the faithful than to shield sinners from publicity. Confessors and penitents were warned repeatedly not to look upon or touch each other. Whether she kneeled before her priest in a confessional box or sat next to him in a private cell, we may be sure that the pious wife faced a man whose training emphasized over and over again the sexually charged nature of the situation.[17]

Bartolomeo de Medina's *Breve instruttione de' confessori*, translated into Italian from the Spanish original, clearly was aimed not at the general public but at priests and confessors. Nonetheless, it differs significantly from its predecessors produced in a scribe culture; its tone is colloquial, and conveys the sense of a book meant less for onetime study at the seminary than for repeated consultation in times of doubt or weakness while on parish duty. Medina expresses sympathy with the temptations involved, and assures his reader that if a confessor accidentally pollutes himself because of hearing libidinous confessions or while studying relevant materials for noble purposes, there is no sin committed. Nor is it sinful if a priest who is forced to talk with a woman in order to carry out his duties involuntarily "feels certain titillations and humidity." [18]

Still, the flesh is weak, and Medina is not fully confident about the remedies he offers. Resist wicked thoughts, he suggests, and always watch over and control the senses, especially the eyes. Work hard and never be idle; remember constantly that God is actively watching you and that to sin in his presence is even more embarrassing than doing so in front of another man. But the most effective remedy is to *flee* all occasions of companionship, familiarity, letters, presents, visits, and thoughts of women of suspect age, even holy ones. Do not even touch women's clothes, because truly the victory over sexual temptation (after the grace of God) consists principally in flight.[19]

Not only must the confessor be constantly on guard against his own stirrings of the flesh, he must be careful not to teach penitents new ways of sinning. Children and unmarried young adults must be questioned carefully about the sins so common to them—telling lies, failing to keep promises, not going to Mass, irreverent behavior in church, disobedience, petty theft, using bad words, and gluttony—but when it comes to sex, proceed "with great discretion and from a distance, so that you do not end up teaching them to sin." [20] Do not probe into every detail of the sexual behavior of married people. So long as ejaculation takes place where it should, pass over problems of libidinous kissing and touching of the dishonest parts. Keep to the standard list of questions; as long as the penitent confesses the wrongdoing and the type of sin, there is no need to explicate the particulars of just how it was done, nor to explore all the circumstances that led up to doing it.[21]

Medina's standard list of questions covers sixteen categories of sexual sin, beginning with adultery, incest, sacrilege, and defloration. Mortal sins contrary to nature are: masturbation, bestiality, and sodomy (male/ male, female/female, and male/female are equally grave). Unnatural positions in heterosexual relations, especially the woman on top, are disorderly, but they remain only venial sins unless the result is ejaculation outside the natural vase. Further sins on which to question the penitent include leading others into carnal vice, for example by exposing oneself at the window or by dressing in a lascivious manner; obtaining sexual favors through gifts or promises; soliciting to sin with words, writings, or through a third party; impeding conception; and reading dirty books.[22]

Two categories appear to apply only to men—having a child with someone else's wife and letting that woman's husband believe the child is his, and adultery by a husband committed with a woman related within the fourth degree to his wife. In both cases, however, the confessor is in a very delicate position because the "property" considerations involved normally would involve restitution as well as penance. But appropriate restitution is not really possible without making matters worse by revealing the sin to the innocent parties, and therefore the confessor should lie if the injured spouse comes around to ask questions.[23]

In advising priests on hearing the confessions of married people, Medina devotes most of his attention to sexual behavior. Nonetheless, the few words he uses to deal with "good governance" are very revealing. The confessor should ask the penitent husband whether he has sinned by failing to provide for the family's economic necessities, by treating his wife badly in word or in deed, by being jealous, or by being sullen and withdrawn. A wife must be questioned about whether she has been disobedient, fastidious, flighty, or negligent in household chores. Does she go out of the house against her husband's wishes? And do they no longer love each other but merely tolerate one another? And do they fail to teach their children good manners? And has she fallen into all the sins of women's vanity and their pomp in dress?[24]

From another sixteenth-century confessor's manual we learn that the effective priest should remind the penitent of her or his guardian angel. Let the angel be named, and shame the sinner into realizing that this Michael, Gabriel, or whoever, was there in the room, in all his winged glory, watching every detail of the sin and feeling deeply distressed by such licentiousness and filth. Harsh penances are in order: mortify the body with fasting, abstinence, disciplines, and a hairshirt; sleep fully clothed on a board or a hard bed; keep vigils; get up early in the morning; go on pilgrimage; do service in a hospital, putting up with the vile stench of unclean places. In this way the flesh will be macerated, mortified, and brought under the dominion of the spirit. But for rich people and others with weak constitutions, who cannot mortify themselves in this way, make them do penance by taking in a spinster or by bringing up and educating an orphan, whatever is within their means.[25]

Another late sixteenth-century pocket-sized manual on how to make a good confession, this one apparently intended both for the clergy and the faithful, addresses the difficult question of intent, one that had plagued theologians and scholastics for centuries and produced volumes of obscure debate, and reduces it to an easily understood set of guidelines. After providing a catalogue of definitions of illicit sexual acts that differs from more scholarly tomes primarily in its greater brevity and clarity, the author turns to sinful desires. "If you consent mentally to carnal desire, you are obligated in confession to name the desire" and the category of person you had in mind—a virgin, a married person, a relative, or whomever. Just as good confession requires telling the circumstances of sinful acts in order that the priest may distinguish between, say, adultery, incest, and simple fornication, so also the specific object of desire determines what sin has been committed. Each occasion of desire must be recounted separately and the penitent must recall whether and with what means she or he tried to ward off the evil thoughts. In the case of someone in love there may be "innumerable sins of thought and desire" and yet each one must be examined diligently. Inducing carnal desire on the part of others toward yourself, what we might call flirting, is also a grave sin. In confessing their sins of desire, the faithful must omit nothing out of shame; nevertheless, their vocabulary always must remain decent and modest, yet not so obscure or genteel that the priest fails to understand exactly what the penitent actually had in mind.[26]

The author then turns to the particular sins of married people, and warns other readers to skip this part of the book. The coverage of illicit acts adds nothing new to what we have been told already by Brother Cherubino da Siena, Father de Medina, and their colleagues. The innovative element, again, is desire. Even if all the physical circumstances are proper, sexual intercourse is sinful if the man or woman is thinking about someone else. Refusal to pay the marriage debt is a grave sin if it is done out of anger, annoyance, excessive piety, or false dignity. If during intercourse you feel such concupiscence that you would enjoy the act even if this were not your spouse, then you are guilty of lust, and the sin is serious. A married woman must not be disobedient or contentious with her husband, but if he asks her to do something she thinks is unseemly, such as being on top during sexual intercourse, she should seek the advice of her confessor and if he says that such a position would be sinful, she must refuse her husband, and if she fails to convince him and gives in, the guilt is hers.[27]

Less explicit but more authoritative than the popular confessional manuals we have been examining thus far is the catechism ordered by the Council of Trent. Catholic Reformation leaders recognized that legalistic doctrines and canons, necessary though they were, could not be expected to infuse the daily lives of the faithful with a proper concern for correct Catholic teaching and practice. Fully cognizant of the power of the printed word, the holy council

> commands all bishops that not only when they are themselves about to administer them [sacraments] to the people, they shall first, in a manner adapted to the mental ability of those who receive them, explain their efficacy and use, but also they shall see to it that the same is done piously and prudently by every parish priest, and in the vernacular tongue, if need be and if it can be done conveniently, in accordance with the form which will be prescribed for each of the sacraments by the holy council in a catechism, which the bishops shall have faithfully translated into the language of the people and explained to the people by all parish priests.[28]

The resulting *Catechism of the Council of Trent* treats the sacrament of matrimony in detail, as it does the sacrament of penance.

Marriage is not merely a human or legal bond, asserts the church, but one established by God and confirmed by sacrament. The people must have explained to them the legitimate reasons for a man and a woman to be married. The first is that during the discomforts of life and in the feebleness of old age, they will provide aid and support to each other. The second is to raise children in the true faith of God. The third is as a remedy against concupiscence. Finally, if these three goals are present, the priest is not to condemn motives such as the desire for a worldly heir or the attractions of wealth, beauty, illustrious descent, and congeniality.[29]

The duty of the husband is to treat his wife courteously and with honor; he must find an honest means to support her and their children; it is he who is in charge and who is responsible for the family's morals. The good wife is subject to her husband in all matters. She was not formed from his feet, an object to be trampled upon, but neither was she formed from his head, and so she must learn to obey, not to command. She must obey willingly and cheerfully in all matters not inconsistent with Christian piety, and, except for God himself, she must love and esteem no one more greatly than her husband. Her proper spheres are the raising of their children in the practice of religion and attending to domestic concerns; she should willingly stay at home and never venture to leave home without her husband's permission.[30]

Priests must instruct their flock on the proper use of the marriage debt. Here great delicacy is in order, lest the clergy offend pious minds or excite laughter by using unseemly language. The lessons are many, but two shall be especially enjoined upon the faithful. The first is that the enjoyment of sexual intercourse must never be an end in itself, for as St. Jerome warned, "There is no greater turpitude than that a husband should love his wife as he would an adulteress." The second injunction is that married couples abstain from sexual activity for three days previous to receiving the Eucharist and "frequently" during Lent.[31]

Great care must be taken by the priest and his parishioners that the holy state of matrimony not be sullied by lust. The origins of lust may be traced back to Adam and Eve, but as a practical matter the faithful must at all times avoid idleness; they must be temperate in food and drink. Women must shun elegance of dress, voluptuous incitements, and loose conversation. Lascivious songs and dances, amatory and obscene books, and indecent images all possess "a fatal influence in exciting to filthy allurements, and in kindling criminal desires in the minds of youth." The most efficacious remedy in the endless war against lust is frequent confession.[32]

In hearing the sins of married persons, the priest must use "extreme caution and prudence," treating "with great delicacy of language a subject which requires moderation rather than copiousness of speech." The good confessor must avoid drawing the penitent into details and topics that may serve to inflame lust rather than to extinguish it. Let all the congregation know of the Tridentine decrees against adultery and the keeping of harlots and concubines, but omit any instruction on the many and varied other species of lust and immodesty, saving this for each individual in private as the circumstances of time and person shall require. By all means speak openly of the biblical destructions wrought upon whole cities of sinners—death, fire, and slaughter—but do not neglect to add the more subtle punishments of internal pangs and tortures, loss of honor and reputation, depression, and melancholy.[33]

The loss of baptismal innocence is akin to a shipwreck, and the faithful have no hope of salvation unless they cling to the plank of penance. No one may gain admittance to heaven unless its gates be opened by the priest, and his power to pardon is unrestrained by civil authority or by the excessive sense of guilt that the contrite sinner still may feel. Church leaders recognized the weakness of their claims to scriptural justification for the sacrament of penance, and perhaps for that very reason, the *Catechism* is unequivocally dogmatic on this point: "The pastor will next teach . . . without any hesitation that . . . this sacrament was instituted by Christ the Lord." The penitent should be prostrate at the feet of the priest, with head uncovered, with face fixed on the earth, and with hands raised in supplication. She or he must be questioned carefully and deeply, so that even sins of desire "buried in the darkest secrecy" will come forth. The mere listing of sins is not satisfactory; the circumstances connected with each sin must be told, and evaluated as to how they aggravate or extenuate the baseness of the evil act.[34]

The psychological dimensions of confession by no means eluded Catholic Reformation prelates. Look for signs of true contrition, and press hard to see that the sinner does not secretly pass the blame onto another. Exhort the bashful to tell everything, reminding them that their faults are common human maladies. Severely rebuke those who have not reflected carefully upon their sins before kneeling in the confessional, and even send them away (in the mildest terms) so that they may return and be more thoughtful another time. But if the priest fears that the sinner may not return at all or for a long time, he should hear the confession anyway, and grant absolution as long as there seems to be at least some disposition to turn over a new leaf. Females especially tend to forget one sin or another, and then they are afraid to return to confession either because they fear people will think them overly pious or just the opposite, guilty of some especially heinous act. Teach the women publicly and privately that no one has such an excellent memory as to be able to recall every sin; they should do their best, and return frequently.[35]

The print revolution of the sixteenth century provided Catholic leaders with new opportunities, and these were exploited fully. At least with regard to developments on the Italian peninsula, historians have given primary attention to the use of the printing press by the papacy's opponents, as well as to the efforts of the Church Militant to suppress, burn, condemn, and confiscate the message of its opponents, along with the messengers themselves. A more complete picture, however, should include as well positive uses of the written word to inculcate Catholic doctrine.

The *Catechism of the Council of Trent* formalized, codified, and publicized correct teaching and belief with an efficacy not possible in earlier centuries. For the first time, the parish priest and his flock would know exactly what was expected of them, and lest there be any forgetfulness or uncertainty, the books were there, in inexpensive vernacular editions available to all. The *Catechism* itself was addressed primarily to the clergy and not the laity, but it repeatedly called upon the utility of the many works widely in circulation for laypeople.

The pious young woman entering upon marriage now had available to her detailed and explicit guides to proper behavior. In earlier centuries she might have stood in a crowd being exhorted by a traveling preacher or listened to the instruction of a particularly conscientious parish priest, but neither one could have provided the kind of specific advice found, for example, in Brother Cherubino's little book. From the many stories of marital tribulations encountered in saints' lives, she could have learned more, some of it explicitly sexual, but with rare exceptions these vitae ended by telling of the dissolution of marriage before the holy woman liberated herself and embarked on a higher spiritual path.

The clarity of the new message, however, carried what may have been a high price. We leave aside for the moment the many young women who were not truly pious and who simply snickered or otherwise remained untouched by the new message. Instead, we consider the unknowable but probably not trivial number of deeply religious brides who attempted to live as they were told that Jesus and the church commanded.

The challenge was one of extraordinary difficulty, for the commands penetrated into every aspect of private life, day and night, into the darkest recesses of the mind. Pay the marital debt and become aroused, your guardian angel is watching and is offended. Obey your husband while feeling a touch of resentment or inadequate cheerfulness, it is a serious sin. Give in to your husband's sexual demands, and be denied the consolation of the Eucharist. Put on a new dress, a splash of perfume, or a bracelet, and be the guilty party if someone looks at you with lust in his heart. Tell your sins openly and fully, and then be coresponsible if your confessor falls into impure thoughts. Trapped in a web of emotionally inhibiting and physically demanding regulations, the pious married woman had little chance of reconciling her spiritual needs with her earthly duties. Only in her later years or in widowhood could she escape the burden of her sex.[36]

NOTES

1    /    Henry Charles Lea, *A History of Auricular Confession and Indulgences in the Latin Church* (Philadelphia, 1896), 1:227–73, is the standard work and is still useful despite its clear prejudices. Oscar Watkins, *A History of Penance: Being a Study of the Authorities*, 2 vols. (New York: B. Franklin, 1961), is excellent on pre–Fourth Lateran matters. For a

crosscultural analysis of confession as practiced in many world religions, see Raffaele Pettazzioni, *La confessione dei peccati*, 3 vols. (Bologna: Forni, 1968 reprint of 1929–1936 orig. ed.).

2 / On medieval penitentials, see John T. McNeill and Helena M. Gamer, *Medieval Handbooks of Penance: A Translation of the Principal* Libri Poenitentiales *and Selections from Related Documents* (New York: Columbia Univ. Press, 1938); also see the excellent introductions in Mary F. Braswell, *The Medieval Sinner: Characterization and Confession in the Literature of the English Middle Ages* (Rutherford, N.J.: Fairleigh Dickinson Univ. Press, 1983), and in Allen J. Frantzen, *The Literature of Penance in Anglo-Saxon England* (New Brunswick, N.J.: Rutgers Univ. Press, 1983). For a legal perspective, see Thomas Oakley, *English Penitential Discipline and Anglo-Saxon Law in Their Joint Influence* (New York: Columbia Univ. Press, 1923). Admirable critical editions of major penitentials of considerable literary interest include: Robert of Flamborough, *Liber Poenitentialis*, ed. J. J. Francis Firth (Toronto: Pontifical Institute of Mediaeval Studies, 1971), and Robert Mannyng of Brunne, *Handlyng Synne* (Binghamton, N.Y.: Center for Medieval and Early Renaissance Studies, 1983). For a modern Catholic perspective, see Paul Anciaux, *Le sacrement de la pénitence* (Louvain and Paris: Editions Nauwelaerts, 1957). Giovanni Cereti, *Divorzio nuove nozze e penitenza nella chiesa primitiva* (Bologna: EDB, 1977), notwithstanding its primary concern with a then current debate in Italy over divorce legislation, provides much useful analysis of early church doctrine.

3 / On traveling confessors, especially from the new mendicant orders, see Lea, *A History of Auricular Confession*, 1:274–311. More explicitly on women, see Carla Casagrande, ed., *Prediche alle donne del secolo XIII* (Milan: Valentino Bompiani, 1978), esp. vii–xxv. On alms and traveling confessors, see Michel Mollat, *The Poor in the Middle Ages: An Essay in Social History*, trans. Arthur Goldhammer (New Haven: Yale Univ. Press, 1986), 126–27.

4 / *Canons and Decrees of the Council of Trent*, trans. H. J. Schroeder (St. Louis and London: B. Herder, 1941), provides a good English translation along with the Latin original. The major decisions on the sacrament of penance were taken during the Fourteenth Session, beginning on 25 November 1551.

5 / Elizabeth L. Eisenstein, *The Printing Press as an Agent of Change: Communications and Cultural Transformations in Early-Modern Europe*, 2 vols. (Cambridge: Cambridge Univ. Press, 1979). Also see Gerald P. Tyson and Sylvia S. Wagonheim, eds., *Print and Culture in the Renaissance* (Newark: Univ. of Delaware Press, 1986), esp. the essays on popular literature by Kyle C. Sessions, Christiane Andersson, and Keith P. F. Moxey.

6 / Thomas N. Tentler, *Sin and Confession on the Eve of the Reformation* (Princeton: Princeton Univ. Press, 1977), esp. 162–232, provides a thorough treatment of the major "official" church writers involved in working out from a theological perspective the proper place of sexuality within marriage. Although the texts that interest me and the questions I am asking are very different, it is also appropriate to note here the fine study by Ian Maclean, *The Renaissance Notion of Woman* (Cambridge: Cambridge Univ. Press, 1980). Richard Lewinsohn, *A History of Sexual Customs*, trans. Alexander Mayce (New York: Harper, 1958), 151–71, provides a useful introduction to the rediscovery of female sexuality by

late Italian humanists. Jean-Louis Flandrin, "Sex in Married Life in the Early Middle Ages: The Church's Teaching and Behavioural Reality," in Philippe Ariès and André Béjin, eds., *Western Sexuality: Practice and Precept in Past and Present Times*, trans. Anthony Forster (London: Basil Blackwell, 1985), 114–29, has influenced my thinking on a number issues that follow.

7  /  Cherubino da Siena, *Regole della vita matrimoniale* (Bologna: Commissione per i testi di lingua, 1969 reprint of 1888 edition by Francesco Zambrini and Carlo Negroni); see v–xxii for the publication history.

8  /  Ibid., 7–25. The matter of familial relations and duties was the subject of numerous sixteenth-century chapbooks, as well as of more detailed works, for example, Nicolò Vito di Gozze, *Governo della famiglia* (Venice: Also Manuzio, 1589), but fuller treatment of these must await another essay.

9  /  Cherubino da Siena, *Regole*, 50 for the quotation.

10  /  Ibid., 60 for the quotation.

11  /  Ibid., 75 for the quotation.

12  /  Ibid., 80–88. On Bonaventure, see Emma Thérèsa Healy, *Woman According to Saint Bonaventure* (New York: Georgian Press, 1955); on Aquinas, see Kari Elisabeth Børresen, *Natura e ruolo della donna in Agostino e Tommaso d'Aquino*, trans. Liliana Lanzarini (Città di Castello: Cittadella, 1979).

13  /  Cherubino da Siena, *Regole*, 91.

14  /  Ibid., 92.

15  /  Ibid., 94.

16  /  Ibid., 96–97. For a lively survey of "situational" sin, see G. R. Quaife, *Wanton Wenches and Wayward Wives: Peasants and Illicit Sex in Early Seventeenth Century England* (New Brunswick, N.J.: Rutgers Univ. Press, 1979), 165–85.

17  /  Lea, *A History of Auricular Confession*, 1:374–95, places expected emphasis on clerical misbehavior but fails to consider the psychological implications for the penitent who is personally known to her confessor and who is the cause of his lustful desires.

18  /  Bartolomeo de Medina, *Breve instruttione de' confessori. Come si debba amministrare il Sacramento della Penitentia* (Venice, 1600), 79b.

19  /  Ibid., 144. A similar set of helpless admonitions followed by the advice to flee all contact with women is found in the anonymous *Methodo di confessione* (Venice, 1572), 217–35.

20  /  Medina, *Breve instruttione*, 153a.

21  /  Ibid., 78b. Michel Foucault, *The History of Sexuality*, vol. 1, trans. Robert Hurley (New York: Vintage Books, 1980), esp. 17–49, places the proliferation of discourse concerned with sex in the eighteenth century, but clearly the argument he is making applies at least back to the mid-sixteenth century.

22  /  Medina, *Breve instruttione*, 163a.

23  /  Ibid., 80a.

24  /  Ibid., 156b.

25  /  Gaspar Loarte, *Avisi di sacerdoti et confessori* (Parma, 1584), 187–92.

26  /  Cherubino da Firenze, *Confessionario* (Fiorenza, 1583), 48–49.

27  /  Ibid., 51–54.

28  /  *Canons and Decrees of the Council of Trent*, sess. 24, pt. 2: Reform, ch. 7.

29 / *The Catechism of the Council of Trent*, trans. Theodore Buckley (London, 1852), pt. 2, ch. 8, question 14 (hereafter, e.g., 2.8.14).

30 / *Catechism*, 2.8.27. On questions of orderly public behavior and wifely obedience, church leaders wrote widely; a rather charming example is Agostino Valerio (Bishop of Verona), *Instruttione delle Donne maritate* (Venice, 1575), a sixty-page little book in the form of a letter to his married sister.

31 / *Catechism*, 2.8.33.

32 / *Catechism*, 2.8.1 and 3.7.11. On the evils of dancing, see Simeon Zuccolo da Cologna, *La pazzia del ballo* (Padua, 1549).

33 / *Catechism*, 3.7.1, 5.

34 / *Catechism*, 2.5.1, 39, 42.

35 / *Catechism*, 2.5.58. For a modern Catholic view, see Andreas Snoeck, *Confession and Psychoanalysis*, trans. Theodore Zuydwijk (Westminster, Md.: Newman Press, 1964). A strident opposing view will be found in G. Rattray Taylor, *Sex in History* (New York: Vanguard Press, 1954). Historical evidence on the response of the female penitent to the confessional situation is hard to come by, but interesting contemporary insights may be found in Gabriella Parca, ed., *Italian Women Confess*, trans. Carolyn Gaiser (London: Allen & Unwin, 1963), for example p. 15 on omitting sexual sins in confession.

36 / Although this is not the place to begin an examination of the nonclerical literature, it is worth noting that the texts analyzed in this essay are far less overtly misogynous than tracts such as Giuseppe Passi, *Dello stato maritale* (Venice, 1602) or his truly vicious *I donneschi difetti* (Venice, 1618). Another source of authoritative and extremely misogynous "information" is the medical text written in the vernacular and in my judgment intended more for consumers of pornography than for physicians, e.g., Gioseppe Liceti, *Il ceva, overo dell'eccellenza et uso de' genitali* (Bologna, 1598).

8

*Keith Moxey*

## The Battle of the Sexes
## and the World Upside Down

ONE DIMENSION OF THE FLOOD OF POPULAR BROADSHEETS produced in Germany during the Reformation is a genre that deals with the subject of marriage. These broadsheets have received scant attention from art historians. The scholarship has been satisfied with a discussion of attribution and dating and has failed to broach issues of interpretation. On the other hand, these broadsheets were incorporated in Steven Ozment's history of the family in the Reformation entitled *When Fathers Ruled*, which was published in 1983. Though not discussed, or even mentioned in the text, these broadsheets were nevertheless regarded as a fitting ornament to a book whose thesis was that Luther's substitution of marriage for celibacy as the ideal form of the Christian life in the temporal world led to a significant improvement in the condition of women. In his conclusion he wrote: "To be 'subject to a man' in the sixteenth and seventeenth centuries did not necessarily mean either the loss of one's identity or the absence of meaningful and rewarding work. . . . In the 'patriarchal' home, authority was shared by husband and wife. A wife's subjection to the rule of her husband was not the subservience of a serf to a lord, or a maid to a master, or a child to a parent; despite male rule an ordered equality existed between husbands and wives."[1]

In the following discussion I want to question whether the social significance of the images and texts of these broadsheets can in fact be reconciled with Ozment's conclusions. In doing so I will approach these images from a radically different perspective. Ozment's failure to discuss them betrays an attitude toward visual representation which suggests that images are concerned only with the record of our perception of the world. In viewing images as the product of the artist's vision, Ozment treats them as transparent, thus implying that their meaning is accessible to any spectator. By contrast, this analysis will assume that images are sign systems analogous to the linguistic sign systems that constitute written documentation. If images are systems of signification, they require as close and as careful interpretation as written documents.

I shall focus on the analysis and interpretation of a single work, namely, the broadsheet entitled *There Is No Greater Treasure Here on Earth than an Obedient Wife Who Covets Honor*, which was published in Nuremberg in 1533 (fig. 1).[2] The woodcut was executed by a follower of Albrecht Dürer named Erhard Schön and the text was provided by Albrecht Glockendon, the broadsheet's publisher. Schön's image represents a man pulling a cart, who is urged onward by a woman holding a whip. This pair is observed by another young couple together with a woman dressed in fool's costume and an old man. The ritual substitution of humans for beasts of burden was a traditional means of symbolizing the inversion of the social order in German carnival celebrations in the late Middle Ages. Women of marriageable age who had no suitors or sometimes old unmarried women were mocked for their lack of husbands by being forced to pull a plough either through or around their villages.[3] Hans Sachs made use of this theme for a broadsheet illustrated by Erhard Schön dated 1532 (fig. 2).[4] In the text which bears the title *The Housemaids Pull the Plough*, Sachs takes the opportunity to moralize against the old carnival custom, saying that instead of rushing into marriage, young people should give it very careful consideration. This carnival practice had been put to revolutionary purposes during the Reformation when monks were forced to pull the plough. In this instance the anticlerical mockery seems to have consisted in equating celibate men with unmarried women who failed to perform what was claimed to be their social duty.[5] In the light of this tradition it is hardly surprising that this form of ritual mockery should have been used to invoke the idea of folly. Albrecht Dürer's woodcut for chapter 47 of Sebastian Brant's *Ship of Fools* (fig. 3) represents a man in fool's costume pulling a cart through an open field. The chapter, which is titled "On the Road to Salvation," is introduced with verses that read

> *Some people persist in folly's road*
> *And draw a cart with heavy load*
> *The right cart awaits in heaven's abode.*[6]

The image of Schön's cart-pulling man with its references to carnival practice and the idea of folly serves to suggest that we witness a situation in which the natural order has been inverted. The carnival practice of attaching women or monks to a plough in order to mock their failure to get married was turned inside out when a man was represented in this position for having done so. This transformation is only comprehensible in terms of the idea of the power of women to which this image also makes reference. During the course of the fifteenth century the image of a man ridden by a woman had been developed as a visual metaphor of the abasement and humiliation to which men were liable as a consequence of their susceptibility to the seductive attractions of women. This may be seen, for example, in an engraving by the Housebook Master representing Phyllis and Aristotle (fig. 4).[7] Illustrations of this thirteenth-century legend, according to which the ancient philosopher was induced to carry a pretty young woman about on his back because of his sexual infatuation with her, formed part of a series of scenes representing the way in which great men were humiliated as a consequence of the evil power of women.[8] Much the same motif was used to satirize marriages in which the woman had usurped her husband's position of authority. This idea was also illustrated by the Housebook Master in a satirical coat of arms in which a peasant woman rides on her husband's back while he is forced to hold her distaff (fig. 5).[9] In this case, the fact that the image represents a violation of the "natural" sexual hierarchy is made explicit by the figure of a peasant standing on his head in the center of the shield.

The inversion of the established marital order is also alluded to by the articles carried in the woman's left hand. These include a sword, a purse, and a pair of pants. All three of these items were used as a means of symbolizing male authority in both the literature and art of this period. For example, the anonymous woodcut frontispiece to the poem *The Evil Smoke* by the Nuremberg playwright Hans Folz (fig. 6) represents a woman beating her husband after having deprived him of his purse, his sword, and his pants.[10] The poem recounts a marital struggle for the right to wear the pants which—then as now—are used as a metaphor of authority.[11] The "battle for the pants" was in fact, one of the more popular images used to satirize wifely insubordination.[12] For example, an engraving by Israhel van Meckenem (fig. 7) represents a woman beating her husband with a distaff while the object of their struggle, the man's pants, lies prominently displayed in the foreground.[13] The demon who aids and abets the woman's efforts makes clear the moral we are to derive from her behavior. The characterization of a dominating woman as evil is also found in the visual tradition of the battle between the old woman and the devil (fig. 8). This theme, which may have its origins in the medieval latin proverb "A bad woman is three times worse than the devil,"[14] was a popular one in fifteenth-century art and literature. An anonymous broadsheet published at Augsburg about 1475 shows an old woman beating a number of devils into submission with a spoon.[15] The text makes a point of equating the fate of the devils with that of a man married to an angry wife. Finally the contents of the barrel which the man pulls in the cart are a reference to the term *Windelwascher* (diaper washer), a derogatory word for a hen-pecked husband.[16] The batlike object perched on top of the load was used as a primitive laundry aid with which one literally beat out the dirt. This object may be identified by means of a woodcut by Hans Schäuffelein (fig. 9), which once illustrated a lost broadsheet by Hans Sachs entitled *Ho, Ho, Diaper Washer.*[17]

The text of Glockendon's broadsheet serves both to articulate more fully the theme of female insubordination as well as to pass judgment on it. The title, *There Is No Greater Treasure Here on Earth than an Obedient Wife Who Covets Honor,* is not only a reference to the Old Testament book of Proverbs, "Who can find a virtuous woman, for her price is far above rubies," but a quotation of a well-known sixteenth-century German proverb, "A devoted wife is worth more than her weight in gold." [18] In invoking the notion of the ideal wife, the title thus offers us the opposite of the unruly woman in the image. The text printed above the man pulling the cart reads in part:

> *Oh woe, oh woe is me, poor fool*
> *How I must work to pull this cart!*
> *And why? Because I took myself a wife*
> *Would that the thought had never crossed my mind!*
> *A shrewish scold has come into my house*
> *She has taken my sword, my pants and my purse*
> *Night and day I have no peace*
> *And never a kind word from her.*[19]

The woman behind him replies:

> *Hey dear boy, what you say is true*
> *But be quiet or I'll hit you over the head*
> *If you want a beautiful and pious little wife*
> *Who obeys you at all times*
> *Then stay home in your own house*
> *And stop carousing about.*
> *. . . If you will not work to support me*
> *Then you must wash, spin and draw the cart*
> *And be beaten on your back*

The couple standing on the right of this argumentative pair pass comment on their behavior in the following exchange. The young man asks the woman whether she would treat him as badly if they were to get married. She replies that she would do no such thing:

> *Boy, believe me on my word of honor,*
> *That I have no desire for such power.*
> *If we have an honest disagreement*
> *You will remain the man in all things.*
> *I only ask you to grant me*
> *Those things that belong to a wife.*
> *That you love, honor and suffer with me in times of need*
> *More I shall not demand.*

The woman standing behind them, who is dressed in a costume of a court fool, warns the young man against marriage, saying that it will only bring him "much anxiety, uncertainty, worry and want." She proposes an alternative that he seek his pleasure with women who will do his will for a bottle of wine. While the image of the court fool had become identified with sinful behavior of all kinds as a result of the publication of Sebastian Brant's *Ship of Fools*, it is significant that it should first have been used as a way of moralizing against lust.[20] An example of this usage is found in an engraving by the anonymous Master E. S. (fig. 10), which represents an allegorical figure of lust being approached by a fool.[21] As a consequence it is fair to conclude that the woman's costume is a comment on the promiscuous way of life she recommends.

The woman's advice is opposed by that of the old man whose speech brings the text to a close:

> *Do not listen to this foolish woman*
> *Beware the wiles of whores*
> *Who will always deceive you*
> *Go and take a wife*
> *God determines how your life together will be*
> *So stay with her in love and suffering*
> *And always be patient*
> *And if you should have much worry and care*
> *Look on it as God's will*
> *Provide for her by the sweat of your brow*
> *As God commanded in the first book of Genesis.*

The broadsheet *There Is No Greater Treasure* is typical of the broadsheets dealing with the subject of marriage in its preoccupation with the need for male authority. In contrast to the allegorical images of female insubordination just discussed, the illustrations to many of the marriage broadsheets are striking in their naturalistic, or mimetic, representation of marital violence. A typical example is Barthel Beham's woodcut for Hans Sachs's broadsheet *The Nine Hides of an Angry Wife* (fig. 11).[22] In this case, the image is a reversal of the iconography of the "battle for the pants" (fig. 7). Instead of depicting female insubordination in allegorical terms, the artist affords the viewer an image of its punishment whose impact depends on its function as an illustration of the text. No longer is the man subjected to the unlikely form of maltreatment illustrated in the image by Erhard Schön (fig. 1). Instead the woman is represented as the victim of a much more probable and all too familiar form of domestic violence. There is a movement, in other words, from allegory to narrative. The ambiguity of the "battle for the pants" iconography, in which it was always possible to view the triumphant woman as victor rather than accept her triumph as a manifestation of improper conduct, has been decisively rejected.[23] The message of this broadsheet was to be univocal.

As we turn to the text of this broadsheet the brutality of the image becomes more comprehensible, for the story of the *Nine Hides* is one of the more sadistic products of a misogynist fantasy. Returning from an inn one evening, where he has been drinking with his friends, a young husband finds that his wife refuses to speak to him. On beating her for this insubordination, he receives no response and comments that his wife's skin feels like that of a codfish. On striking her a second time, she reacts like a raging bear, on receiving a third blow she resembles a hissing goose, on the fourth a barking dog and so forth until having reached the ninth skin, his wife becomes human again and implores his forgiveness, promising never to question his authority again. Despite the fact that Sachs closes the poem advising against such violence and argues that women must be ruled with reason rather than force, the appeal of the broadsheet undoubtedly lay in the sadistic humor with which this account of marital strife is described. The ambiguity of the poet's position is perhaps best discerned by examining his own words:

> *So punish your wife modestly*
> *And if there is any honor in her*
> *She will become an obedient wife*

*As one says, "A devoted husband*
*Can bring forth a devoted wife."*
*But if she remains self-willed*
*And refuses you in all your requests*
*Ever disobedient and rebellious*
*On those occasions when she spurns cooperation*
*You may punish her with blows*
*Yet do it still with reason and discretion*
*So that no harm is done to either of you*
*Use both carrot and stick*
*To bring about companionship*
*As befits an honorable man.*[24]

What did Sachs mean when he advised punishing one's wife "modestly"? How were "blows" to be administered "with reason and discretion"? How were "carrot and stick" to bring about "companionship"? The tone of disinterested concern masks a defense of physical violence.

There was nothing new about the misogynist humor just described. Such themes were a commonplace of late medieval art and literature. However, the satirical imagery of the battle of the sexes, which had been developed in an age that regarded marriage as spiritually inferior to celibacy, had different implications in a context that regarded marriage as the most desirable form of social life. In contrast to the orthodox church, Luther believed that there was no form of life on earth that could lead to spiritual perfection. Since he regarded the sexual drive as an overpowering force from which no human was exempt, the association of sex with lust brought about as a consequence of the Fall, meant that there was no escape from sin. These views led him to reject orthodoxy's regard for celibacy as the highest form of the Christian life. If human nature was in its essence sinful, then there was no possibility of living a wholly virtuous life. Rather than pursue a hopelessly flawed ideal, it was better than Christians should consider the married rather than the celibate life as the natural condition of human existence. "For this word which God speaks, 'Be fruitful and multiply,' is not a command. It is more than a command, namely, a divine ordinance which it is not our perogative to hinder or ignore. Rather, it is just as necessary as the fact that I am a man, and more necessary than sleeping and waking, eating and drinking and emptying the bowels and bladder."[25] While the married state did not eliminate sin from sexual relations, it provided a context in which lust could be contained. In Luther's eyes the function of marriage as a means by which the sinful power of the sexual drive could be restrained and controlled was as important as its role in procreation. "Therefore [because of the Fall], the married state is now no longer pure and free of sin. The temptation of the flesh has become so strong and consuming that marriage may be likened to a hospital for incurables which prevents the inmates from falling into graver sin." [26]

If God's punishment of Adam and Eve was responsible for calling the institution of marriage into existence, it also determined its structure. Like the medieval theologians before him, Luther regarded the wife's subordination to her husband as God's curse on the female of the species for the sin of Eve.[27] "Hence it follows that if the woman had not been deceived by the serpent and had not sinned, she would have been the equal of Adam in all respects. For the punishment that she is now subjected to the man, was imposed on her after sin and because of sin, just as other hardships and dangers were: travail, pain and countless other vexations." [28]

Luther's views regarding the role of women in marriage were incorporated in the reformed wedding ceremony. In *The Order of Marriage,* Luther ordained that the following words be included in the minister's blessing of the couple before the altar: "Wives submit yourselves unto your own husbands, as unto the Lord. For the husband is head of the wife, even as Christ is the head of the church: and he is Saviour of the body. Therefore as the church is subject to Christ, so let wives be subject to their husbands in everything." [29] The subordination of women as a consequence of Original Sin was regarded by Luther not only as the justification of her inferior position in marriage, but as the foundation of all worldly authority. According to his "two world" theory, secular authority was a part of the natural law to which man was subject in the temporal world. Wives were subject to their husbands just as men were subject to the secular authorities.[30] Commenting on the fourth commandment "honor thy father and mother," Luther described the relationship in the following terms:

> Therefore everything that one calls master stands in the place of the parents and must draw from their power to rule. It is for this reason that according to Scripture, they are all called fathers whenever they fill the post of father in their governments and must carry a fatherly heart towards their subjects. Just as since antiquity the Romans and other peoples called the lord and mistresses of the house *Patres et matres familias,* which means housefather(s) and mother(s), therefore they also called their princes and ruler *Patres patriae,* that is, father(s) of their country. It is a great shame that we who want to be Christians do not do the same or at least regard and honour them in that way.[31]

The consequences of Luther's teaching on the subject of marriage made themselves felt in Nuremberg shortly after the town council introduced the new faith in the early 1520s. Following the Religious Disputation of 1525 in which the council stage-managed the defeat of the Catholic theologians by the Lutheran ministers, it took measures to close the city's monastic institutions.[32] While most of the monastic orders were dissolved and their property placed at the disposal of the city's poor relief by the end of that year, the Franciscans and the convents of St. Clare and St. Catherine held out. The surviving orders were prohibited from taking novices, from preaching, and from celebrating Mass. As a consequence they gradually died out in the course of the sixteenth century.[33] Significantly enough, the convents were the last to go.

The council also took the administration of marriage out of the hands of the ecclesiastical authorities. Marital cases were henceforth dealt with in the city courts. The new marriage ritual, commissioned by the council from the Lutheran pastors, gave new importance to the ceremony.[34] Whereas orthodox marriages had in most instances, been blessed at a ceremony held before the church doors, a symbol of the church's unwillingness to accept full responsibility for what it regarded as a secular institution, the Nuremberg marriage ordinance of 1525 decreed that the ceremony was now to take place inside the church, before the altar.[35] Unlike the orthodox church, which still recognized the validity of marriage vows taken outside of the church even though it disapproved of them, the Lutherans were determined to make the religious ceremony the only recognized form of marriage. They thus put into practice Luther's views regarding the importance of the sexual hierarchy in marriage as a natural metaphor of the social hierarchy. The degree to which the interests of church and state intersected in this matter can be gauged by the fact that by 1537 the council no longer recognized marriages that had not been performed in the church.[36]

What is the significance of this interpretation of the social function of the marriage broadsheets as a means of validating the political order of Nuremberg society for the ongoing debate about the consequences of the Reformation for the status and role of women?[37] First, the role played by marriage broadsheets in the construction of an orderly Lutheran society can only have had an adverse effect on the economic independence of women. Neither the size of Nuremberg, estimated at between 40,000 and 50,000 inhabitants in the period 1500–1550, nor its economic power can be regarded as an indication of the wealth of its inhabitants.[38] While the great merchant families, in whose hands the political power of the city was concentrated, lived like princes, they constituted only a tiny fraction of the population. More than half the inhabitants were artisans who lived a more or less precarious existence that was constantly threatened by unemployment and inflation. It has been calculated that while the wages of unskilled laborers doubled and those of artisans' apprentices tripled during the course of the sixteenth century, living costs rose by an average of 400 to 600 percent in the same period.[39] The economic autonomy of the artisan class was further threatened by the introduction of a capitalist organization of labor. Wealthy artisans banded together to finance the production of their fellows in such a way as to control the prices demanded for their wares. By extending loans or guaranteeing prices they established a monopolistic control over certain crafts. Since the new arrangements tended to keep prices artificially low, many artisans suffered a gradual erosion of their standard of living. It is in this context that women, who had once been represented in a wide variety of occupations, were gradually but systematically excluded from the world of employment.[40] A slow "professionalization" is discernible in which the highest-paying positions became the posts from which women were barred.[41] This process ultimately confined women to occupations that were low in both status and pay. While the ways in which these trends are related to each other are not immediately obvious, it can be argued that the reinforcement of patriarchal values that took place as a consequence of the social teaching of the Reformation, teaching which is vividly expressed in the marriage broadsheets, can only have encouraged impoverished male artisans in seeking to eliminate female competitors from the job market by confining their sphere of activity to home.

The "battle of the sexes" represented in the marriage broadsheets may not only have fostered the competition for jobs, it may also have added impetus to changes taking place in the age of marriage. Historical demographers have shown that the age of marriage grew progressively later during the course of the sixteenth and seventeenth centuries. The medieval pattern of marriage at puberty was replaced by one in which marriage took place when both partners were in their late twenties or early thirties, the man being usually older than the wife.[42] This change, which has been associated with the need for families of all classes to ensure their social status by means of accumulation of capital, would have enhanced the authority of the husband at the expense of that of the wife. The violence of the imagery of the marriage broadsheets would thus have served to promote male supremacy in a situation that was psychologically loaded. It seems unlikely, in other words, that women who entered marriage at mature age would have found that their personal and social views necessarily coincided with those of their husbands, and as a consequence the potential for conflict must have increased.

An approach to the marriage broadsheets as systems of signs reveals the complexity of the social meaning they served to create. The social function of the misogynist satires of the late Middle Ages which depended on the notion of the "world upside down" was transformed from one of provocation to affirmation. Instead of disparaging the institution of marriage by pointing out the abuses to which it was subject, they now served to affirm its validity. The importance of the "battle of the sexes" in these broadsheets, whether it takes the allegorical form of the "world upside down" or a narrative display of male violence (figs. 1 and 11), indicates that reformed marriage did not depend, as Ozment suggests, on an "ordered equality" between husbands and wives. The intensity of the violence of these confrontations indicates that the social teaching of the Reformation had less to do with the equality between the sexes, less to do with the promotion of the social status of women, and more to do with their continued social and economic oppression.

## NOTES

This chapter is adapted from chapter 5 of my book *Peasants, Warriors, and Wives: Popular Imagery in the Reformation* (Chicago: Univ. of Chicago Press, 1989), © 1989 by The University of Chicago, all rights reserved, and appears here with the permission of the publisher.

1 / Steven Ozment, *When Fathers Ruled: Family Life in Reformation Europe* (Cambridge: Harvard Univ. Press, 1983), 99.

2 / Max Geisberg, *The German Single-Leaf Woodcut*, 4 vols., trans. Walter Strauss (New York: Hacker Art Books, 1974), vol. 3, cat. no. 1176.

3 / Hans Moser, "Die Geschichte der Fastnacht im Spiegel von Archivforschungen: Zur Bearbeitung bayerische Quellen," in *Fasnacht*, ed. Hermann Bausinger (Tübingen: Tübinger Vereinigung für Volkskunde, 1964), 15–41; idem, "Städtische Fasnacht des Mittelalters," in *Masken: Zwischen Speil und Ernst*, ed. Hermann Bausinger (Tübingen: Tübinger Vereinigung für Volkskunde, 1967), 135–202, esp. 186–89.

4 / Geisberg, *Woodcut*, vol. 3, cat. no. 1181. Heinrich Rottinger, *Die Bilderbogen des Hans Sachs* (Strasbourg: Heitz, 1927), cat. no. 561. For the text see Heinrich Adelbert von Keller and E. Goetze, eds., *Hans Sachs*, 26 vols. (Hildesheim: G. Olms Verlagsbuchhandlung, 1964; 1st ed. Stuttgart, 1870), 5:179–83.

5 / See Bob Scribner, "Reformation, Carnival, and the World Turned Upside Down," *Social History* 3 (1978): 303–29.

6 / Sebastian Brant, *The Ship of Fools*, trans. and ed. Edwin Zeydel (New York: Columbia Univ. Press, 1944), 170.

7 / Jan Piet Filedt Kok, ed., *Livelier than Life: The Master of the Amsterdam Cabinet or the Housebook Master*, exhibition catalog, Rijksmuseum, Amsterdam, 1985, cat. no. 54. The Housebook Master was active on the

Middle Rhine in the late fifteenth century. The engraving is usually dated in the 1480s.

8 / For the iconography of the power of women in the late Middle Ages see Friedrich Maurer, "Der *Topos* von den Minnesklaven: Zur Geschichte eine thematischen Gemeinschaft zwischen bildenden Kunst und Dichtung im Mittelalter," *Deutsche Vierteljahrschrift für Literaturwissenschaft und Geistesgeschichte* 27 (1953): 182–206; and Susan Smith, " 'To Woman's Wiles I Fell': The Power of Women *Topos* and the Development of Medieval Secular Art," Ph.D. diss. Univ. of Pennsylvania, 1978.

9 / Filedt Kok, *Livelier than Life*, cat. no. 89. For other examples see the engravings by Master b. x. g., cat. nos. 95 and 102.

10 / For the text of this poem see Heinrich Adelbert von Keller, ed., *Fastnachtspiele aus den funfzehnten Jahrhundert*, 4 vols. (Stuttgart, 1853–58), 2:1278–82. The poem was first published about 1480.

11 / The theme of the battle for the pants is already found in a French tale dating from the thirteenth century. See Theodore Neff, *La satire des femmes dans la poésie lyrique française du Moyen-Age* (Geneva: Slatkine Reprints, 1974; 1st ed. Paris, 1900), 21. The metaphor is widely used in European literature from at least the fourteenth century. Among its earliest occurrences in German literature is the following passage from Heinrich Wittenwiler's poem the *Ring* of about 1400 (my translation):

> *Be master in your house!*
> *If your wife wears the pants,*
> *She'll be your scourge and your curse*
> *Since this defies God and his law*
> *You will become a laughing stock.*
> *(Bis du herr in deinem haus!*
> *Wiss, and träyt dein weib die pruoch,*
> *Sey wirt dein hagel und dein fluoch*
> *Wider Got und sein gepott;*
> *Hier zuo wirst den leuten spott.)*

Quoted by Frans Brietzmann, *Die böse frau in der deutschen Litteratur des Mittelalters* (Berlin: Mayer and Muller, 1912), 128. In the Middle Ages pants seem to have been an exclusively male garment. See C. Willet and P. Cunnington, *The History of Underclothes* (London: Gordon Press, 1981; 1st ed. 1951), chap. 1.

12 / See Lené Dresen-Coenders, "De strijd om de broek: De verhouding man/vrouw in het begin van de moderne tijd (1450–1630)," *De Revisor* 4 (1977): 29–37, 77; also Walter Gibson, "Some Flemish Popular Prints from Hieronymous Cock and his Contemporaries," *Art Bulletin* 60 (1978): 673–81.

13 / Max Lehrs, *Geschichte und kritischer Katalog des deutschen, niederländischen und französischen Kupferstichs im XV Jahrhundert*, 10 vols. (Nendeln: Kraus Reprints, 1969; 1st ed. Vienna, 1908), vol. 9. cat. no. 504. Israhel van Meckenem was active at Bocholt at the end of the fifteenth century.

14 / Hans Walther, ed., *Proverbia sententiaeque latinitatis medii aevii: Lateinische Sprichwörter und Sentenzen des Mittelalters*, 6 vols. (Göttingen: Vandenboeck and Ruprecht, 1959–67), vol. 3, part 2b, cat. no. 9016: "Femina demonio tribus assibus est mala peior."

15 / W. L. Schreiber, *Handbuch des Holz und Metallschnitte des XV Jahrhunderts*, 8 vols. (Leipzig: K. W. Hiersemann, 1926–30), vol. 4, cat.

no. 1974m. See also Walter Gibson, "Bruegel, Dulle Griet and Sexist Politics in the Sixteenth Century," in *Pieter Bruegel und seine Welt*, ed. O. von Simson and M. Winner (Berlin: Mann, 1979), 9–16.

16 / Jacob Grimm and Wilhelm Grimm, *Deutsches Wörterbuch*, s.v. "Windelwascher."

17 / Geisberg, *Woodcut*, vol. 3, cat. no. 1107; Röttinger, *Bilderbogen*, cat. no. 719; Nuremberg, Stadtgeschichtlichen Museen, *Die Welt des Hans Sachs*, exhibiton catalog, Nuremberg, 1970, cat. no. 168. The broadsheet was probably published in 1536.

18 / Proverbs 30:10. Sebastian Franck, *Sprichwörter, Schöne, Weise, Klugreden* . . . (Frankfurt am Main, 1548), cited by Joyce Irwin, *Womanhood in Radical Protestantism, 1525–1675* (New York: Mellen, 1979), 69.

19 / My translation has been adapted from that provided by Ozment, *When Fathers Ruled*, 52–53.

20 / See Keith Moxey, "Master E. S. and the Folly of Love," *Simiolus* 11 (1980): 125–48.

21 / Lehrs, *Katalog*, vol. 2, cat. no. 213. Master E. S. was active on the Upper Rhine from about 1450 to 1466.

22 / Geisberg, *Woodcut*, vol. 1, cat. no. 158; Röttinger, *Bilderbogen*, cat. no. 900. Sach's text, which was entered into his collected works with the date 1589, is thought by Röttinger to have been composed earlier.

23 / For a discussion of the way in which the image of the unruly woman was used for revolutionary purposes in this period, see Natalie Davis, "Women on Top," in *Society and Culture in Early Modern France* (Stanford: Stanford Univ. Press, 1965), 124–51, esp. 131.

24 / My translation is based on that provided by Ozment, *When Fathers Ruled*, 76–77.

25 / "The Estate of Marriage," 1530, trans. Walter Brandt in *Luther's Works*, vol. 45, ed. J. Pelikan and H. Lehmann (Philadelphia: Concordia, 1962), 18. For Luther's views on marriage see Waldemar Kawerau, *Die Reformation und die Ehe* (Halle, 1892); Reinhold Seeberg, "Luthers Anschauung von den Geschlechtsleben der Ehe und ihre geschichtliche Stellung," *Luther Jahrbuch* 7 (1925): 72–122; Lilly Zarnke, "Die naturhafte Eheanschauung des jungen Luther," *Archiv für Kulturgeschichte* 25 (1935): 281–305; idem, "Der geistliche Sinn der Ehe bei Luther," *Theologische Studien und Kritiken* 106 (1934): 20–39; Olavi Lahteenmaki, *Sexus und Ehe bei Luther* (Turku: Schriften der Luther-Agricola-Gesselschaft, 1955); Roland Bainton, "Changing Ideas and Ideals in the Sixteenth Century," in *Collected Papers in Church History*, 3 vols. (Boston: Beacon Press, 1962–64), 1:154–82; Klaus Suppan, *Die Ehelehre Martin Luthers* (Salzburg: Universitatsverlag A. Pustet, 1971).

26 / "A Sermon on the Estate of Marriage," 1519, trans. James Atkinson, in *Luther's Works*, vol. 44 (Philadelphia: Concordia, 1966), 9.

27 / For medieval teaching on this subject, see Kari Elisabeth Borresen, *Subordination and Equivalence: The Nature and Role of Women in Augustine and Thomas Aquinas*, trans. Charles H. Talbot (Washington, D.C.: University Press of America, 1970, 1st ed. Oslo, 1968).

28 / "Lectures on Genesis," 1535–36, trans. George Schick, in *Luther's Works*, vol. 1 (St. Louis: Concordia, 1958), 115.

29 / "The Order of Marriage," 1529, trans. Paul Zeller Strodach and Ulrich Leupold, in *Luther's Works*, vol. 53 (Philadelphia: Concordia, 1965), 114.

30 / See Franz Lau, " 'Ausserlich Ordnung' und 'Weltlich Ding' " in *Luthers Theologie* (Göttingen: Hubert, 1932); Johannes Heckel, *Lex charitatis: Eine juristische Untersuchung über das Recht in der Theologie Martin Luthers* (Cologne: Bayerischen Akademie der Wissenschaften, 1973).

31 / "Der Grosse Katechismus," 1529, ed. D. Albrecht, D. Brenner and J. Luther, in *D. Martin Luthers Werke: Kritische Gesamtausgabe*, vol. 30, pt. 1 (Graz: Akademische Druck- und Verlagsanstalt, 1964; 1st ed. Weimar, 1910), 152: "Also das alle die man herrn heisset an der eltern stad sind und von yhn krafft und macht zuregieren nemen müssen. Daher sind auch nach der schrifft alle Veter heissen, als die ynn yhrem regiment das vater ampt treiben und veterlich hertz gegen den yhren tragen sollen. Wie auch von alters her die Römer und andere sprachen herrn und frawen ym haus Patres et Matres familias, das ist haus veter und haus mutter, genennet haben. Also auch yhre landsfursten und oberherrn haben sie Patres patriae, das ist veter des gantzen lands geheissen und die wir Christen sein wöllen, zu grossen schanden, das wir sie nicht auch also heissen oder zum wenigsten dafur halten und ehren."

32 / Gerhard Pfeiffer, "Entscheidung zur Reformation," in *Nürnberg: Geschichte eine europäischer Stadt* (Munich: Beck, 1971), 152–54.

33 / For the history of the order of Saint Clare see Nuremberg, Kaiserburg, *Caritas Pirckheimer, 1467–1532*, exhibition catalog, Nuremberg, 1982.

34 / See Gerhard Müller, ed. *Andreas Osiander d. Ä. Gesamtausgabe*, 6 vols. (Gütersloh: Gütersloher Verlagshaus G. Mohn, 1975–81), 2: 195 ff., 290 ff.

35 / Judith Harvey, "The Influence of the Reformation on Nurnberg Marriage Laws, 1520–25," Ph.D. diss., Ohio State University, 1972, 55. For the situation before the Reformation see Rudolph Sohm, *Das Recht der Eheschliessung* (Aalen: Scientia Verlag, 1966; 1st ed. Weimar, H. Böhlan, 1875), chap. 5; Richard Köbner, "Die Eheauffassung des ausgehenden deutschen Mittelalters," *Archiv für Kulturgeschichte* 9 (1911): 136–98, 279–318; Augus Jegel, "Altnürnberger Hochzeitsbrauch und Eherecht besonders bis zum Augsang des 16. Jahrhunderts," *Mitteilungen des Verein für Geschichte der Stadt Nürnberg* 44 (1953): 238–74.

36 / Harvey, "Influence of the Reformation," 60.

37 / For recent evaluations see Natalie Davis, "City Women and Religious Change in Sixteenth-Century France," in *A Sampler of Women's Studies*, ed. Dorothy McGuigan (Ann Arbor: Univ. of Michigan Press, 1973), 18–45; Jane Dempsey Douglass, "Women and the Continental Reformation," in *Religion and Sexism: Images of Women in the Jewish Christian Traditions*, ed. Rosemary Ruether (New York: Simon and Schuster, 1974), 293–318; Eleanor McLaughlin, "Male and Female in Christian Tradition: Was There a Reformation in the Sixteenth Century?" in *Male and Female: Christian Approaches to Sexuality* (New York: Random House, 1976), 39–52; Lawrence Stone, *The Family: Sex and Marriage in England, 1500–1600* (New York: Harper and Row, 1977), ch. 5: "The Reinforcement of Patriarchy"; Ozment, *When Fathers Ruled*.

38 / Rudolf Endres, "Zur Einwohnerzahl und Bevolkerungstruktur Nürnberg im 15. und 16. Jahrhundert," *Mitteilungen des Verein für Geschichte der Stadt Nürnberg* 57 (1970): 242–71.

39 / Rudolf Endres, "Zur Lage der Nürnberger Handwerkerschaft zur Zeit von Hans Sachs," *Jahrbuch für Fränkische Landesforschung* 37 (1977): 107–23.

40 / See Karl Bücher, *Die Frauenfrage im Mittelalter* (Tübingen: H. Laupp'sche Buchhandlung, 1910); Luise Hess, *Die deutsche Frauenberufe des Mittelalters* (Munich: Neuer Filser-Verlag, 1940); Merry Weisner Wood, *Working Women in Renaissance Germany* (New Brunswick, N.J.: Rutgers Univ. Press, 1986); Martha Howell, *Women, Production, and Patriarchy in Late Medieval Cities* (Chicago: Univ. of Chicago Press, 1986).

41 / Wood, *Working Women*, 189–90.

42 / J. Hajnal, "European Marriage Patterns in Perspective," in *Population in History*, ed. D. Glass and D. Eversley (Chicago: Aldine, 1965), 101–43.

Der arm götze

Ach weh ach weh mir armen narren
Wie hart zeuch ich in disem karren
Darzu hat mich weybnemen bracht
Ich wolt ich het mirs nie gedacht
Se man ist kumen in mein hauß
Zeucht mir schwert / bruch vn tasche auß
Nacht vnd tag hab ich kein rhu
Vnd kein gutes wort darzu
Mein trew ist jr nicht angenehm
Meine wort sind jr gar widerzehm
Also geschicht noch manchem man
Der nichts hatt / waiß oder kan
Wil doch bey zeyt ein frawen han.

Die fraw spucht.
Ey lieber gesell ists aber war?
...
Mit spülen / waschen / kochen vnd keren /
Ich wolt ehe weybnemen verschweren.

Der geselle.
Was sagt jr darzu junckfraw seyn /
Wolt jr auch also Sy man seyn
Vnd selbs haben in ewr bende
Schwert / bruch / taschen vnd regiment
Mit wort beissen / schnarre vn schneide
Das kund vnd möcht ich re nicht leide
Sole ich mit euch rauffen vn schla:
Villeycht müst ich in einen wagen gen
Wie diser man im karren leyden
Vnd alle freud vnd kürtzweyl meyden
Sol ich mein fres leben verteren /
Ich wolt ehe weybnemen verschweren.

Die junckfraw.
Gesel glaube mir bey meiner eh:
Sölches gewalts ich nicht beger
Wann jr wöllet nach eben ringen
So seyd selb man in allen dingen
Vnd wenn jr mich allein gewert
Was einer frawen zugehert
Zu lieb vnd layd notdürffte vnd ehren
So will ich anders nicht begeren
Dann allzeyt ewren willen thun
Daran solt jr kein zweiffel han
In ewrem dienst wil ich ye ben
Vnd euch in stäter freundschafft lieben.
Wil euch mit keinem wort betrieben.

Die Nerrin.
Hüt dich bey leib du junger knecht
Ich arme nerrin sag dir recht
Man sagt vil gutes von der Ee
Sy hiess vil göllicher das wehe /
Du müst leyden biß in den tode
Vil angst / sorg / kummer vnd auch not
Das dir kein mensch nicht wenden kan
Findstu doch sunst wol frewlein schan
Die geren thun den willen deyn
Nur vmb ein kenblein mit weyn
Darnach magst du sie faren lan
Vnd ein andere nemen an
Eyn ehweyb müstu ewig han.

Der weiß man.
Gesel ich wil dich bessers leren
Thu dich nicht an ein nerrin keren
Hüt dich allzeyt vor büren list
Du wirst betrogen zu aller frist
Nym dir ein frewlein zu der Ehe
Got geb wie es dir mit je gehe
So bleyb bey jr in lieb vnd leyt
Vnd biß gedultig alle zeit
Ob dir begegnet kummers vil
Gedenck dir es sey Gottes wil
Ner sie im schweyß deyns angesicht
Wie Got am ersten Genesis spricht
Gedult vnd leyden ist ein port
Durch die wir kumen an das ort
Da die Engel wonung han
Also spricht Albrecht Glockendan.

Fig. 1. Erhard Schön, *There Is No Greater Treasure Here on Earth than an Obedient Wife Who Covets Honor*, woodcut, 1533. (Photo, Max Geisberg, *The German Single-Leaf Woodcut*, 4 vols., trans. Walter Strauss (New York, 1974), vol. 3, cat. no. 1176)

Fig. 2. Erhard Schön, *The Housemaids Pull the Plough*, woodcut, 1532.
(Photo, Geisberg, Vienna, Albertina)

Vil dünt jnn dorheyt hye beharren
Vnd zießen vast eyn schweren karrßen
Dort würt der recht wag naßer faren

## võ dē weg der sellikeit

Gott laßt eyn narren nit verston
Syn wunder / die er hat gethon
Vnd täglich důt / dar vmß verdyrßt
Gar mancher narr / der zittlich styrßt

Fig. 3. Albrecht Dürer, *On the Road to Salvation*, woodcut illustrating chapter 47 of Sebastian Brant's *Ship of Fools* (Basel, 1494). (Photo, Hans Koegler ed., *Das Narrenschiff* [Basel, 1913])

Fig. 4. Housebook Master, *Phyllis and Aristotle*, engraving. (Photo, Amsterdam, Rijksprentenkabinet)

Fig. 5. Housebook Master, *Coat of Arms with a Peasant Standing on His Head*, engraving. (Photo, Amsterdam, Rijksprentenkabinet)

**Eyn lieb genant der pöß rauch**

**Jn der flam weis**

Fig. 6. Anonymous, *Battle for the Pants*, woodcut frontispiece to Hans
Folz's poem *The Evil Smoke*. (Photo, Gustav Konnecke, *Bilderatlas zur
Geschichte der deutschen Nationallitteratur* [Marburg, 1895], 101)

Fig. 7. Israhel van Meckenem, *Battle for the Pants*, engraving. (Photo, Berlin, Kupferstichkabinett, Staatliche Museen Preussischer Kulturbesitz)

Ich kam auff ein gewilde weyt
Do sach ich zů der selben tzeit
Ein übel weyb das ist war
Strepten mit des teuffels schar
Es geschach auff ein morgen frü
Die teuffel seczte des übeln weib zů
Mit mangerley schalckhait
Einer schwůr auff seinen eyd
Er wölt grousse ding began
Wölt das übel weib allein bestan
Sie hyelten gegen einannder
Die teuffel mit prem pancz
Das übel weib stůnd allein dort
Vnd sprach greuweliche wort
Wol her ir teuffel alle gemein
Beyde grouß vnd auch klein
Wir wöllen an annder peyssen
Zerren grymmen vnd teyssen
Sie zerriß in kurtzer stund
Der teuffel mer dann tausunt
Ir aller meyster der lag tot
Do hůb sich angst vnd not
Vber das übel weib also
We we sie thůt vns allen also
Do sprach ein teuffelischer man
Von dem strept sullen wir lan
Vnnd wider in die helle faren
Da müge wir vns wol bewaren
Vnd wo sie in die helle komen
Ir einer sprach bey namen
Vn were wir lenger hie gewese
Vnser kainer wer vor ir genesen

Von der bösen vnseligen dyet
Ir aller syn in das wo ryet
Wol vns lieben gesellen mein
Das wir also entrunnen sein
Wann wer mit übeln weiben
Sein tzeit můß hye vertreyben
Dem wer vil weger der tod
Denn das er köme in solhe not
Ist sie übel vnnd arg von art
We im das er ye geboren wart
Ist er traurig so ist sie fro
Wil er denn sunst sie will so
Wil er gen sie wil lauffen
Wil er strelen sie wil rauffen
Wil er traben sie wil tzelten
Wil er kpfeln sie wil schelten
Wil er essen sie wil trincken
Wil er springen sie wil hincken
Wil er denn ligen sie wil sitzen
Wil er auffsten sie wil schwitzen
Wil er denn kalt sie wil heyß
So er sie narrt so läst sy ein scheiß
Sy gat tzů einem pfaffen
Also kan sie es geschaffen
Darumb wer ein übel weyb hab
Der thů sich ir bey tzeit ab
Vnnd füre sie da in die hellen
Zů den teuffelischen gesellen
Das ist von den übeln weyben
Die tugenthafften leyd vertreyben
Des das übel weyb nit enkan
Darumb hasset sie yederman

Fig. 8. Anonymous, *The Old Woman and the Devil*, woodcut. (Photo, Eugen Diederichs, *Deutsches Leben der Vergangenheit in Bildern*, 2 vols. [Jena, 1908], vol. 1, fig., 462)

Fig. 9. Hans Schäuffelein, *Diaper Washer*, woodcut to lost poem *Ho, Ho, Diaper Washer* by Hans Sachs, 1536? (Photo, Coburg, Kupferstichkabinett, Kunstsammlungen, Veste Coburg)

Fig. 10. Master E. S., *Lust and the Fool*, engraving. (Photo, Dresden Kupferstichkabinet)

# Die Meünerley beüt einer bösen Frawen/sampt jren neün aygenschafften.

Als ich eins abents gieng spacieren
Ward einer sach nach fantasieren
Gieng auff vnd ab die Haller wisen
Kein gsellen einer der sich zwar
Verhayrat het in disem Jar
Er war zerkratzet vns zerkrelt
Den grüst ich vnd zü red jn stelt
Wo er gewest wer vntern katzen
Er sprach/du darfst mich nit seer fatzen
Die katzen haben mein nicht gfelt
Mein Fraw die hat mir also gstrelt
Ich sprach/wie hat sich das begeben
Er sprach/nun hör vnd merck mich eben
Mein weyb ist nicht wie ander leut
Dann sie hat wol neünerley beüt
Beinander/des hat sie pur
Jn jr auch neünerley natur
Des müß yegkliche baut allein
Besonderbar geschlagen sein
So wil kein schlagen an jr flecken
Ich sprach/thü mir die sach entecken
Was ichs verstee/ich bitt dich drum
Ich sprach/in Summa summarum
Als ich am Montag kam vom wein
Vnd was ich fragt die Frawen mein
So wolt sie mir kein antwort geben
So dacht ich bey mir selbert eben
Ich hab offt ghört von alten leuten
Dich weyber sind von neün beuten
Er mit zü teyl ist eine worten
Also ergrimet ich in zoren
Vnd thet jr die Stockfisch baut plewen
Am nechsten sich vor mir zü schewen
Antwort zü geben auff mein frag
So bald ich jr gab noch ein schlag
So thet ichs auff Bernbaut troffen
So kam ich tör jr her geloffen
Vnd fieng beymlichen an zü prummen
Diewol ich kein wort hab vernummen
Hab jr noch ein güts an schlaff
Vnd sic gleich auff Genßhaut diaff
Ist fieng sie an ein solches schnadern
In schwatzen klapern vnd thadern
Ich ein ein wort antworten thet
Es thet die weyl wol siebne gredt
Thet mit hönworten mich fast essen
Irst thet ichs auff die Hunzbaut treffen
Irst fieng sie hefftig anzü pellen
Vnd bieng mit an vil schamper schellen

Ich wer ein Esel/Narr vnd tropff
Ich gab jr noch ein güts an kopff
Do traff ichs auff den Hasen palck
Sie loff darüon vnd schray du schalck
Du Hüren jeger vnd Eebrecher
Du Spilgur vnd du wein zecher
Stach mich mit der gleich worten spitzig
Ich luff jr nach wurd wider hitzig
Vnd stach sie wider zü den oren
Traff sie gleich auff die rofbaut voren
Do schlugs auff sam der windt her wehet
Vnd stieß mich das ich mich verdrehet
Erst traff ichs auff die baut der katzen
Do fiels auff mich mit kreln vnd kratzen
Also wölt sie mich zü flecken reissen
Das schreyen kundt ich kaum verpeissen
Ich zuckt ein prügel lanck genüg
Damit ichs auff die Sew baut schlüg
Tantzt jr auff dem rück vnd den armen
Das sie sich selbert thet erbarmen
Vnd fieng an zü greynen vnd röln
Als ich sie war noch baser knüln
Erst traff ichs auff die menschen baut
Do rüfft sie vmb gnad gar laut
Vnd sprach mein hertz lieber Man
Irst auff ich wil sein nymmer than
Mich hat ein nachpawrin verfürt
Zü handlen das sich nicht gebürt

Der wil ich volgen nymmer mer
Hab dir zü pfandt mein weyblich eer
Vnd fiel mir weynend vmb den hals
Ich sprach/es sey vergeben alß
Doch kum nymmer das rat ich dir
Dich auff zübaumen gegen mir
So macht wir mit einander freide
Wie lang es wert das waiß ichnit
So hat der bader sich angspunnen
Wie wol ich hab die schlacht gewunnen
Ist mir mein teyl auch tückisch woren
Im angsicht hals vnd vmb die oren
Das ich der schlacht nicht laugnen mag
Ich sprach/mein gsell merck was ich sag
Jr jungen Eemänner seyt zü gech
Zü mütwillig/doll/dum vnd feech
Wenn euch ein weyb nit schön ansicht
Oder nach ewerm sinn zü spricht
Oder nicht aller sach recht geyt
Wenn jr schon gar vnheuflich seyt
Wölt jrs mit schlagen als auß richten
Das zimpt ein biderman mit nichten
Vngraten Ee werden darauß
Man müß mit krieg nit halten hauß
Sonder mit frid vnd freündschafft mer
Paulus vns mannen geyt ein ler
Die weyb mit vernunfft zü regieren
Nit pollern/grob tyrannisieren

Weyl sie der schwechst werckzeug sein
Derhalben straff dein weyb allein
Mit vernünfftigen güten worten
Zwischen euch beyden an den orten
Mein liebes weyb/das sol nicht thon
Vnd jhenes steet dir übel an
Schaw diß ist schand/vnd jbens ist schad
Wilt haben mein gunst vnd genad
So stee des müssig/vnd volg mir
Dargegen wil ich volgen dir
Wo mir ein ding steet übel an
Wil handlen als ein redlich Man
Vnd wil kein böß wort dir mer geben
So müg wir wol vnd freündlich leben
Bey leyb laß niemandt dich verhetzen
Das du dich gegen mir wölst setzen
Der gleich sol niemandt mich verfüren
Zü handlen das nicht thü gepüren
Was dir selt solu klagen mir
Was mir bricht wil ich sagen dir
Du darfst dich vor mir gar nicht schweren
Kein mesch maint vns mit gantze trewen
Als wir zwey gböten ye züsamen
Was wolt wir zancken vnd grißgramen
Füren ein solch Teuffelisch leben
Vnd vns vnter die leut aufgeben
Die halten dann nichts von vns beyden
Schaw also straff dein weyb bescheyden
Ist denn ein eer jn jrem leyb
So zeudst auff jr ein ghorsam weyb
Wie man dein spricht ein ein frumer Man
Ein frumes weyb im zieben kan
Wo sie aber blieb aygenwillig
Nicht handlet das wer gleich vnd billig
Wolt dir gar nicht sein vntbenig
Vngehorsam vnd widerspennig
Wo sie rümoret noch dar gegen
So magstu straffen sie mit schlagen
Doch mit vernunfft vnd wol bescheyden
Das es vnschedlich sey euch beyden
Also went süß vnd sawers für
Wie einem biderman gepür
Biß jr zületzt eins synnes werdt
Dardurch euch bie in zeyt auff erdt
Frid/freüp vnd freündeligkeyt erwachs
Im Keling standt / das wunscht Hans
                                    (Sachs

¶ Gedrückt durch Hans
        Guldenmundt.

Fig. 11. Barthel Beham, *The Nine Hides of an Angry Wife*, woodcut.
(Photo, Geisberg, *Woodcut*, vol. 1, cat. no. 158)

9

Thomas Head

## The Religion of the *Femmelettes:* Ideals and Experience among Women in Fifteenth- and Sixteenth-Century France

WOMEN OF THE EARLY SIXTEENTH CENTURY from virtually every class and nationality were passionately interested in the changes of religious belief and practice introduced by the reform movements. A few examples will suffice to illustrate this breadth of female religious concern. The Memmingen city council issued an order prohibiting servant women from discussing religion when fetching water from the wells.[1] The notes made by Elizabeth Kensam, an Englishwoman of the merchant class, in the endpapers of her Book of Hours suggest that she ranked the change of the language of Sunday services from Latin into English as an event of similar import to the birth of her children.[2] King Henri de Navarre on occasion slapped his wife Marguerite and, in the words of their daughter, "forbade her sharply to meddle in matters of doctrine."[4]

Most historians who have surveyed the role of women in the Reformation have concluded that women benefited from it, most particularly in the area of marriage and the family. In a pioneering study, Jane Douglass concluded, "It is difficult to find evidence that any conscious effort was made by the Reformation to change the social status of women. Yet the new theology did contribute to greater freedom and equality for women."[4] Douglass emphasized that such gains occurred primarily in the domestic sphere. Nancy Roelker went further: "By permitting wives as well as husbands to instigate divorce proceedings, Calvin elevated their dignity and increased their legal rights. Enacted into Genevan law, this could not help but raise the position of women to a higher level. . . . The special responsibility of the mother for family worship . . . became a feature of French Calvinism in succeeding generations. Woman is thus not relegated to separate and unequal status in the family or confined to the 'calling of domesticity,' even though *le chemin de la foi* runs through the kitchen and the nursery as through all places of useful work."[5] Roger Stauffenegger, however, pointed out the dangers of evaluating social change on the evidence of theological abstraction or the experience of the high nobility.[6] Divorce, for example, was only rarely allowed in Calvinist communities and marriage practice seems to have changed little.[7] Taking such social historical research into account, Natalie Davis tempered earlier conclusions by contrasting the varying achievements of reformed and Catholic solutions to the relations between the sexes, although she implied that the former, despite its problems, went further in promoting equality.[8] More recent evaluations have been even less sanguine.[9]

Virtually all historians agree that one important social fact did not change: church institutions, and those of society more generally, continued to be governed by misogynistic assumptions. The subordinate position of women may be effectively illustrated by the fact that, in French religious treatises, female audiences were addressed by male and female writers alike as *femmelettes,* or "little women."[10] Whether it was German serving women being silenced by a Lutheran city council or French noblewomen by their Catholic husbands, women did not have any sanctioned public authority. Even in the private sphere of the family, they were governed by their spouses. A recent survey of Lutheran pamphlet literature on marriage and the family is entitled *When Fathers Ruled.*[11] While the works of such male reformers as Luther and Calvin did provide a new religious value for the married state, their attempt to eliminate the option of the celibate life as found in monasticism eliminated one of the important private spheres of authority open to women and thus limited their potential role almost exclusively to the sphere of the family. In Dagmar Lorenz's telling phrase, the Lutheran Reformation moved women "from the cloister to the kitchen."[12]

Merry Wiesner has warned that a narrow focus on the development of the family in writing the history of the sixteenth century threatens to ignore this continuation of misogyny in religious and social institutions.[13] In order to write the history of women in the Reformation, historians must listen not only to the voices of male religious writers but also to the voices of women themselves in their numerically few, but quite powerful, religious writings. They must attempt to discover not only what the spiritual ideals offered to women were but also how women received those ideals and put them into practice. In the present study we will examine three works written by or for bourgeois women in the early stages of the reform movement in French-speaking lands. This examination will help to suggest the insufficiency of certain assumptions about the religious benefits brought by the reformers to women.[14] While I do not mean to claim that the experience of the women described here was duplicated in other ethnic, geographic, or class contexts, I do think that these insufficient assumptions are common to much historiography concerning women in arenas of the Reformation.

First it is necessary to place women's experience of the Reformation, like the work of male theologians, in late medieval perspective. The women of the early sixteenth century inherited from the late Middle Ages a distinctively female spirituality. This tradition was distinct from male spirituality both in terms of the ideals which male clerics offered to women by means such as sermons and the literature of spiritual advice and in terms of the ways in which women actually experienced those ideals and put them into daily practice. Within this theological and pastoral tradition, marriage was seen as a device for propagating the human race, created by God in recognition of human fraility. In sermons, women were bombarded with references both to their inferior nature and to the inherent temptation which they provided by their supposed sexual insatiability. John Bromyard, for example, castigated the woman who "in a single day, by her dancing or her perambulation through the town, inflames with the fire of lust—it may be—twenty of those who behold her, damning the souls whom God has created." At the same time preachers urged their audiences to practice chaste marriages, by which they meant unions in which sexual intercourse was practiced only rarely and within the confines of canon law.[15] Childbearing became the defining fact of women's nature. It was a process fraught with danger and pain, and women were urged to turn to other women for help, both saintly intercessors, such as St. Margaret, and to midwives, perhaps the only predominantly female profession.[16] The examples of female saints—such as Mary Magdalene, a repentent prostitute, and Elizabeth of Hungary, a queen who rejected suitors—were held up as correctives to the inherent faults of female nature.

The only escape provided women from complete subordination in the marital relationship was a life vowed to virginity, described for both men and women as a marriage to Christ. This ideal was offered to women as a means of transcending their nature. One late medieval preacher claimed that the Old Testament ideal for women had been fecundity, but that fecundity had been replaced and thus perfected in the New Testament by the ideal of virginity.[17] The ideal of marriage to Christ was interpreted with particular literalness when applied to women. In a sermon directed to nuns on the feast of the Virgin Mary, Stephen Langton described the spiritual attainments of his audience in terms of the various vestments and ornaments of a secular bride.[18] In an English vernacular text, *Hali Maidenhead*, a clerical author told the anchoresses of his audience that Christ was a more handsome lover and a better provider than any earthly spouse.[19] Jean Gerson, one of the most influential writers of late medieval France, noted that virginal female souls became pregnant with Christ.[20] Women, for their part, often embodied these ideals in their experience. Hildegard of Bingen had her nuns dress in nuptial garb as brides of Christ.[21] Christina of Markyate used her betrothal to Christ as the basis of a legal claim to avoid marriage to a man.[22] The belly of Dorothy of Montau swelled in a mime of pregnancy when she took the Eucharist.[23]

The research of Caroline Bynum and others has shown how late medieval women in France and elsewhere reinterpreted the rituals and symbols provided for them by male clerics.[24] Most of these women did so in the context of the convent, but some few, like Dorothy of Montau and Margery Kempe, did so within secular marriages. Their use of such metaphors as the maternity of Jesus or the marriage to Christ was different from that of their male contemporaries.[25] In particular they developed a set of pietistic practices related to the preparation and consumption of food as ritualized in the Eucharist. One of the most dramatic of these was severe fasts in which the woman attempted to live solely on the sustenance provided by the Eucharistic elements. Such fasts were an attempt to use the sacrament of the Eucharist, which had to be consecrated by a male cleric, in a manner not available to those male clerics. One of the most important services of Bynum's research is to point out that such piety was not a denial of the physical body. These women rather used their bodies as a means for gaining salvation. The sexual was denied, but the writings of female mystics, far more than their male contemporaries, celebrated the bodily in writings infused with an almost erotic quality.

This distinctively female spirituality of the later Middle Ages was intimately bound up with a concern for salvation achieved through penitence and pietistic action. Women were particularly dependent upon such bodily oriented means of salvation because they were seen in the theological, philosophical, and medical traditions as being in their very essence physical, as opposed to spiritual or rational, beings.[26] Such means were readily available in the highly praxis-oriented penitential and sacramental systems of late medieval Christianity. That mode of seeking salvation, however, came to be labeled "works righteousness" and rejected by Luther and his fellow reformers. Nevertheless it was just such forms of "works righteousness" that stood at the center of women's experience of Christianity through the early years of the Reformation.

As we have seen, there were two spheres of action open to late medieval women, both defined by marriage: one the physical marriage to a spouse, the second the metaphorical marriage to Christ. As both social and religious beings women were defined in terms of their relationships to men. Neither the kitchen nor the cloister offered much in the way of sanctioned public authority. As Herlihy has concluded, "By many social indicators—access to property, power or knowledge—the position of women deteriorated across the long centuries of the Middle Ages. Women in fact fared better in barbarian Europe of the sixth or seventh centuries than they did in the cultured Europe of the fifteenth and sixteenth." The social institution of marriage was, however, undergoing major social changes during the fifteenth and sixteenth centuries, particularly in demographic terms that had little to do with religion. In a process that is still understood only for certain regions, the average age of marriage for both men and women was on the increase. Nevertheless, in reconsidering Joan Kelly-Gadol's famous pronouncement that women did not have a Renaissance, Herlihy has been forced to look to "charismatic" women, such as Catherine of Siena and Joan of Arc, who exercised public authority outside of, and in virtual opposition to, traditional institutions.[27]

In particular, women were barred by canon law, based on the well-known Pauline prohibitions (1 Corinthians 14:34; 1 Timothy 2:11-12), from having a public voice in church. In one of the most commonly printed glosses on those verses, Nicholas of Lyra stated that women were prohibited from all public religious speech, including prophecy, because such was "repugnant to the female gender."[28] Even Jean Gerson—a man praised by Christine de Pisan as a defender of women—denied women any teaching role within the church: "Every teaching of women . . . is to be held suspect . . . because women are too easily seduced, because they are too obstinately seducers, because it is not fitting that they should be knowers of divine wisdom."[29] Certain forms of female authority were recognized, however, in indirect manners or in exceptional circumstances. Some preachers, such as Thomas of Chobham, assumed that women would play a didactic role in the home, for "no priest is able to soften the heart of a man the way his wife can."[30]

Moreover, the Acts of the Apostles provided—both in the person of Priscilla who converted her husband to Christianity and in the quotation of Joel 2:28 ("your sons and your daughters will prophesy")—a warrant for severely limited forms of public religious authority for women. Thus the Franciscan theologian Eustachius of Arras admitted that *mulieres sanctes,* such as Mary Magdalene and Catherine of Alexandria, could be specially ordained by the Holy Spirit to speak authoritatively in a manner similar to preaching.[31] In commenting on these verses Nicholas of Lyra was forced to admit, in seeming contradiction of his gloss on the Pauline passages, that the gift of prophecy was given "indifferently" to both sexes.[32] Numerous female visionaries within the celibate life—some who were regarded as saints, others as heretics—cited the inspiration of the Holy Spirit as a license to preach and teach. One of the most successful, Hildegard of Bingen, advised a fellow female visionary to speak in the manner of a trumpet, allowing the breath of the Holy Spirit to blow through her.[33]

French sermons from the generation immediately preceding the reform confirm that theological discourse—that is, authoritative discussion of religious matters—was barred to women.[34] Oliver Maillard, a Franciscan, attacked the unfortunate tendency of women to get interested in theology, labeling such women *semi-theologicales*.[35] The phrase implied that women were by nature unfit for such discourse. He ended his sermon with reference to the good example of Catherine of Alexandria, who spoke publicly only on the extraordinary authority of the Holy Spirit. A younger colleague, Michel Menot, chastized those women "who have all of theology available in French, even a library full. They go off to the Carmelites and Augustinians and other convents for as much advice as they can get, but they do nothing about it."[36] For him it was those women who avoided sin who were *bonnes theologiennes*.[37] Both men viewed vernacular translations of the Bible with suspicion, equating popular desire for reading the Scriptures with the contemporary fad for secular romances. Furthermore they saw both types of literature as being particularly appealing to, and hence dangerous for, women.[38]

Whatever the distinctive qualities of female piety and sanctity in the late Middle Ages, women were regarded with profound suspicion within ecclesiastical institutions. The achievements of such exceptional women as Catherine of Siena and Dorothy of Montau remained at odds with the inferior position of women within the church, a position based upon the traditional Pauline prohibitions against speaking in church. Recourse to a claim of prophetic authority only worked for certain exceptional women. These two issues—a distinctively female piety based upon a highly physical attraction to and relationship with Christ and the inability of women to exercise public religious authority without recourse to a claim of a prophetic mandate—would continue to remain at the heart of female religious experience during the early generations of the Reformation.

Both can be detected in the first work of the Reformation period to be examined here, an account of the reform of the city of Geneva composed by Sister Jeanne de Jussie, a Franciscan nun.[39] By 1535 the prince-bishop, Geneva's traditional ecclesiastical and secular lord, had been expelled in favor of a city council packed with members sympathetic to the reform. Catholic ecclesiastical institutions were systematically closed or transformed. In July two prominent reformers, Guillaume Farel and Pierre Viret, went to the Franciscan convent along with senior civic officials in order to convert the nuns. When they gathered the nuns into the chapter room for a sermon, the prioress protested vehemently and so was led from the room. The men spoke with gusto concerning the freedoms provided by marriage, but when they discussed what Jussie termed "carnal corruption," these women vowed to a life of celibacy began to cry out at the top of their lungs. Hearing this the prioress beat on the walls with her fists, shouting encouragement to those within. The older nuns stuffed wax into their ears so that they could not hear the preachers. Farel and Viret left in confusion.[40]

A few weeks later another delegation came to the convent to demand the provision of a dowry for one Sister Blaisine, the only nun who had converted and decided to marry. In their company was a former nun who took it upon herself to speak to the nuns about marriage. Years later Jussie recalled the vehement reaction of her community:

> In that company was one false abbess, wrinkled and of diabolical language, possessing a husband and child, named Marie d'Entière of Picardy, who mixed herself up in preaching and in perverting the people from devotion. She placed herself among the sisters. . . . But because of the desire she had of perverting someone, she did not take note of [their] reproaches and said, "Alas, poor creatures! if only you knew how good it was to be next to a handsome husband, and how God considers it pleasing. For a long time I lived in those shadows and hypocrisy where you are, but God alone made me recognize the abuse of my pitiful life, and I was brought to the light of truth. Considering with regret how I lived, for in these orders there is nothing but sanctimoniousness, mental corruption and idleness . . . I took about five hundred ducats from the treasury of the abbey, and I left that unhappiness. Thanks to God I have five handsome children and I live wholesomely." The Sisters shrank back from these words of error and deceits, and they spat at her in hate.[41]

Beating on walls, stuffing wax in one's ears, and spitting at speakers—all forms of behavior which might safely be assumed as unusual for Franciscan nuns—graphically illustrate the profound emotional attachment to traditional female spirituality which continued to enliven the religious lives of some women.

In describing the events of the following years, Jussie emphasized the centrality of the Eucharist and the patronage of the Virgin Mary to the religious life of her community.[42] The nuns struggled against increasing odds to keep their ritual and symbolic universe alive. In the absence of priests, for instance, the abbess placed ashes on the heads of the nuns at the beginning of Lent in 1533.[43] The struggle over that symbolic order can be graphically seen in the events around Easter of that year. When the Catholic population held their traditional processions on the feasts of Easter and Pentecost, Protestant women stood by and ostentasiously continued to do their clothes mending and washing, thereby denying the validity of that ritual behavior. In its place they openly celebrated the domestic sphere. Nor was Dentière the only Protestant woman to preach to the Catholic nuns.[44] Catholic women for their part attempted to deny the Protestants the symbols of their new domestic ethic: they threw the washing into the Rhone river and one Protestant woman died when she was hit on the head with her distaff.[45] Still later Catholic women—and according to Jussie women remained more steadfastly Catholic than did men—used other ritual practices such as sanctified burial and the Eucharist to defy Protestant authority.[46] Even the miracles which she cited as defenses of the Catholic faith concerned the resurrection of the physical body and the protection of the body of Christ as found in the transubstantiated elements.[47] Despite this fierce defense of treasured religious symbols, the Catholic women shunned the public teaching role denied them by canon law. Jussie quoted her abbess, "It is not the trade of women to dispute, since such is not ordained for them. You will find that they ought not to dispute seeing that it is forbidden for unlettered people to meddle in speaking about Holy Scriptures."[48]

These vignettes illustrate how the reformers, both male and female, tried to invert and subvert the symbolism and ideals of late medieval spirituality.[49] Dentière, for example, had in effect extracted a dowery from the treasury of her abbey and transformed her marriage to Christ into a marriage to a secular spouse.[50] Farel and Viret, for their part, had gone to the Franciscan convent on the Sunday following the feast of the Visitation of the Virgin Mary to the house of her cousin Elizabeth (July 25). Jussie recalled that they interpreted the traditional gospel reading for that feast (Luke 1:39–56) as "saying that the Virgin Mary no longer held to a solitary life, but was diligent to help and give service to her aged cousin, and on the basis of this passage dismissed the life of the holy cloister, monasticism, and the state of holy chastity."[51] Dentière similarly stressed the pregnancies of Mary and Elizabeth as part of her defense of the public role of women.[52] In contrast late medieval preachers, such as Johannes Herolt, had interpreted the passage from Luke on the visitation as suggesting that Mary went "in haste" because the virgin did not want to be seen in public. Herolt also stressed that the pregnancies of a virgin, Mary, and a sterile elderly woman, Elizabeth, were miracles which reaffirmed God's desire to overturn the norms of human society. For him the services rendered by Mary were examples of her humility and obedience, rather than a call of women to an active life.[53] Such messages concerning the virtues of the traditional virginal marriage to Christ had molded the lives of the nuns reared in the late medieval spiritual tradition. Thus their hearts were "pierced," to use Jussie's phrase, by the reformer's rejection of that late medieval piety and their insistence that the nuns enter into more conventional marriages.[54]

If Catholic women such as Jussie perceived the reformers as inverting the traditional symbolic order of female spirituality, it was not accidental, for the reformers themselves consciously sought to do so. It is fortunate that two pamphlets survive by Marie Dentière, the former abbess and wife of a reform preacher who preached to Jussie's community. In her history of the reform of Geneva, Dentière sarcastically described a Dominican preacher's sermon:

> [He said] that Jesus had been in the belly of Mary like an ant and that the priest was more dignified than the Virgin Mary, having the power to make Jesus come from the sky by breathing on a piece of bread, forged between two hot irons, by means of saying "Hoc est corpus meum." His adversaries were scandalised by him, listening to him speak against the pure word of God, which teaches us to believe that Jesus Christ sits at the right hand of God the Father until he comes to judge the living and the dead. He would have to blow right well if, from a little bit of bread and pastry, he was to forge such a body. . . . Never did any alchemist so magnify his work.[55]

While the issues marked by Dentière in this passage were all common to reform polemic, the language is in many senses distinctively feminine. The image of a metaphorical pregnancy, the symbolic stature of the Virgin Mary, and the description of the Eucharist in terms of food preparation are all drawn from traditional female spirituality. Although Dentière sought to deconstruct the theological basis of that spirituality, her categories of thought were still informed by it.

Dentière composed that passage in 1536, the year in which Geneva officially declared itself in allegiance with the reform and in which Jean Calvin arrived in the city. Two years later the city council expelled Calvin, Farel, and Viret from the city in a dispute over the ecclesiastical control of public morals. The next year Dentière composed a defense of these men and of reform theology in the guise of an open letter to Queen Marguerite de Navarre.[56] She recognized a central role for women in the events of the reform: "Everyone . . . desires to know and hear how they ought to live in these most dangerous times; so, too we women ought to know how to flee and avoid all errors, heresies, and false doctrines."[57] She devoted particular attention to the rejection of the doctrine of transubstantiation and the cult of the saints, which were the pillars of Jussie's piety, claiming that such practices "turn into idolators the poor people who adore bread and wine as their real God."[58] In her discussion of both tithing and clerical celibacy she exhibited a sophisticated knowledge of canon law which she turned against the Catholic positions.[59] She continued to show a particular genius for inverting symbols. Countering male theologians who cited Eve's responsibility for the fall of humankind, she stated, "It was not a woman who sold and betrayed Jesus, but a man, named Judas." She also turned women's lack of education to advantage, by claiming that they defended the gospel, whereas the educated only defended the works of university professors.[60]

Much of Dentière's invective betrays the formative influence of the cloister, but she completely rejected the cloister as a proper expression of Christianity. She was, however, unwilling simply to retreat into the domestic sphere of the kitchen. Rather she attempted to create a sphere of religious authority for women outside the home, to replace the rejected sphere of the cloister. Her sense of this new sphere was probably in some sense based on the authority she had enjoyed as an abbess. Since the traditional works-oriented piety that had grounded female spirituality had lost its veracity, a new spirituality had to be constructed in its place. Dentière described the religious authority of women in bold terms:

> For we ought not, any more than men, hide and bury within the earth that which God has . . . revealed to us women. Although we are not permitted to preach in assemblies and public churches, nevertheless we are not prohibited from writing and giving advice in all charity one to the other. I have wished to write principally for those poor *femmelettes* who desire to know and hear the truth; they do not know which road, which path they ought to follow. . . . Even to the present day it seemed that women ought not read anything or listen to the Holy Scripture. . . . [I hope] in God that henceforth women will no longer be scorned as in the past. . . . If God has given graces to some good women, revealing to them something holy and good through His Holy Scriptures, should they, for the sake of the defamers of truth, refrain from writing down, speaking, or declaring it to each other? Ah! it would be too impudent to hide the talent which God has given to us.[61]

*Not viewed through my lens.*

To overcome the Pauline prohibitions against women speaking in church, Dentière consciously developed Old Testament women, such as Deborah and Ruth, to serve as female role models in place of the virginal saints of the medieval church.[62] Lest her claim appear too bold, she later turned to glossing the famous passage from Paul (Galatians 3:28), "Do we have two Gospels, one for men and the other for women? One for the educated and the other for the multitude. . . . We are all one in Jesus Christ, there is neither male nor female, nor serf, nor freeman. I do not speak here of the body, for there exists in physical terms . . . the husband and the wife, the first for loving, the other for holding him in esteem."[63]

*Yes!*

Dentière was not alone in her attempt to construct some new form of limited, public religious authority for women. Over a decade earlier Katerina Zell, the wife of a reform preacher in Strasbourg, had addressed in German a defense of women's authority to the Catholic hierarchy which was based not on Paul, but on the Old Testament authority of Joel (2:28, quoted in Acts 2:17), "You remind me that the Apostle Paul told women to be silent in church. I would remind you of the word of this same apostle that in Christ there is no longer male nor female and of the prophecy of Joel: 'I will pour forth my spirit upon all flesh and your sons and your daughters will prophesy.' I do not pretend to be John the Baptist rebuking the Pharisees. I do not claim to be Nathan upbraiding David. I aspire only to be Balaam's ass castigating his master."[64] She attempted to give a new, "protesting" twist to the claim of prophetic authority previously used by such medieval monastic women as Hildegard of Bingen.

*Aspire*

French noblewomen focused on the right of women to read, and hence implicitly to interpret, Scripture. Marguerite de Navarre, the addressee of Dentière's treatise, had Oisille, heroine of the *Heptameron*, read Scriptures to a private assembly of nobles. This group, both men and women, took her reading to be an "excellent teaching."[65] Jeanne d'Albret, her daughter and a convinced Huguenot, later exclaimed, "Those who say it's not for women / To look at Holy Writ / Are evil men and infamous / Seducers and antichrist."[66] These noble women, perhaps supported by their position in the social hierarchy, eschewed any reference to prophecy.

Male clerics—Protestant or Catholic—did not easily accede to the wishes and visions of these women. In the middle decades of the sixteenth century, French Catholics criticized the Huguenot movement for improperly providing women too prominent a place in religious affairs. Both Jean Guéraud and Claude Haton expressed amazement at the fact that women and men were allowed to mingle socially and even to mingle their voices together in singing the psalms during the liturgy. The former called Huguenot services "diabolic" and a "bacchanal."[67] Gabriel de Saconay, a somewhat eccentric theologian from Lyon, went even further, darkly suggesting that reformed ministers used their attempts to teach women doctrine as a cover for more lascivious pursuits. His descriptions of meetings for bible study took on a resemblance to contemporary renderings of the witches' sabbath: "These fine nocturnal assemblies have been transformed by those very satyrs who introduced them into religious practise. After the sermon charity is exercised when the candles are extinguished and brothers mingle with their sisters in Christ."[68]

More mainstream Catholic voices accused Calvinist women of "mixing themselves" (*se mesler*) up in matters that did not concern them.[69] Noel Taillepied, a Franciscan, provided a sarcastic account of how the place of women put the Protestant faith outside the natural order. "I do not wish to speak of women who desire to become abbesses, but instead abbots and bishops, and to mix themselves up in preaching in the company of men."[70] In the view of Florimond de Raemond, a jurist who had briefly joined the reformed faith, "Lutheran" missionaries to France had intentionally preyed on women and their most useful convert had been Marguerite de Navarre. Like the Franciscan preachers of previous generations, he saw the vernacular Scriptures as a dangerous novelty that led unsuspecting Christians—lured by their semblance to the romances—into error. The worst problem was that the uneducated laity, including women, thought empowered to interpret scripture for themselves and even to preach. He complained, "One sees in many places that women not only mix themselves up in theology, but even in the public function of the office of minister or deacon." He apparently had such German women as Argula von Grumbach in mind. Raemond went on to complain that "it is not right that simple little women (*femmelettes*) . . . wish to see the holy Bible trotted out with no dignity on the tables of a cabaret just as glasses are."[71] Both men explicitly cited the Pauline prohibitions against women speaking in church against their Huguenot foes.[72] This did not mean that women could not have any teaching office. In commenting on 1 Corinthians 14:34, the most influential Catholic exegete of the period, Cardinal Cajetan, emphasized that mothers had a duty to teach their children, both male and female, on religious matters.[73]

Ironically, male reformers agreed in large measure with their Catholic clerical counterparts on the need to keep women from preaching publicly on religious matters. The antagonistic reception which Dentière and her treatise received in Geneva during the years following its pub-

*[margin handwritten note: Catholic allowed women to teach their kids but not men]*

lication points out the male reformers' desire to place severe limits on the sphere of female religious authority. As early as 1538, Guillaume Farel—whom Dentière herself had earlier described in glowing terms—was writing dark reports to Calvin concerning Dentière's bad influence on her husband, the preacher Antoine Froment.[74] Six weeks after the publication of Dentière's *Letter to Queen Marguerite*, the civic authorities of Geneva seized all available copies of the work.[75] Some pastors, that is, the Genevan clergy, chose to ignore the fact that the work was by a woman and accused her husband, Antoine Froment, of having written the allegedly seditious tract. They did so despite Dentière's explicit request in the colophon of the work that her husband not be blamed for her writing.[76] Other clerics decried the work simply because it was by a woman. Béate Comte, for instance, replied to the inquiries of the City Council of Berne that the book contained nothing contrary to Scripture, but as it was an inopportune work and by a woman, who was barred by gender from the office of prophesying, it ought not be published.[77] Froment himself later remarked that the greatest regret of the council members was that they had been "so wounded, piqued, and dishonored by a woman."[78]

A year after the seizure of the work Froment unsuccessfully tried to have the copies released.[79] Shortly thereafter the exiled reformers, whom Dentière had defended in the work, returned to positions of power within Geneva. In August of 1542 Froment once again sued for the release of the work, only to have such action blocked by Calvin.[80] Although Dentière was in most respects in close theological agreement with Calvin and Farel, and although she clearly saw herself as a member of their reforming party, these males saw her message concerning the religious authority of women as subversive. The Genevan church did not provide women with any significant institutional voice, even of the sort of quasi-public role advocated by Dentière. She and her husband appear to have been pushed to the margins of Genevan society.

In 1546 Calvin wrote to Farel with what he termed "an amusing story." He had found Dentière speaking publicly in long robes, in the supposed fashion of Old Testament prophets. When Calvin tried to silence her, she claimed to be speaking on the authority of the Holy Spirit. Apparently Farel had earlier had a similar experience with her. Calvin concluded that he had sent Dentière away, "just as I ought to have done."[81] Having failed in her attempt to construct some alternative to the cloister and the kitchen, Dentière found herself forced to rely—like anabaptist contemporaries whom she despised and Catholic nuns whose life she had rejected—on a claim of charismatic or prophetic, rather than institutional, authority. In 1561 Dentière died in almost tragic circumstances, a year after the trial of her husband on charges of adultery.[82]

It is hardly surprising to find Calvin taking practical steps to silence Dentière and deny the preaching role to a woman. To be sure, Calvin was less blatantly antifeminist than many of his contemporaries.[83] He accepted, for example, the spiritual equality of women and men before God. By associating sin with the higher, or rational, faculties of Aristotelian psychology, he freed women from the charge of being essentially sinful because they were essentially carnal. Such an attitude had negative consequences for women as well. He firmly endorsed the social subordination of women to men and developed a theology of marriage based on that hierarchical ordering. While women could sue for divorce on the basis of adultery, they could not do so on the basis of physical abuse. Any equality was simply spiritual and not physical, or hence social. Calvin's general attempt to look past the physical world in favor of the spiritual realm of divine omnipotence tended to negate any form of female piety based on physicality or sensuality. Thus, while women might in theory have a more privileged position in the thought of Calvin than in the writings of many contemporaries, their position in a Calvinist church or community differed little. As Davis has observed, "The social thrust of the Reformation, as [Calvin and other members of the Venerable Company of Pastors] saw it, was to overthrow the hierarchical priestly class and administer the church instead by well-trained pastors and sound male members of the Consistories. That was enough topsy-turvy for them."[84]

Douglass has correctly stressed that Calvin placed the Pauline prohibitions against women speaking in church among the *adiaphora,* or indifferent things. These were to be decided by a church community according to its circumstances.[85] Calvin, however, did not envisage any woman of his own time, such as Dentière, preaching in the church of Geneva or any other reformed congregation. He used one of the Pauline prohibitions (1 Corinthians 14:34) as an occasion to note that Paul himself had judged the Corinthian community an unsuitable context for women speaking in church.[86] Commenting on two women, Priscilla and Aquila, who expounded the Scriptures to Apollos (Acts 18:26), he noted simply that women should be acquainted with Scripture, while emphasizing that they should speak on it only in private: "We also see that at that time women were not so unacquainted with the Word of God as the Papists wish to have them, since we see that one of the chief teachers of the church was taught by a woman. Yet we must remember what I said, that Priscilla carried out this instruction at home, and within private walls, so that she might shake as little as possible the order prescribed by God and by nature."[87] As Bouwsma has pointed out, Calvin had an inherent horror of mixing categories. He condemned men for "feminine" conduct; so, too, he would condemn a woman for taking up "masculine" activities. Moreover, his description of the already marginalized Dentière of 1546 suggested that he saw the threat of anabaptist antinomianism in her actions.[88] Any possibility of women preaching would remain forever theoretical in Calvin's mind, as his treatment of Dentière eloquently attested. As Douglass herself concludes, "Reason has been given to assume that Calvin knew that at least some Renaissance supporters of the women's cause were suggesting that women should have the right to preach; Calvin does not agree in practice, but he does not exclude that possibility in principle."[89]

In practical terms, the religious and intellectual inheritance of Calvin left Geneva with a judicial system that treated women with surprising equality to men, but an educational system which largely ignored them and a church in which they held no authoritative positions.[90]The major teaching office held open to them was a domestic one, responsibility for providing the religious formation of their own children, and perhaps even the children of others in elementary schools. Reformed theologians such as Pierre Viret did not sound terribly different from Catholics such as Cajetan on this point. The only writer of the reformed tradition to press for significant inclusion of women in the orders of the church was a layman, Jean Morély, in his *Treatise of Christian Discipline and Governance*. He wished to reinstitute the order of deaconesses found in the early church. These women would serve, in contrast to the "lazy" order of nuns, as a group dedicated to social service, such as the care of the sick and the poor. Even Morély, however, dismissed any possibility of women preaching. His suggestions do not seem to have been incorporated by any reformed congregations. In fact the controversy surrounding the publication of his work may have prevented the inclusion of female deacons in the Genevan church.[91]

Far more common was the attitude of Peter Martyr Vermigli, a former Augustinian monk who became a prominent theologian and exegete in the reformed church. Like Dentière, Vermigli admitted that there was a tension between the prohibitions found in the Pauline correspondence against women speaking in church and the fact that women could be found acting as prophets in both Testaments of Scripture. Vermigli, however, distinguished between the prophetic office, which was a "special privilege" (*peculiarium privilegium*) given directly by God, and the "ordinary law" (*ius ordinarius*) of the church, which had been laid down by Paul. "It should not be deduced . . . that that which God does in some particular case of privilege should be made by us a model of behavior." If women were to take the suggestions of the prophet Joel too seriously and commonly teach in public, it might lead men to be seduced by the devil.[92] Elsewhere, commenting directly on 1 Corinthians 14:34, he concluded, "[The ordinary ministry] is in no way permitted to women, [although] for an extraordinary reason it sometimes happens that women prophesy."[93] Vermigli's exegesis of that verse did not differ greatly from that of a somewhat younger Jesuit, Cornelius a Lapide.[94]

Even if reformed churches did not meet the highest expectations of such women as Marie Dentière and Katherina Zell in constructing a new sphere of authority for women, they did provide a welcome religious alternative to the strictures of traditional Christianity for a large number of literate women. The urban kitchen became, as Calvin suggested Priscilla's once had been, a significant arena for religious discourse. Moreover, convents suffered from a general lack of popularity in France.[95] Thus the Catholic clergy in France found that they had to pay more attention to the religious lives of laywomen in the middle years of the sixteenth century. No longer was it possible simply to reprint manuals designed for a monastic audience.[96] An excellent example of the piety which literate women were taught is provided by *A Little Instructional Manual on Living for a Laywoman*, which was published in Paris and elsewhere in northern France in those years.[97] The work was written by an anonymous author whose gender is uncertain but who was certainly in a monastic order. In the long-standing tradition of both the *devotio moderna* and the use of Books of Hours, that author tried to inculcate the *femmelettes* of the audience in an abridged form of monastic life and devotions.[98] The wide publication of the work suggests a substantial audience of women who were literate, bought books, and used texts. The author urged the reader to "extract from [this book] those things which are to be said every day such as the preparations which you make in the morning and the manner of attending Mass, and the preparations for receiving the Lord Jesus Christ. Write these onto a small piece of paper and put this within the Book of Hours which you bring to church."[99] Despite the author's assumptions about literacy and reading, the practices of works-oriented piety were still emphasized in obvious reaction to the reformed stress on the private reading of Scripture. The author urged, "Realize that in order to make such gain it is not sufficient to write and read something which is not then fully put into practice."[100]

The practices so encouraged were designed to lead to the goal of salvation: "Consider that you are in this world only for saving your soul."

The reader was well advised to worry about salvation for even "the pain of purgatory is greater than all the other torments which one can suffer in this world." That goal, however, was not easily attained by a laywoman: "I nevertheless have compassion for you, considering that you stand among the dangers to salvation which exist in the world." Among the dangers which could threaten such a woman's soul was her own family: "I beg you to put yourself at pains . . . not to incline too much either to worldly good or to your children or to your other carnal friends, for all these are not able to help you in your greatest need, which is death." [101] The center of the daily practices advised by the author was Mass and the reception of the Eucharist.[102] This was anchored in a deep devotion to the human, and most particularly to the suffering, Jesus. The reader was encouraged to meditate upon images. Jesus was made to address the reader directly as a knight: "When [the devil] sends you some temptation to evil and sin, then enter into your room, that is into your heart, and gaze upon my weapons all bloodied, that is the Cross, the nails, the lance, the sponge, and the crown of thorns which sat on top of my soft human body all covered with great sores." The sensuality of the image is unmistakable; the characterization of Jesus as a knight an obvious inversion of the secular romances which the reader of the *Manual* might also have in her library. That reader was not only provided with male religious models: "Read also what St. Cecilia did, as well as St. Natalie." [103] The Virgin Mary, and particularly the prayer Ave Maria, also played a strong supporting role.[104]

The author of the *Manual* included an exemplary story about a young laywoman who approached a university professor of theology, which is very revealing of attitudes toward the public status of married women in Catholic society.[105] The master at first treated this young woman with scorn because "he was more accustomed to having many great clerics request his counsel than such *femmelettes*." When he asked the woman if she were married, she replied "Yes sir, I am bound in marriage but, if I were freed from this bond, I would not allow myself to be bound to this world again. Now that I am bound there, I firmly believe that God has called me there and ordained me to that estate for my salvation. I would well like to introduce my husband and my small infant children to everything which is good to do." Then she outlined her daily spiritual exercises, which included the use of mental images like those discussed above, such as "bath[ing] myself every day in the ruby-colored wounds of Our Saviour . . . having full confidence that He purified all my faults by His blessed Passion." When she finished, the master replied, "I have held this cap for fifty years and am called a Master of Sacred Theology;

all that while I have never found such perfection." Here a limited sphere of authority has been returned to laywomen, but only to those who had essentially tried to turn their kitchens into cloisters.

The Huguenots had clearly alerted the Catholic hierarchy to the presence of a large public of laywomen who both raised children and read religious books. They themselves were aware of the dangers posed by traditional piety. It is worthwhile noting that at this time the reformed theologian Pierre Viret, in an influential catechism, pointedly denied the efficacy of the canonical hours, of the Ave Maria, and of invocation of the angels and saints. As he succinctly put his case, "All the prayers which the papists address to the Virgin Mary or to the other saints, such as the 'Obsecro te,' the 'O intemerata,' the 'Ave maris stellis' and other similar forms of prayers and invocations, addressed to others than God are full of execrable blasphemies." [106] The author of the *Manual* attempted to respond to the literate lay audience by enlarging the traditional sense of the Catholic cloister to include a wider audience of laywomen within the changed circumstances of the Reformation. This author encouraged the development of a distinctively female spirituality grounded in the traditional theology of salvation by works. In this context marriage was seen as a possible hindrance to salvation, but, as with the physical body, it could also present the possibility of penitential actions which would lead to ultimate salvation.

Whether or not women as a group generally benefited from the various reform movements has been much debated. There is no doubt that the reformers instituted salubrious changes. In numerous small German municipalities Lutheran reformers instituted clerical marriage, made divorce possible in certain restricted circumstances, and founded civic schools for girls. On the other hand, they shut down beguinages and convents, drastically curtailed the cult of the Virgin and other female saints, and forbade women from gathering and discussing religion. In the case of Zwickau, for instance, Karant-Nunn has concluded that the "Lutheran Reformation as imposed by prince and city council confined women's contributions to religion more closely than had Catholicism." [107] Such large-scale assessments, however, do not face the fact of continued misogynism in the basic institutions of Christianity. Those quantitative assessments also beg the questions of how gender conditioned people's experience of the reform and, conversely, of how religious institutions helped to construct gender as a social category.

While there were seeds of a public religious authority for women in both Catholic and reformed theologies, both sets of church institutions continued to be resolutely misogynistic in practice. Moreover, the competing claims of the two clergies threatened to disenfranchise the women of sixteenth-century Europe from any possibility of such public authority. Like the late medieval women studied by Bynum, the Catholic women studied here—Sister Jeanne de Jussie and her contemporaries, along with the readers of the *Manual*—could achieve salvation, and even a severely limited sense of authority, by works based within their quotidian physical environment. To be sure they had to ignore the certain demands of marriage and child-bearing in favor of the call of their true spouse, Jesus. By washing away their sins in his "ruby-colored wounds" such women still clung to the physically oriented and even erotic female spirituality noted by such French feminist theorists as Irigary.[108] Such a spirituality could, at its best, transcend the deep sense of dualism that devalued women as physical, and therefore inferior. It did little, however, to alter the governing misogyny of social and religious institutions. By continuing to denigrate secular marriage as inferior to marriage to Christ, the social roles of Catholic women within marriage remained little changed by the Reformation. There was, for instance, no avenue for divorce, although that alternative was in practice little used by Protestant women. More strikingly, Catholic women have still to achieve a public role of ordained clerical authority in their church.

On the other hand, Protestant women such as Marie Dentière could not achieve salvation through child-bearing and marriage. They merely avoided religious error by being married and shunning the cloister. The basic Protestant doctrine of salvation by faith alone denied the efficacy of the physical in terms of salvation. Jean Calvin dismissed the traditional piety of women with a contemptuous nod, "There are foolish little women who run from altar to altar and then do nothing but sigh or mutter till the middle of the day. By the pretext [of piety], they free themselves from all domestic duties. On returning home, if everything is not to their liking, they take offense, disturb the whole household with senseless cries, and sometimes come to blows."[109] The result was that women— who were seen by their society as being primarily physical rather than spiritual beings—lost the sort of distinctive piety provided by the cloister and its analogues in Catholicism. At the same time marriage was no longer a second-class institution and the theology of the reformers certainly paved the way to certain basic gains in that specific social sphere for women. The male reformers did little or nothing, however, to replace the private sphere of the cloister with other privileged arenas of religious action for women. In the very first years of the reform, as the institutions of the traditional religious order were being deconstructed along with their governing theology, Marie Dentière felt empowered to demand a new sphere of religious activity for women outside of the kitchen. Such a new sphere of authority was denied by her male superiors. Like medieval nuns and contemporary anabaptist women, Dentière had to defend her public speech as being inspired by the Holy Spirit, not sanctioned by ecclesiastical custom. Ironically Jeanne de Jussie found encouragement and advancement in her more limited and traditional role, as she was eventually promoted to abbess of her community in their new quarters at Annency.[110] Dentière's experience, like that of the German peasants in 1525, points out that, while reform or revolutionary movements create opportunities for subordinate classes in their initial stages, new institutions with new agenda of suppression frequently take the place of the rejected institutions.

The Protestant reformers did not undo the misogyny of Catholic religious institutions. Rather, after a brief period of openness during the polemic battles of the reform, two competing sets of misogynistic religious institutions—one Catholic, the other reformed—continued to govern the Christian church. Within that context the Protestant doctrine of salvation by faith led to a somewhat improved social situation for women, but denied the efficacy of a distinctively female spirituality. The Catholic emphasis on salvation by works allowed the continuation of just such a distinctively female spirituality by which women could transcend certain governing misogynistic assumptions in theology and philosophy by seeking salvation through the body.

## NOTES

I would like to thank the Association of Theological Schools for a grant which aided in my research. I would also like to thank Jane Dempsey Douglass, Virginia Reinburg, Elizabeth Robertson, and Merry Wiesner for their encouragement and advice.

1 / Merry Wiesner, *Working Women in Renaissance Germany* (New Brunswick, N.J.: Rutgers Univ. Press, 1986), 111.

2 / The book is currently preserved at the Hunnold Library of the Claremont Colleges, Crispin 22, fols. 174v–175. For a full description, see Consuela Dutschke and Richard Rouse, *Medieval and Renaissance Manuscripts in the Claremont Libraries* (Berkeley and Los Angeles: Univ. of California Press, 1986), 44–47.

3 / The description is that of their daughter, Jeanne d'Albret; see Nancy Roelker, "The Appeal of Calvinism to French Noblewomen in the Sixteenth Century," *Journal of Interdisciplinary History* 2 (1972): 400.

4 / Jane Douglass, "Women and the Continental Reformation," in *Religion and Sexism: Images of Woman in the Jewish and Christian Traditions*, ed. Rosemary Ruether (New York: Simon and Schuster, 1974), 292–318 (the quotation is on 303).

5 / Roelker, "Appeal of Calvinism," 391–413 (the quotation is on 406–7).

6 / Roger Stauffenegger, "Le mariage à Genève vers 1600," *Mémoires de la société pour l'histoire du droit* 27 (1966): 317–29 (esp. 327–28).

7 / For a survey of the social status of women in Europe by region, see *Private Lives? Women in Reformation and Counter-Reformation Europe,* ed. Sherrin Marshall (Bloomington: Indiana Univ. Press, in press).

8 / Natalie Davis, "City Women and Religious Change," in idem, *Society and Culture in Early Modern France* (Stanford: Stanford Univ. Press, 1965), 65–96 (esp. 89–94, 90 in response to Roelker).

9 / See esp. Merry Wiesner, "Women's Response to the Reformation," in *The German People and the Reformation,* ed. R. Po-Chia Hsia (Ithaca: Cornell Univ. Press, 1988), 148–71.

10 / For example, Marie Dentière, *Epistre très utile, faicte et composée par une femme chrestienne de Tornay, envoyée à la Royne de Narvarre, seur du Roy de France, contre les Turcz, Juifz, Infideles, Faulx chrestiens, Anabaptistes et Lutheriens* (Geneva: Jean Gerard, 1539), fol. A3v; *Un petite instruction et maniere de vivre pour une femme seculiere* (Paris: Guillaume Merlin, n.d.), fol. A3v. Such self-references to the weakness of women were topoi in medieval literature. Hildegard of Bingen, one of the most influential prophetic and intellectual voices of the twelfth century, referred to herself as *paupercula feminea forma* (a poor little figure of a woman); see Barbara Newman, *Sister of Wisdom: St. Hildegard's Theology of the Feminine* (Berkeley and Los Angeles: Univ. of California Press, 1987), 2.

11 / Steven Ozment, *When Fathers Ruled: Family Life in Reformation Europe* (Cambridge: Harvard Univ. Press, 1983). Despite the subtitle, Ozment is concerned almost exclusively with German areas.

12 / Dagmar Lorenz, "Vom Kloster zur Küche: Die Frau vor und nach der Reformation Dr. Martin Luthers," in *Die Frau von der Reformation zur Romantik: Die Situation der Frau vor dem Hintergrund der Literatur- und Sozialgeschichte,* ed. Barbara Becker-Cantarino, Modern German Studies, 7 (Bonn: Bouvier Verlag Herbert Grundmann, 1980), 7–35.

13 / Merry Wiesner, "Beyond Women and the Family: Towards a Gender Analysis of the Reformation," *Sixteenth-Century Journal* 18 (1987): 311–21.

14 / For a more general consideration of women's public voice in the German Reformation, which provides an instructive parallel to the present case study, see Wiesner, "Women's Response to the Reformation."

15 / For a useful summary of English vernacular preaching on women in the fourteenth and fifteenth centuries, see George Owst, *Literature and the Pulpit in Medieval England,* 2d ed. (Oxford: Basil Blackwell, 1966), 376–406 (the quotation from Bromyard is on 395). On the attitudes toward women and marriage of Jean Gerson, one of the most influential writers on pastoral subjects in France, see D. Catherine Brown, *Pastor and Laity in the Theology of Jean Gerson* (Cambridge: Cambridge Univ. Press, 1987), 209–38.

16 / On the cult of Margaret as the patron of pregnancy, see Davis, "City Women," 76. For a typical late medieval sermon on Margaret, see Johannes Herolt, *Sermones de sanctis cum promptuario exemplorum et miraculis Beatae Virginis* (Reutlingen: Michel Greyff, c. 1482), sermon 26. On midwifery, see Wiesner, *Working Women,* 55–73.

17 / Owst, *Literature and the Pulpit,* 378.

18 / Phyllis Roberts, "Stephen Langton's *Sermo de Virginibus,*" in *Women of the Medieval World: Essays in Honor of John Hine Mundy,* ed. Julius

Kirshner and Suzanne Wemple (Oxford: Basil Blackwell, 1985), 103–18.

19 / John Bugge, *Virginitas: An Essay in the History of a Medieval Ideal,* International Archives of the History of Ideas, series minor 17 (The Hague: Martinus Nijhoff, 1975), 87–90.

20 / Jean Gerson, *Collectorium super Magnificat* in *Oeuvres complètes,* ed. Palemon Glorieux, 10 vols. (Paris: Desclèe Brouwer, 1960–73), 8:397–98.

21 / Newman, *Sister of Wisdom,* 221–22.

22 / I have discussed this topic at greater length in an unpublished paper: "Marriage as Contract in the Vita of Christina of Markyate," presented at the International Congress of Medieval Studies, Kalamazoo, May 1987.

23 / Caroline Walker Bynum, *Holy Feast and Holy Fast: The Religious Significance of Food to Medieval Women* (Berkeley and Los Angeles: Univ. of California Press, 1987), 136.

24 / See esp. Caroline Walker Bynum, *Jesus as Mother: Studies in the Spirituality of the High Middle Ages* (Berkeley and Los Angeles: Univ. of California Press, 1982); idem, "Women's Stories, Women's Symbols: A Critique of Victor Turner's Theory of Liminality," in *Anthropology and the Study of Religion,* ed. Frank Reynolds and Robert Moore (Chicago: Center for the Scientific Study of Religion, 1984), 105–25; idem. *Holy Feast and Holy Fast*; Rudolph Bell, *Holy Anorexia* (Chicago: Univ. of Chicago Press, 1985); Michael Goodich, "The Contours of Female Piety in Later Medieval Hagiography," *Church History* 50 (1981): 20–32; idem, "*Ancilla Dei:* The Servant as Saint in the Late Middle Ages," in *Women of the Medieval World,* 119–36; Jane Schulenburg, "Sexism and the Celestial Gynaeceum, from 500–1200," *Journal of Medieval History* 4 (1978): 117–33; Richard Kieckhefer, *Unquiet Souls: Fourteenth-Century Saints and Their Religious Milieu* (Chicago: Univ. of Chicago Press, 1984).

25 / See, for example, Bynum, *Jesus as Mother,* 160–63.

26 / Ian MacLean, *The Renaissance Notion of Woman: A Study in the Fortunes of Scholasticism and Medical Science in European Intellectual Life* (Cambridge: Cambridge Univ. Press, 1980).

27 / Joan Kelly, "Did Women Have a Renaissance?" in *Becoming Visible: Women in European History,* ed. Renate Bridenthal and Claudia Koonz, (New York: Houghton Mifflin, 1977), 137–64. David Herlihy, "Did Women Have a Renaissance? A Reconsideration," *Medievalia et Humanistica,* n.s. 13 (1985): 1–22 (the quotation is on 1). For a more general discussion of the public role of women, see Merry Wiesner, "Women's Defense of Their Public Role," in *Women in the Middle Ages and Renaissance: Literary and Historical Perspectives,* ed. Mary Beth Rose (Syracuse: Syracuse Univ. Press, 1986), 1–27.

28 / Nicholas of Lyra, *Postillae super totam bibliam* (Strasbourg: Johannes Mentelin, 1472).

29 / Brown, *Pastor and Laity,* 223.

30 / On the attitude of Thomas of Chobham and his contemporaries to women in their audiences, see Sharon Farmer, " 'Persuasive Voices': Clerical Images of Medieval Wives," *Speculum* 61 (1986): 517–43; and idem, "Softening the Hearts of Men: Women, Embodiment, and Persuasion in the Thirteenth Century," in *Embodied Love: Sensuality and Relationship as Feminist Values,* ed. Paula Cooey, Sharon Farmer, and Mary

Ellen Ross (New York: Harper and Row, 1987), 115–33 (the quotation is on 124).

31 / *Quaestiones quodlibetales*, bk. 2, question 5, edited in Jean Leclercq, "Le magistère prédicateur au XIIIe siècle," *Archives d'histoire doctrinale et litteraire de moyen âge* 15 (1946): 120.

32 / Nicholas of Lyra, *Postillae super totam bibliam*, on Acts 2:17–18.

33 / On Hildegard's preaching and claim to visionary authority, see Newman, *Sister of Wisdom*, 1–41 (the advice to Elizabeth of Schönau is quoted on 36).

34 / On late medieval Franciscan preaching in France, see A. J. Krailsheimer, *Rabelais and the Fransciscans* (Oxford: Oxford Univ. Press, 1963), esp. 19–32.

35 / Oliver Maillard, *Sermones de Adventu, dominicales et de peccati stipendio et gratie premio* . . . (Lyon: S. Guèygnard, 1503), fol. 2v.

36 / Michel Menot, *Sermons choisis de Michel Menot*, ed. Joseph Nève, Bibliothèque de XVe siècle, 29 (Paris, 1924), 157.

37 / Menot, *Sermons choisis*, 145.

38 / Maillard, *Sermones de Adventu*, fols. 6v and 58v; Menot, *Sermons choisis*, 199.

39 / Jeanne de Jussie, *Le levain du calvinisme, ou Commencement de l'heresie de Geneve*, ed. Ad.-C. Grivel (Geneva, 1865).

40 / Jussie, *Le levain du calvinisme*, 135–40.

41 / Ibid., 167–74 (the quotation is on 173–74). The traditional assumption that Marie was an abbess is based upon this passage. The list of abbesses, however, from Sancta Maria de Pratis, the Augustinian convent in her home of Tournai, does not include her name. See *Gallia Christiana*, 2d ed., 16 vols. (Paris, 1715–1865), 3:301–2.

42 / For example, Jussie, *Le levain du calvinisme*, 9–10, 23–24, and 40–48. Jane Dempsey Douglass has offered a differently shaded reading of many of the events discussed here. See "Women and the Continental Reform," 309–14, and *Women, Freedom, and Calvin* (Philadelphia: Westminster Press, 1985), 98–102.

43 / Jussie, *Le levain du calvinisme*, 60.

44 / Ibid., 91–92, 185–86.

45 / Ibid., 62, 95.

46 / Ibid., 106, 108, 113–15.

47 / Ibid., 89–90, 107–8.

48 / Ibid., 125.

49 / Similar examples could, of course, be found in other locales. The most striking parallel to the experiences of Jussie and her sisters was the attempted dissolution of the Franciscan convent in Nuremburg. The efforts of the reformers there were vigorously, and for a while successfully, opposed by the abbess, Caritas Pirckheimer. A woman of remarkable education who was well connected in humanist circles, Pirckheimer recorded her experiences in a work entitled the *Denkwürdigkeiten*. For an edition, see *Die "Denkwürdigkeiten" der Caritas Pirckheimer*, ed. Josef Pfanner (Landshut: Solanus-Druck, 1962).

50 / On evidence from Germany on women leaving the cloister, see Ozment, *When Fathers Ruled*, 9–25.

51 / Jussie, *Le levain du calvinisme*, 137. The incipit of the gospel passage ("exurgens Maria abiit in montana") is misprinted in this edition. See Johannes Herolt, *Sermones de sanctis*, sermon 25.

52 / Dentière, *Epistre très utile*, fol. A4v.

53 / Johannes Herolt, *Sermones de sanctis*, sermon 25.

54 / Jussie, *Le levain du calvinisme*, 137.

55 / Marie Dentière, *La guerre et déslivrance de la ville de Genesve. Fidèlement faicte et composée par ung marchant demourant en icelle* (Geneva: N.p., 1536) as published from the surviving manuscript copies by Albert Rilliet, "Restitution de l'écrit intitulé: *La guerre de deslivrance de la ville de Genesve* (1536)," in *Mémoires et documents publiées par la société d'histoire et d'archéologie de Genève* 20 (1881): 337–76 (the quoted passage may be found on 353). See the description of this same sermon provided by Jussie, *Le levain du Calvinisme*, 79. On Dentière also see Thomas Head, "A Propagandist for the Reform, Marie Dentière," in *Women Writers of the Renaissance and Reformation*, ed. Katherina Wilson (Athens: Univ. of Georgia Press, 1987), 260–83.

56 / Dentière, *L'epistre très utile*, fols. B2v–B5v, C4–C8, D5. The only known copy of this work is preserved in the Musée historique de la Réformation in Geneva, where it bears the number D. Den. 1. Excerpts have been published by Rilliet, "Restitution de l'écrit," 377–384, and by Aimé-Louis Herminjard, ed., *Correspondance des réformateurs dans les pays de langue française*, 9 vols. (Geneva, 1866–97), 5:295–304. I have translated these excerpts into English in "A Propagandist for the Reform," 275–80.

57 / Dentière, *L'epistre très utile*, fol. A2.

58 / Ibid., fol. B1.

59 / Ibid., fols. C1–C3. Cf. her use of *Decretals, distinctio* 34 to that made by her husband, Antoine Froment, in a sermon of 1533 which he recorded in his *Les actes et gestes merveilleux de la cité de Genève*, ed. Gustave Revilliod (Geneva, 1854), 41.

60 / Dentière, *Epistre très utile*, fol. A5 (Rilliet, "Restitution de l'écrit," 379).

61 / Dentière, *L'epistre très utile*, fols. A3v and A5 (Herminjard, *Correspondance*, 298, Rilliet, "Restitution de l'écrit," 380).

62 / Dentière, *L'epistre très utile*, fol. A4 (Rilliet, "Restitution de l'écrit," 378). Cf. this use of Old Testament models to that of Hildegard of Bingen discussed by Newman, *Sister of Wisdom*, 39.

63 / Dentière, *L'epistre très utile*, fol. D1.

64 / Quoted in Roland Bainton, *Women of the Reformation in Germany and Italy* (Boston: Beacon Press, 1971), 55. On Zell and other female pamphleteers who wrote in German, see Paul Russell, *Lay Theology in the Reformation. Popular Pamphleteers in Southwest Germany, 1521–1525* (Cambridge: Cambridge Univ. Press, 1985), 185–211.

65 / Marguerite de Navarre, *Heptameron*, ed. Simone de Reyff (Paris: Flammarion, 1982), bk. 6, prologue, 389–90.

66 / Quoted in Davis, "City Women and Religious Change," 78.

67 / Jean Guéraud, *La chronique lyonnaise de Jean Guéraud, 1536–1562*, ed. Jean Tricou (Lyon: Imprimerie Audinienne, 1929), 66, 147; Claude Haton, *Mémoires de Claude Haton*, ed. F. Bourquelot, 2 vols. (Paris, 1857), 1:50.

68 / Gabriel de Saconay, *Genealogie et la Fin des Huguenaux, et descouverte du Calvinisme* (Lyon: Benoît Rigaud, 1573), 64b.

69 / In contrast, a Huguenot, Claude de Rubys, made fun of the fact that Catholic women "do not wish to mix themselves up in . . . disputes over religion." (*Histoire veritable de la ville de Lyon* [Lyon: Bonaventure Nugo, 1604], bk. 1, c. 21, 84).

70 / Noel Taillepied, *Histoire de l'Estat et Republique des Druides* (Paris: Jean Parant, 1585), fol. 33.

71 / Florimond de Raemond, *L'histoire de la naissance, progrez et decadence de l'hérésie de ce siècle* (Rouen: Estienne Vereul, 1623), bk. 7, c. 3, pts. 3–4, 847–49 and bk. 7, c. 7, pts. 4–5, 874–77 (the quotation is on 875).

72 / Taillepied, *Histoire de l'Estat de Druides*, fols. 38v–39; Raemond, *L'histoire de la naissance de l'hérésie*, bk. 7, c. 7, pt. 5, 876–77. Taillepied's citation is partially mistaken, making reference to 1 Tim. 3, rather than 1 Tim. 2. See also De Saconay who said (*Genealogie et la Fin des Huguenaux*, 60a), "There is no need for any woman or artisan to distract themselves from their work and labor in order to take up their time by reading the Old and the New Testaments as translated into the vernacular. . . . Women ought to keep silent in church, says St. Paul (1 Corinthians 14). It is no longer permitted for them to speak, rather they ought to be silent."

73 / Tommasso de Vio, *Epistolae Pauli et aliorum apostolorum . . . iuxta sensum literalem enarratae* (Paris: Carol Guillard, 1540), fol. 161.

74 / Herminjard, *Correspondance*, 5:151. See also the similar language used in a letter of 1541 in 6:173.

75 / Jean Gerard had printed 1,500 copies under her name but also under a false imprint of Antwerp (*Anvers, chez Martin Lempereur*) designed to circumvent regulations on printing in Geneva. The reports of the ensuing trials, maneuvers, and legislation can be found in Geneva, Archives d'Etat, *Registres du Conseil*, 33:103, 108–11, 113v–115v. See also Théophile Dufour, *Notice bibliographique sur le Catéchisme et la Confession de Foi de Calvin (1537) et sur les autres livres imprimés à Genève et à Neuchatel dans les premiers temps de la réforme (1533–1540)* (Geneva, 1878), 155–6.

76 / Dentière, *Epitre très utile*, fol. D8v. Having been asked by Genevan authorities to judge the work, the Council of Berne deemed "Froment's" work acceptable; see Herminjard, *Correspondance*, 5:321–23 and 332–33.

77 / Transcription of a minute of the Berne council quoted in Herminjard, *Correspondance*, 5:332–33, nn. 2–3. In 1536 Dentière had chosen to publish her history of the reformation battles in Geneva under the guise of a male pseudonym: "Ung marchant demourant en icelle [Geneva]." See Rilliet, "La restitution," 337.

78 / An unpublished passage from the *Actes et gestes* cited by Herminjard, *Correspondance*, 5:456–57.

79 / *Registres du Conseil*, 33:413v.

80 / *Registres du Conseil*, 36:96, partially printed by Herminjard, *Correspondance*, 5:322, n. 6.

81 / Jean Calvin, *Opera quae supersunt omnia*, ed. G. Baum, E. Cunitz, and E. Reuss (Brunswick and Berlin, 1863–1900), 12:377–78.

82 / Dentière is mentioned as Froment's wife at his trial in January of 1561; see Geneva, Archives d'Etat, *Procès criminal*, 2d ser., no. 1223. On November 28 of that year he requested permission to leave the city of Geneva to go to Flanders to visit the parents of his wife and commiserate with them over her death.

83 / For a positive, if qualified, assessment of Calvin's attitude toward women, see Roelker, "The Appeal of Calvinism," 406–8, Douglass, *Women, Freedom, and Calvin*, and, more generally, William Bouwsma, *John Calvin: A Sixteenth-Century Portrait* (Oxford: Oxford Univ. Press, 1988), 52–54, 76–77, 136–38.

84 / Davis, "City Women and Religious Change," 83.
85 / Douglass, *Women, Freedom, and Calvin,* esp. 51–65.
86 / Jean Calvin, *Commentarius in Epistoli Pauli ad Corinthos 1* (for 14:34), *Opera omnia,* 49:532–33.
87 / Jean Calvin, *Commentarius in Acta Apostolorum* (for 18:26), *Opera omnia,* 48:437–38. Translation as in Douglass, *Women, Freedom, and Calvin,* 54.
88 / Bouwsma, *John Calvin,* 34–37.
89 / Douglass, *Women, Freedom, and Calvin,* 82.
90 / E. William Monter, "Women in Calvinist Geneva (1550–1800)," *Signs* 6 (1980–81): 189–209 (esp. 204–5, on education).
91 / Robert Kingdon, *Geneva and the Consolidation of the French Protestant Movement, 1564–1572* (Madison: Univ. of Wisconsin Press, 1967), 43–62; Douglass, *Women, Freedom, and Calvin,* 90–92.
92 / Peter Martyr Vermigli, *Loci communes* (London: John Kyngston, 1576), bk. 4, c. 1, pt. 11, 842–43.
93 / Ibid., bk. 1, c. 3, pt. 6, 10.
94 / Cornelius a Lapide, *In omnes divi Pauli epistolas commentaria* (Paris, 1638), 296.
95 / This was not the situation throughout Europe. Those in Tuscany, for example, flourished in a situation created by the demographic and social vagaries of the marriage market. Virtually all unmarried women in the patriciate, and many of lesser classes, had the alternative of a marriage to Christ arranged by their families. In 1552 approximately 15 percent of the women in Florence were nuns (Richard Trexler, "Le célibat à la fin du Moyen Age: Les religieuses de Florence," *Annales: Economies, sociétés, civilisations* 27 [1972]: 1329–50.
96 / For example, a vernacular translation of the *Epistola de virginitate servanda* of Georges d'Esclavonie was printed three times in the first decade of the sixteenth century: *Le chasteau de virginité* (Paris: Anthoine Vérard, 1505); *Le chasteau de virginité* (Paris: Jehan Trepperal, 1506); *La vierge sacrée* (Paris: Simon Vostre, n.d.). This work had originally been composed in 1411 by a canon of Tours for a learned young nun in the convent of Beaumont-les-Tours. It covered topics relevant almost exclusively to monastic women and made no attempt to adapt that monastic piety for a domestic environment.
97 / The copy I have used of *Cy commence une petite instruction et maniere de vivre pour une femme seculiere* was printed by Guillaume Merlin in Paris and is currently in the Bibliothèque national, Réserves, p.D. 107. For a brief introduction to the work, a list of other editions, and a partial translation, see Thomas Head, "A Sixteenth-Century Devotional Manual for Catholic Laywomen," *Vox Benedictina* 4 (1987): 40–59.
98 / For a brief survey of the devotional use of Books of Hours, see W. A. Pantin, "Instructions for a devout and Literate Layman," in *Medieval Learning and Literature: Essays Presented to Richard William Hung,* ed. J. J. G. Alexander and M. T. Gibson (Oxford: Clarendon Press, 1976), 398–422, esp. 412–13; Susan Groag Bell, "Medieval Women Book Owners: Arbiters of Lay Piety and Ambassadors of Culture," *Signs: Journal of Women in Culture and Society* 7 (1982): 742–68, esp. 753–60; and Virginia Reinburg, "Prayer and the Book of Hours," in *Time Sanctified: The Book of Hours in Medieval Art and Life,* ed. Roger Wieck (Baltimore and New York: The Walters Art Gallery and George Bra-

ziller, 1988), 39–44. In its various printings, *Une petite instruction* was sometimes bound together with copies of Books of Hours as an appendix.

99 / *Une petite instruction*, fol. A2v.

100 / Ibid., fol. A2.

101 / Ibid., fols. A4v, C1, A1v, A5.

102 / A daily of prayers and meditations may be found ibid., fols. A7v–B7v.

103 / Ibid., fols. A6 and A3.

104 / For instructions on how to pray the Ave Maria, see ibid., fols. C6v–C8v.

105 / Ibid., fols. A3v–A4v.

106 / Pierre Viret, *Exposition familiere des principaux poinctes du Catechisme et de la doctrine chrestienne* ([Lyon]: N.p., 1562), fols. 75–78 (the quotation is on 77v–78).

107 / Susan Karant-Nunn, "Continuity and Change: Some Effects of the Reformation on the Women of Zwickau," *Sixteenth-Century Journal* 12 (1982): 42.

108 / See, for instance, Luce Irigaray, "La Mysterique," in *Speculum de l'autre femme* (Paris: Editions du minuit, 1974), 238–52. I am grateful to Elizabeth Robertson for her observations on this subject.

109 / Jean Calvin, *Commentarius in Epistolam ad Timotheum I*, (for 5:5), *Opera omnia*, 52:307; translation as in Bouwsma, *John Calvin*, 53.

110 / Douglass, "Women and the Continental Reformation," 310.

## 10

*Alexander Sedgwick*

# The Nuns of Port-Royal: A Study of Female Spirituality in Seventeenth-Century France

THE HISTORY OF THE NUNS OF PORT-ROYAL AND THEIR EFFORTS throughout the seventeenth century to maintain their spiritual integrity in the face of intense social pressures and of a hostile church and state has been told many times since the convent was destroyed in 1711 on orders from Louis XIV. It will be my purpose in this paper to examine that history in order to identify those elements inherent in the spirituality of Port-Royal that enabled it to have such an impact in its time and to determine what may be essentially female attributes of that spirituality. I will be primarily concerned with those nuns who were members of the Arnauld family. Over the course of seventy-five years they were the dominant influence within the convent, and it was through their magnetic piety that the Arnauld family became the driving force in the Jansenist movement. Indeed the history of French Jansenism can be said to have begun with the efforts of Angélique Arnauld (1591–1661), who became abbess of Port-Royal in 1602, to reimpose the Cistercian Rule on the convent.[1] Angélique was able to acquire her position at the tender age of eleven because of her family's political connections so that the indissoluble link between the Arnaulds and Port-Royal was established at the beginning of the century as the impact of the Counterreformation made itself felt on France.

Angélique's father, Antoine, was a lawyer attached to the Parliament of Paris. At the time of her birth in 1591, Antoine's situation was precarious. He had been loyal to Henry III and had not joined the Catholic League, but when that king was assassinated in 1589, it was not entirely clear whether the Huguenot heir to the throne, Henry of Navarre, would be able to secure his rule given the fierce resistance of the league to that rule. However as the political fortunes of Henry IV improved, so did those of Antoine Arnauld, aided in part by the close ties that existed between his two Huguenot brothers and the duc de Sully, superintendent of finances. In 1591 Antoine was not particularly well off, and so four years later after the birth of two more daughters he accepted the invitation of his father-in-law, Simon Marion, a prominent lawyer also attached to the Parliament of Paris, to become part of his household in the capital city.

By 1600 Antoine and his wife Catherine had produced five daughters and only two sons. Simon Marion, the head of the household until his death in 1605, decided that his granddaughters would have to be placed in convents in order to sustain the family fortune. Because of his good relations with Henry IV, he was able to obtain the promise of the position of abbess of Port-Royal for his granddaughter Angélique and a similar position at the Convent of Saint-Cyr for another granddaughter, Jeanne (1593–1671). The initial application for papal approval of Angélique's appointment was denied on the grounds that she was too young, but a second application asserting that she was seventeen years old when she was only eleven and still too young, according to the canon of the Cistercian order, was approved in 1601. A year later she was installed as abbess of Port-Royal.

The decision to place Angélique and three of her sisters in a convent was based entirely on family interests. The Arnaulds were religious only in a conventional sense, and like many families with social and political ambitions, they understood that success depended on the careful management of family assets. Too many daughters each requiring a substantial dowry in order to marry advantageously would make it difficult for the male head of the household to invest the family resources in the careers of the sons. Of the eighteen children borne by Catherine Arnauld between 1588 and 1612, ten lived to adulthood, six females and four males. Five of the daughters entered convents at an early age. The eldest daughter, Catherine (1590–1651), ironically the most religious of all the daughters as a child, was married to another lawyer, Isaac Le Maistre. The oldest son of Antoine and Catherine Arnauld, Robert Arnauld d'Andilly (1588–1674), moved into the financial administration, a preferred avenue to social and political advancement, as the protégé of his uncle Isaac Arnauld. Another son, Henry (1597–1692), was launched in a diplomatic career, and a third son, Simon (1603–1639) embarked on a military career. The youngest son, Antoine (1612–1694), was intended for a brilliant if worldly career in the church. In short, the Arnauld family was on the make, and like other families in similar circumstances, they saw nothing wrong in falsifying Angélique's application for the position of abbess of Port-Royal or in forcing a monastic life upon an unwilling child of eleven.

Angélique on the other hand, was not in the least happy about her new life at Port-Royal in the Valley of Chevreuse, just outside of Paris. She was restless and found even her minimal monastic responsibilities distasteful. She preferred Plutarch's *Lives* to sacred texts, and she amused herself by entertaining guests from the world she was compelled to abandon. So convinced was she that monastic life was diametrically opposed to her aspirations that she even considered escape, urged on by two Huguenot aunts who told her that her vows were against God's intention. At the same time her parents spent much time at Port-Royal managing the estate and seeing to it that Angélique was as comfortable as it was possible for her to be, given her unhappy state of mind.

Six years after her installation as abbess in 1608. Angélique heard a sermon preached by a monk visiting the convent. As she described the event over fifty years later, "God touched me in such a way that as of that moment I was happier to be a nun than I had been unhappy at being one." [2] As a result of this conversion experience, she began to regard herself as an instrument of God's purpose, which was, she thought initially, that she renounce her position as abbess to devote herself entirely to her own spiritual needs. However, she soon realized that it was her duty to reform not only herself but the convent. Her decision to reimpose the Cistercian rule at Port-Royal met with opposition from many of the nuns and from her family as well. Her parents were disturbed by the possibility that the harsh monastic atmosphere would do her bodily harm, and her older brother, Arnauld d'Andilly, then at the threshold of a brilliant career, was of the opinion that Angélique's extravagant intention was detrimental to family interests.[3]

Worn out by fasting and discouraged by her family's attitude, Angélique was at the point of renouncing her intention to reform Port-Royal when she heard another sermon based on the text from the Gospel according to St. Matthew, "Blessed are they that are persecuted for righteousness sake" (5:10). Realizing that God's grace was bestowed on those who resisted worldly influences in whatever form, Angélique resolved once again to initiate Cistercian reforms at Port-Royal. These included strict cloister, control of what had been the nuns' personal property, and maintaining an atmosphere of austere piety, poverty, and simplicity.[4]

Antoine Arnauld was not at all reconciled to his daughter's inclinations. He and his wife objected to cloister because, as Angélique explained, "my mother said that it was necessary that she be admitted [to the convent] so that she could see I was behaving myself. In a certain sense she was right because it was useful and even necessary during my childhood, and because I was only seventeen years old, she didn't have much confidence in me."[5]

The quarrel reached a climax on 25 September 1609. Antoine Arnauld, his wife, and eldest son paid a visit to Port-Royal. When they arrived they were refused admission, but Angélique appeared at a small window from which she invited them into an adjoining parlor—the only room to which visitors were now admitted. Antoine was furious and insisted that he be let into the building proper. She refused whereupon her father vowed that he would never see her again. He was distressed, he told her, by how much her "mind had become perverted."[6] When one of the nuns who happened to witness the confrontation admonished Angélique for her treatment of her father, she retorted, "My parents did not consult me when they made me a nun. Why should I consult them when I wish to live like one."[7] She was so upset by the effect of her intransigence that she fainted. When she had recovered, her parents agreed to respect her reforming intentions.

But rather than causing a definite family break, the episode of 25 September 1609 began a process by which the spirituality of Port-Royal for which Angélique was primarily responsible gradually drew most of the members of the Arnauld family away from worldly pursuits to a life of solitude and prayers in and around Port-Royal. Antoine had begun to provide material support for the convent as his financial situation improved, and he continued to do so throughout his life.[8] As larger numbers of women sought admission to Port-Royal, it became clear that the facility had become incapable of accommodating them. In 1624 Madame Arnauld, now a widow, purchased an estate in Paris to which the community was moved a year later.[9]

The worldly goods of the Arnauld family were soon augmented by their spiritual resources. All the daughters of Antoine and Catherine Arnauld entered the convent. Angélique was joined by her sister Agnes, who had served briefly as abbess of Saint-Cyr, and three other sisters. Anne-Eugénie (1592–1653), Marie de Saint-Claire (1600–1642), and Madeline de Saint-Christine (1607–1649) took their vows at Port-Royal at an early age. After separating from her Huguenot husband, Angélique's older sister, Catherine Le Maistre, moved into the Port-Royal-de-Paris. When her children were no longer dependent on her, Madame Arnauld herself, having distributed her wealth to her progeny and to the convent, took her vows as a novice in 1629.

One of the sisters, Anne-Eugénie, became in effect a pawn in the power struggle between the worldly interests of the Arnauld family and the spiritual demands of Angélique. Installed at Port-Royal at an early age, Anne was removed by her father in 1605 because the improvement in his material fortunes enabled him to contemplate the possibility of an advantageous marriage for her. Anne showed the same signs of discontent and restlessness that her older sister had experienced before her conversion, and under the influence of the Huguenot aunts who had encouraged Angélique to escape, she too came close to converting to Protestantism. An attack of smallpox in 1613 apparently contributed to the conversion experience that caused her to return to the cloister. According to Angélique, who exerted considerable pressure on Anne to return, "God moved her to become a nun and to have such a great contempt for the world" that she overcame her parents' objection and returned to Port-Royal in 1616.[10]

Angélique's powerful spirituality, which infused the atmosphere of Port-Royal and drew the women of the Arnauld family to it, had a similar effect on its men. Although her father remained in the world, his son, Arnauld d'Andilly, during the 1620s became increasingly preoccupied with spiritual concerns. Letters from his sister Agnes, another dominant figure among the nuns at Port-Royal, reveal her efforts to influence d'Andilly and other male relatives to eschew worldly ambitions. "You are," she wrote in 1634, "without ambition and without anxiety, which also makes you more dependent on divine Providence. . . . Who would have thought that solitude . . . should be so agreeable to a person of your condition."[11] In another letter written in the same year Agnes refers to "the perpetual contradiction between faith and feeling, and consequently a continual separation between one and the other."[12] This distinction between faith, which draws one away from the world, and feeling, which draws one toward it, was an essential characteristic of the spirituality of Port-Royal. In counseling her brother, Agnes was very conscious of gender. "This time my dear brother," she wrote, "I am playing the part of preacher as if I had forgotten that I am a woman and your little sister. But you have told me on numerous occasions not to keep my condition in mind as far as you are concerned."[13]

Agnes also used her influence to draw her nephew, Antoine Le Maistre (1608–1658), away from the world. Le Maistre, the oldest son of Isaac Le Maistre and Catherine Arnauld, had embarked on a successful career as a barrister and had become a protégé of the chancellor Pierre Séguier. When his aunt learned that he was about to be married, she did not hesitate to express her disappointment. That decision, she insisted, was based on self-interest and not on devotion to God. "Thus have I spoken to you about marriage, which is not contemptible in itself, but in comparison to the ecclesiastical order, which is an association of the living whereas the other [marriage] constitutes the company of the dead." [14] In 1637 Le Maistre declared his intention to withdraw from the world in a letter to Séguier: "I renounce once and for all my claims to ecclesiastical as well as to civil offices; I am not merely changing my ambition. I have none at all." [15] Instead of entering the clergy, however, Le Maistre became one of the first of a group of men known as the *solitaires,* who lived a secluded life around Port-Royal-des-Champs, where they performed manual labor, penitential exercises, and read and translated sacred texts. Le Maistre was soon joined by his brothers, Le Maistre de Sericourt (1611–1650) and Le Maistre de Saci (1613–1684). After his wife's death and having made various arrangements for his children, the new patriarch of the family, Robert Arnauld d'Andilly also became a *solitaire* in 1643. He was joined by his youngest brother, Antoine (le Grand Arnauld), and a son, Arnauld de Luzancy (1623–1684). All of d'Andilly's daughters became nuns at Port-Royal.

Thus in a very real sense Port-Royal became an Arnauld family enterprise. The women became nuns, and most of the men became *solitaires.* Two, Le Grand Arnauld and Le Maistre de Saci, were confessors to the nuns, and Angélique's brother Henry, who became bishop of Angers in 1649, remained in close touch with the convent. The struggle between Angélique and her parents eventually resulted in the Arnaulds investing their considerable talents and abilities in the service of the spiritual interests of Port-Royal instead of Port-Royal serving the worldly interests of the family.

Angélique Arnauld's struggle to reform Port-Royal was no less intense than the one with her family. At the time she assumed her position as abbess, many of the nuns had little if any religious commitment; they led comfortable lives, enjoying their personal property and entertaining their friends and relatives. Thus Angélique's decision to reestablish the Cistercian rule met with substantial opposition within the convent itself. By forcing nuns without a vocation to leave the establishment and by admitting only those who believed themselves to be called to monastic life, Angélique and Agnes were able to create a community that conformed to their ideals.

The proper governance of Port-Royal was essential to the implementation of monastic reform. In that regard, Angélique worked long and hard to make the office of abbess elective. The ancient right to choose the head of the monastic household had long since disappeared as secular rulers acquired the authority to nominate candidates to high ecclesiastical office subject only to papal confirmation. This authority was sustained by the Council of Trent on the grounds that women in particular were weak and inconstant and therefore incapable of governing themselves. It is a tribute, therefore, to Angélique's tenacity and to the reputation that she had acquired as a reformer that she was able to make her position elective by 1630.[16]

While reviving the rule of Cîteaux, Angélique was able to rely on the support and encouragement of the abbot of the Cistercian order, Dom Boucherat, who was also committed to monastic reform. After his death in 1625, she decided to remove the convent from the jurisdiction of the Cistercian order because she believed his successor to be far less responsive to the needs of the establishment. In 1627 she succeeded in obtaining papal approval to place Port-Royal under the jurisdiction of the archbishops of Paris and Sens and the bishop of Langres. This complicated and ultimately unsatisfactory arrangement resulted from Angélique's association with the bishop of Langres, Sébastien Zamet. Zamet, another reformer, had encouraged the abbess to leave the Cistercians and to place Port-Royal under his direction as the nucleus of a new order, the Institute of the Holy Sacrament, which he proposed to establish. Because the institute was to be located in Paris, Zamet realized that its directorship would have to be shared with local episcopal authority.

The new arrangement had significant consequences for Port-Royal. It first came under suspicion of heresy when Bishop Zamet persuaded Agnes Arnauld to write a special prayer for the new order. The prayer was denounced as heretical by theologians at the Sorbonne, who saw in it a mystical element that was unacceptable to Catholic orthodoxy. Alarmed by these accusations, Zamet invited the abbé de Saint-Cyran, a learned and devout theologian, to defend Agnes's prayer. Saint-Cyran's brief succeeded in warding off condemnation, but the furor created by the charge of heresy led to the dissolution of Zamet's institute and in 1636 the placing of Port-Royal under the sole jurisdiction of the archbishop of Paris. In her account of these events, Angélique wrote that "this persecution . . . was so great that the Court became involved, and there we were described as visionary heretics; and some even went so far as to call us witches."[17] However, the most significant consequence was the involvement of the abbé de Saint-Cyran in the affairs of the convent, first as its defender and then as its spiritual director.

Placing Port-Royal under proper governance also required a devout spiritual director or confessor. For Angélique, proper spiritual direction was essential to the community and to her own needs. She was acutely aware of her own imperfections. Perhaps her greatest struggle throughout her life was with herself. In 1620 she wrote to Jeanne de Chantal: "I am all imperfection, and my grief is that I am unable to see at all the means of correcting myself." [18] To the same person she complained seventeen years later "I . . . am miserable in the continuance of my infidelities and resistance to [God's] grace. I am unable to tell you what I suffer knowing as I do that the depths of my soul do not belong to God but to its own interests, against which it never gives any real resistance for the purpose of a genuine submission to God. I believe that my life is nothing but lies and hypocrisy." [19] Her suffering was all the greater because the potential confessors whom she encountered were unable to serve her needs. For a brief period of time she found some relief in unburdening her soul to the bishop of Annecy, François de Sales, but after his death in 1622, her spiritual life became increasingly internalized to the point where even when she wanted to confess to Saint-Cyran she was unable to do so at first. Finally after several encounters with the abbé, Angélique found it possible to submit to his direction because "God had given him the grace by means of solid truths to touch hearts with the love and respect they owed God in such a way that it gave birth to grief for having offended Him and a great desire to satisfy him." [20]

In contrast to the spirit of independence that Angélique displayed to her parents and to ecclesiastical authorities of one sort or another, she and the nuns submitted to the spiritual authority of the abbé de Saint-Cyran, as did her brothers Arnauld d'Andilly and Antoine Arnauld *fils*. In him they all saw an instrument of God's purpose. When Saint-Cyran was arrested and imprisoned in 1638 because of his opposition to Cardinal Richelieu's policies, the community of Port-Royal was deeply distressed. Its members saw in this event yet another example of the world's persecution of the righteous. Saint-Cyran remained in prison until 1643, after the deaths of Richelieu and Louis XIII, during which time he continued to provide spiritual direction to the nuns of Port-Royal and others through correspondence. Shortly after his release from prison the abbé died of a stroke, and the nuns made a cult of the man whom they regarded as a saint. Pictures of him were to be found in their cells and relics such as bits of his hair and the water in which he had washed his hands were venerated.

At the time of his death, Saint-Cyran's penitential theology was under attack. A book written by Cornelius Jansen, bishop of Ypres, entitled *Augustinus* published in 1640, was denounced by several ecclesiastical officials. Jansen had been a close friend of Saint-Cyran's and had collaborated with him in developing his theological ideas. Another book, *De la*

*Frequente Communion*, published by a protegé of Saint-Cyran and one of his successors as spiritual directors of Port-Royal, Le Grand Arnauld, had become equally controversial. Both works were suspect because they advocated a penitential discipline that seemed excessive to some leaders in the church. Eventually several propositions allegedly drawn from Jansen's opus were condemned by Pope Innocent XI on the grounds that they came too close to the Calvinist doctrine of predestination.

Supporters of the *Augustinus* came to be known as Jansenists. They included Antoine Arnauld, who wrote several works in defense of Jansen's theology, which led to his being expelled from the faculty of the Sorbonne in 1655. As one might expect, the nuns of Port-Royal were horrified that the beliefs of the man whose memory they cherished were pronounced as heretical and that the brother of Angélique Arnauld was repudiated by the Sorbonne. Once again they saw in these developments further examples of the blessed being persecuted for righteousness sake by the wicked.

The quarrel caused by the works of Jansen and Arnauld took place during the time of the civil war known as the Fronde. After Cardinal Mazarin regained control of the French government in 1653, he decided to suppress what came to be known as the Jansenist movement in the interests of political order and tranquility. He obtained from the Assembly of Clergy a formulary, to be signed by all clergy including nuns, that professed obedience to the pope's decision to condemn the propositions allegedly drawn from Jansen's work. For political reasons the formularly was not circulated until 1661, when the young king, Louis XIV, took over the government after Mazarin's death.

Consternation was widespread among the nuns of Port-Royal. By signing the formulary, each nun would personally condemn what she devoutly believed to be the theology of the abbé de Saint-Cyran. By not signing each nun would be proclaiming her disobedience to both church and state. There were essentially two responses within Port-Royal to the crisis of conscience produced by the formulary. The position taken by Angélique, who was on her deathbed when the crisis occurred, was that although persecution was a sign of God's mercy, to engage in public dispute was to be guilty of the sin of pride. Therefore one should sign the formulary out of a sense of humility. In other words, the nuns should suffer persecution in silence. On the other hand, the position taken by her niece, Angélique de Saint-Jean, the eldest daughter of Arnauld d'Andilly and the dominant personality within Port-Royal after the death of her aunt, was that signature of the formulary was in effect, a repudiation of the reform movement launched by her aunt and sanctified by Saint-

Cyran. Angélique de Saint-Jean had no intention of remaining silent, and she encouraged the publication of memoirs and correspondence that depicted the struggle of Port-Royal against the world so that the heroism of the nuns might inspire others to do likewise. After unsuccessful attempts to work out a compromise with various ecclesiastical authorities, the new archbishop, Hardouin de Péréfixé, who had assumed his position in 1664, made a series of visits to Port-Royal-de-Paris during which he interrogated each nun individually. Alone in the presence of such an august personage, each was forced to decide whether to sign the formulary in obedience to the archbishop's command. When he met with resistance from one nun he lost his temper. "Shut up! You are nothing but a little obstinate, headstrong person with no intelligence, and you take it upon yourself to judge things about which you know nothing. You are nothing but a stuck-up girl, a little goose, a know-nothing." [21] On another occasion, when he met with the nuns as a group, Péréfixé complained: "You are as pure as angels but as proud as Lucifer." [22] The wrath of the archbishop was enough to convince a number of nuns to sign the formulary. However, twelve, including Agnes Arnauld, and her nieces, Angélique de Saint-Jean and Marie-Angélique (1630–1670), refused to submit. They were taken from Port-Royal, placed in other convents around the city, where they were supervised by unsympathetic nuns, and deprived of the sacraments.

The psychological hardships endured by the nuns are described in individual accounts that were later published. In her account, Marie-Angélique describes the doubt and confusion that she experienced as a result of being deprived of both the sacraments and the right to confess that initially caused her to recant and sign. But once having yielded to the pressures put on her by the archbishop and her guardian nuns she felt such remorse that she wrote to Péréfixé retracting her signature. "I was unable to escape the reproaches of my conscience which became my accuser and my judge." [23] Agnes Arnauld aged and infirm at the time of her removal, remained unalterably convinced that the persecution she endured was a sign of God's favor.

The most dramatic account of the confrontation with Péréfixé, the removal from Port-Royal, and the suffering endured in the hostile atmosphere within the convent in which she was placed, appears in the account of Angélique de Saint-Jean. As she was being removed from her own convent, she was asked to state her family name by one of her guards. "I said it [the name of Arnauld] aloud, without blushing, for in such a circumstance it is almost like confessing the name of God to confess our own when it is being dishonored for His sake." [24] In her mind, the Arnauld family, once honored for its worldly achievements, was now to be honored for the persecution that its members suffered in service to God. Cut off from the sacraments, Angélique de Saint-Jean experienced within her a "struggle between grace and nature, without any arms to defend myself except the shield of truth." She was able to survive, she tells us, by reestablishing Port-Royal within herself. She chanted portions of the Mass, and subjected herself to the sort of intense introspection advocated by Saint-Cyran that served as a form of confession. She found that she was able to do without the sacraments. As she explained it, "We benefit" from participation in the sacraments, "the love and desire for which increases every day when we are deprived of them for a long time. Nevertheless, if they were restored to us, it might occasion perilous temptations, and if we were permitted to confess without a free choice of confessor, nothing could do us greater harm." [25]

In July 1665 almost a year after the nuns were dispersed from Port-Royal-de-Paris, Archbishop Péréfixé installed all the nuns who refused their signature at Port-Royal-de-Champs, where they continued to be denied sympathetic confessors and the sacraments.[26] Angélique de Saint-Jean and the others remained adamant in the refusal of their signature because, in their minds, they had made a distinction between the true church of God and the false church dominated by worldly officials, a distinction that appears in a prayer written by the nuns in 1664. "It is from these pastors [the Apostles] who have not wanted to dominate their flock that we ask justice against our pastors [the Archbishop of Paris and others] who rise up against us with a power that [God has] not given them because [such power] tends to be destructive and not [for] the edification of souls." [27]

A compromise between the papacy and the French government, on the one hand, and the Jansenists, on the other, was eventually worked out in 1669. The arrangement called for an end to all public discussions of the issues relating to the *Augustinus* and the circulation of a new formulary, which permitted mental reservations as to whether Jansen's work was heretical. The nuns at Port-Royal-des-Champs signed despite the profound misgivings of Angélique de Saint-Jean, and they were then allowed to partake of the sacraments. The Jansenist controversy flared up once again during the 1680's to the point where Louis XIV, exasperated by the political and religious unrest caused by war, ordered the destruction of Port-Royal-des-Champs in 1711 and the dispersal of the nuns who were left.[28]

What was left of Port-Royal-des-Champs is now faced with extinction as highrise apartment houses, shopping centers, and other forms of suburban culture threaten to finish the job begun by Louis XIV's soldiers. But the copious record of the nuns' activities, their religious experiences, and their struggles constitute an indestructible monument to their spirituality. We must ask ourselves, on the basis of that record, what were the particular attributes of their spirituality that enabled the nuns to withstand pressures from family, church, and state, and were these attributes related to gender? After her conversion experience, Angélique Arnauld sought to detach herself from her family and from the world. Indeed her entire life as a nun consisted of a struggle against worldly influences as she sought to become entirely attached to God. "It is certain," she wrote, "that attachment to creatures is the greatest obstacle to our progress toward [spiritual] reflection. We must attach ourselves to God alone. When we distance ourselves from creatures, we approach God. . . . In God we find every good thing, and, without God, we find nothing good. This ought to require us to attach ourselves to Him alone." [29] As Angélique and the nuns of Port-Royal became ever more dependent on God's grace in order to become attached to God, they asserted their independence from worldly influences.

Attachment to God required submission to God's purpose and to those who were clearly motivated by God's grace. Hence Angélique eventually submitted to the spiritual direction of the abbé de Saint-Cyran and his protégés. However those to whom she had submitted were compelled to suffer persecution for righteousness' sake as she had done at the time of her initial quarrel with her family. Did obedience and submission to saintly persons such as Saint-Cyran signify disobedience to those who oppressed them? If such disobedience took a public form, then it was unacceptable to Angélique because public displays of any kind were but manifestations of pride. However for her niece, Angélique de Saint-Jean, who took pride in her family's association with a holy cause, disobedience to unjust authority was but a manifestation of submission to God.

All Jansenists, male and female, struggled to detach themselves from the world and submit themselves to God, and beyond the walls of Port-Royal they struggled against what they perceived to be the corrupt forces of the century in which they lived. However dependency and submission are attributes historically associated with women. It was their apparent independence and their inclination toward disobedience that caused the nuns to be accused of being witches, stuck-up girls, and obstinate geese and eventually led to the violent destruction of Port-Royal-des-Champs. Independence and insubordination on the part of women were particularly offensive to Archbishop Péréfixé and Louis XIV. Like their oppressors, the nuns of Port-Royal were always sensitive to their status as women as is made clear, for instance, in Agnes Arnauld's letters to her brother, and in their awareness at all times of their monastic vows. Their behavior with respect to family, church, and state was based entirely upon what they believed to be a more perfect dependency and submission than the outside world—with the exception of the Jansenists—was capable of understanding.⟩

## NOTES

1 / Alexander Sedgwick, *Jansenism in Seventeenth-Century France: Voices from the Wilderness* (Charlottesville: Univ. Press of Virginia, 1977), 14–21.

2 / Louis Cognet, ed., *Relation ecrite par la Mere Angélique de Saint-Jean sur Port-Royal* (Paris: B. Grasset, 1949), 40.

3 / Louis Cognet, *La Réforme de Port-Royal, 1591–1618* (Paris: Sulliver, 1950), 95. This is the most important book on the early career of Angélique Arnauld and her family. An essential work for those interested in the subject is Sainte-Beuve's classic *Port-Royal*.

4 / For a discussion of the relationship between Port-Royal and the Cistercian order, see F. Ellen Weaver, *The Evolution of the Reform of Port-Royal from the Rule of Citeaux to Jansenism* (Paris: Beauchesne, 1977).

5 / Cognet, *Relation ecrite par la Mere Angélique*, 50.

6 / Ibid., 61.

7 / Quoted in Cognet, *La Réforme de Port-Royal*, 116–17.

8 / For the best discussion to date of the financial support that the Arnauld family provided Port-Royal, see William Ritchey Newton, "Port-Royal and Jansenism: Social Experience, Group Formation, and Religious Attitudes in Seventeenth-Century France," Ph.D. diss., Univ. of Michigan, 1974.

9 / Port-Royal now consisted of two establishments: Port-Royal-de-Paris, to which the community was removed in 1625, and Port-Royal-des-Champs, which remained empty until the Fronde, when Angélique and a handful of nuns returned.

10 / Cognet, *Relation ecrite par la Mere Angélique*, 70; idem, *La Réforme*, 195–238.

11 / M. P. Faugere, ed., *Letters de la Mere Agnes Arnauld, Abbesse de Port-Royal* (Paris, 1858), 1:36–37.

12 / Ibid., 57.

13 / Ibid., 67.

14 / Ibid., 55.

15 / Quoted in Sedgwick, *Jansenism*, 24.

16 / Weaver, *Evolution of Reform*, 44, 53.

17 / Cognet, *Relation ecrite par la Mere Angélique*, 138–39.

18 / Augustin Gazier, *Jeanne de Chantal et Angélique Arnauld d'aprés leur correspondence, 1620–1641* (Paris: H. Champion, 1915), 129.

19 / Ibid., 153–54.

20 / Cognet, *Relation ecrite par la Mere Angélique*, 146–47.

21 / Quoted in Henry de Monterlant, *Port-Royal* (Paris, Gallimard 1954), 16.

22 / Quoted in Weaver, *Evolution of Reform*, 106.

23 / *Divers actes, letters, et relations des religieuses de Port-Royal du Saint-Sacrement touchant la signature du formulaire* (Utrecht, 1735), vol. 1. These volumes are unpaginated.

24 / Ibid., vol. 2.

25 / Ibid.

26 / Port-Royal-de-Paris was now separated once and for all from Port-Royal-des-Champs. It contained the nuns who signed the formulary whereas Port-Royal-des-Champs contained the intransigent nuns.

27 / *Divers Actes*, vol. 1.

28 / Port-Royal was denied the right to receive postulants as of 1679. This act on the part of the archbishop of Paris in effect denied the convent a future.

29 / Gazier, *Jeanne de Chantal et Angélique Arnauld d'apier in correspondance*, 143.

## 11

*Rosemary Skinner Keller*

## Calling and Career:
## The Revolution in the
## Mind and Heart of
## Abigail Adams

WHAT DO WE MEAN BY THE AMERICAN REVOLUTION? Do we mean the American War?" queried John Adams in a letter to his friend Hezekiah Niles in 1818, long after the War for Independence was completed. He responded to his own thoughtful question with a brilliantly provocative answer that is classic in the literature of the revolutionary era.

"The Revolution was effected before the war commenced," Adams continued. "The Revolution was in the minds and hearts of the people; a change in their religious sentiments of their duties and obligations. . . . This radical change in the principles, opinions, sentiments, and affections of the people was the real American Revolution." [1]

The revolution "in the minds and hearts of the people" marked the crucial turning point in the vision held by New England patriots, a vision inherited from their Puritan forebears of the Massachusetts Bay colony as a restored Jerusalem committed to devotion and service to God. It led them to a modern conception of the United States as a secular nation undergirded by religious principles of public morality and civic virtue. If not avowedly identified as a Christian country, the United States would always incorporate sacred principles to justify its nationalistic mission.

Adams's sense of inner revolution as a "radical change in [people's] duties and obligations" points to a historic shift in the Puritan idea of calling and career. Writing from the Continental Congress in Philadelphia to his wife Abigail, at their home in Braintree, Massachusetts, in October 1775, he declared: "My opinion of the Duties of Religion and Morality comprehends a very extensive Connection with society at large, and the great Interest of the public. Does not natural morality, and much more Christian Benevolence, make it our indispensable Duty to lay ourselves out to serve our Fellow Creatures to the Utmost of our Power, in promoting and supporting those great Political systems. . . . Public

Virtues, and political Qualities, therefore should be incessantly cherished in our children."[2]

During the revolutionary era, men began to select professions with greater freedom than was possible for their Puritan fathers. Occupational decisions now became the first steps in a career including different kinds of work that contributed service to the public while also bringing personal fulfillment to the individual. Because of their overarching religious worldview and a belief that they were set apart to fulfill God's will, male patriots could not yet choose their work based upon self-aggrandizing ambition and upward mobility.

The merging of calling from God and personal choice in the motivations underlying John Adams's professional life exemplified the model of the age set before the sons of the revolutionary generation. His decision to become a lawyer was finally reached out of his conviction that law could be as effective as the ministry in serving his fellow citizens in the name of God, while at the same time responding to his own interests and need for esteem and status in the eyes of others.[3] His long years of service to his country, from representative to the Continental Congress and architect of the Declaration of Independence to the vice-presidency and presidency, symbolized the evolution from the earlier Puritan belief in the ordained ministry as the highest expression of calling to the conviction of the revolutionary generation that political service was both the most exalted calling from God and the most satisfying personal career.

Though less acknowledged, the American woman's life also has been defined historically by a careerist orientation, just as a man's has been. Until the late twentieth century, the proper role and work of a middle-class white woman has been circumscribed within the home, literally as a career, in President Theodore Roosevelt's words, "more worthy of honor and . . . more useful to the community than the career of any man, no matter how successful."[4]

The encasement of woman's function within the home gained almost unquestioned acceptance until the present day because her purpose was deemed not only a personal career but also a calling from God. The link between woman's calling and career was stated with conviction by a primary advocate and female educator of the nineteenth century, Catharine Beecher. She sought to uplift and sanctify the female's domestic role and to bring her social, political, and religious purposes together by stating a domestic ideology to justify woman's full-time role as homemaker:

> The woman . . . contributes to the intellectual and moral elevation of the
> country, even the humble domestic whose example and influence may be

moulding and forming young minds, while her faithful services sustain a prosperous domestic state; each and all may be animated by the consciousness, that they are agents in accomplishing the greatest work that ever was committed to human responsibility. It is the building of a glorious temple, whose base shall pierce the skies, whose splendor shall beam on all lands; 'and those who hew the lowliest stone, as much as those who carve the highest capital, will be equally honored, when its top-stone shall be laid, with new rejoicings of the morning stars, and shoutings of the sons of God.[5]

This essay seeks to analyze the union between calling and career in the experience of Abigail Adams. It posits that the era of the American Revolution marked a turning point in understanding woman's role not exclusively as a calling from God but as a career that gained its sanction from God. The essay first describes the nature of personal calling which Abigail Adams inherited from her Puritan ancestors. Second, it portrays the revolution in her own mind and heart that marks the origins of a careerist orientation, undergirded by calling from God, in modern American womanhood. The essay integrates the sense of calling and career in Abigail Adams's experience and background with that of John's life and ancestry. For her identity can only be understood in relationship to his, both as her life was subsumed under his and as she sought to become a person of equal stature and interdependence with her husband.

The most striking quality of Abigail and John Adams's family ancestry is the deep sense of calling from God that pervaded their lives. Further, their heritage personifies the distinct roles Puritan society delegated to men and women for the fulfillment of those callings.

Abigail Smith Adams descended on her mother's side from the Quincy family, a long line of natural or untitled aristocracy of landed gentry in Massachusetts history. The first Quincys to arrive in Boston were Edmund and Judith, with one son and six servants in the Puritan migration led by church divine John Cotton and his wife, Sarah, in 1633. They were among the earliest colonists admitted to membership in the First church of Boston with the Cottons in July of that year.[6]

Edmund Quincy received one of the few large land allotments of several hundred acres by the Massachusetts General Court in its effort to raise up a landed gentry alongside the predominant class of small farmers. He was immediately elected to the first General Court, and multiplied his land holdings until he owned a sizable part of the shoreline known today as Quincy Bay. All this was accomplished in his four short years in America before he died in 1639, still a young man in his thirties.[7]

The career pattern for men of subsequent generations of the landed gentry was public service, civic and religious, to their town and province, following that of the first Edmund Quincy. The gentlemen had underlings to carry on daily management of their estates, enabling them to commit themselves to voluntary public duty, representing Braintree on the General Court, serving on the Massachusetts Provincial Council, and holding provincial judgeships and justices of the peace. Further, they all carried the essential pedigree of a Harvard degree. The career of John Quincy, Abigail Adams's grandfather, was typical. He received Braintree's most distinguished appointment, representative to the Massachusetts General Court, at the age of twenty-eight. Between 1717 and 1756, the town delegated him to that same high post thirty-one times. It was fitting that the name of Braintree was changed to Quincy in his honor, as well as others in the family line, in 1792.[8]

John Adams's family were sturdy New England yeomen, a strand of the Quincys. His original American ancestors were Henry and Edith Adams, a part of the first settlement of English Puritans to emigrate directly to the Braintree area in the early 1630s.[9]

To stress the social and class distinctions between the Quincys and Adamses is to miss the essence of life in the small New England town of Braintree. The town records from the founding of the village until 1760, when John Adams came onto the scene of public life, point to the close interrelationship of the two families from generation to generation. Adams men attained an unprecedented total of thirty-five accumulated years as selectmen, moving from the most menial positions in the community to the top level. The community created its own self-styled gentry, amounting to a union between the Quincy and Adams families long before the marriage of Abigail Smith and John Adams was consummated.[10]

The most immediate and direct influence upon Abigail Smith as she grew up was religious commitment. Her father, the Reverend William Smith, came to Weymouth, Massachusetts, in 1734 as a Harvard graduate, twenty-seven years old, to enter the ministry. He lived the rest of his days there, remaining as minister of the small First Church of Weymouth, a few miles south of Braintree, for forty-nine years until his death in 1783. Six years after arriving in Weymouth, he married Elizabeth, the daughter of John and Elizabeth Quincy. During the next ten years, the couple had three daughters and one son.

By outward social standards, William Smith seemed to be the logical man to marry into the Quincy family. His father was a wealthy mariner and merchant who owned large land holdings, particularly an eighty-acre farm on the Mystic River. Probably as a result of inherited wealth, Abigail's father had an economic status above that of most families in his Weymouth parish.[11]

At least two deep impressions of Smith's ministry must have had abiding influences on Abigail's life. One was his staying quality, the ability to persist in the regular and unexceptional tasks placed upon him. The records of the Weymouth Church and Smith's diary indicate that he was a minister of middling sorts who was content to live out his days and his calling in the small village. Second was his emphasis on doctrinal Christianity, the liberal precepts of a rational and practical Christianity including freedom of the will and the right of private judgment. During the American Revolution, Abigail's life was characterized by its diligence in fulfilling rigorous but ordinary homefront responsibilities. Further, throughout her life, she upheld the reasonableness of Christianity, remained within the liberal wing of Congregationalism, and applied its precepts to the rights of women and blacks.[12]

No diaries or letters of Abigail's mother or grandmother are extant. Comparable sources within the Quincy papers, however, give insight into the expectations placed upon women in the family. The three men in the Quincy line whose wives were living when their wills were executed designated their wives as executors and named no male overseers, suggesting that these women had assumed joint responsibilities in managing the business transactions of their large estates. It was equally uncommon for men in colonial society to grant real property in their wills to wives and daughters. While Quincy men granted the "use and improvement" of land to wives, as was typical, they usually gave real property to daughters. Those shares of land were bequeathed equitably to daughters and sons in the Quincy families.[13]

The letters of Edmund Quincy IV, Abigail's uncle, to his three daughters, her close associates in Braintree, provide further rare and significant insights into the attitudes in the family toward women. The understanding of life as weighty, purposeful, and committed to God is the overriding theme of Quincy's correspondence. Writing his daughter Katy when she was seventeen years old in 1750, the father admonished her to recognize the utter seriousness of life while she was in her youth and to use and improve her time to greatest advantage. He stated this stark perception of life in a letter to her twenty-five years later when, in his later years, he contemplated the momentous consequences of the impending revolutionary conflict: "Ah, my Friends while we laugh all things are Serious round about us. . . . *God* is serious who exerciseth patience toward us, *Christ* is serious who sheds his blood for us; the *holy Ghost* is serious who continually strives ag.t the obstinacy of our hearts: the *holy Scripture* . . . bring[s] to our eyes tears the most serious things in the world; the *holy Sacraments* represent the most serious and awful *truths;* . . . All that are in *Heaven* or *Hell* are Serious, how then can we be gay." [14]

Quincy believed that the preparation of his daughters for their adult role was as important a task as was that of his son. As he wrote Katy in 1750: "To prepare for your Succeeding Future State . . . is as necessary as it would be for a Soldier to Furnish himself with all accoutrements of war." His key admonition to Katy was this: May your ornament of a "meek and Quiet Spirit . . . be that which you most delight in, and may you learn to look on Every other only as Tinsel or Triffles." [15]

Edmund Quincy's words that Katy maintain a "meek and Quiet Spirit" were counsel that she fit into the traditional Puritan image of the female as subordinate to men and restricted to the private framework of the home. In reading more deeply into his correspondence to his daughters, however, both the style and content of the letters reveal a sense of equality in his relationship to them. He wrote Katy in 1783: "I treat you as a friend and therefore use no ceremony." He closed his letters to his daughters with the words "your friend and father." [16] To latter-day Puritans of the Enlightenment, "friend" signified equality.

In one sense there is a paradoxical quality to the instructions Quincy gave his daughters. He admonished them, first, to maintain a "meek and Quiet Spirit," a subordinate, private role that was expected in a woman of Puritan descent in the eighteenth century. On the other hand, he addressed them as near equals. He expected these women to think and to commit themselves to religious and civic duty just as men would do.

The differing goals were not actually paradoxical. Though clearly limited to the domestic sphere, Quincy women were expected to support their husbands' work and to be able to express themselves and their thoughts on public issues. Quincy sought to mold strong and intelligent women, suitable companions for men whose lives were geared to public service. Through their designated private sphere, women of the family were to be as committed to religious and political responsibility as men.

The consuming religious dedication of the Quincy women is reflected in one of the few statements in the family papers written by females. Mary Quincy, daughter of the second Edmund and his wife, Elizabeth, wrote a paper in 1712 that sheds light on the outlook on life and the educational level of Abigail Adams's female ancestors. Both Mary's parents had died not long before, and she had just recovered from a serious illness that had threatened her life. The stress of such circumstances impelled Mary Quincy to write a personal credo. Her statement is pervaded with a deep sense of religious faith communicated through her Puritan heritage: "It pleased God to help me in my childhood with a religious education and to this day with the means of his grace and my salvation. . . . I was moved to think more closely and seriously on my condition than I thought I had done before thereupon I made my promise that if God pleas'd to recover mee I would amend my ways and walk more closely with him than before I had done. . . . I hope I can truly say I am sick of sin and desire to loath and abhor my self for it and to rely only on the merits of xt [Christ] for pardon." [17]

This significant statement, drawing upon scriptural citations, demonstrates that her self-knowledge, and the ability to articulate it, were comparable to those of men within the Quincy line. Though the women were tutored at home while their brothers attended Harvard, it is clear that the family emphasized female education. Mary Quincy was a strong woman who demonstrated the capabilities and training both to think and act for herself.


After Abigail Smith and John Adams were married on October 25, 1764, by Parson Smith in the First Church of Weymouth, they moved into the square salt-block house in Braintree that John inherited from his father. In some respects the early years of their marriage were a time of domestic peace and felicity in which both partners engaged in traditional marital roles. "We do pretty much as We used to of old," Abigail wrote her sister-in-law, Mary Smith Cranch, in 1766. "Marry and give in Mariage, increase and multiply all in the old fashioned way." [18]

Abigail bore their one daughter and three sons who lived to adulthood, and two daughters who died in infancy. She maintained primary responsibility for the home, while John rode the Massachusetts and eastern Maine court circuits, establishing a creditable reputation as a lawyer. He was also active in Braintree local government, serving as selectman, surveyor of highways, assessor, and overseer of the poor.

Abigail and John Adams brought into their marriage the rich heritage of calling from God that had been transmitted to them through the several generations of their Puritan ancestors on Massachusetts soil. Had the War for Independence not impinged upon their lives, they likely would have lived out their callings "pretty much as We used to of old . . . in the old fashioned way" of their forebears in the small Braintree world. The patterns of their lives seemed set, as they began marriage just a score of years before independence was declared. John would express his calling through a career in law and local public service, and Abigail would support him on the domestic scene as did all latter-day Puritan women to fulfill their callings.

"The real American Revolution," which, as we have seen, Adams described as "a change in their religious sentiments of their duties and obligations," occurred as deeply and personally within Abigail Adams as in her husband during the decade preceding the Declaration of Independence, beginning in 1765. Between 1765 and 1776, her thinking incorporated the arguments for independence, leaving her British heritage for the sake of a new American identity.

Because of her deep spiritual conviction and belief in calling from God, Abigail became convinced that the War for Independence was a holy war, that God was on the side of the American patriots, and that the "Lord Jehovah" would lead them to victory through military revolution. Such a religious persuasion caused her to internalize a political purpose for her life at home during the American Revolution and enabled her to commit her daily life to the war effort with the same intense conviction that motivated her husband during his ten years as a delegate to the Continental Congress, as American diplomat to Europe, and as peace negotiator with Great Britain.

Both continued to believe that their lives were defined by calling from God. But as surely as John incorporated an emerging idea of a man's career into the traditional understanding of calling that pervaded the lives of his ancestors, Abigail's role also evolved from the traditional idea of the Puritan woman's calling. Her life during the American Revolution exemplifies an emerging belief that women on the domestic scene also had a political and religious purpose—to provide the moral undergirding of a new secular nation.

Abigail Adams's revolution of loyalty within her heart and mind was grounded, most immediately, in her own and her family's daily experience after 1765. The Adamses lived both in Boston and in nearby Braintree during these years in the shadows of an armed camp. By 1768 British artillerymen had landed in Boston harbor and drilled daily in Brattle Square in front of their residence. Abigail felt indignation at the stationing of troops during peacetime, recognizing it as an ominous threat that Great Britain was determined to subjugate the American colonies. Newspaper articles described the city as a perfect garrison: "All the troops landed under cover of the cannon of the ships of war, and marched into the Common, with muskets charged, bayonets fixed, colours flying, drums beating, and fifes, &c, playing." The Common was covered with soldiers and tents. The House of Representatives, Court House, and Fanueil Hall were occupied by troops. Daily accounts in newspapers told of scuffles between innocent citizens and soldiers, which resulted in shootings, knivings, and confinement without lawful warrants of citizens in jail. Townspeople of patriot persuasion retaliated against military rule by tarring and feathering tory informers, beating customs officials, raiding stores for food and supplies, and destroying local guardhouses.[19]

A second major influence on Abigail's revolution of loyalty was her husband's central role in the Continental Congress, from its opening sessions in September 1774, until independence was declared. No person was more responsible for turning that body from conciliation with Great Britain to advocacy of independence. He was one of five delegates originally chosen by the Massachusetts House of Representatives to serve in the first Congress of the colonies. After his election, he rapidly shifted his focus from law and part-time public service to national offices and concerns. Adams has rightly been considered one of the leading protagonists in the struggle for the congressional mind and the chief architect, along with Thomas Jefferson, of the Declaration of Independence.[20]

The final major influences that led Abigail Adams to a commitment to American independence were the readings of secular historians and political propagandists and the sermons of patriot ministers. Her letters are laced with her personal commentaries on the writings of histories of Great Britain and the Greek and Roman empires, by such persons as James Burgh, Catharine Macaulay, and Charles Rollins, who influenced patriot leaders toward a revolutionary commitment.

Abigail read these histories for what they taught her generation and was moved by their application of lessons from the past to the British and American scene. The writers interpreted history as a sermon on the text that nothing is more dangerous than power without responsibility, and feared that the downfall of Greece and Rome was being repeated in modern-day England. To guard against the abuse of power, the people must be virtuous. Rome fell because its people became engrossed in private ambition and succumbed to luxury, ease, and pleasure. Virtuous citizens, on the other hand, were not private persons. The lesson of history was that the "greatness of Soul" of Athens and Sparta was found in the virtues of love of courage and labor, disregard of self-interest, and zeal for liberty.[21]

These historians told the story of the past as if it were a morality play, written in terms of good and bad, virtue and vice, whig and tory. Being able to interpret history in absolute terms enabled Abigail Adams to persuade herself more easily that the British position was categorically wrong and the American right. American pamphleteers, such as John Dickinson and John Adams, applied the same technique to the revolutionary crisis. So did Boston ministers, including Jonathan Mayhew, Charles Chauncy, Samuel Cooper, and Andrew Eliot, whom Abigail referred to in her letters, as well as her own father, William Smith.[22]

The clergy's contention that God must approve of the American cause was the most powerful sanction for rebellion in the eyes of a religious person like Abigail Adams. Subjects were to be dutiful and peaceable, never using their liberty as a cloak for licentiousness. On the other hand, the Christian's primary loyalty was "to the supreme RULER of the universe, *by whom kings and princes decree justice.*" Submission of the citizen was a criminal act if the ruler usurped unwarranted power and oppressed the people. After careful and rational deliberation, the true patriot might be required to rebel.[23]

The revolution within Abigail Adams's heart and mind reached its final stage by early 1775. Her own experience of living in the armed camp of Boston, her husband's involvement in the Continental Congress, her readings in secular history and propaganda tracts, and her attention to the sermons of patriot preachers led Abigail to a shift of allegiance from Great Britain to America. During the last year of her intellectual revolution, she developed a rationale to justify war and independence to herself and to convince other people to accept her radical views. A letter written to her husband at the Congress in November 1775 testifies to her revolutionary commitment. In as forceful language as any patriot propagandist could have employed, Abigail called upon the Lord to defeat the designs of the British: "I could not join to day in the petitions of our worthy parson, for a reconciliation between our no longer parent State, but tyrant State, and these Colonies.—Let us separate, they are unworthy to be our Breathren. Let us renounce them and instead of suplications as formorly for their prosperity and happiness, Let us beseech the almighty to blast their counsels and bring to Nought all their devices."[24]

More than simply an intellectual conversion from British to American loyalty, Abigail's revolution was a commitment of her whole self, her feelings and will along with her mind, to the patriot cause. She stated this total involvement well in describing a celebration of American independence which she attended in Boston on July 18, 1776. After hearing a sermon on Thursday, "I went with the multitudes into Kings Street," she wrote to John, "to hear the proclamation for independence read and proclaimed." It was a great and joyful occasion, much as anniversaries of American independence have been celebrated since then. Troops marched, artillery pieces were displayed, the cry "was God Save our

American States and then 3 cheers which rended the air, the Bells rang, the privateers fired, the forts and Batteries, the cannons were discharged, the platoons followed and every face appeared joyfull." The event was climaxed by removal of the king's arms from the State House. Symbols of the British rulers were brought together and burned in King Street. Abigail's final commentary signified her total commitment to the American cause of independence: "Thus ends royall Authority in this State and all the people shall say Amen."[25]

Abigail Adams's conversion gave her endurance to fulfill the demanding jobs that lay ahead during the Revolution. Without her strong commitment to the American cause, she would have found it even more difficult to accomplish patriot tasks on the homefront and take responsibility for property and family management during her husband's long absence.

She saw her primary patriotic and religious duty in tending the family's private affairs with frugality and in releasing her husband for service on high levels and in distant places. "Doubled in Wedlock," Abigail raised their children and managed the home and farm alone.[26]

"All domestick pleasure and injoyments are absorbed in the great and important duty you owe your Country," Abigail wrote to John. Her function was a sacrificial one, to release him from cares and responsibilities of the home and family so that his life could be given to the "Secondary God" of country. The honors that public service brought to John were to Abigail "badges of unhappiness" from which she gained "a pleasure in being able to sacrifice my selfish passions to the general good, and in imitating the example which has taught me to consider myself and family, but as small dust of the balance when compared with the great community."[27]

While her Puritan ancestors saw the home as a "little church," with religious training at its core, the revolutionary generation began to envisage it as a training ground to mold their sons and daughters into good citizens. "The only sure and permanent foundation of virtue is Religion," she wrote her son, John Quincy, when he was only thirteen years old and studying in Europe. Training him from his earliest years to become a great statesman, she undergirded his emerging vision of career with a calling from God. Her letter continued: "Every new Mercy you receive is a New Debt upon you, a new obligation . . . in the first place to your Great Preserver, in the next to Society in General, in particular to your Country, to your parents and to yourself."[28]

In the upbringing of her daughter, Nabby, Abigail Adams strongly advocated a more liberal and comprehensive education for girls. Yet she believed that the young woman's primary calling and career in the new nation for many years to come would be to stand behind, rather than alongside, men. As she put it: "If we mean to have Heroes, Statesmen, and Philosophers, we would have learned women."[29]

Characteristic of many women of any age, Abigail Adams conceived her purpose in two ways. Besides her primary understanding and function of living her life through her husband and children, she evaluated her responsibilities during the war: "I hope in time to have the Reputation of being as good a *Farmeress* as my partner has of being a good Statesmen." Abigail knew that, in fact, she was functioning as an autonomous being in an equal and interdependent relationship with her husband, with a career, even an identity, of her own. She still lived primarily out of the meaning of a woman's calling from God as understood and transmitted by her Puritan ancestors. As a "good wife" of the late eighteenth century, Abigail would never have been able to identify herself as other than her husband's surrogate.[30]

Her appeal to John at the Continental Congress in 1776 to "remember the Ladies and to [be] more generous and favourable to them than your ancestors . . . in the new Codes of Law" is a striking example of the disjunction between Abigail's perception of herself and the reality of her existence. Her appeal was to both reason and revelation, like that of the Declaration of Independence. She, too, was asking the governing authorities to act "in immitation of the Supreme Being" to use their power to write the full humanity of women into the laws of the nation.[31] John Adams responded to his wife that he could not but laugh at her "Extraordinary Code of Laws." He knew that the American struggle with Britain had set an example and "loosened the bands of Government everywhere." Children, apprentices, Indians, and "Negroes grew insolent to their Masters." But, as he jokingly dismissed her plea, "your letter was the first Intimation that another Tribe more numerous and powerfull than all the rest were grown discontented."[32]

In a more serious tone, he expressed fear of the dynamic principle behind her ideas in a letter to John Sullivan, delegate to the Massachusetts Provincial Assembly, shortly after his exchange with his wife:

> Depend upon it, Sir, it is dangerous to open so fruitful a source of controversy and altercation as would be opened by attempting to alter the qualifications of voters; there will be no end of it. New claims will arise; women will demand a vote, lads from twelve to twenty-one will think their rights not enough attended to; and every man who has not a farthing, will

demand an equal voice with any other, in all acts of state. It tends to confound and destroy all distinctions, and prostrate all ranks to one common level.[33]

Six years later, in the summer of 1782, as John was in the midst of peace negotiations with Great Britain, Abigail again wrote him concerning the rights of women and the patriotic effort they had displayed during the war. She began by expressing the same strong commitment to American independence that she had articulated when the Declaration was signed. Reports reaching New England indicated that disappointing terms, providing a peace settlement unfavorable to America, were being framed in Britain. Abigail told John that the states were instructing their Congressional delegates "to consider every offer as an insult from Britain . . . if Independence is not made the Basis." She tenaciously advanced the same conviction: "I cannot feel the least inclination to a peace but upon the most liberal foundation."[34]

To maintain such a determination, Abigail had to cast aside her desires for John's return. Her point was that such unselfish sacrifices were demanded of all women during the war. Her avowal of a suitable peace agreement was a springboard from which to discuss a subject of important personal consequences—the incongruity between the unselfish wartime commitment of women and their lack of rights:

> Patriotism in the female Sex is the most disinterested of all virtues. Excluded from honours and from offices, we cannot attach ourselves to the State of Government from having held a place of Eminence. Even in the freest countrys our property is subject to the controul and disposal of our partners, to whom the Laws have given a soverign Authority. Deprived of a voice in Legislation, obliged to submit to those Laws which are imposed upon us, is it not sufficient to make us indifferent to the publick Welfare? Yet all History and every age exhibit Instances of patriotick virtue in the female Sex; which considering our situation equals the most Heroick of yours.[35]

Abigail stated directly that women's contribution to the war had been as important as men's. The passion of pain pervaded her words regarding the failure of Congress to grant legal rights to women. There was a sense of resignation, for she had lost hope that Congress would carry out the personal implications of freedom. Finally, there was a tone of loftiness and deserved self-pride. For Abigail told John that women had done their job well, even though society had not acknowledged it.

The revolution in the mind and heart of Abigail Adams led her to conceive that women, as well as men, had a political role in the American Revolution. Women's purpose was to be in charge of the home and the homefront in the absence of their husbands, and to mold their children's education to prepare them for life and leadership in the new republic. This political role amounted to an emerging career for women as domestic managers and agents of moral and religious uplift in home and society.

This political function has remained the primary socially approved career for middle-class white women until the late twentieth century. The need for a wartime crisis to provide the generating power behind such a sanction evaporated. For woman's career within the home became her unquestioned purpose, generation after generation, to be inhaled as the air she breathed.

As in Abigail Adams's day, authorization of calling from God continued to undergird women's domestic function throughout the nineteenth and twentieth centuries. Divine sanction has proved to be a forceful power, carrying stronger legitimization than any human agent could provide.

The revolution in Abigail Adams's mind and heart also led her to conceive that women and minorities have natural rights to live equally and fully with white men. She understood this as a God-given natural right and recognized that it conflicted with the inherited Puritan belief that God called persons to remain in socially prescribed subordinate positions, including careers. Her more expansive understanding of the relationship between calling and career has remained a prophetic vision of a crosscurrent of women and men throughout American history.

The relationship between calling and career continues to be ambiguous and tenuous. But in the late twentieth century, larger numbers of people of religious persuasion are acting upon the prophetic vision that God is calling men and women to liberation. Through Abigail Adams we gain more sensitive understanding of the deeply pervading hold of the currents of calling and career—and of the tenacity and courage needed to claim equality in the name of God and human nature.

### NOTES

1 / John Adams to Hezekiah Niles, 1818, quoted in Bernard Bailyn, *The Ideological Origins of the American Revolution* (Cambridge: Belknap Press of Harvard Univ. Press, 1967), 160.

2 / John Adams to Abigail Adams, Oct. 29, 1775, L. H. Butterfield, ed.,

*Adams Family Correspondence*, 4 vols. (Cambridge, Belknap Press of Harvard Univ. Press, 1963–73), 1:316, 317.

3 / John Adams's conflicts over the choice of a career, and their resolution, can be traced through his own words in Butterfield, ed., *The Earliest Diary of John Adams* (Cambridge: Belknap Press of Harvard Univ. Press, 1966), 66, 70–77, and Butterfield, ed., *Diary and Autobiography of John Adams*, 4 vols. (New York: Atheneum, 1964), 1:7, 15, 31, 37, 72, 78, 82, 87, 96–100, 108, 118.

4 / Quoted in Barbara Ehrenreich, *The Hearts of Men: American Dreams and the Flight from Commitment* (New York: Doubleday Anchor, 1984), 9.

5 / Quoted in Kathryn Kish Sklar, *Catharine Beecher: A Study in American Domesticity* (New Haven: Yale Univ. Press, 1973), 160.

6 / Quincy Papers, Manuscript Collection, Massachusetts Historical Society; Adams Family Papers, Microfilm Edition, Massachusetts Historical Society (Boston: 1954–59), Reel 603 (Genealogical Material).

7 / Quincy Papers; Edward Salisbury, *Seventeen Pedigrees from "Family Memorials"* (New Haven, 1885), 297, 300, 309; "Memoir of Edmund Quincy," by Eliza Susan Quincy, *New England Historical and Genealogical Register* (April 1884): 4–7.

8 / Quincy Papers; Salisbury, *Family Memorials*, 297–362; John Langdon Sibley and Clifford K. Shipton, *Biographical Sketches of Graduates of Harvard University, in Cambridge, Massachusetts*, 13 vols. (Boston, 1873), 5:444–49, 6:491–95, 7:106–16, 8:463–75; Samuel Bates, ed., *Records of the Town of Braintree, 1640–1793* (Randolph, Mass., 1886).

9 / Other published sources of Braintree area history, besides the most comprehensive coverage by Charles Francis Adams, Jr., *Three Episodes of Massachusetts History*, 2 vols. (1894; reprint New York, Russell & Russell, 1965), include his *An Historical Address*, Proceedings of the 250th Anniversary of the Permanent Settlement of Weymouth (Boston, 1874), 3–34; Daniel Munro Wilson, *Three Hundred Years of Quincy: 1625–1925* (Boston: Wright & Potter, 1926), ch. 1, and *Where American Independence Began* (New York: Houghton Mifflin, 1902), ch. 2; Marion Sophia Arnold, *A Brief History of the Town of Braintree in Massachusetts* (Boston, Press of Thomas Todd, 1940); and Charles M. Andrews, *The Colonial Period of American History*, 4 vols. (1937; reprint New Haven: Yale Univ. Press, 1964).

10 / Compilation made by Rosemary Keller from Samuel Bates, ed., *Records of the Town of Braintree 1640–1793*. Also see Kenneth Lockridge, *A New England Town, the First Hundred Years* (New York: Norton, 1970), ch. 3.

11 / Adams Papers, reel 603; Sibley & Shipton, *Sibley's Harvard Graduates*, 7:588–91; Gilbert Nash, *Historical Sketch of the Town of Weymouth, Massachusetts, from 1622 to 1804* (Weymouth, 1885), 101–3, 168, 169; Adams, *Historical Address*, 40–56.

12 / Book of Records, First Church in Weymouth, 1734–1825, Microfilm Edition, Massachusetts Historical Society; "Diaries of Rev. William Smith and Dr. Cotton Tufts, 1738–1748," *Proceedings of the Massachusetts Historical Society*, vol. 42 (June 1909), 444–70; Adams, *Historical Address*, 250th Anniversary of Weymouth, 41; Sibley & Shipton, *Sibley's Harvard Graduates*, 7:590.

13 / Quincy Papers; Adams Papers: Reel 603; Daniel Scott Smith, "Inheritance and the Position and Orientation of Colonial Women" (paper pre-

sented at the Second Berkshire Conference on the History of Women, Oct. 27, 1974).

14 / Edmund Quincy to Katherine Quincy, Jan. 25, 1750; Feb. 9, 1777, Quincy Papers.

15 / Ibid., Jan. 25, 1750, Quincy Papers.

16 / Ibid., Oct. 3, 1763, Jan. 9, 1775, Dec. 21, 1774; Edmund Quincy to children, Apr. 9 (no year given); Edmund Quincy to Dorothy Hancock, Sept. 30, 1775, Feb. 8, July 22, 1776; Edmund Quincy to Esther Sewell, Aug. 22, 1777, Quincy Papers.

17 / Mary Quincy, Mar. 19, 1712, Quincy Papers.

18 / Abigail Adams to Mary Smith, Oct. 13, 1766, Jan. 12, 15, and 31, 1767, *Adams Family Correspondence*, 1:56–62.

19 / *Boston under Military Rule, 1768–1769 as revealed in A Journal of the Times*, compiled by Oliver M. Dickerson (Boston, Chapman & Grimes, 1936) provides a compilation of these newspaper accounts; *Diary and Autobiography of John Adams*, 3:289, 290.

20 / Charles Francis Adams, *The Life of John Adams*, 2 vols. (New York, Haskell House, 1968), 1:201–3; Edmund C. Burnett, *The Continental Congress* (New York, Macmillan, 1941), 20; *Journals of the Continental Congress, 1774–1789*, Worthington C. Ford et al, eds., 34 vols. (Washington, D.C.: U.S. Govt. Printing Office, 1904–37), 1:13; Allen French, *The First Year of the American Revolution* (Boston: Houghton Mifflin, 1934), 277.

21 / James Burgh, *Political Disquisitions: or an Enquiry into Public Errors, Defects, and Abuses* (London, 1774–75); Catharine Sawbridge Macaulay, *The History of England from the Accession of James I to the Elevation of Hanover*, 5 vols. (London, 1766); Charles Rollin, *The Ancient History*, 4 vols. (London, 1768).

22 / Rollin, *The Ancient History*, 1:78, 79; James Dickinson, *Letter from a Farmer in Pennsylvania, to the Inhabitants of the British Colonies* (1768; reprint New York: Outlook Co., 1903); John Adams, *Novanglus and Massachusettensis*, in *The Political Writings of John Adams*, ed. G. A. Peek (1774–75; reprint Indianapolis: Bobbs-Merrill, 1954), 27–79; Andrew Eliot, *A Sermon Preached before his Excellency Francis Bernard, Esq.; Governor, The Honorable, His Majesty's Council, and the Honorable House of Representatives, of the Province of the Massachusetts Bay in New-England, May 29, 1765* (Boston, 1765); Charles Chauncy, *Civil Magistrates must be just, Ruling in the Fear of God* (Boston, 1749); Samuel Cooper, *A Sermon upon Occasion of the Death of our late Sovereign, George the Second, Preach'd before His Excellency Francis Bernard, Esq.* (Boston, 1761); Jonathan Mayhew, *A Discourse concerning Unlimited Submission and Non-Resistance to the Higher Powers* (Boston, 1750).

23 / Mayhew, *Unlimited Submission*.

24 / Abigail Adams to John Adams, Nov. 12, 1775, *Adams Family Correspondence*, 1:324.

25 / Ibid., July 21, 1776, 2:56.

26 / Abigail Adams to Mercy Warren, Apr. 13, 1776, *Adams Family Correspondence*, 1:377.

27 / Abigail Adams to John Adams, Dec. 23, 1782, Butterfield, ed., *The Book of Abigail and John*, (Cambridge: Harvard Univ. Press, 1976), 333.

28 / Abigail Adams to John Quincy Adams, *Adams Family Correspondence*, 3:310.

29  /  Abigail Adams to John Adams, Aug. 14, 1776, ibid., 2:94.

30  /  Abigail Adams to John Adams, Apr. 11, 1776, ibid., 1:375.

31  /  Abigail Adams to John Adams, Mar. 31, 1776, ibid., 1:370.

32  /  John Adams to Abigail Adams, Apr. 14, 1776, ibid., 1:382.

33  /  John Adams to John Sullivan, *Works of John Adams*, 10 vols. (Boston, 1856), 9:375–78.

34  /  Abigail Adams to John Adams, June 17, 1782, *Adams Family Correspondence*, 4:328.

35  /  Ibid.

## 12

*Elizabeth Fox-Genovese*

# Religion in the Lives
# of Slaveholding Women of
# the Antebellum South

FOR MANY CONTEMPORARY FEMINISTS, Christianity, in its emphasis on a male divinity and savior, threatens women's sense of self-worth, although historically Christian women have turned to it as their principal source of self-worth. Southern slaveholding women, like many other women throughout the United States and Western Europe, drew upon their faith and its promise of salvation to forge standards of a personal calling. In addition, they drew upon it for assurance that their social role as slave-holders was ordained of God. They saw no denial of their own value in the celebration of a male God and his Son, for they viewed their own vocation as particular to their condition as women within a society and ideology dominated by men. They sought not to rebel against but rather to realize that vocation through their best efforts at personal piety within the world that they knew.

From the start Christianity has been informed by a powerful current of criticism—a view of the world as inherently imperfect. In the next and better world the last shall be first. In Christ, all are equal: "There is neither Jew nor Greek, there is neither slave nor free, there is neither male nor female; for you are all one in Christ Jesus." [1] And many Christians have drawn upon this current to insist that the kingdom of God can and must be realized—or at least more nearly approximated—on earth. For black slaves Christianity held out the promise of freedom in this world as well as of salvation in the next. For them, the predominant message of the Bible was, "For freedom Christ has set us free; stand fast therefore, and do not submit again to a yoke of slavery." [2]

Many other Christians have staunchly rejected the egalitarian message of their faith, insisting that the righting of wrongs (if wrongs there be) must be left to God. Some of this persuasion have nonetheless sought to attain the greatest possible personal purity through mysticism and personal denial of the claims of the flesh and the world without challenging the prevailing social order. Still others have favored the reform of the world in order to bring it closer to what they understand to be the teachings of the Bible. Such was the position of many of the more thoughtful and pious antebellum southern slaveholders. But for the overwhelming majority the abolition of slavery—or what they would have called radical reform, Yankee style—did not figure among the ranks of biblically mandated and desirable reforms. To the contrary, they viewed slavery as ordained of God and sanctified by the Bible. They sought, in other words, not slavery's abolition but its reform—sought the realization of a Christian slaveholding society.[3]

The slaveholders' position may now seem inadequate, but we should sadly mistake them if we dismissed the depth or seriousness of their faith. In their view, the Bible did not sanction the kind of systematic individualism that was beginning to appear in some northern circles and that would justify the leveling of ranks or the homogenization of conditions. Rather, it visibly sanctioned hierarchy and particularism, including slavery and the subordination of women to men. Indeed, for slaveholding women, who largely accepted the sanctity of slavery and the inferiority of black people, their entire social system was grounded in inequality. More important, slaveholding women fully understood that, from the perspective of their society and, especially, their clergy, the arguments for slavery depended on and were grounded in the prior argument for woman's subordination to man.[4]

Religion lay at the core of slaveholding women's identity. It provided their most important standard for personal excellence and legitimated their sense of self in relation to the other members of their society. For the overwhelming majority, religion meant a general version of Bible-based Protestant Christianity. Many slaveholding women harbored a special allegiance to their own church; many others, who in essential respects considered themselves Christian members of a Christian society, never joined a church. Their deeply religious sensibility in this respect transcended denominational identification, and even, though less often, transcended church attendance. From their earliest consciousness until their deaths, most thought of their own lives with reference to Christian precepts, developed their personal ideals in conformity with Christian ideals, and envisioned their society as both embodying and legitimated by Christian principles. Their religious identities, in other words, were barely distinguishable from their personal identities, which themselves were barely distinguishable from the gender and social relations through which they were realized.

In general, slaveholding women experienced religion as the warp of their lives—as a natural structure that linked all other aspects of their being. They took it as much for granted as the complementary definitions of themselves as privileged, white, female members of a slave society. To be a slaveholding woman was to be a Christian woman. But many slaveholding women also viewed religion as the outstanding measure of personal worth and continually monitored their own progress toward greater personal and spiritual fulfillment. Religion thus represented a calling, the realization of which demanded constant struggle and vigilance. Religion informed and permeated their lives, notwithstanding tremendous variation in denomination, church attendance, and personal piety.

The best evidence for the influence of religion both as general ideology and personal standard lies in the diaries, journals, and letters of slaveholding women of different ages, denominations, regions, and wealth.[5] For many of these women, personal narratives offered a privileged vehicle for exploring the state of their own souls and for assessing their worth as members of this world and potential members of the next. They looked to their journals and diaries to ground their consciences, to help them to attain their own standards of personal excellence. They did not normally intend these writings as exemplary portraits for a public audience, although they frequently did intend them to be read by their own children, notably their daughters. Their autobiographical writings sought a delicate balance between forthright confession and the creation of a public persona. And in this context slaveholding women frequently privileged religion—as they understood it—as the premier standard of personal worth.

In the absence of systematic figures, it is impossible to write with certainty of slaveholding women's propensity to join and to attend church. Even were such figures available, they would hardly provide a complete picture of the place of religion in the lives of slaveholding women, who sought in their faith something more than correct institutional observance. For most slaveholding women, religion included church attendance, although they were often not as faithful as they might have wished, whether because of inclement weather, long distances, poor roads, family responsibilities, or poor health. For many slaveholding women, religion included church membership, although many who considered themselves devout believers or even regular attenders never joined a church. But for the majority of slaveholding women, religion consisted above all in the careful monitoring of their own spiritual states, including what many of them referred to as the quest for spiritual delights; regular reading of the Bible; ubiquitous concern with their and their near ones' prospects for salvation; and a wish to see a greater realization of the Christian spirit in their own society.

Sarah Gayle of Alabama, for example, implicitly viewed religion as the anchor for her sense of herself in her world, yet she died without ever having joined a church. For all her conviction about the centrality of religion, Sarah Gayle found the struggle for faith unending. She had no difficulty in accepting God as the supreme being upon whom all humans depended for salvation. She had no trouble in accepting the principle that the church necessarily mediated between God and his people. But she never could fully commit herself to joining a church, or even to accepting a single theology. She continually reminded herself that lip service to religious principles and facile observances would not satisfy the requirements of an all-powerful God, who could scrutinize the secret crannies of a recalcitrant heart. Faith, she fully understood, could not be faked. The issue, she wrote her husband, had little to do with the choice of one or another denomination, but everything to do with the quality of a faith that could, by its own sincerity, triumph "over the fear of death," and look "with hope and confidence beyond the grave."[6]

Yet she also knew that church membership betokened a commitment she was unable to make. Once, watching two of her friends take the Sacrament, "in its sacred awfulness," she found herself overcome by feelings of her own inadequacy. She wished that she could accept participation in that communion. Even more, she "wanted the pride and vanity, rioting at my heart to be destroyed, and humility and faith and hope to be implanted in their place." But even when her fears of death most overwhelmed her, she admitted she could not feel "the humility, the adoration of a Christian." She, like many others, suspected that her resistance to church membership derived from a too great attachment to the world. Her language further suggests that she found it difficult to subordinate her will to God's, that she remained bedeviled by a recalcitrant pride. She also had difficulty in accepting some of the specific tenets of Christianity, notably the doctrine of atonement. The Fall of Man especially troubled her. If she could satisfy herself on that point, "why man should have fallen at the first," she could accept atonement as "a splendid instance of love and gracious compassion, calling for gratitude from every creature." She knew full well that her train of thought led to "what seems little better than impiety," but could not shake it.[7]

Many other women, who did not share Sarah Gayle's theological doubts, understood church membership as an important element of their social and personal identities and frequently prayed for other members of their family to convert and join their church. Anne Turberville Davis captured the singular importance many women attached to their personal identification with a church when she noted that she would have greatly preferred "death to having my name erased from the church of my choice." Even though her husband was a minister and, accordingly, her religious identification was deeply intertwined with her social and family situation, that choice represented a central affirmation of self—a personal choice in the full sense. And she trusted that she would retain her place in the Methodist Episcopal Church, "which is militant, until I join the church triumphant in Heaven." But, like Sarah Gayle, she also understood the need to continuously struggle for her faith and prayed, "O Lord, keep thy unworthy child faithful until death." [8]

Ministers' wives especially concerned themselves with church affairs, encouraged membership, and worried about the size and fervor of the congregation, but they were not alone in identifying their own well-being with the vitality of the church to which they belonged. Wives and mothers worried about the conversions of husbands and children, concerned both to ensure their salvations in the next world and to share with them the delights of church fellowship in this world. Eliza Clitherall mightily wished for the most precious "of all tidings, the conversion of all my dear Children." She shuddered at the thought of the temptations that beset her dear grandchildren "—these, such as they have not the strength to resist of their own and left to themselves, no Pious friend or relative to lead them to the right." Despairing that her daughters' "reckless sons and daughters will be sav'd," she could only lift up her heart to God who had, thus far, placed her family beyond the worst temptations of fashion and the world. [9]

Martha Jackson, a devout Baptist, constantly worried about her husband, Henry, who, although an exemplary man and devoted husband, continued to resist conversion. During one of their unavoidable separations, she wrote to him that she would spare no effort "(through assisting grace)" to make their household "a terrestrial paradise to ourselves and our children." But, she warned him, her efforts could avail nothing "without the presence of *bible religion,* candid examination of its real value, of its intrinsic truth." Such religion alone could "place the *capstone* on the superstructure of our temporal as well as our spiritual enjoyments." [10] Meta Morris Grimball, an Episcopalian, who shared little of Martha Jackson's evangelical fervor, expressed deep satisfaction when her younger daughters, Charlotte and Gabriella, finally joined her church. On Communion Sunday, the day of their confirmation, she enjoyed "the great comfort of having my 3 daughters with me partaking of that Sacrament. —I pray that they may earnestly walk in a Christian life." [11] But her greatest joy came with her husband's conversion—a source of great comfort, for "since my marriage 32 years ago Mr. Grimball's not being a member of the Church has been a trouble to me & now that in spite of his prejudices he has joined the Episcopal Church, I consider this the answer to my prayers." Not least she rejoiced because she knew that his example would lead her sons to church membership.[12] Mrs. Erwin, in contrast, suffered the terrible burden of a husband who resolutely opposed her even joining a church. How, Sarah Gayle wondered, could a man who loved his wife as Mr. Erwin incontrovertibly loved his "inflict the pain Mr. Erwin does by his opposition to her joining the Church?" [13]

Many slaveholding women shared something of Sarah Gayle's sense that the differences among denominations did not carry overwhelming significance. Time and again they visited different churches, normally to hear a new or especially vaunted preacher, but sometimes out of simple curiosity or convenience. Frequently, they welcomed news of a successful revival even when not of their own denomination, for revivals betokened a quickening of the Christian spirit in their communities. For most, the progress of that spirit overshadowed denominational allegiances and brought renewed conviction about the essential worthiness of their society. Thus Lucilla McCorkle, the wife of a Presbyterian minister, commented favorably upon a protracted Methodist meeting. "If no other good is accomplished—the church is aroused & revived—but I hope many sinners may be brot in & many backsliders reclaimed." And she especially prayed that "the different denominations provoke one another to love & good works," prayed God to "forbid that green eyed jealousy or envy or malice or vile speaking should once be named or felt among us." Concluding with the wish that each denomination feel secure in the knowledge that there "is a sphere for each and that God rules over us in wisdom," she nonetheless prayed that He "bless our dear little flock of Presbyterians." [14]

Lucilla McCorkle's special concern for her own church found echoes among other women, who did not share her special interest in its prosperity. For many, the general commitment to Protestant Christianity coexisted with a special feeling for the church to which they belonged. Eliza Carmichael, a Presbyterian, enjoyed church attendance and good preaching of whatever denomination, but after a summer of attending the Episcopal church with her children, she privately noted that she did "long to go to my church again," thus underscoring the belief that church membership represented a very special anchor to her personal identity.[15]

If church membership offered many women a strong personal grounding, church attendance offered even more the sense of participation in the fundamental values and network of their society. One slaveholding woman after another punctuated her private writings with references to having attended, or having failed to attend, services. Indeed some women took the regular recurrence of church service as the governing structure of their writings. Fannie Bumpas, the wife of a Methodist minister, never wrote on Sundays, although she scrupulously recorded Sunday's events on Monday, for she regarded even a journal devoted to an account of her spiritual state as too secular an activity for the Sabbath.[16] Lucilla McCorkle, another minister's wife, dated all her journal entries by reference to the Sabbath. Others, not married to ministers and as different as Kate Carney in Tennessee, Elizabeth Ruffin and Fannie Page Hume in Virginia, Eliza Clitherall in North Carolina, and Mahala Roach in Mississippi regularly noted the church they attended, who preached, and the text of the sermon. Just as scrupulously, they noted their failure to attend church, their reasons, and the reading they had done during the day. This tendency to take careful note of their Sabbath observances testified to their recognition of the centrality of church in their society, and beyond it to a more personal conviction that respect for religious precepts and sensibilities alone could order their lives.

Sarah Gayle, persisting doubts notwithstanding, regularly attended services and commented extensively in her journal on the quality and content of the preaching. After moving to Tuscaloosa from Greensboro, she met with numerous inquiries as to what church she planned to frequent. She consistently replied that she planned to "hear all the ministers, and then select the one whose preaching I preferred."[17] Several weeks later she still had not decided, but, since she had heard that the preachers at the Methodist church were excellent, decided to go there. In the event, the performance of Dr. Cannon, the minister, sorely disappointed her by attempting "by any and every means, to operate on the feelings of his audience. so as to cause them to shout and weep and make great outcries." As he succeeded with others, her own good feelings dissipated to be replaced by "distrust and scorn of the little arts employed."[18] The Episcopalian minister, Mr. Lewis, whom she heard on another occasion, also disappointed her by reading a letter instead of delivering a proper sermon. "I tried to feel the solemnity of the service, but could not, and do not hesitate to say, I have more pleasure in attending the Presbyterian and the Methodist Churches, than any other."[19]

Later that month she heard Judge Taylor preach "a most excellent sermon" at the Methodist Church. He especially brought her to understand, more clearly than she normally did, "the appropriateness of atonement," which she had always found "a dark subject." The experience reminded her of how beneficial it was for one such as herself, "who reads the Bible sparingly," to attend church.[20] She profited similarly from a sermon that Dr. Woods preached at the Baptist Church. "Death was his solemn subject, and well and unaffectedly did he manage it, bringing to the comprehension of every hearer, yet never coming below his own dignity."[21] Sarah Gayle resembled other slaveholding women throughout the South in expecting the most of preachers and rewarding them with heartfelt approval when they met or surpassed expectations.

Slaveholding women expected their ministers simultaneously to touch their hearts and enlighten their minds. For all the respect they were prepared to grant them, they did not gracefully tolerate intellectual vacuity or an uncouth manner. Elizabeth Ruffin held a low opinion of Methodism in this regard, believing that it had little to offer in the way of edification. She especially reproached the widespread belief among Methodists that theological attainments were unnecessary for clerical duties. She could not accept that "our own personal feeling, conviction, and conversion should be as powerful an instrument in convincing the reason and enlightening the understanding as a greater degree of Biblical knowledge would be."[22] For Elizabeth Ruffin, intellectual attainments and theological sophistication constituted necessary signs of social and religious standing. Other slaveholding women, even if not as intellectually demanding as she, looked to their ministers to represent in their demeanor and words the highest personal standards of the slaveholding class, even as they looked to them to inspire that spiritual conviction which would confirm the members of that class in their aspiration to serve a higher purpose.

These concerns with propriety and tone testify to the fundamental contradiction in many slaveholding women's attitudes toward religion as a social network. Elite women, in particular, were wont to be exacting in their requirements that religion embody the social standards of their immediate circle. Too much bombast, too little learning, above all too much pandering to the undisciplined sensibility of those whom they viewed as their social inferiors immediately elicited their harsh condemnation. Yet they, like others who were in the matter of social tone less exacting than they, also insisted that good preaching must touch the heart—must not settle for cold formality. Gertrude Clanton Thomas, who belonged to a wealthy slaveholding family but was herself a Methodist, noted approvingly, after having heard the Reverend Benjamin Morgan Palmer preach in the Presbyterian Church in Augusta, Georgia, that he had given a real "Methodist revival sermon—Oh Gospel preaching is the most effective after all—Give to me the preaching that touches the heart." She fully appreciated intellectual accomplishments, but insisted that "the mind may be edified while the heart remains cold as an iceberg but the 'Heart in waking woke the Mind.' "[23] Believing, nonetheless, that some lines had to be drawn in order to maintain acceptable decorum, they frequently tended to draw them at the more extravagant manifestations of evangelical fervor, especially camp meetings.

Juliana Margaret Conner, a Charlestonian Episcopalian who visited a camp meeting in North Carolina, could not believe her eyes or ears. Having to sit "melting with heat and covered with dust" merely reinforced her disgust with the "ranting bombastic speaker." Yet once clear of the scene itself, she reflected that "these meetings doubtless have a beneficial influence on minds of a certain cast," although "what pleasure they can afford or how they can be endured by well informed, intelligent people is to me inexplicable."[24] Six months later she visited another in Alabama at which the style of the preacher "exceeded anything I ever heard and if there was any regular gradation by which *nonsense* could be measured this (I think) would have reached the highest degree." His discourse manifested "neither connection, good sense, or even pertinent remarks." But then, she recognized "his sole aim, end and object was to make the people groan."[25] The next day, while visiting in Marion, Alabama, she proved somewhat more tolerant of the performance of Mr. Stiles, "a celebrated Presbyterian Preacher," whom she had the opportunity of hearing. Mr. Stiles benefited from an "extremely handsome and prepossessing" appearance, "a full and sweet voice, a distinct and elegant pronunciation united with a graceful easy manner." The "solemnity" of his address additionally commended him to her. But later the same evening Mr. Stiles preaching at the courthouse to a more motley audience forfeited some of her esteem. Specifically, she found his illustrations of his points "too familiar," although she acknowledged that "they were doubtless calculated to make an impression on the minds of many of his hearers."[26]

Other slaveholding women, notably Baptists and Methodists of various degrees of wealth, proved more tolerant of overt religious enthusiasm and frequently attended camp meetings themselves. Mary Jeffreys Bethell, a member of the planter class by virtue of her husband's seventy-five or so slaves and a pious Methodist, welcomed camp meetings precisely for their numbers and their fervor, both of which, in her mind, bore witness to the progress of the gospel.[27] Lucilla McCorkle, as a minister's wife, had special reasons for enjoying camp meetings, although she recognized that those who attended might have mixed motives ranging from the desire that "the heart of christians may be enlarged and warmed up with fresh spirit & grace," to the hope of impressing their families with the importance of seeking the Lord and encouraging the conversion of sinners, to simple enjoyment of the exciting scene, to clerical ambition to increase the membership of specific churches.[28] Anne Turberville Davis, also the wife of a minister and of a somewhat higher social background than Lucilla McCorkle, professed even greater enthusiasm upon her return from a "glorious" camp meeting, which she believed would long "be impressed forcibly on the tablet of my memory." In her eyes, the meeting had indeed been "a time of the outpouring of the Holy Spirit of our merciful God, in the awakening and conversion of sinners, and the sanctification of believers." Originating in the preacher's tent, "the fire of Divine love . . . rushed from heart to heart until each one in the tent was blessed with perfect love."[29]

Notwithstanding significant differences in the extent to which their social attitudes influenced their tolerance for overt religious enthusiasm and indiscriminate contact with those they considered social inferiors, the vast majority of slaveholding women attached great importance to the substance of religion as developed in the sermons they heard and carefully noted the texts of those they heard. In March of 1840 Susan Davis Hutchinson attended both the Baptist and Lutheran churches. In her opinion, Mr. Pritchard, the Baptist minister, preached "profitably on the faith once delivered to the saints."[30] She also thought highly of the Lutheran Mr. Hoover's sermons. But she particularly enjoyed the sermon of Mr. Snyder, another Baptist minister, who, preaching an afternoon sermon at the Lutheran Church, took as his text Romans 8, and showed "that all who were truly called would certainly be brought in and that God had from the beginning chosen some to eternal life." Mr. Hoover, she reflected, must surely have felt as if the discourse were directed at him, "for he had taken God to witness that he had in the name of his divine Master extended the invitation to all," whereas Mr. Snyder was now asserting "that none were truly called save such as would eventually come."[31]

In 1837 Susan Davis Hutchinson had had the opportunity to hear the Reverend Mr. Thornwell, one of the greatest southern theologians, preach "an admirable sermon upon the offices and person of the blessed Redeemer in which he showed how necessary it was that he should be human and divine." She was particularly impressed with Thornwell's feeling discussion of Christ's human nature and his relationship to his people. The sermon left her "newly impressed upon the subject of justification," which, he had convinced her, "surely must be prior to the moment in which the gracious Spirit comes to dwell in the heart." But it also left her worrying whether Christ "can dwell with us while vain thoughts dwell with us?"[32]

Susan Davis Hutchinson did not always explore the theological implications of the sermons she heard, although she regularly noted the text. But even those who normally confined themselves to the brief notation of a text, might also write at length about a particular theological point that concerned them. Fannie Page Hume normally settled for the laconic textual notation, as on the two occasions at which she heard Bishop Johns preach. On the first occasion, he took no text, but took the consecration as his subject; on the second, he preached from Luke 13:23.[33] But as the secession crisis intensified, she began to write more about the sermons she heard. In November 1860 Mr. Davis "gave us one of the very best of sermons," which he very beautifully applied "to the present troublous times," taking as his text Matthew 10:8–31. Two weeks later Mr. Davis preached another fine sermon "admirably suited to the occasion. The subject was 'the judgment pronounced upon Ninevah by the prophet Jonah,'" the text Jonah 3:5–10. And, on 15 November 1861, when President Jefferson Davis set a day of fasting and prayer, the Reverend Mr. Davis again delivered a "solemn discourse," after reading the thirteenth chapter of 2 Chronicles and drawing a parallel "between the Children of Israel under *Abijah* & *Jeorboan* & our National difficulties."[34]

Fannie Page Hume, like so many others who wrote before the great crisis of the 1860s, apparently counted upon the reference to the text to jog her memory about the substance of the sermon. Presumably, she, like others, also relied upon a certain continuity of religious discourse. Having been reared as a churchgoing Christian, she knew what to expect from sermons on particular texts and only felt prompted to write about the sermon when it unexpectedly stretched her thinking by presenting a new perspective on a familiar or especially troubling topic. Others occasionally wrote about sermons that displeased or confused them. Lucilla McCorkle, for example, found little to praise in Mr. Scales's sermon on sanctification. "I did not rightly get the drift of his discourse—I was going to say argument—but he presented none except his own experience."[35]

Lucilla McCorkle, who, to her own chagrin, hardly ranked among the most intellectually sophisticated slaveholding women, insisted as firmly as Elizabeth Ruffin did that serious faith had to be grounded in texts and arguments. Even those who focused on personal experience regarded the keeping of a journal as a personal affirmation of the importance they attached to their own participation in that literate culture. Indeed, most of them viewed their journals primarily as accounts of personal, intellectual, and spiritual progress. Some used journals to copy from the books they were reading, but even those who did not do so noted their reading and often assessed its contribution to their models of female excellence. And for them, as for so many women until the very recent past, the Bible constituted the primary text.

From earliest childhood, slaveholding girls at their mothers' knees learned to read from the Bible. Charlotte Beatty's daughter, Sara, finished the New Testament for the first time before she was five. At seventeen, Kate Carney had finished the New Testament for the eighth time and immediately began to read it again. Mature women regularly turned to the Bible for instruction and solace. Susan Davis Hutchinson, who frequently devoted Sundays, especially those when she did not attend church, to reading her Bible, was especially drawn to Job, which she read at least twice in one year. In her case, marital difficulties in which she felt herself sorely tried may have contributed to the specific choice of text, but did not account for her lifelong habit of Bible reading. Lucy Fletcher, a minister's wife who enjoyed regular exposure to Bible reading, especially noted her private reading of 2 Galatians. Many, like Sarah Adams and Elizabeth Ruffin, devoted much of their Sundays, instead of or after church, to reading the Bible.[36]

The Bible transcended slaveholding women's variations in personal piety, their differences in age and situation. For one woman after another, the Bible constituted the bedrock of their religious and personal identity—the premier standard of personal excellence, the premier consolation against travails and disappointments, the premier promise of the life to come. The more pious complemented Bible reading with religious tracts and church history. Many had a special feeling for John Sargent's *A Memoir of the Rev. Henry Martyn, B. D.*, to which they invariably referred as "The life of Henry Martyn." Mary Moragne believed it "the most delightful memoir that I ever read—such a breathing of piety; & such varied information it imparts." Eliza Clitherall found in it the confirmation of her own sinfulness "contrasted with the sweet humble strains of these righteous men."[37] Other favorites included Lanvin's sermons and, invariably, the works of Hannah More. Many slaveholding women also read various histories of Christianity, in particular histories of the Reformation and Protestantism.[38] Some, like Fannie Hume, read at least a little theology; others read widely in religious fiction from which they drew models of exemplary behavior.[39]

Reading merged with writing in a continuing quest to make sense of life, to fit a sometimes troublesome reality into a meaningful pattern. Living in a world fraught with violence, living among people—white and black—who frequently disappointed their expectations, slaveholding women frequently turned to their journals to gain a sense of control over their lives, as well as to investigate how well they were living up to their own standards. Their frequent references to religion—whether in practice, through reading, or in self-chastisement—suggest how deeply they accepted Christian principles as the proper guide for their lives and as a standard to which they could properly hold others. The faith of slaveholding women simultaneously provided a source of reassurance and consolation and a standard of excellence for themselves and their world. It was thus motivated and informed by a complex combination of fear and idealism, both derived from the specific character of their lives.

Slaveholding women regularly wrote of the fears that beset them, especially of their pervasive fear of death. Sarah Gayle depicted that fear as her constant companion, the dark shadow of a generally happy life. Living in frontier Alabama in the 1820s and early 1830s, she worried about the inevitable deaths of her husband and children, as well as about her own. Haunted by the loss of both of her parents and two infants, she had direct experience of the grief of losing those whom she considered essential to her own identity.[40] Only the prospect of a future reunion in heaven permitted her to stave off melancholia and to transform that grief into mourning. Her continuing struggle for faith merged with her continuing struggle to accept death as but a temporary separation. The ferocity of her struggle testified to her unshakable sense of death as a daily companion, ever ready to pounce on another member of her family. Any untoward occurrence could remind her of the enormity of the risks she faced: random violence, runaway horses, unexplained illnesses, epidemics, the dentist. Her journals suggest that her wonderful ability to enjoy her life coexisted with a pervasive anxiety that, while never engulfing her, colored her experience the way gray skies can accentuate the colors of a landscape. She sought in religion, especially in its promise of a life hereafter, the only solid bulwark she could imagine against the inevitable losses she confronted.

For most slaveholding women the most oppressive fears derived from their personal experience, especially childbirth and the loss of infants. Each confinement, no matter how many had preceded it, revived women's terror of not surviving.[41] In the face of such fears, many turned to personal pacts with God: if He spared them, they would consecrate themselves to ever more perfect observance of his Word; if he spared them and the child, they would dedicate the child to his service. Both

Susan Davis Hutchinson and Lucilla McCorkle privately dedicated their infant sons to God, promising to raise them up to be preachers. Lucilla McCorkle entered into her private promises following the child's baptism; Susan Davis Hutchinson, doubtless worrying as so many did about the necessity for infant baptism, made her promise before the official baptism, confiding him to God's special care whether he lived or died.[42] They like others wrestled with the secret fear that they were called to suffer death of an infant, or worse an older child because of some failing of their own.

The fear of the cost of personal failings prompted many slaveholding women carefully to monitor their own spiritual states. Most of them privately admitted their recognition of their own tendencies to sinfulness—to quarrelsomeness, to short temper, to vanity, to greed, to too great attention to the opinions of the world, to too little attention to God's teaching. Some approached obsessiveness in their repeated self-examinations. Most simply attempted to maintain a regular vigilance on the state of their souls. Sarah Gayle especially valued religion for precepts on how to fulfill her allotted role, how best to meet her responsibilities. In this respect, she saw religion as an important standard for her identity as a woman, notably her own performance as a mother. Her temper too frequently got the better of her, causing her to discipline her children erratically. Her own lack of conversion accounted for her failure to lead her children into church membership and thus properly to safeguard their souls.[43]

Recognition of small failings thus imperceptibly merged with the great questions of life, death, and salvation, leading slaveholding women to see their entire lives in reference to religious values. They might go for days without questioning their own impatience with their children, much less their tendency to leave much of the care of those children to black slaves. But when misfortune struck, or simply when they engaged in searching self-assessment, they suddenly confronted the inescapable connections between their habits of everyday life and their ultimate fate. Drawing these connections encouraged many of them to view their entire lives as a progress toward—or falling off from—spiritual worth.

Mary Jeffreys Bethell chastised herself for having permitted her daughter to attend a dancing party. More seriously, she obsessively rehearsed the childhood death of another daughter, repeatedly trying to reassure herself that she had not caused it by her negligence. Mary Henderson, who lost several children, yet more vociferously berated herself for possible negligence. For these, as for so many other slaveholding women, the frequent deaths of children offered the recurring confirmation of the precariousness of all human life and could only be accepted as the will of God. Peace with that will did not come easily, especially for those who worried that God's will in this instance represented a judgment on them. They continued to struggle for that confident faith which would enable them to stave off the fears that a death had been willed by God as a sign of their own sinfulness and to replace it with the certainty he had willed it because he so loved their child that he had taken it unto himself to await their own arrival in heaven.[44]

Their fears and aspirations normally coalesced around their specific roles as wife, mother, and mistress. Lucilla McCorkle explicitly requested that God grant her "the grace to perform my duty as *wife*." In addition, "as a *mother* I hourly need divine assistance," and "as a *mistress* I so need patience, forbearance, meekness, mercy."[45] She, like many others, nourished a deep conviction of particularism, namely, that if she was to be a good Christian she could only be one by being a good Christian, slaveholding woman—a wife, a mother, a mistress. In addition, slaveholding women frequently associated religion with family feeling in general, experiencing it as an articulation of parental love and validation. Attending church and hearing an excellent sermon reminded Caroline Lee Hentz of her childhood when she "used to hear my dear mother's voice joining in, that fervent hymn of morning praise."[46]

Most slaveholding women, even when they chafed at specific irritations, found their prescribed roles neither imprisoning nor incompatible with a quest for spiritual excellence. In their journals they moved naturally from their worldly accomplishments and failings to the state of their souls. Even the ministers' wives rarely hinted that they felt themselves constrained to love God in man, to carry their subordination to men in the affairs of this world over into their faith. They all assumed independent relations between their souls and God: they were accountable for their failings, but would reap the rewards of their devotion. God asked that they fulfill the particular roles he had ordained, not that they accept men as mediators between them and himself. Ever mindful of their personal responsibility for the state of their souls, these women often wrote of their lives as if they constituted above all a spiritual journey or a calling.

Eliza Clitherall, noting "the last day of another month—The last day of another week!" asked her heart, "What spiritual Progress I have made— do I feel the conviction that I am on my last journey, travelling on to the last place of rest—approaching my journey's *end*?" She was especially concerned with having soon to render her account "at the Bar of eternal Justice," with having to face the judgment on whether her time "has been employ'd good or evil . . . 'twill be a solemn an awful reckoning."[47] Charlotte Beatty believed that "self-examination and communion with one's own heart," by which she meant private communion with God, were essential to her well-being. She opened her journal with the observation that "religion is a part of human nature not inseparable from it." It was, accordingly, her responsibility to war with the doubt and skepticism that might weaken her faith.[48] Fannie Webb Bumpas constantly worried about her "hard, cold heart" and her "unfaithfulness." She prayed the Lord to move her, to "revive thy work in this cold heart and make me entirely thine."[49]

As Fannie Webb Bumpas agonized about her cold resistance to the workings of divine grace, others worried about their susceptibility to the temptations of the world. Martha Foster believed herself to have strayed, "vanity has filled my mind: the great object of life is seldom remembered." Pride of a kind she had not previously known consumed her. "I have established a reputation for piety, and considerable intelligence. I am mortified when I hear of others doing better than I! A *christian* to carry selfishness so far! Nothing can save me but Jesus."[50] A month later she still bemoaned "the depth into which I am plunged." For her, "prosperity—the smiles of the world—are too alluring." And she prayed for a dose of adversity—"for some stroke to lay low my pride, vanity, worldliness—and—I cannot utter it." She recognized her danger but felt herself powerless to avert it, "the syren still lures me on, farther and farther from duty. I cannot feel a sickness and disgust at the world—cannot see clearly my different relations."[51]

Anne Turberville Davis proved more reticent than most, even in her journal, in acknowledging the specific sins she believed that she had committed. But sinful she assuredly believed herself to be. In her intense spiritual self-examination, she confessed to "my adorable Master" in "shame and confusion" that " 'I have most unfaithful been.' " Her unspecified "sinfulness and unworthiness" left her feeling "cast down into the very dust" and unable to "claim any portion with Thy people." "My Master," she continued, "thou knowest and I know, that without holiness of heart I cannot please Thee. . . . I sometimes awfully fear that I have instead of advancing in the Divine Life, retrogressed."[52] Similarly, Lucilla McCorkle viewed herself as "a poor irresolute slothful mortal," who felt "as though, if ever saved from degradation & wretchedness in this world & from endless ruin in the next, it will be through the abounding love of God & the merits of Jesus Christ alone."[53] Months later she prayed to her "Heavenly Parent" to give her "grace, to control myself and thus the authority to control others."[54]

For twenty years, Mary Jeffreys Bethell kept a journal primarily devoted to her spiritual state, in which she regularly agonized about her preoccupation with the things of this world and her consequent failure to make "that progress in divine life" which she might have. Temptations constantly bedeviled her, even interfering with her prayers.[55] If she, like others, highly valued the comfort of prayer and the emotional confirmation of God's love, she also valued divine assistance in meeting her designated worldly obligations, especially the ability appropriately to manage and discipline the children and servants over whom she had authority. The responsibilities of children and servants weighed heavily on slaveholding women. Fannie Bumpas spoke for many when she prayed for the "grace to enable me to govern my family aright."[56]

Governance, especially of servants, did not always come easily to slaveholding women, who knew themselves to be subject to the temporal authority of men and the spiritual authority of God, but they fully recognized the obligations of their station and tried to do their best. Many interpreted proper governance to include the responsibility to bring their servants, or at least those of their immediate household, to a sincere acceptance of religion. Lucilla McCorkle, chastising herself for what she found "amiss" in her family, particularly fretted about her servants "who have immortal souls," and found "the responsibility . . . greater than I can bear."[57] Mary Jeffreys Bethell said a daily prayer that "*all* my children should become christians, my *servants* also."[58] In 1856 she took her child and his thirteen-year-old nurse, Betty, with her to camp meeting. During the ride home in the carriage Betty suddenly broke out, "Oh! Miss Mary I believe God will have mercy on me." An astonished Mary Jeffreys Bethell assured Betty that God would indeed bless her if she continued to have religion after returning home. Betty's conversion made her thankful. "I hope God will convert all of my negroes. I am praying for it." And to hasten the conversions, she made it her practice to "read the bible to them Sunday nights and instruct them, and sing and pray with them."[59]

Many others read the Bible to their favorite servants in the hope of converting them. Clarissa Town had a literate slave, Rose, whom she encouraged to read a little from the Bible every night. "I hope it may have a good influence on her, though it seems to be hoping against hope, she is so perverse."[60] In 1857 Eliza Magruder noted that she had "commenced sunday school for the darkeys."[61] Eliza Clitherall, who felt an obligation to offer religious instruction to her slaves, regularly assembled all who were interested for Bible reading and religious discussion. Throughout the South, others did the same.[62]

Whatever their frustrations with their everyday relations with slaves and whatever their discomfort with their own inadequacies as mistress, the overwhelming majority of slaveholding women did not fundamentally doubt the legitimacy of slavery. Not uncommonly, they also became deeply attached to a number of their slaves, especially to those who had worked in the house or who had known them from childhood.[63] They assuredly did not worry that the enslavement of blacks was in any way incompatible with Christianity. For them, Christian order rested upon and articulated necessary social order—a recognition of rank and station, the proper subordination of some to others. Some suspected that heaven might dispense with the stratifications of earth and recognize the equality of souls, but others apparently assumed—as, however improbably, some of their ministers did—that the order of heaven would reflect the stratified order of earth, assumed, as one woman put it in her journal, that the Lord himself could not but prefer refinement and eloquence to the run of the mill. "Is it possible," a plantation mistress asked the Reverend Francis Le Jau in 1711, "that any of my slaves could go to Heaven & must I see them there?"[64]

Acceptance of the prescribed order of their world did not lead slaveholding women into a complacent acceptance of its virtue. Many professed deep concern about the lamentable state of society at large; others professed specific concern about what they saw as the growing tendency toward "fashionable" religion—toward facile observance without conviction or substance. Eliza Clitherall was very much distressed that "the vanity—dress—& shew at the large church quenches devotion—and precludes the comforts of sanctuary."[65]

If slaveholding women remained primarily interested in the religious state of the members of their own households, and if they did not themselves get much drawn into associations for reform, they nonetheless cared deeply about the general religious tenor of their society. Hence many of them welcomed revivals, even if not in their own denomination, as evidence of a growing attention to religious values. Julia Gilmer applauded the progress of religious sentiment in her congregation. Giving special thanks for the conversion of her own son, she added, "May our hearts be continually drawn out in love & praise to God for his unspeakable goodness—many of the children of our neighbors & friends have made professions & united themselves with the church."[66] Others worried that the absence of religious conviction in their communities invited harsh judgments from God. Epidemics caused particular concern. In 1832 Sarah Gayle trembled at the reports of cholera. "Were the Destroying Angel to approach me visibly, my fears could not be more harrowing." Her only hope lay in placing "my destiny where at last it has to be placed, in the hands of a good God, who does not idly or wantonly afflict his creatures."[67] Hearing, in 1853, of the progress of yellow fever in New Orleans, "that second Babylon, that city of revelry & crime," Eliza Clitherall saw less reason to hope for God's mercy and feared what might befall her city of Mobile, which did not lag far behind "in religious neglect—oh that the Minister 'wou'd cry aloud and spare not.' "[68]

The crisis of secession and war intensified some slaveholders' concerns that God might indeed be passing judgment on their ways. The ministers who led the appeal to reform before it was too late did not preach the abolition of slavery. They called for its reform.[69] Their message conformed closely to the feelings of pious slaveholding women, whose highest aspirations lay in meeting their full responsibilities as members of a Christian slave society. The shock of defeat sorely shook the faith of those who had most completely accepted the potential virtue of the society they cherished. By destroying the slave society that the Bible purportedly legitimated, the Civil War sharply challenged at least some slaveholding women's confidence in the faith of their fathers.

Ella Gertrude Clanton Thomas, for whom a personal conversion during her teens had anchored a devout faith, faced the social and economic uncertainties of the aftermath of the war as a young wife for whom religion no longer offered its accustomed comforts. Not until the abolition of slavery had she recognized "how intimately my faith in revelations and my faith in the institution of slavery had been woven together." She had previously suspected the evils of slavery, but had brushed off her doubts in confidence that "if the *Bible* was right then slavery *must be*." But with slavery abolished, "my faith in God's Holy Book was terribly shaken."[70] For a time she "doubted God. The truth of revelations, all— every thing—" and "no longer took interest in the service of the church." Throughout the summer of 1865, she faced the fears of another pregnancy with none of her accustomed longing for religious support, with "no desire for increased spiritual faith." Prayer could not comfort her. "When I opened the Bible the numerous allusions to slavery mocked me. Our cause was lost. Good men had had faith in that cause. Earnest prayers had ascended from honest hearts— Was so much faith to be lost? I was bewildered— I felt all this and *could not* see God's hand."[71]

The measure of Gertrude Thomas's despair reflects the measure of faith that she and other slaveholding women had had in the justice of their society. It testifies to the inextricable links that bound their faith in the abstract to the specific relations of that society. Bible-based Christianity had permitted many slaveholding women to link personal quests for sanctification and salvation to the fulfillment of prescribed roles within a particular world. Their faith contained its share of contradictions, but for them the very concreteness of its referents—its direct relevance to their everyday lives—endowed it with tremendous power and linked their personal lives to a larger divine purpose.

NOTES

The Research for this essay was supported by a research grant from the National Endowment for the Humanities.

1 / Galatians 3:28.
2 / Galatians 5:1. For discussions of Afro-American Christianity, see Eugene D. Genovese, *Roll Jordan, Roll: The World the Slaves Made* (New York: Pantheon, 1974); Albert J. Raboteau, *Slave Religion: The "Invisible Institution" in the Antebellum South* (New York: Oxford Univ. Press, 1978); Lawrence Levine, *Black Culture and Black Consciousness: Afro-American Folk Thought from Slavery to Freedom* (New York: Oxford Univ. Press, 1987); Jean E. Friedman, *The Enclosed Garden: Women and Community in the Evangelical South, 1830–1900* (Chapel Hill: Univ. of North Carolina Press, 1985); Donald G. Mathews, *Religion in the Old South* (Chicago: Univ. of Chicago Press, 1977); Donald Blake Touchstone, "Planters and Slave Religion in the Deep South," Ph.D. Diss., Tulane Univ., 1973.
3 / Eugene D. Genovese and Elizabeth Fox-Genovese, "Religious Ideals of Southern Slave Society," in Numan V. Bartley, ed., *The Evolution of Southern Culture* (Athens: Univ. of Georgia Press, 1988), 14–27; idem, "The Divine Sanction of Social Order: Religious Foundations of the Southern Slaveholders' World View," *Journal of the American Academy of Religion* 55, no. 2 (June 1987): 201–23; Eugene D. Genovese, *"Slavery Ordained of God": The Southern Slaveholders' View of Biblical History and Modern Politics*, The Fortenbaugh Memorial Lecture (Gettysburg, Pa.: Gettysburg College, 1986).
4 / For a fuller development of these arguments, see Elizabeth Fox-Genovese, *Within the Plantation Household: Black and White Women of the Old South* (Chapel Hill: Univ. of North Carolina Press, 1988), and Genovese, *"Slavery Ordained of God."*
5 / For a general discussion of slaveholding women, see Fox-Genovese, *Within the Plantation Household*. For a general discussion of slaveholding women and religion, see, Friedman, *The Enclosed Garden*. See also, Mathews, *Religion in the Old South*; Anne Firor Scott, *Making the Invisible Woman Visible* (Urbana: Univ. of Illinois Press, 1984). We as yet have no comprehensive study of slaveholding women's church membership and church attendance. Even the personal evidence on which I draw here cannot be regarded as a scientific sample. My arguments are based on extensive reading in a particular universe—the papers of literate, introspective women who kept diaries and journals or wrote letters. I do, however, believe that this evidence is representative of the beliefs of women of that particular group.
6 / Sarah Ann (Haynsworth) Gayle, Journal, Bayne and Gayle Family Papers, Southern Historical Collection, Univ. of North Carolina at Chapel Hill (hereafter SHC), 19 July 1835, 28 Oct. 1832.

7 / Sarah Ann (Haynsworth) Gayle Diary, Gayle and Gorgas Family Papers, William Stanley Hoole Special Collections, Amelia Gayle Gorgas Library, Univ. of Alabama, Sunday [25 July], 1831, 1 Feb. 1830.

8 / Anne Turberville (Beale) Davis Diary, SHC, [date smudged, but between 7 and 26] Dec. 1838.

9 / Eliza Clitherall Autobiography, Eliza Carolina (Burgwin) Clitherall Books, SHC, 5–10 Aug. 1860.

10 / Martha Jackson to Henry Jackson, Jackson-Prince Family Papers, SHC, 31 July 1831.

11 / Meta Morris Grimball Journal, Grimball Family Papers, SHC, 25 June 1862.

12 / Ibid., 9 Sept. 1863.

13 / Sarah (Haynsworth) Gayle Journal, Bayne and Gayle Family Papers, SHC, 10 Aug. and 19 July 1833.

14 / Lucilla Agnes (Gamble) McCorkle Diary, William Parsons McCorkle Papers, SHC, 23 Sept. 1847.

15 / Mara Eliza (Eve) Carmichael Diary, Carmichael Family Books, SHC, 27 Sept. 1826 (clearly a typographical error, the date must be 1840).

16 / Ibid., 18 Apr. 1839, 6 May 1843; Frances Moore (Webb) Bumpas Diary, Bumpas Family Papers, SHC, 12 Mar. 1842.

17 / Sarah (Haynsworth) Gayle Journal, Bayne and Gayle Family Papers, SHC, 24 Mar. 1833.

18 / Ibid., 2 May 1833. On the same morning she sent her husband and the children to the Episcopal church, "in consideration of the heat and the crowd."

19 / Ibid., [29 Apr. or early May, torn page] 1833.

20 / Ibid., May 1833.

21 / Ibid., 26 May 1833.

22 / Elizabeth Ruffin Diary, SHC, 25 Feb. 1827.

23 / Ella Gertrude Clanton Thomas Diary, Perkins Library, Duke Univ., 13 Dec. 1861.

24 / Diary of Juliana Margaret Conner, SHC, 5 Aug. 1827.

25 / Ibid., 4 Aug. 1827.

26 / Ibid., 14 Oct. 1827.

27 / See, e.g., Mary Jeffreys Bethell Diary, SHC, 16 Oct. and 3 Dec. 1856, 12 Oct. 1862. She attended camp meetings almost every year.

28 / Lucilla Agnes (Gamble) McCorkle Diary, William Parsons McCorkle Papers, SHC, 23 Aug. 1847.

29 / Anne Turberville (Beale) Davis Diary, SHC, 28 Oct. 1838.

30 / Susan Davis (Nye) Hutchinson Journal, SHC, 8 Mar. 1840.

31 / Ibid., 29 Mar. 1840.

32 / Ibid., 14 May 1837.

33 / Fannie Page Hume Diary, SHC, 20 and 21 June 1860.

34 / Ibid., 23 Dec. 1860, 4 Jan. 1831, 15 Nov. 1861.

35 / Lucilla Agnes (Gamble) McCorkle Diary, William Parsons McCorkle Papers, SHC, 4th Sab. Sept. 1847.

36 / Charlotte Beatty Diary, Taylor Beatty Papers, SHC, 30 Dec. 1843; Kate S. Carney Diary, SHC, 16 and 17 Mar. 1859; Susan Davis (Nye) Hutchinson Journal, SHC, 15 July 1838, 12 May 1839; Lucy Muse (Walton) Fletcher, Sabbath Notebook for 1841; Elizabeth Ruffin Diary, 18 Feb. 1827; Susan Davis (Nye) Hutchinson Journal, SHC, 3 Oct. 1831, 9 Dec. 1832.

37 / Mary Moragne, *The Neglected Thread*, ed. Del Mullen Craven (Colum-

bia: Univ. of South Carolina Press, 1952), 42, 15 Jan. 1842. Henry Martyn was chaplain to the East India Company and a pioneer missionary to India; he translated the New Testament into Hindustani.

38 / Anne Turberville (Beale) Davis Diary, 11 Nov. 1838; Sarah Eve Adams Diary, 5 and 19 Dec. 1813; Susan Davis (Nye) Hutchinson Journal, SHC, 11, 13, 16 Feb. 1827; Eliza Clitherall Autobiography, Eliza Carolina (Burgwin) Clitherall Books, 9 May 1853; Fannie Page Hume Diary, 3 Feb. 1861, 12 Feb. and 19 Aug. 1860.

39 / Fannie Page Hume Diary 16 Jan., 5, 6, 7 Feb. 1860. "That sweet book, 'Edith's Ministry,'" prompted Fannie Page Hume to bemoan her own failure to match the heroine's "lovely Christian graces." Such books always made her acutely aware of her "own unworthiness." Her progress in religion was not what it could have been, her heart remained inhabited by "worldliness & pride." And she prayed for strength to do better. The next month she began "Kate Vinton or Sunshine," another "sweet book" and again aspired to "greater holiness." Such reading almost made her doubt her own ability to feel true religion.

40 / Sarah (Haynsworth) Gayle Diary, Gayle and Gorgas Family Papers, William Stanley Hoole Special Collections, Amelia Gayle Gorgas Library, Univ. of Alabama, 14 Sept. 1832, 3 Jan. and 4 Sept. 1829.

41 / Anne Turberville (Beale) Davis Diary, 19 May 1839; Frances Moore (Webb) Bumpas Diary, Bumpas Family Papers, SHC, 6 Feb. 1844; Lucilla Agnes (Gamble) McCorkle, William Parsons McCorkle Papers, SHC, 27 Dec. (4th Sab.) 1846; Mary Jeffreys Bethell Diary, SHC, Introductory Autobiography, 12 Dec. 1853, 6 June 1855, 9 Dec. 1857, 10 Feb. 1862; Mary S. F. Henderson Journal, 15 Aug. 1855. See also Susan Davis (Nye) Hutchinson Journal, SHC, 19 Oct. 1831, 16 Feb. 1832.

42 / Susan Davis (Nye) Hutchinson Journal, SHC, 26 Aug. 1827; Lucilla Agnes (Gamble) McCorkle Diary, William Parsons McCorkle Papers, SHC, 27 Dec. (4th Sab.) 1846.

43 / Sarah (Haynsworth) Gayle Journal, 2 July and 31 June 1832.

44 / Mary Jeffreys Bethell kept reminding herself that trouble worked for her spiritual good, that we are but "pilgrims, traveling to a better country, to a home in our Fathers house in heaven." Trials served to cut "the cords that bind us to earth." Yet she could hardly bear the loss of her lovely child, Phereba Hinton. Mary Henderson could not recover from her grief at the loss of her son Baldy that "overshadows me with gloomy foreboding and shuddering dread." Anna Matilda King died of grief a year after the death of her adult son, Butler. Mary Jeffreys Bethell Diary, Introductory Autobiography, SHC; Mary Steele Ferrand Henderson Diary, John Steele Henderson Papers, SHC, 1855 throughout, especially Oct.; Thomas Butler King Family Papers, SHC.

45 / Lucilla Agnes (Gamble) McCorkle Diary, William Parsons McCorkle Papers, SHC, 9 Sept. 1847. See also, Lucilla Agnes (Gamble) McCorkle Diary, William Parsons McCorkle Papers, SHC, 24 (4th Sab.) Jan. 1847, Monday morning after the 1st Sab. of Apr. 1847, 6 June (1st Sab.) 1847.

46 / Caroline Lee Hentz Diary, SHC, 21 Feb. 1836.

47 / Eliza Clitherall Autobiography, Eliza Carolina (Burgwin) Clitherall Books, SHC, 31 Jan. 1852.

48 / Charlotte Beatty Diary, Taylor Beatty Papers, SHC, n.d., 1843, 20 and 21 Jan. 1845.

49 / Frances Moore (Webb) Bumpas Diary, Bumpas Family Papers, SHC, 12 Mar. 1842.

50 / Martha E. Foster Diary, Perkins Library, Duke Univ., 25 Sept. 1850.

51 / Ibid., 17 Oct. 1850.

52 / Anne Turberville (Beale) Davis Diary, SHC, 18 Oct. 1840.

53 / Lucilla Agnes (Gamble) McCorkle Diary, William Parsons McCorkle Papers, SHC, 2d Sab. Jan. 1847.

54 / Ibid., 10 Oct. (2d Sab.) 1847.

55 / Anne Turberville (Beale) Davis Diary, SHC; Lucilla Agnes (Gamble) McCorkle Diary, William Parsons McCorkle Papers, SHC, 2d Sab. Apr. 1850, 1st Sab. May 1850. See also, Anne Firor Scott, *The Southern Lady: From Pedestal to Politics, 1830–1930* (Chicago: Univ. of Chicago Press, 1970), 10–11; Anne Scott, "Women, Religion, and Social Change in the South, 1830–1930," in her *Making the Invisible Woman Visible*, 175–211.

56 / Mary Jeffreys Bethell Diary, SHC, 12 Jan. 1858; Frances Moore (Webb) Bumpas Diary, Bumpas Family Papers, SHC, 24 Apr. 1845; Mahala Roach Diary, 28 and 29 Mar., 28 April, 24 June 1853.

57 / Lucilla Agnes (Gamble) McCorkle Diary, William Parsons McCorkle Papers, SHC, 29 Nov. (5th Sab.) 1846.

58 / Mary Jeffreys Bethell Diary, SHC, 9 Dec. 1857.

59 / Ibid., 3 Dec. 1856.

60 / Clarissa E. (Leavitt) Town Diary, Louisiana and Lower Mississippi Valley Collections, Louisiana State Univ. Library, 1 Feb. 1853.

61 / Eliza L. Magruder Diary, Louisiana and Lower Mississippi Valley Collections, Louisiana State Univ. Library, 13 July 1857.

62 / Eliza Clitherall Autobiography, Eliza Carolina (Burgwin) Clitherall Books, SHC. See also, Fannie Heck, *In Royal Service: The Mission Work of Southern Baptist Women* (Richmond, Va.: Southern Baptist Convention, 1913), 69–70.

63 / Sarah (Haynsworth) Gayle Journal, 4 May 1834.

64 / F. J. Klingberg, ed., *The Carolina Chronicle of Dr. Frances Le Jau, 1706–1717* (Berkeley: Univ. of Calif. Press, 1956), 102.

65 / Eliza Clitherall Autobiography, Eliza Carolina (Burgwin) Clitherall Books, SHC, 4 Dec. 1853.

66 / Julia A. Gilmer Diary, SHC, Aug. 1859.

67 / Sarah (Haynsworth) Gayle Journal, Bayne and Gayle Family Papers, SHC, 6 July 1832.

68 / Eliza Clitherall Autobiography, Eliza Carolina (Burgwin) Clitherall Books, SHC, 17 Aug. 1853.

69 / Genovese, *"Slavery Ordained of God"*; Touchstone, "Planters and Slave Religion."

70 / Ella Gertrude Clanton Thomas Diary, Perkins Library, Duke Univ., 8 Oct. 1865.

71 / Ibid.

## 13

*Mary Walker*

## Between Fiction and Madness:
## The Relationship of Women
## to the Supernatural in
## Late Victorian Britain

THE MOST INTERESTING AND CHARACTERISTIC RESPONSE of the Victorians to the supernatural was their attempts to reconcile it directly with science. The twentieth-century mind tends to regard the supernatural as either disproved by modern science or irrelevant to it, but many Victorians were reluctant to abandon either their traditional perception of the transcendent or their new faith in science and tried instead to prove one by means of the other. The two most important products of this response were spiritualism and psychical research. Both of these approaches attempted to prove empirically that the nonmaterial was real, spiritualism by means of séances and psychical research by experimentation and statistical surveys. Even though neither movement ever became part of the mainstream of Victorian thought, the very vehemence with which both were denounced by the establishment of the day shows how close they came to winning serious consideration.

The role of women in psychical research has not been as thoroughly analyzed as has their participation in spiritualism. The role of women in spiritualism, especially as mediums, has been described by R. Laurence Moore in his book on American spiritualism, and there is no reason to suppose that his findings do not hold true for Great Britain as well. Spiritualism held that one may verify the existence of an afterlife, and even communicate with a deceased loved one, through the agency of a person sensitive to supernatural influence called a medium. Spirit voices, raps, music with no apparent source, the materialization of fruit or flowers out of nowhere, or a vision of the spirit itself were all supposed to be common occurrences at séances. It was the spirits, not the mediums, who were held to be responsible for these phenomena, the medium only acting as a conduit for the spirits' activities. Consequently the best mediums were held to be people without strong wills or marked personalities of their own. Given Victorian assumptions about women's essentially passive nature, it is easy to see why many spiritualists regarded women as more naturally given to mediumship than men.[1]

Psychical research was distinguished from spiritualism by greater scientific rigor and fewer religious preconceptions. Psychical researchers were interested in all types of inexplicable phenomena. They approached their subject of study with a more open mind than the spiritualists and included among their number many people with scientific training. Psychical research was similar to spiritualism, however, in that much of the most important testimony in its favor came from women.

The predominance of female witnesses in the evidence gathered by the psychical researchers in their first attempts to study the supernatural created problems for them, both in terms of traditional notions about women and the supernatural and in terms of the new ideas about women and sanity being developed by the emerging field of psychology. The prevalence of female testimony in the documents of psychical researchers also invites speculation on the reasons why Victorian women saw and reported supernatural phenomena more consistently than their male contemporaries.

Psychical research was born in Britain with the founding of the Society for Psychical Research (SPR) in 1882. The society's early years—from its founding to the death of its principal theorist, Frederic W. Myers in 1901—were concerned with defining a basic agenda, methods of research, and an overall approach.[2] During this time it produced four important bodies of evidence for the existence of the supernatural. The first two were *Phantasms of the Dead*, a survey of sightings of ghosts, the results of which were analyzed in the *Proceedings* of the SPR for 1885, and *Phantasms of the Living*, which dealt with "point of death" experiences—that is, seeing the apparition of a person within twelve hours before or after that person's death.

Criticism of the methodology of *Phantasms of the Living* led to the more ambitious *Census of Hallucinations*, which recorded 1,622 cases of all types of sightings of the unreal, the findings of which were summarized in the *Proceedings* of the SPR for 1894.[3] That all of these surveys were done among middle-class people is obvious from the level of education demonstrated by the written responses and from the accounts themselves, which invariably describe large houses with many rooms and a domestic staff. The reasons most frequently given for not coming forward with the information more readily were the fear that the value of a house might be depreciated or that servants would refuse to stay if it got a reputation for being haunted. The SPR obviously preferred to record the experiences of educated ladies and gentlemen who were assumed to be unsuperstitious and incapable of telling a lie. If the veracity of working-class people was given the benefit of the doubt, it was usually because they were assumed to lack the imagination necessary to fabricate a story.[4] Domestic servants, most of whom were women, are the only working-class people to appear in the documents with any frequency, and their reports are often given at second hand by their employers.

The last important research project begun by the SPR before the turn of the century was the investigation of the American medium Mrs. Leonora Piper of Boston. As of 1904 Mrs. Piper had been under investigation by the SPR for fifteen years.[5] Obviously Mrs. Piper was a female source of information for SPR, but the other three published sets of research findings also relied heavily on the testimony of women. In *Phantasms of the Dead* approximately 70 percent of the percepients (the SPR term for the witness of a supernatural occurrence or the receiver of information in a telepathic communication) were women.[6] In *Phantasms of the Living*, 58 percent of the respondents were female,[7] and in the *Census of Hallucinations* the society reported that "the number of men who experience sensory hallucinations and remember them is to women who do so in the ratio of nearly 2 to 3,"[8] while the proportion of women reporting visual hallucinations was twice that of men.[9]

This dependence on evidence provided by female observers was a problem for the SPR, especially in light of the rapid maturing of the field of psychology, a field of which the SPR liked to consider itself a part. Psychologists, especially those associated with Charcot, regarded most psychical phenomena as the result of mental illness and shared the prejudices of the lay public in regarding women as more mentally fragile than men. The SPR was therefore faced with the problem of having many of its findings dismissed as the products of hysteria.

For example, one critic of psychical research, Dr. Hugo Munsterberg, found psychical research not only scientifically indefensible but sordidly ludicrous: "What a difference between the mediaeval monk who becomes convinced of the mystical sphere because the Virgin appears to him in the clouds, and the modern scholar, who is converted because a pathological woman is able to chat about his personal secrets at the rate of twenty francs a sitting."[10] He also viewed psychical research as a threat to personal faith, not a support of it, because "our ethics and religion may be shaken tomorrow by any new result of laboratory research and must be supported today by the telepathic performances of hysteric women."[11]

The strategy adopted by the SPR to deal with these kinds of attacks was either to ignore the gender bias in their data or to argue that it arose from a bias in the evidence-gathering process itself, not from any special facility in women for seeing the unseen. In *Phantasms of the Dead*, the author, Eleanor Sidgwick, observed in spite of the preponderance of women witnesses in the study that "as to the seers of ghosts we can lay down no rules. The power is not limited by sex, age, or professions." [12] Sidgwick did not deal directly with the issue of hysteria, though she does say a few words in defense of hallucinations: "It would be a great pity if anyone thought that hallucinations, when not veridical [i.e., truth-telling] were indications of anything seriously amiss with the brain. Hallucinations are, no doubt, sometimes produced by overwork or other causes, but so are headaches, and no one is either ashamed of a headache, or particularly alarmed." [13]

In the *Census of Hallucinations* the authors attempted to explain the high percentage of women reporting visual hallucinations by citing recent studies that implied that women were better visualizers than men and might, therefore, remember visual hallucinations more clearly and report them more consistently. They admitted that much of their evidence supported the notion that women hallucinate more frequently than men, but they included the proviso "or remember them better" in their summing up. [14]

In *Phantasms of the Living* the 16 percent greater response of women to the survey was dismissed as insignificant. "The preponderance of female percepients cannot be assumed to indicate any superior susceptibility in that sex to telepathic impressions." [15] The authors did not feel that it indicated any mental inferiority, either, as they made clear in a response to the attacks of an "eminent physiologist" who had asserted that the SPR's evidence came mostly "from a class of persons given to hallucinations, especially clergymen and women, who are naturally inclined to believe marvels." [16] The SPR claimed that the greater number of female percepients was not large enough to support this assumption and argued instead that "the slight predonderance of female informants may probably be due to their having as a rule, more leisure than men for writing on matters unconnected with business."

This explanation for the preponderance of women in the survey is weak and suggests the lengths to which the SPR was willing to go to avoid any implication that their evidence was coming mostly from women, whose mental stability would be regarded as automatically suspect in many quarters. When the charge could not be avoided, the SPR often had to resort to the countercharge that it was unfair to assume that if a woman reported supernatural phenomena she was automatically a fitting subject for a study on abnormal psychology.

Alexander Lang, a prominent writer and president of the SPR in 1911, made this very point in an article in the *Proceedings* on the visions of Joan of Arc: "The vague and question begging term 'hysterical' can only be applied to Jeanne if we argue, 'all visionaries are hysterical. Jeanne was a visionary. Therefore Jeanne was hysterical.'"[17] Lang mentions the fact that Joan of Arc's visions began at puberty, a time of life supposedly prone to mental aberration, and that she frequently fasted, but only to dismiss these as inadequate explanations for her experiences.

In an earlier and more important article, Frederic Myers had discussed Joan of Arc as part of a larger discussion of the Daemon of Socrates. By pairing Joan of Arc with a respected male thinker, who also claimed to have heard guiding voices, Myers may have hoped to dismiss gender as an issue in Joan of Arc's case. In fact the only distinction he made between Socrates and Joan of Arc was the difference in their levels of education and intellectual attainments.[18]

The accusation of hysteria was an obvious threat to the evidence provided by Mrs. Piper. Critics of spiritualism had long regarded those mediums who were not frauds to be mental cases, especially if they were female. Michel Sage, a French psychical researcher, tried to cope with these criticisms in the first chapter of his book on Mrs. Piper which he entitled "Is Mediumship Neurosis?" Like Lang, he taxed his critics with assuming too readily that mediumistic activity was the result of hysteria or epilepsy without even bothering to investigate. When discussing the fact that Mrs. Piper's special gifts had only become apparent after her recovery from a serious illness, Sage admitted that "many persons will be disposed to believe that Mrs. Piper's tumor is the true explanation of her mediumship, particularly as the mediumship only appeared after the tumor. It is rather difficult to prove them wrong."[19] He countered by arguing that her powers declined rather than improved when she was unwell, while her recovery from her illness had "favoured the developing and perfecting of [her] mediumship." He finished this chapter with the rather flimsy observation that "after all, are there not famous men of science who declare that genius itself is only a neurosis? In their eyes the bandit is only a sick man; but the genius also is only a sick man."[20]

Why did the SPR strive to avoid the issue of hysteria by de-emphasizing the disproportionate contribution made by women to their research rather than arguing for a special relationship between women and the supernatural like the spiritualists? The SPR had been founded by spiritualists anxious to give their creed greater respectability among the scientific community and the general public. Thus one might expect that the SPR would ascribe the frequency of female observation of supernatural phenomena to a special facility in women in the same way spiritualists regarded women as the most likely subjects for mediumship. After all, both spiritualists and psychical researchers would have shared the same cultural assumptions about women's role as society's custodian of spiritual values and the common perception of women as more intuitive than men. Some may also have been aware that the visionary tradition in relgous mysticism was stronger for women than for men. Joan of Arc was only one example of numerous female saints and mystics who from the early Middle Ages on had claimed to hear and see things revealed by God.

Obviously the SPR was more concerned with the good opinion of psychologists than of spiritualists, an orientation explained by a look at the internal history of the SPR in its early years.[21] Although founded by spiritualists, the early leadership of the SPR was recruited from among a group of Cambridge thinkers that included Henry Sidgwick, first president of the SPR, his wife Eleanor, Frederic Myers, and Edmund Gurney. These people had been recruited to give the new organization greater credibility with the scientific community, and the Cambridge group did have comparatively higher standards of intellectual rigor. So much so, in fact, that the spiritualists began to find themselves squeezed out of their own organization almost from the beginning. For example, Henry Sidgwick, in his presidential address, ruled out at once experimentation with professional mediums.[22]

The spiritualists' inclination to assume that the evidence of their own eyes and ears sufficed to prove the existence of the supernatural, and their a priori assumption that they were dealing with the activities of spirits of the dear departed, quickly became intolerable to the Cambridge group, whose methods and philosophical outlook were more sophisticated. Eleanor Sidgwick remarked in one letter to her husband, "I really think the Spiritualists had better go. It seems to me that if there be truth in Spiritualism their attitude and state of mind distinctly hinder its being found out."[23] The Cambridge group's indifference to the opinion of the spiritualist community, which eventually deserted the SPR, and their active participation in international conferences of psychologists demonstrates clearly which group they considered to be their constituency.

The SPR's approach to the issue of hysteria and mental illness as a factor in their research findings may also have been influenced by the activity of its leadership in the cause of higher education for women.

Henry and Eleanor Sidgwick were two of the founders of Newnham College, Cambridge, one of the earliest colleges for women, and Frederic Myers had been one of their most active supporters in this work. Eleanor Sidgwick, herself an outstanding mathematician, had written a work disproving the contention that strenuous mental effort adversely affected the health of women students. In this study she compared the medical histories of a group of women college students with their sisters who did not attend college and found that the health of the women students was, in fact, better than that of their sisters who had not undergone the rigors of a higher education.[24] The SPR was, therefore, led by individuals who did not assume that women were mentally and physically fragile creatures whose testimony must always be viewed with suspicion.

The character of the rank-and-file membership of the SPR, which was roughly 40 percent female, possibly reinforced this attitude.[25] Forty percent was a very high percentage compared to other British learned societies, many of which did not admit women. Of these female members, many had a connection with the women's movement. Eleanor Sidgwick was a onetime president of the Cambridge branch of the Conservative and Unionist Women's Franchise Association and her sister-in-law was Lady Frances Balfour of the national executive of the National Union of Women's Suffrage Societies. Agnes Garrett, cousin of Millicent Garrett Fawcett, president of the N.U.W.S.S., was a member, as was Dr. Elizabeth Blackwell, the first Anglo-American woman doctor. Anna Cobden Sanderson, daughter of Richard Cobden and later a militant suffragette, was briefly associated with the SPR in its early years. Dame Edith Lyttelton, whose husband Alfred was one of suffrage's most active supporters in the House of Commons, became the SPR's second woman president in 1933 (the first was Eleanor Sidgwick in 1908) and Lady Henry Somerset, best known for her work in the temperance movement but also a suffragist, was a long-time member.

Other women associated with women's higher education who were active in the SPR apart from Eleanor Sidgwick were Constance Jones and Miss C. Jebb of Girton College. Mrs. Juliet Mylne, a pioneer among women poor-law guardians and an active member of the Women's Local Government Society, belonged to the SPR, as well as Lady Mabel Howard, an early woman county councillor, who claimed to be able to do automatic writing.[26]

The inclusion of some feminists in the membership rolls of the SPR was probably due to the fact that many feminists moved in the same social and intellectual circles as the psychical researchers and does not imply any special affinity between the two schools of thought. It is only suggested that this feminist contingent in its ranks may have reinforced the SPR's stance that women could be credible witnesses and reliable observers. Theosophy appears to have been the occult practice of choice for feminists in this period. Theosophy claimed to offer a more profound understanding of nature than that offered by the empirical sciences, an understanding that claimed to encourage the development of an individual's own latent psychic abilities. This makes for an interesting contrast with spiritualism, which viewed the medium as only an instrument with no real supernatural abilities of her own.[27]

While madness was the most serious charge that could be brought against the evidence contributed by women, a simple excess of imagination and love of the dramatic also presented a minor threat to its credibility. A natural inclination to "believe marvels" was the second part of the criticism leveled at women's evidence by the unnamed physiologist cited in *Phantasms of the Living*, and E. Ray Lankester, the zoologist and an active opponent of spiritualism, characterized the SPR as a group of "enthusiasts . . . eagerly collecting ghost stories and records of human illusion and fancy."[28] As one SPR committee report admitted, many "regard 'ghost stories' as more suited to the amusement of a firelight hour in the drawing room or the nursery, than the subject of serious and painstaking research."[29] The drawing room and the nursery were of course the territory of women and children. "True" ghost stories were a common feature in popular magazines and the telling of ghost stories on Christmas Eve, preferably those alleged to be true, was a popular Victorian custom. The narrative frame for the most famous ghost story of the Victorian period, *The Turn of the Screw*, is just such a holiday gathering. Interestingly, much of the literary debate about this story is over whether the female protagonist is really seeing ghosts or just hallucinating.

Women were not only regarded as the sort of people most likely to believe such stories, but also the people most likely to tell them. Women, especially one's grandmother or old nurse or maiden aunt, were the traditional tellers of ghost stories.[30] One of Mrs. Gaskell's ghost stories is called "The Old Nurse's Tale" while one of Sir Walter Scott's is called "My Aunt Margaret's Mirror." Women even predominated as the writers of fictional ghost stories for the literary market. During the middle decades of the century, writers like Mrs. J. H. Riddell, Amelia Edwards, Rosa Mulholland, and Mrs. Molesworth produced dozens of ghost stories for the Christmas annuals of popular periodicals.[31]

The SPR was aware of this association and took note of it in its discussion of its findings. One SPR committee report cautioned that allowance had to be made for the "instinctive tendency of the imagination towards dramatic unity and completeness" in reconstructing an incident.[32] For this reason Eleanor Sidgwick considered the uninteresting behavior of most of the ghosts reported to be one of the strongest features of the evidence in *Phantasms of the Dead*: "There is a total absence of any apparent object or intelligent action on the part of the ghost. If its visits have an object it entirely fails to explain it. It does not communicate important facts. It does not point out lost wills or hidden treasure" or otherwise behave like a fictional ghost.[33]

This preference for a dramatically uninteresting ghost story goes a long way toward explaining the SPR's initially negative reaction to one of the best-known "true" ghost stories of the period, the book *An Adventure*. This book, published in 1911, recounted the experiences of two women who, while walking in the gardens of Versailles close to the Petit Trianon claimed to have witnessed a scene from the life of Marie Antoinette.

The book was published under the pseudonyms "Miss Morrison" and "Miss Lamont." The real authors were Miss Charlotte Moberly, principal of St. Hughes College, Oxford, and Miss Eleanor Jourdain, vice-principal of the same institution and Moberly's eventual successor as principal. The American branch of the SPR, which was more heavily influenced by spiritualism than its British counterpart, gave the book an overall favorable review and called it a "story as romantic and incredible as any ever told in the annuals of psychic research."[34] It seems to have been this very "romantic and incredible" aspect of the story that alienated the British SPR. In its review of the book, which appeared in the *Proceedings* for 1911, the reviewer concluded that

> while gladly admitting that Miss Morrison and Miss Lamont have produced a very readable book and have taken praiseworthy trouble in looking up historical facts and traditions, we cannot honestly say that they appear to us to have added anything of interest to the positive side of psychical research. The foundations on which the supernormal claims of the "Adventure" are built are too slight, and too little allowance is made for the weakness of human memory both in adding and subtracting from facts—weaknesses which there is no reason to think the writers of this book suffer less than the rest of the world.[35]

The reviewer was Eleanor Sidgwick, herself principal of another women's college.[36] The real identities of the writers were not publicly announced until many years after the death of Jourdain in 1924, but this information was known to the SPR before the review appeared. The authors' account had been submitted to SPR investigator Alice Johnson for evaluation. Johnson regarded the case as too weak to merit investigation and said so in a series of acrimonious letters exchanged with Moberly.[37] Therefore Eleanor Sidgwick knew when she wrote the review that the writers were two of her colleagues in the work of women's higher education, and it is interesting to speculate how this may have influenced her reception of the book. One suspects that she may have been very much annoyed by it, feeling that it might damage the cause of higher education for women while doing nothing for psychical research. Characteristically, the deficiencies in the book are ascribed to tricks of memory from which men might suffer as easily as women, not to hallucinations.

Madness, imagination, a bias in the evidence-gathering process, or a special relationship with the supernatural all were reasons given by the Victorians for the prevalence of testimony by women for the existence of the supernatural. Other reasons that suggest themselves are a desire for attention and the validation of one's special experience, as well as the satisfaction of participating in what was viewed as an important scientific study. To have a body of distinguished people interested in one's story must have been gratifying to many men as well as many women, though one suspects that the pleasure of being taken seriously was a probably a more novel experience for the women.

It is probably also true that in many cases if a woman reported supernatural phenomena she might be greeted with a condescending smile, but not actual disapproval, while a man reporting the same phenomena might be met with outright derision since as a man he was expected to know better. A man might be more fearful of the damage to his public reputation as a hardheaded man of business or a trained professional if he reported seeing supernatural occurrences.

A desire for excitement is another possible explanation why women reported psychical phenomena more often than men in this period. With a ghost in the house a woman could add a little adventure to her life without ever venturing into the public sphere; in fact, Victorian ghosts seem to have been like many middle-class Victorian women: home-loving creatures who were rarely seen in places of business. While most of the ghost stories reported by women in *Phantasms of the Dead* are uninteresting apart from their claim to be true, two stories reported by female observers describe their haunting as events posing a challenge to be overcome. In the first case a house was supposed to be haunted by among other things, a man who kept appearing on the stairs. The lady narrating the story, which is taken from her diary, emphasized that the man's sudden disappearance whenever she and her elder daughter attempted to confront him could not be explained by normal causes since they were not frightened by the occurrences and there was no delay on their part which might allow him to make a hasty retreat: "There is no misapprehension, because no fear quells our courage; no cowardice prevents the full action of our powers of perception; no alarm frustrates our intention of grappling with him if we can, or of pursuing him or of holding him if we can come up with him. We are on our guard against surprise, and our nerves steady, prepared to make a decided and unequivocal effort to find out who and what this nocturnal intruder may be."[38] This description sounds like something more appropriate to an old soldier's memoirs than a Victorian lady's diary.

We find a similar sense of conflict in the account given of a haunting associated by the percepients with the death of a child in the house. The nurse hired to attend the child wrote in her account, "I always feel when called here to nurse that I am to do battle for the life of my patient with a foe whose exact power I do not understand, and have always striven to defeat an influence which I felt was evil, by soliciting the protection of One who is Almighty."[39] After recounting the appearance to herself and her young patient, who died a few days later, of a lady in a black dress, the nurse concludes with the remark that "more than once since then I have asked myself this question, 'Was she frightened to death?'"

Sightings of the supernatural may therefore have been in some cases a sign, not only of stress caused by conflict but stress caused by the lack of it. Many Victorian ladies felt, consciously or unconsciously, bored and frustrated with the limited opportunities for experience allowed them, and sightings of the supernatural may have been one strategy for bringing a challenge into their lives. One is reminded of Florence Nightingale's novel fragment "Cassandra," where she insists that suffering is to be preferred to apathy. Nightingale, of course, claimed that voices from God told her to become a nurse and go to the Crimea.

Finally one might speculate on how the testimonies of these women relate to the larger context of psychical research, namely, the Victorian crisis of faith. In light of the fact that religion was considered more central to the lives of women than of men, one might ask in what way women's responses to the climate of religious doubt differed from those of men. For many men and women the loss of religious faith was a liberating experience, but for many others it was one rife with fear and anxiety. If religion was expected to play a larger role in women's lives than in men's, would the anxiety and the fear created by religious doubt have been greater? Many middle-class women, even those with some education, would have lacked the training necessary to find an intellectual and scholarly response to the issues raised by Darwin or the Higher Criticism, and it is questionable whether a purely intellectual response would have been adequate if it had been available. Were women, then, more likely than men to seek reassurance of a belief in something beyond this life in a figure of a gray lady in their drawing room or the sound of footsteps on the staircase at night?

## NOTES

1 / R. Laurence Moore, *In Search of White Crows: Spiritualism, Parapsychology, and American Culture* (New York: Oxford Univ. Press, 1977), 105–18.

2 / John Cerullo, *The Secularization of the Soul: Psychical Research in Modern Britain* (Philadelphia: Institute for the Study of Human Issues, 1982), ch. 5. I am heavily indebted to Cerullo for much of the background material for this paper.

3 / "Report on the Census of Hallucinations" (hereafter cited as *Census*), *Proceedings of the Society for Psychical Research* 10 (1894): 168 (hereafter *SPR*).

4 / SPR Archives, BG 51, cited in R. C. Finucane, *Appearances of the Dead: A Cultural History of Ghosts* (Buffalo, N.Y.: Prometheus Books, 1984), 207–8. This observation was made in a paper on reports by farm laborers of supernatural phenomena in the Vale of Evesham.

5 / Michel Sage, *Mrs. Piper and the Society for Psychical Research*, trans. from the French by Noralie Robertson with a preface by Sir Oliver Lodge (New York, 1904), 1–2.

6 / Mrs. Henry (Eleanor Balfour) Sidgwick, "Notes on the Evidence, Collected by the Society, for Phantasms of the Dead," *SPR* 3 (1885): 69–150. No breakdown by age, gender, or other categories is provided by the author and the accounts quoted are sometimes vague. In those cases, 101 of them, where the gender of the percipient was indicated, I counted seventy-two women and twenty-nine men.

7 / Edmund Gurney, Frederic W. H. Myers, and Frank Podmore, *Phantasms of the Living* (London, 1886) 2: 723.

8 / *Census*, 152.

9 / Ibid., 153. Finucane, who reviewed the same materials as well as the archives of the SPR, reached the conclusion that in the Victorian period "overall most percipients were women" (*Appearances*, 211).

10 / Hugo Munsterberg, "Psychology and Mysticism," *Atlantic Monthly* 83 (1899): 67.

11 / Ibid., 81.

12 / *Phantasms of the Dead*, 145.

13 / Ibid., 149.

14 / *Census*, 153–54.

15 / *Phantasms of the Living*, 2:723.

16 / Ibid., 1:3 n. 1.

17 / Alexander Lang, "The Voices of Jeanne D'Arc," *SPR* 11 (1895): 199.

18 / Frederic W. H. Myers, "The Daemon of Socrates," *SPR* 5 (1889): 543.

19 / Sage, *Mrs. Piper*, 4–5.

20 / Ibid., 6.

21 / Cerullo, *Secularization of the Soul*, ch. 4.

22 / *SPR* 1 (1882–83): 11, cited in Cerullo, 60.

23 / Ethel Sidgwick, *Mrs. Henry Sidgwick: A Memoir by Her Niece* (London: Sidgwick & Jackson, 1938), 99.

24 / Mrs. Henry (Eleanor Balfour) Sidgwick, *Health Statistics of Women Students of Cambridge and Oxford and Their Sisters* (Cambridge, 1890), cited in Rita McWilliams-Tulberg, *Women at Cambridge: A Men's University—Though of a Mixed Type* (London: Victor Gollancz, 1975), 103.

25 / This rough estimate was arrived at through random sampling of membership lists, published with every volume of the *SPR* for several years between 1882 and 1914.

26 / *SPR* 9 (1893–94): 44.

27 / See Janet Oppenheim's discussion of Annie Besant and Dr. Anna Kingsford in *The Other World: Spiritualism and Psychical Research in England, 1850–1914* (Cambridge: Cambridge Univ. Press, 1985), 185–93. Jonathan Rose, in *The Edwardian Temperament, 1895–1919* (Athens: Ohio Univ. Press, 1986), 11, observed that "Theosophy attracted a small following among bohemians, suffragettes, and men of the Irish Renaissance."

28 / Oppenheim, *Other World*, 241. These remarks were made by Lankester during his presidential address to the British Association for the Advancement of Science in 1906. Thirty years earlier Lankester and Dr. Horatio Donkin had successfully prosected a fraudulent medium in the famous Slade case.

29 / *SPR* 1 (1882–83): 105.

30 / This was a tradition of long standing. "When I was a child (and so before the Civill Warres) . . . the fashion was for old women and mayds to tell fabulous stories nightimes, of sprights and walking of ghosts, etc. This was derived down from mother to daughter" (John Aubrey, *Brief Lives*, cited in Finucane, *Appearances*, 124).

31 / Julia Briggs, *Night Visitors: The Rise and Fall of the English Ghost Story* (London: Faber & Faber, 1977), 44.

32 / *SPR* 1 (1882–83): 105.

33 / *Phantasms of the Dead*, 142–43.

34 / James H. Hyslop, "Reincarnation and Psychical Research," *Journal of the American Society for Psychical Research* 5 (1911): 411.

35 / [Mrs. Henry (Eleanor Balfour) Sidgwick], "Review: An Adventure," *SPR* Supplement, pt. 63 (1911): 360.

36 / The original review is unsigned. The reviewer is identified as Eleanor Sidgwick by Edith Olivier in her preface to *An Adventure* (London: Faber & Faber, 1947), 26.

37 / Lucille Iremonger, *The Ghosts of Versailles: Miss Moberly and Miss Jourdain and Their Adventure: A Critical Study* (London: Faber & Faber, 1957), 157–67.

38 / *Phantasms of the Dead*, 129. These accounts often give vivid glimpses of middle-class Victorian domestic life since in the course of telling their stories the witnesses often reveal details about the layout of their houses, their daily routines, and their family relations.

39 / Ibid., 125.

## 14

*Vanessa D. Dickerson*

## A Spirit of Her Own:
## Nineteenth-Century Feminine
## Explorations of Spirituality

THE VICTORIANS EXPERIENCED A CRISIS of faith.[1] Scientific, industrial, and material advances on which the era prided itself threatened the older sense of mystery, of a priori truths, of providential design. But despite the Benthamism, empiricism, and scientism of the times, the Victorians were most reluctant to let the numinous, traditionally conveyed by the church, wane. Their preoccupation with spirituality and otherworldliness revealed itself in less dogmatic and formalistic ways. Thus, a record number of ghost stories were written during this period.[2] Mesmerism—a pseudo-scientific session of minds in which a controller or person with a strong will (usually a man) exerted an uncanny hypnotic power over a weaker-willed patient (usually a female) supposedly with medically beneficial results—and later spiritualism—the belief that the living communicated with the dead through a medium—became popular.[3] By the end of the nineteenth century the Society for Psychical Research was established to investigate reports of supernatural incidents or sightings. According to Ronald Pearsall, the Victorians' concern with matters spiritual pervaded their very homes and furnishings: "The Victorian period was not only a haunted age; it was also, in every sense of the word, a hallucinatory age, lending itself to every type of illusion even at the level of bricks and mortar. . . . [There were] money-boxes disguised as books, substantial-looking doors that on examination was [sic] merely cunning paintwork, solid-looking chairs that were, in fact, featherlight, being manufactured from papier mâché."[4] Such haunted materialism called into question the very results of the "real" and mechanical accomplishments of the nineteenth century.

Another and more interesting way in which the Victorians may be said to have reinvested their spirituality was through their women. For it was during this period that woman was socially acclaimed, after the ideal woman in Coventry Patmore's poem, "the angel in the house."[5] Her ethereality thus lauded and her person pedestaled, woman was granted the power "to soften and to attract," to be a gentle moral force in the home.[6] And so long as she ministered to the comfort of her husband, tended the children, managed the household, all was well. However, when she began to assert herself beyond the domestic realm, her special powers became equivocal. At best her ultradomestic energies were hysterical; at worst these energies were seen, Nina Auerbach argues, as demonic.[7]

One of the ways in which nineteenth-century British women themselves addressed, manifested, and explored the spirituality their age granted them was through their writings about and their participation in such supernatural phenomena as mesmerism and spiritualism. The ascendancy of heart, soul, and sympathy in the feminine sex, whether indeed innate or merely culturally ingrained, seemed to make women the ideal disseminators of spiritual beliefs and experiences. In her *Women in Nineteenth Century* (1845), Margaret Fuller, later Ossoli, credits nineteenth-century woman with an "especial genius" that is "electrical in movement, intuitive in function, spiritual in tendency," an ability to seize causes instinctively, and a talent for the "simple breathing out of what she receives, that has the singleness of life, rather than the selecting and energizing of art."[8] Elsewhere Fuller emphasizes the special spiritual nature of the female, remarking how the great Italian poets "saw that, in cases where the right direction had been taken, the greater delicacy of [woman's] frame and stillness of her life left her more open than is Man to spiritual influx."[9] Equally, if not more, attuned to the distinct spirituality of the female, Catherine Crowe in *The Night Side of Nature* (1845) explains:

> The circumstances, too, that phenomena of this kind [dreams, presentiments, ghost-seeing] are more frequently developed in women than in men, and that they are merely the consequence of her greater nervous irritability, has been made another objection to them—an objection, however, which Dr. Passavent considers founded on ignorance of the essential difference between the sexes, which is not merely a physical but a psychological one. Man is more productive than receptive. . . .
>
> Thus the ecstatic woman will more frequently be a seer, instinctive and intuitive; man, a doer and a worker; and as all genius is a degree of ecstasy or clear-seeing, we perceive the reason wherefore in man it is more productive than in woman.[10]

Crowe apparently felt no qualms in remarking the distinctions between the spiritually receptive female and the materially productive male. "It is alleged, then," she writes elsewhere, "that these phenomena never appear spontaneously, or can be evoked, except in persons more or less diseased, or in weak women and impressionable children. . . . But what of these?"[11] Women, who more easily entered into mesmerism and spiritualism, were regarded as being more open to "higher truths" than men;[12] they were hailed for being more open to spiritual knowledge.

One case Crowe held forth that evidenced the legitimacy of the supernatural and that further documented woman's special role and powers was her translation of Justinus Kerner's *Die Seherin von Prevorst* (1845). The German doctor Kerner kept the seer Frederica Hauffe under close surveillance, at one point moving her into his own home. He witnessed the mesmeric trances during which the seer conversed with her guardian spirit, the efficacy of the cures she, while deep in mesmeric sleep, prescribed for ailing neighbors who sought her medical advice, her preternatural powers of prevision and vision. On occasions, in experimenting with her powers, he noted how the "nipples of a horse, the tooth of a mammoth, bezoar, a spider's web, a glow-worm, &c. &c., all produced specific effects on being placed in her hand."[13] Other experiments he conducted on the seer centered in water, gravity, "imponderable substances," the human eye, the pit of the stomach, to name a few areas. Through Frederica Hauffe, Kerner became more convinced that "there is a super-terrestrial world."[14]

With her clairvoyant powers and her inner hotline to the dead, the simple, sensitive, mountain-bred Frederica Hauffe amazed and impressed Doctor Kerner. But what apparently most amazed and troubled even this open-minded medical observer was the seer's sex. "It is certainly hard," complained Kerner, "and we cannot wonder at the annoyance it occasions, that a weak silly woman should thus disturb the established systems of the learned, and revive persuasions that it has long been the aim of the wise among men to erradicate." But Kerner availed himself of a biblical touchstone for reassurance, Paul's first Epistle to the Corinthians (1: 27, 28): "But God hath chosen the weak things of the world to confound the things which are mighty."[15]

While Kerner bemoaned the fact that "a weak silly woman" should challenge "the established systems of the . . . wise among men," Catherine Crowe, whose translation of *Die Seherin* helped to make the seer a legend among spiritualists, had elsewhere offered a scientific explanation for the faculties of the clairvoyant female: "It is, doubtless, from the greater development of the ganglionic system in women, that they exhibit more frequent instances of such abnormal phenomena [presentiments, dreams, ghost-seeing, etc.] as I am treating of, than men."[16]

At least one medical journal, the *Lancet*, was skeptical of mesmerism and the seer who practiced it. Launching an attack on mesmerism, the *Lancet* singled out the spiritual proclivity of females as an aberration:

> All the malingering of the age has a natural determination towards mesmerism. Of such imposters the sisters OKEY may be considered the type. In some cases there is no actual deceit, but merely a morbid desire to parade these disorders, real or imaginary, before the public eye; or they deceive themselves, and really believe in the existence of diseases and the occurrence of cures. Affected by a depraved appetite, like that which impels certain descriptions of patients to eat the dirt of the most loathsome corners . . . so these semi-patients and semi-dupes, affected by a moral pica, delight to dwell upon disgusting or indelicate details. . . . In this way the celebrated authoress of the preventive check parades her diseased vagina and os uteri as it were in a public speculum before the general gaze, and other ladies write and publish pamphlets about their uterine symptoms and their disorders of sex, in a manner to have made our grandmothers sink into the earth for shame. The sensations, disorder, credulity, cunning, and self-deceptions of this class of subjects, and the simplicity of the great number who credulously believe in them, form the other great division of the mesmeric array.[17]

The attack on mesmerism becomes an ad hominem attack on women. The *Lancet* article pointedly fails to mention any male dupes; instead, it centers its vituperative sexual assault on women, depicting them as "diseased" and feeble-willed trash receptacles rather than as receptive human beings. These presumably hysterical women were, the journal suggests, the gulls and "semi-dupes" of abominable, bogus fads like mesmerism and spiritualism not only because of their psychologically "morbid desires" and "depraved appetites," but also because of the very things that made them female—"the vagina" and "os uteri."

As the *Lancet* article suggests, some Victorian males soon became highly uneasy about such female modes of escape as mesmerism and spiritualism. While female practitioners of these phenomena initially seemed to be minding their own ethereal business and leaving worldly affairs to men, they also were threatening to subvert the patriarchally designated Christian roles of the quiet, obedient, homebound angel. The exhibitionism the *Lancet* writer derides may be exaggerated, but it is undeniably true that things spiritual afforded Victorian women an outlet for self-assertion as well as notoriety, attention, and a means of capitalizing on the intuitive powers with which they were credited by a society that regarded them otherwise as intellectually barren. A writer like Charlotte Yonge, who, as Katherine Moore notes, was a firm believer in the "subjection of women," nonetheless insisted that such subjection by no means extended to spiritual matters: "Women are not only allowed but encouraged to call their *souls* their own and so they retain their dignity in spite of all the meek obedience demanded of them."[18] The supernatural could provide women with new contexts for speech and action, a freed voice for their conscious and unconscious feelings, a higher regard for their persons and for their neglected minds. What women want, wrote Margaret Fuller, is "the freedom, the religious, the intelligent freedom of the universe to use its means, to learn its secret as far as Nature has enabled them, with God alone for their guide and their judge."[19] The debate over the legitimacy of mesmerism and spiritualism, indeed even of ghosts, would afford women the opportunity not only to publicize their personal experiences and beliefs in the weird phenomena and, in some instances, to investigate the role of the church, but also to enlist, consciously and unconsciously, the attention of a popular audience as well as a professional and scientific one.

Interestingly enough, Harriet Martineau, a noted rationalist and writer on religion, economy, and government, vehemently decried any form of supernatural hocus-pocus, though she staunchly credited the mesmer-ism the *Lancet* denounced. Disparaging the mysteries of providence and supernaturalism as figments of a mind slipped back into black and ob-scure error, Martineau wondered, "How many entire ghosts have thus presented themselves from the mere fragments of resemblance to the human form! How many gleams of moonlight, how many nodding twigs, how many scudding clouds have inspired needless terror!"[20] One road that might lead from the dusty darkness of unreality to empirically sub-stantial reality was, as Martineau suggested, to be found in nature: "And what a *feeling* it is,—that which grows up and pervades us when we have fairly returned our obedience to Nature! What a healthful glow animates the faculties! . . . One seems to have even a new set of nerves, when one has planted one's foot on the broad common of Nature, and clear day-light, and bracing breezes are about one, and there are no more pitfalls and rolling vapors,—no more raptures and agonies of selfish hope and fear,—but sober certainty of reliance on the immutability of Nature's laws."[21] With her Wordsworthian love of nature, and her eighteenth-century Lockean belief in the senses and reason, Harriet Martineau could decide that "the philosopher is safe in his conclusion that as the material frame cannot be renovated, and as the spiritual one is not recognisable by the senses, the dead do not appear to the living."[22] Instead ghosts, deities, and other such superstitious folly, the agnostic Martineau insisted, were often the work of a "few individuals who, by skill or accident, . . . [having] anticipated scientific facts now generally known turned their knowledge to profitable account by imposing on the imaginations of the ignorant many." [23]

Martineau not only attacked the supernatural that thinkers like Crowe and later De Morgan sought to "palliate" with science and reason, but she also attacked religious supernaturalism and its proponents. The clergy, as Martineau saw it, also had a hand in nursing supernaturalism: "We still find the devil the bugbear, and the clergy the managers. We still find that the ignorant are cajoled, and that orthodoxy is propped up by the false supports of superstition." [24] In her *Society in America* (1837), Martineau goes one step further and accuses clergymen of taking particularly shameless advantage of women who

> in all matters relating to religion . . . naturally reverence and cling to those who show them respect and deference. The clergy, from understanding this point in their nature, possess great and deserved influence over them; and they have only to interest their feelings, to insure success to any clerical or charitable purpose. . . . And will she not toil for days, scarcely raising her eyes from the work, to assist in purchasing an organ, a new altar-cloth, or in cleaning and painting a church?
>
> So great is the tax, now, on a woman's time, for these and for other religious purposes, such as the "educating young men for the ministry," that the amount is frightful and scandalous. [25]

Such exploitation of women in the name of God, as well as the supernaturalism of charlatans and clergymen, could not be disposed of until "every man ascertains and applies his Christianity for himself" and until people came "to expose indefatigably the machinery of spiritual illusion; to frown upon all spiritual monopoly; to reveal to the ignorant their own rights and to protect their claim." [26]

For the philosophical, agnostic Martineau, the only apparitions that plagued mankind were those projected by imposture or by a malfunctioning nervous system or overheated brain. "Apparitions, then," she determined, "are seen when ideas are so vivified as to overpower actual impressions," and this vivification of ideas often results from illness or mental excitement. [27] She was sympathetic to the idea that people in bereavement, affected by illness, or merely eager to enrich daily existence imaginatively could yearn for such things as ghosts, but that they should actually believe these superstitions was more than any sensible person could countenance.

Yet the hardheaded rationalist and professionally reputable Harriet

Martineau who explicitly attacked supernaturalism gave hearty credence to mesmerism, that shady phenomenon with decided supernatural overtones. Admittedly, she saw nothing supernatural in mesmerism, but then neither did men like Charles Dickens and Dr. John Elliotson of the University of London, who both practiced it. She set all the theories proposed to explain the phenomenon at naught and was, in spite of her philosophical turn of mind, quite content for the time being simply to relish its effectiveness without actually knowing its origin and cause.[28] In the final analysis, she supposed this miraculous phenomenon one of the natural but heretofore uncultivated powers of man, and, having thus explained away what smacked of the supernatural, proceeded herself to mesmerize some of her sick neighbors in the Lake District. Still, this phenomenon which Martineau so gratefully credited in her *Letters on Mesmerism* (1845) was the very same which the previously cited *Lancet* article attacked, only two years later, as the "professed science" of hysterical women, a bogus, and an "infamy."[29]

Despite such attacks on the phenomenon by fellow skeptics, Harriet Martineau remained firmly anchored in the ranks of the credulous. "My recovery now," she proclaimed, "by means of mesmeric treatment alone, has given me the most thorough knowledge possible that Mesmerism is true."[30] The horrible internal disease that had imprisoned her in a room for five years was cured in miraculous mesmeric sessions to which she attributed a supernatural aura quite similar to that "machinery of illusion" she had so vehemently denounced in others: "Twenty minutes from the beginning of the *séance*, I became sensible of an extraordinary appearance, most unexpected, and wholly unlike anything I had ever conceived of. Something seemed to diffuse itself through the atmosphere . . . most like a clear twilight, closing in from the windows and down from the ceiling, and in which one object after another melted away, till scarcely anything as visible before my wide-open eyes . . . then . . . the busts re-appeared, ghost-like."[31] The rationalist who had earlier praised the "clear daylight" now finds herself in "a clear twilight." Obviously, Martineau did not feel the disgust for mesmerism that another great agnostic writer, George Eliot, would later feel. If anything, Martineau's mesmeric experience gave her a sympathetic understanding of how mesmerism could be interpreted supernaturally.

Perhaps Martineau's mesmeric experiences allowed her to come as close as she ever could to a type of religious ecstasy she could enjoy and accept as sanctioned by her intellect. She was clearly thrilled by more than a release from pain; the new sense she had discovered helped her to compensate for her impaired ones. Mesmerism revealed a new faculty that would enable her to apprehend more of the nature around her, and it opened up new vistas of that freedom and knowledge she had always valued: "Ignorant as we yet are,—hardly able yet . . . to snatch a glimpse of the workings of Nature . . . obvious as it is that our condition is merely that of infant-waking upon the world of existence, the privilege of freedom, as far as we are able to go, is quite inestimable." [32] Finally, with its promise of a communication achieved without the use of the ordinary senses, mesmerism must have also afforded her a psychologically gratifying communion with fellow creatures from whom she must inevitably have felt cut off by the handicap of her deafness. Probably the most eminent member of that numerous class of Victorian women, the professional invalid, to whom mesmerism appealed, [33] Martineau nonetheless defies the easy stereotyping of *The Lancet*. Whatever the reasons for her belief in mesmerism, Martineau was hardly a hysteric. And yet this unique and skeptical woman was far closer than she realized, or would have liked, to many a naive believer in the supernatural.

Whereas Harriet Martineau put her faith in a verifiable "daylight" of nature and natural causes, Catherine Crowe believed that the phenomena labeled supernatural were glimpses of a side of nature usually hidden from view. Crowe, who never claimed personally to have experienced the efficacy of mesmerism or to have seen a ghost, had, nevertheless, witnessed strange phenomena. She had seen "tables move without any hand touching them" and "candles extinguished" unaccountably. She had also "held a guitar" while "chords were struck" mysteriously. "Being desired by the invisible Intelligence to sing," writes Crowe, "I was regularly accompanied through several songs." [34] On 15 October 1858, Crowe declined to say publicly whether she had ever seen a ghost. [35] About halfway into her *Ghosts and Family Legends* (1859), she does, however, give an account of her visit to a haunted house. Though she sees no ghosts herself, by holding the hand of a clairvoyant young female, Crowe perceives strange "waves of white light." [36] Of this honestly stated but rather anticlimactic jaunt to a haunted house, Catherine Crowe comments at length:

> You see our results were not great, but the visit was not wholly barren to me. Of course, many wise people will say, I did not see the lights, but that they were the offspring of my excited imagination. But I beg to say that my imagination was by no means excited. If I had been there *alone,* it would have been a different affair; for though I never saw a ghost nor ever fancied I did, I am afraid I should have been very nervous. But I was in exceedingly good company, with two very clever men, besides the lawyer, a lady, and the clairvoyante [*sic*]; so that my nerves were perfectly com-

posed, as I should not object to seeing any ghost in such agreeable society. Moreover, I did not *expect* any result; because, there is very seldom any on these occasions, as ghosts appear we know not why; but certainly not because people wish to see them. They generally come when least expected at least thought of.[37]

Catherine Crowe's candor, her truthful and understated account of the particulars of her visit to the haunted house, reminds one of Martineau's equally factual defense of mesmerism. By discounting the idea of female hysteria or an "excited imagination" and by engaging the notable company of "two very clever men, besides a lawyer" as well as two other persons, Crowe seeks to validate the significance of "results" that others— lawyers, doctors, and priests, would be disposed to set aside.

Clearly nothing of a spiritual nature could be "wholly barren" to a Catherine Crowe, who devoted so much time and effort to championing supernaturalism in the face of disbelief, of materialism, of the "Persons in authority, in this case . . . the scientific world."[38] Crowe herself became an authority on what is called the supernatural. Her *Night Side of Nature*, which covers every form of spiritual manifestation from dreams to ghosts, is a Victorian bible of supernaturalism. In the preface to the work, Crowe, who notes that science in this country has "put [the supernatural] aside as beneath its notice," is careful to relate her undertaking to the writings of German authors like Henrich Schubert, who wrote, in Crowe's words, "a sort of cosmogony of the world, written in a spirit of philosophical mysticism—too much so for English readers." Denying the "pretension of *teaching* or of enforcing opinions," Crowe seeks "to suggest enquiry and stimulate observation," and "to induce a few capable persons, instead of laughing at these things, to look at them."[39]

Though she never claimed to be a spiritualist, eleven years after the publication of *Night Side*, at the request of her English and American friends, Catherine Crowe became one of the first to write on "the vexed question of Spiritualism." In her *Spiritualism and the Age We Live In* (1859), Crowe not only argues characteristically for open-mindedness on this topic, but she, like Martineau, also uses this opportunity to criticize dogmatic religion, which was fast becoming dry, worldly, and ineffective.

> Nor can we wonder at the small moral influence or dogmatic religion, and the inefficiency of these promises and threats to make men virtuous, when they cannot fail to observe how little their pastors themselves are affected by them. Ambition, love of dominion, too eager desire for wealth and worldly advantages, jealousy, intolerance, are the characteristics of all churches; insomuch, that it is the constant care of wise governments to

avoid throwing too much power into their hands. That church that has the most, makes the worst use of it; priests, of whatever denomination, are no better than other men; and religion is, in fact, rather an engine of government, and a reinforcement to the police, than a saving health to men's souls.

Spiritualism seemed an invitingly viable alternative to the "empty formalism" of dogmatism. While it corresponded to the "rapid advance of physical science," it also had a "tendency to generate or revivify the essentials of Religion, which are the emotions of the soul and its consciousness of immediate intercourse with God." [40] As Mary Howitt, who coedited with her husband a history of the supernatural, would also note, what she initially thought a delusion had "in many cases . . . produced such beautiful and sincere religious faith and trust." [41] Spiritualism, which was based on communication with the dead through a medium, purportedly by means of some electrical field, seemed what a religion should be—"an emotion arising out of knowledge, not a form founded on prescription." [42]

One writer who actually adopted and defended spiritualism as a religion was Florence Marryat, daughter of author and naval officer Captain Frederic Marryat. Calling, as Crowe had earlier, for open-mindedness as well as for the right of people to decide for themselves, Marryat soon declares how she herself has decided: "Let us resolve to know everything, and judge for ourselves! If we find Spiritualism does us harm, prevents our doing our duty in this world, or saps our health and strength, by all means abandon its pursuit, for it is not for us. But if it gives us comfort and pleasure, more faith in the goodness of God, and courage to do the work He has appointed us on earth, then cling to it as the greatest solace He has allotted Man. . . . *I* believe it to be an unmitigated blessing." For Marryat, the "umitigated blessing" of spiritualism was "a subject which is a religion to me." In her spiritualistic manifesto *The Spirit World* (1894), Marryat writes, "If Spiritualism is wrong, God is wrong, and the Christ is wrong, and the Bible is wrong, and you have nothing left to cling to for time or eternity." While spiritualism thus incorporates elements of orthodox religion, there nonetheless remains a recognized antagonism between the two:

> The dead are not dead! They stand in our midst to-day. I, who write for you, have seen them, conversed with them, and handled them; and I would not part with the knowledge thus gained for all the good this world could give me. I allow that, in these days, it is not a common experience. Would

that it were! For centuries Spiritualism has been banned by the Church and thrust out of sight as an unclean thing. The Church, which encourages the State in upholding laws which are totally opposed to the teaching of its professed master Christ; which solemnizes marriages which are nothing less than prostitution; which permits divorce, capital punishment, actions at law, winks at simony, and allots enormous revenues to its bishops and arch-bishops, whilst the poor rot and starve—this same Church forbids us to have any communication with spirits, who are the very first to denounce its corrupt practices.

According to Marryat, established religion affords no comfort to the harried classes of people, amongst whom women are numbered, but rather encourages or condones the state in oppressing these people.[43]

Fervent as Marryat was in her convictions about spiritualism, she was not so sentimental or irrational as to overlook the need for organization and revenue in the spiritual cause:

> I contend that the Spiritualist should no more expect to enjoy the privileges of *his* religion for nothing than the Christian. We live in an age of greed and heavy expenses. Nothing is to be had for nothing in the year of our Lord 1894, and the time is past when congregations could assemble under the green-wood tree to hold their meetings of prayer and praise. A Spiritualist Society must have a room to assemble in, and preachers to conduct its services, just like the Christians, and such luxuries have to be paid for.
>
> . . . And why should mediums, who expend far more strength on the exercise of their profession than any of the clergy, be grudged the reward due to their great work?[44]

The Spiritual Society Marryat proposes would create a new profession— that of the medium, and thereby open up new social and religious horizons.

Marryat herself claimed modest powers as a medium: "I am a physical medium, and though I cannot procure materializations by myself, I am said to impart much force to those I set with."[45] Her argumentative and persuasive powers in *There Is No Death* (1891) and *The Spirit World* (1894) proved even more formidable, it would seem, than her mediumistic powers. Helen Black, a contemporary of Florence Marryat, reported that Marryat "numbers her converts [to Spiritualism] by the hundreds and they are all gathered from educated people; men of letters and of science have written to her from every part of the world, and many clergymen have succumbed to her courageous assertions."[46]

Spiritualism was just one of the means through which Victorian women could present their profoundly ambivalent responses to Christianity. For while Christianity, as Martineau shrewdly pointed out, filled the vacuity in some women's lives,[47] and while some women saw in Christianity a release from the narrowness of their roles, others felt that Christianity with its emphasis on obedience and self-sacrifice reinforced the limiting role of angel in the house. As we have seen, Catherine Crowe recognized it as an "engine of government"; later Florence Marryat would see it as the tool of a paternalistic state.

Yet it was science that remained the prime antagonist. Uncomfortable with the notion of instinct and spirit, scientists, according to Catherine Crowe, were limiting their knowledge. "Reason," she writes, "is a very valuable endowment certainly; but till it can teach us the way to truth, it is quite evident that, either we do not know how to use it, or that it is not so supreme a gift as the despised gift of instinct." An excessive reliance on reason, according to Crowe, could only lead to the materialism which she despised. "At a period when life has grown into a struggle and a contention for material existence that threatens to disorganize society, and render all the restraints of morality and religion utterly nugatory," a phenomenon like spiritualism or a belief in spirits and ghosts becomes absolutely necessary, Crowe insisted. Nor does she fail to note the special attraction of such a phenomenon to women. Classed among that "weak and foolish part of the world," truly at disadvantage since not allowed to contend for their "material existence," finding their supposed moral and religious "influence" rendered "nugatory" by the very "struggle and contention for material existence," women, she implies, should be seers capable of pointing beyond that deadening materialism.[48]

To convince nineteenth-century skeptics of a world beyond mammon and matter, two English matrons wrote major books, published in the same year, faithfully recording and defending spiritual manifestations and powers. Sophia De Morgan's *From Matter to Spirit* (1863) was an informative work on the types and functions of the spiritual medium. Supposedly written at the behest of the spirits themselves, Emma Hardinge's (later Emma Hardinge Britten's) *Modern American Spiritualism* (1863) proclaimed the glories of the spiritualist movement while presenting a thorough record of the movement's progress in America. In their books De Morgan and Hardinge tried to accommodate the Victorian dualisms of insight and conception, darkness and light, intuition and reason. "Never has any way been made," states the prefacer of De Morgan's work, "by observation alone. Facts have sometimes started a theory; but until sagacity had conjectured, divined, guessed, surmised . . . what they pointed to, the facts were a mob, and not an army." [49] Both women called for a union between God as the preternatural agent of the soul's immortality and science as the ordering agent of matter. For Emma Hardinge, spiritualism was a marriage of scientific reason and supernatural belief that yielded a spiritual science.

Sophia De Morgan not only felt that God was manifested in the progress from matter to spirit—"We should not undervalue the raps and movements, strange and childish as they appear: they form but the lowest step of a ladder whose base is on the earth, and whose top rests at the feet of the Lamb in the centre of the Throne" [50]—but she also contended that incredible phenomena such as ghosts merited the attention of the scientists as well as the theologian. Thus, in hopes that Victorian scientists and rationalists would find the preternatural phenomena more acceptable and credible, she sought a connection between spiritualism and the more objectively verifiable mesmerism. Hardinge, who likewise believed that science could substantiate the belief in God, declared, first, that chemistry, physiology, phrenology, magnetism, and clairvoyance were all revealing precursors of nature's supernatural mysteries,[51] and, second, that the new spiritual science was "placing religion no longer on the foundations of fleeting human opinion, human assertion, or theory, but on the enduring basis of scientific facts." [52] Denied the possibility of being doctors, scientists, or priests, women writers like De Morgan and Hardinge, nevertheless, in defining and underlining the supernatural experience with scientific as well as theological explanations, took a step from kitchen and boudoir toward the laboratory and the seminary.

For the time being, however, the parlor served as laboratory and seminary for those women who were seers or mediums. These individuals drew the dead and the living into their parlors to hold séances that became so popular that Queen Victoria even participated in them. During these bewitching gatherings, tables rose and sometimes floated through the air; rappings or knockings were heard on various pieces of furniture and at different places in the room; and at times a spirit would use the body of the medium to write, to draw, or, as in the case of the great Daniel Homes, to levitate through the air. In the thicket of these supernatural happenings, women who had supposedly always exerted a subtle spiritual guidance in the home, now, as seers and mediums, sat at the head of the table: they now became acknowledged spiritual guides, supernaturally chosen disseminators of spiritualism.

In England, Eliza Finch, Florence Cook, Miss Fay, and Miss Chandos were a few of the more prominent mediums. One Miss Elizabeth Squirrell achieved such recognition of her visionary and spiritual powers that

William Howitt in his *History of the Supernatural* (1863) pronounced her "The Seeress of Shottisham" in honorable emulation of the renowned seer of Prevorst. The first to introduce the séance into England was an American woman, a Mrs. Hayden, of whom a prominent English states- man was said to have declared that she "deserved a monument, if only for the conversion of Robert Owen." [53] Herself a medium, Emma Hardinge catalogues the active female mediums in America, where spiritualism had been, according to Howitt, stronger than in England:

> Amongst the more distinguished professional or public mediums were Mrs. Coan, the excellent test rapping medium; George Redman, a rapping, writing, and test medium . . . Mrs. Cora Brown, Miss Middlebrook, and Miss Sarah Irish, admirable mediums for tests by rapping, seeing, writing, trance, etc.; Mrs. Bradley and Mrs. Townsend . . . Mrs. Kellog, one of the best clairvoyant, personating, seeing and writing mediums in the country; Mrs. Harriet Porter . . . Miss Seabring . . . Miss Mildred Cole, a child scarcely twelve years of age . . . the still famous Miss Leah Fish, of the Fox Family.[54]

As this list indicates, the ranks of the spiritualist movement swelled with women: Mr. Redman seems buried amongst this heap of matrons and maidens. Supernaturalism indeed had an infectious appeal for those ladies who, despite the disapprobation of disbelieving husbands, doc- tors, and priests, persisted in their séances and supernatural belief. That the bitter attacks of rationalists could not weaken the appeal suggests a special feminine rebellion that stemmed from deep-seated needs for action and self-expression, the urge to communicate, and the longing for public and professional recognition. By eagerly opening their minds to what the seer of Prevorst had called the inner life, female mediums and believers of the supernatural were making headway in their outer lives: being seen, heard, and studied. Then, too, spiritualism was a new area of knowledge in which women, for the most part, had outstripped the scientists. "Observation," wrote Catherine Crowe, "[is] a faculty, by the way, which our scientific men appropriate wholly to themselves. On this occasion, however, they have certainly yielded their pre-eminence to the 'weak and foolish' . . . for it is women and unscientific persons that have hitherto carried out these experiments, and satisfied themselves of their soundness." [55] Through spiritualism, mesmerism, and supernaturalism, the Victorian woman probed the nature and the extent of her spirituality and discovered expression, freedom, and power.

NOTES

1  /  For the best discussion of this crisis of faith see the chapter "Anxiety" in Walter E. Houghton's landmark work *The Victorian Frame of Mind, 1830–1870* (New Haven: Yale Univ. Press, 1957). See also "Religious Movements and Crisis," in Richard D. Altick's *Victorian People and Ideas: A Companion for the Modern Reader of Victorian Literature* (New York: Norton, 1973).

2  /  See Julia Briggs, *Night Visitors: The Rise and Fall of the English Ghost Story* (London: Faber & Faber, 1977).

3  /  "Why was this? Why were people—and, as time went on, these included people of the highest intellect and sophistication—so eager to accept, or impose, the so much less likely supernatural explanation [for phenomena like spiritualism and mesmerism]?" queries Ruth Brandon in *The Spiritualists: The Passion for the Occult in the Nineteenth and Twentieth Centuries* (New York: Knopf, 1983), 7. One insightful response Brandon offers is that people were seeking to blur "the boundaries between life and death" (10). In other words, people wanted to affirm the afterlife for which Florence Marryat would argue in her book *There Is No Death* (New York, 1891). In his *Dickens and Mesmerism* (Princeton: Princeton Univ. Press, 1975), Fred Kaplan rightly notes the "utopian" aspects of mesmerism that "appealed to the heart as well as to the head," a mesmerism that "had not only a strand of scientific but also an elaborate weave of Romantic and revolutionary utopianism that contained threads from western society's inheritance of religion and magic." With its similar magnetic and electrical basis, spiritualism, too, appealed to the "heart as well as the head."

4  /  Ronald Pearsall, *The Table-Rappers* (London: Joseph, 1972), 139.

5  /  Coventry Patmore, *The Angel in the House*, 4th ed. (London, 1866).

6  /  I have borrowed this phrase from Mary Shelley's *Frankenstein, or the Modern Prometheus*, ed. M. K. Joseph (London: Oxford Univ. Press, 1969), 38.

7  /  See Nina Auerbach, *The Woman and the Demon: The Life of a Victorian Myth* (Cambridge: Harvard Univ. Press, 1982).

8  /  Margaret Fuller Ossoli, *Women in the Nineteenth-Century, and Kindred Papers Relating to Sphere, Condition and Duties, of Women*, ed. Arthur B. Fuller (Boston, 1855), 115.

9  /  Ossoli, *Women*, 69.

10  /  Catherine Crowe, *The Night Side of Nature: or, Ghosts and Ghost Seers*, 2 vols. (1848; rpt. Folcroft Library Editions, 1976), 1:383–84.

11  /  Catherine Crowe, *Spiritualism and the Age We Live In* (London, 1859), 91.

12  /  Ibid., 13.

13  /  Justinus Kerner, *The Seeress of Prevorst, Being Revelations Concerning the Inner-Life of Man, and The Interfusion of a World of Spirits in the One We Inhabit*, trans. Catherine Crowe (London, 1845), 68.

14  /  Ibid., 151.

15  /  Ibid., 4.

16  /  Crowe, *Night Side*, 1:104–5.

17  /  "Mesmeric Deceptions—The Whipton Prophetess," *Lancet*, I (1847): 178–79.

18  /  Katherine Moore, *Victorian Wives* (London: Allison and Busby, 1974), 150.

19 / Ossoli, *Women*, 63.
20 / Harriet Martineau, "Demonology and Witchcraft," in *Miscellanies*, 2 vols. (Boston, 1836), 2:98–99.
21 / Harriet Marineau and Henry George Atkinson, *Letters on the Laws of Man's Nature and Development* (Boston, 1851), 290.
22 / Martineau, "Demonology and Witchcraft," 95.
23 / Ibid., 96.
24 / Harriet Martineau, "On Witchcraft," in *Miscellanies*, 2:402.
25 / Harriet Martineau, *Society in America* (New York, 1837), 415.
26 / Martineau, "On Witchcraft," 402.
27 / Martineau, "Deomonology and Witchcraft," 109, 112.
28 / Harriet Martineau, *Miss Martineau's Letters on Mesmerism* (New York, 1845), 22.
29 / "Mesmeric Deceptions," 178.
30 / Martineau, *Letters on Mesmerism*, 4.
31 / Ibid., 5.
32 / Martineau and Atkinson, *Man's Nature and Development*, 290.
33 / Pearsall, *Table-Rappers*, 24.
34 / Crowe, *Spiritualism and the Age We Live In*, 106–7.
35 / Catherine Crowe, *Ghosts and Family Legends: A Volume for Christmas* (London, 1859), vi.
36 / Ibid., 135–42.
37 / Ibid., 142.
38 / Crowe, *Spiritualism and the Age We Live In*, 105.
39 / Crowe, *Night Side*, 1:vii–viii.
40 / Crowe, *Spiritualism and the Age We Live In*, [i], 23, 48, 54.
41 / Mary Howitt, *Mary Howitt, An Autobiography*, ed. Margaret Howitt, 2 vols. (Boston, 1889), 2:105.
42 / Crowe, *Spiritualism and the Age We Live In*, 54.
43 / Florence Marryat, *The Spirit World* (Leipzig, 1894), 26, 8, 39, 38. Quotations in this paragraph are taken from this text.
44 / Ibid., 286–87.
45 / Ibid., 120.
46 / Helen Black, *Notable Women Authors of the Day* (London, 1906), 89.
47 / See Nancy Cott's *The Bonds of Womanhood* (New Haven: Yale Univ. Press, 1977), 137.
48 / Crowe, *Spiritualism and the Age We Live In*, 132, 131, 141. Quotations in this paragraph are taken from this text.
49 / Sophia De Morgan, *From Matter to Spirit* (London, 1863), xxiv.
50 / Ibid., 380.
51 / Emma Hardinge [Britten], *Modern American Spiritualism* (1870; rpt. New Hyde Park, N.Y.: University Books, 1970), 22.
52 / Ibid., 520.
53 / Ibid., 147.
54 / Ibid., 149–50.
55 / Crowe, *Spiritualism and the Age We Live In*, 138.

# Contributors

RUDOLPH M. BELL received his Ph.D. from the City University of New York. He is Professor of History at Rutgers University. Professor Bell is the author of *Holy Anorexia*; (with Donald Weinstein) *Saints and Society: Two Worlds of Western Christendom, 1000–1700*; *Fate and Honor, Family and Village: Demographic and Cultural Change in Rural Italy since 1800*; and *Party and Faction in American Politics: The House of Representatives, 1789–1801*. He is currently at work on daily life in sixteenth-century Rome and sixteenth-century Italian gender images as reflected in popular literature.

ELIZABETH CLARK received her Ph.D. from Columbia University. She is currently John Carlisle Kilgo Professor of Religion at Duke University. Professor Clark is the author of *Clement's Use of Aristotle: The Aristotelian Contribution to Clement of Alexandria's Refutation of Gnosticism*; *Women and Religion: A Feminist Sourcebook of Christian Thought*; *Jerome, Chrysostom, and Friends: Essays and Translations*; *The Golden Bough, the Oaken Cross: The Virgilian Cento of Faltonia Betitia Proba*; *The Life of Melania the Younger: Introduction, Translation, and Commentary*; *Ascetic Piety and Women's Faith: Essays on Late Ancient Christianity*. She is currently at work on a book on the Origenist controversy.

GRACIELA DAICHMAN received her Ph.D. from Rice University. She is currently a lecturer in the Departments of English and of Spanish, Portuguese, and Classics at Rice. She is the author of *Wayward Nuns in Medieval Literature*. Professor Daichman is currently at work on medieval medicine and superstition in the *Libro de Buen Amor*.

VANESSA D. DICKERSON is Assistant Professor of English at Rhodes College. She has forthcoming articles on Toni Morrison's *The Bluest Eye* and on the Victorian ghost stories by late nineteenth-century British women authors. She is currently collaborating on a critical volume about women's art, property, and professions. Professor Dickerson is also at work on essays about Zora Neale Hurston's *Their Eyes Were Watching God* and Paula Marshall's *Brown Girl, Brownstones*.

ELIZABETH FOX-GENOVESE received her Ph.D. from Harvard University. She is Director of Women's Studies and Professor of History at Emory University. Professor Fox-Genovese is the author of *Within the Plantation Household: Black and White Women of the Old South*; *The Divine Sanction of Social Order: Religious Foundations of the Southern Slaveholder's World View*; *The Origins of Physiocracy: Economic Revolution and Social Order in Eighteenth-Century France*; (with Eugene Genovese) *Fruits of Merchant Capital: Slavery and Bourgeois Property in the Rise and Expansion of Capitalism*. She is currently examining the social creation of woman.

SUSAN ASHBROOK HARVEY received her Ph.D. from the University of Birmingham. She is Assistant Professor of Religious Studies at Brown University. She is the author of *Asceticism and Society in Crisis: John of Ephesus and the "Lives of the Eastern Saints"*, and coauthor with Sebastian P. Brock of *Holy Women of the Syrian Orient*. Professor Harvey is currently working on the imagery of early Syriac asceticism, and particularly on the understanding of stylitism.

THOMAS HEAD received his Ph.D. from Harvard University. He is Assistant Professor of History at Yale University. His *Hagiography and the Cult of the Saints in the Orleanais, 800–1200* is forthcoming. He is the coeditor with Richard Landes of *Essays on the Peace of God: The Church and the People in Eleventh-Century France*. Professor Head is currently at work on women's voices in medieval Christianity.

ROSEMARY KELLER received her M.A. from Yale Divinity School and her Ph.D. from the University of Illinois at Chicago. She is Professor of Religion and American Culture at Garrett-Evangelical Seminary. She is the coeditor, with Rosemary Ruether, of *Women and Religion in America*; the coeditor of *Women in New Worlds: Women in the Wesleyan Tradition*. Professor Keller is currently examining the relationship of work and calling, and also writing a biography of Georgia Harkness.

DIANE MOCKRIDGE received her Ph.D. from Duke University. She is Associate Professor of History at Ripon College. Professor Mockridge's dissertation is entitled *From Christ's Soldier to His Bride: Changes in the Portrayal of Women Saints in Medieval Hagiography*. She is currently at work on gender in saints' lives.

KEITH MOXEY received his Ph.D. degree from the University of Chicago. He is Professor of Art History at Barnard College and Columbia University. He is author of *Pieter Aertsen, Joachim Beuckelaer and the Rise of Secular Painting in the Context of the Reformation* and *Peasants, Warriors and Wives: Popular Imagery in the Reformation*. He is also coeditor (with Norman Bryson and Michael Holly) of *Visual Theory: Painting and Interpretation*.

DUANE J. OSHEIM received his Ph.D. from the University of California at Davis. He is Associate Professor of History at the University of Virginia and author of *An Italian Lordship: The Bishopric of Lucca in the Late Middle Ages* and *A Tuscan Monastery and Its Social World, San Michele of Guamo*.

ALEXANDER SEDGWICK received his Ph.D. from Harvard University. He is Professor of History at the University of Virginia. Professor Sedgwick is the author of *The Ralliement in French Politics, 1890–98*, *The Third French Republic, 1870–1914*, and *Jansenism in Seventeenth-Century France: Voices from the Wilderness*. He is currently at work on a history of the Arnauld family in seventeenth-century France.

MARY WALKER received her Ph.D. from the University of Virginia. Her Ph.D. dissertation is on women in English local government, 1914–1919. She is currently working on Catholic women in the English suffrage movement as well as esoteric religions in the British Empire.

# Index